Writing under the Raj

Writing under the Raj

GENDER, RACE, AND RAPE IN THE BRITISH COLONIAL IMAGINATION, 1830–1947

NANCY L. PAXTON

Library of Congress Cataloging-in-Publication Data

Writing under the Raj : gender, race, and rape in the British colonial imagination, 1830–1947 / Nancy L. Paxton.
p. cm.
Includes bibliographical references and index.
ISBN 0-8135-2600-0 (cloth : alk. paper). — ISBN 0-8135-2601-9 (pbk. : alk. paper)
1. India—History—British occupation, 1765–1947. 2. India—Politics and government—1765–1947. 3. English literature—19th century—History and criticism. 4. English literature—20th century—History and criticism.
DS479.W75 1999
954.03—dc21   98-19522
                                                                                              CIP

British Cataloging-in-Publication data for this book is available from the British Library

Manufactured in the United States of America

1001701677

To my husband, Richard Stockinger,
and in memory of our mothers

CONTENTS

ACKNOWLEDGMENTS

I began this book more than twelve years ago, inspired, in part, by E. M. Forster's fascinating *A Passage to India*, but it would not have developed into its final form without the financial support of a number of institutions, as well as the ongoing interest and generous efforts of many colleagues and friends. First of all, I cannot adequately express my gratitude for being selected in 1986 as a participant in the Fulbright-Hayes Summer Seminar in India, which allowed me to learn so much about Indian culture in six dizzying weeks of travel throughout the subcontinent. Sharada Nayak, the director of our seminar, could not have been a more gracious and delightful host. She arranged for us to meet many of India's finest scholars, to see unforgettable art and architecture, and to attend superb music and dance performances, and she worked tirelessly behind the scenes to make our travels effortless as well as rewarding. My experiences in India were deepened immeasurably by the conversations and continuing friendship of Cyndi Wasko, Sue Light, Sue Standing, Carol Oldham, and Robert Croonquist.

Significant and timely support for my research on this project also came from the Andrew W. Mellon Faculty Fellow Program at Harvard University, where I was awarded a teaching fellowship in 1988–1989. I would especially like to thank Richard M. Hunt, the program's director; Susan Lewis, director of the Freshman Seminar Program; and Marjorie Garber, director of the Center for Literary and Cultural Studies, who provided office space and welcome invitations to many of the center's lectures and seminars. Barbara Johnson, Lewis Wurgaft, Deena Goodman, Joanna Drucker, Mary Berg, Virginia Davidson, and Elizabeth Goodenough all helped to make that year especially productive and stimulating.

The Mary Ingraham Bunting Institute provided invaluable support by awarding me a fellowship in fall of 1990. I owe an enormous debt of gratitude to Florence Ladd, director of the Bunting Institute, for her inspiring leadership, for her personal interest in my work on India, and for several introductions to scholars who were instrumental in advancing my research on rape law and on Indian history and culture. Bina Agarwal, Lynn Wilson, Mary Wilson Carpenter, Beverly Grier, Gail Hershatter, Amy Lang, Selem Mekuria, Connie Soja, and Zhu Hong all read portions of early drafts of this book and offered many kind and discerning suggestions.

I am also grateful for the financial and intellectual support provided by the Davis Humanities Institute, which offered me a fellowship during the spring of 1991, and to its director, Michael Hoffman, as well as to Kay Flavel, who organized our seminars. Special thanks go to Jan Gouldner, Kari Lökke, Anna Kuhn, Roger Rouse, and the other institute fellows for their comments and continuing interest. Thomas Metcalf, Barbara Metcalf, Lata Mani, and Valerie Matsumoto offered particularly helpful suggestions that deepened my understanding of current trends in Indian history.

I have also benefited from the financial and intellectual support provided by the National Endowment of the Humanities, for a travel grant in 1988 and for a summer stipend in 1994. The John D. Rockefeller Foundation provided funding for an important scholar-in-residence program at the Southwest Institute for Women at the University of Arizona in April 1992. I would especially like to thank my host, Karen Anderson, and Ann L. Stoler for their warm encouragement and perceptive comments about rape, feminist theory, and colonial history. Philippa Levine, Leslie Flemming, Margaret Strobel, Antoinette Burton, Cynthia Talbot, and Ali Behdad have all offered invaluable research advice on various aspects of Indian history and culture. Special thanks also go to Catharine Stimpson, Nancy K. Miller, and Barry Qualls for their ongoing support, and to Richard Dellamora for several enlightening discussions about E. M. Forster. I owe a personal debt of gratitude to Nanette Eichell, Diane Marting, Marie Logue, and Bobbi Greene for the hospitality that made my research trips to libraries in New York and Boston so much more pleasant. I also want to thank Lindy Flynn, Karen Myers, Julie Roller, Glo Edwards, Georgia Taylor, and Debbie Hill for helping me maintain a sense of balance and delight that allowed me to keep writing.

Since I started this project shortly after I began teaching in the English Department at Northern Arizona University, many colleagues have provided financial and intellectual support for my research and writing about colonial novels about India. I would like to express my thanks, first of all, to the Organized Research Committee of Northern Arizona University, which has generously provided support for this project over a number of years. Past and present colleagues have been instrumental in contributing material and moral support, including Henry Hooper, Karl Webb, Susan Foster-Cohen, Sharon Crowley, and Geoff Chase. While it is impossible to list all the colleagues and students in the English Department and the Women's Studies Program who have helped me sharpen my thinking about British literature, Indian history, colonialism, and feminist theory, I gratefully acknowledge the unfailing interest and steadfast support of Alison Brown, Irene Matthews, Bryan Short, Kit Hinsley, Victoria Enders, Julie Schimmel, Susan Deeds, Karen Powers, Geeta Chowdhry, Sheryl Lutjens, and Linda Shadiow. Malathi Sandhu, Sanjay Joshi, Jim Wilce, Flower Darby, and Thäis Morgan all read portions of this manuscript and offered critical help during my final revisions. Joe Boles, who succeeded me as director of Women's Studies at Northen Arizona University, deserves particular recognition for his important bibliographical suggestions, his computer assistance, and his cordial willingness to read yet another draft of the endlessly revised manuscript.

Writing under the Raj would not have found its way into print without Leslie Mitchner's enthusiastic support and patience over far too many years. I also want to thank Joseph A. Boone, who was an ideal reader for this book. His always generous, informed, astute, and extraordinarily helpful suggestions helped to make this a shorter and, I trust, a more coherent book.

Finally, I want to thank my father and sister for their understanding and patient support and my husband, Richard Stockinger, who was there from the beginning and has always known what I needed most. He has offered an endless supply of love, advice, and comfort, and has cheerfully provided conversation, proofreading, or dinner, whenever the need arose.

Writing under the Raj

Introduction

ORIENTALIZING RAPE

In "A Letter to a Member of the National Assembly," written in 1772, Edmund Burke describes the colonial relationship between England and India as poised between courtship and rape: 1767, he declared, marked the year when the "administration discovered that the East India Company were guardians to a very handsome and rich lady in Hindostan. Accordingly, they set parliament in motion; and parliament . . . directly became a suitor, and took the lady into its tender, fond, grasping arms, pretending all the while that it meant nothing but what was fair and honourable; that no rape or violence was intended; that its sole aim was to rescue her and her fortune out of the pilfering hands of a set of rapacious stewards, who had let her estate run to waste, and had committed various depredations."[1] By 1787, Burke amplified his criticism of Warren Hastings, the Governor General of Bengal between 1774 and 1785, charging him not only with promoting the economic rape of India but also with the literal rape of Indian women. Moved by his inflammatory rhetoric, Burke's colleagues in the House of Commons initiated proceedings to remove Hastings from the seat he then occupied in the House of Lords.

During the trial, Burke enumerated his charges against Warren Hastings, proclaiming not only that he had countenanced the use of sexual violence as a strategy of control by his colonial subordinates but that he had also personally "undone women of the first rank" in India, noting especially his humiliation of the Princesses of Oude in 1772–1773. In one speech, Burke vividly catalogued the barbaric treatment that Indian women received at the hands of Hastings and his men:

1

Virgins, who had never seen the sun, were dragged from the inmost sanctuaries of their houses, and in the open court of justice, . . . (but where no judge or lawful magistrate had long sat, but in their place the ruffians and hangmen of Warren Hastings occupied the bench), these virgins, vainly invoking heaven and earth, in the presence of their parents, . . . publicly were violated by the lowest and wickedest of the human race. Wives were torn from the arms of their husbands, and suffered the same flagitious wrongs, which were indeed hid in the bottoms of the dungeons in which their honour and their liberty were buried together. . . . But it did not end there. Growing from crime to crime, ripened by cruelty for cruelty, these fiends . . . these infernal furies planted death in the source of life, where that modesty, which, more than reason, distinguishes men from beasts, retires from the view, and even shrinks from the expression, there they exercised and glutted their unnatural, monstrous, and nefarious cruelty.[2]

In short, Burke charged Hastings with implementing policies that destroyed "the honour of the whole female race" in India.

Burke's criticism of the rapaciousness of British colonial policy in India was a minority voice at the time. Though his powerful descriptions of Hastings's unspeakable colonial acts inspired agitation in the large audiences attracted to the trial, Burke failed, nonetheless, in his efforts to convict Warren Hastings, and, after a trial that lasted seven years, the latter was acquitted in 1795.[3] Burke died two years later, so, by 1797, his inimitable and inflammatory rhetoric about the rape of India by the lawless agents of the East India Company was silenced forever.

One of the features that made Burke's speeches about colonial policy in India so memorable was that they skillfully exploited the rhetoric of surprise, since most English readers, regardless of whether they endorsed or opposed state sponsorship of the East India Company or the colonial wars in India conducted in its name, were more likely to have read Oriental tales that focused on seduction rather than reports of the violently transgressive acts of rape that he so vividly described.[4] A second feature that made Burke's speeches so important was, as Sara Sulieri has argued, that they also initiated a new period in British discourse about India because they were informed by his extensive reading of new English translations of major Sanskrit texts.[5]

For contemporary postcolonial readers and critics, however, Burke's use of rape as a tactic and metaphor to describe England's guilty traffic with the women—and men—of India may seem unexceptional. Beginning with Frantz

Fanon's critiques, nearly fifty years ago, authors as diverse as Edward Said, Octave Mannoni, Laura E. Donaldson, Jenny Sharpe, and Malek Alloula have identified rape as a master trope of colonial discourse and a sign of the colonizers' bad faith.[6] If we look more closely, however, at the participants in the "rape script" that these critics have identified in colonial discourse about India, we can see some fundamental differences. In *Orientalism*, for example, Said uses rape as a discreetly understated metaphor to describe the relationship between West and East. He argues, for example, "A certain freedom of intercourse was always the Westerner's privilege: because his was the stronger culture, he could penetrate, he could wrestle with, he could give shape and meaning to the great Asiatic mystery, as Disraeli once called it" (44). Passages like this make it abundantly clear that Said is primarily interested in highlighting the epistemic rather than the more material or personal forms of domination, violence, and rape authorized by the language and habits of mind that he calls "Orientalism."

More recent literary critics, especially those who endorse Said's anti-imperial politics, often invoke rape to characterize the Occident's relation to the Orient. Eric Meyer, for example, argues that British Romantic poetry about the Orient is defined by the following "meta-grammatical" sentence: "The thrust of the narrative enacts the colonization of the Orient, as the imperious male European ego penetrates the feminized space of the East; and the subjection of the veiled feminine other becomes an image of the submission of the Oriental to the Occidental principle" (668). In other words, critics who follow Said usually read Orientalist texts as organized by a rape scenario involving white colonizing males who rape Indian women in order to reduce them, and Indian men as well, to a state of enforced submission.

Colonial critics from earlier generations, including Fanon and Mannoni, argue, instead, that the rape of a colonizing woman by a native man is the master trope of colonial discourse, and they generally exclude the indigenous woman from their analysis. Laura Donaldson's *Decolonizing Feminisms* illustrates a more contemporary example of this critical approach. Though she offers an important feminist critique of Mannoni's assumptions about colonizing women, by offering alternative readings of texts about virginal European women who imagine themselves as threatened with rape by indigenous Calibans and defended by powerful fathers, she reproduces a configuration of colonial desire in her formulation of the "Miranda Complex" that reinstalls a triangular Freudian paradigm similar to Mannoni's, even as she criticizes it. Likewise, though Jenny Sharpe establishes a very different critical platform for her analysis of nineteenth-century English and Anglo-Indian texts about

India, she does not, to my mind, offer an adequately theorized explanation of why white women necessarily replace native women in the colonial texts that she discusses as "allegories of empire" during the British Raj. What all these commentators on colonial discourse have in common with Said is that they erase at least one of four possible participants in the colonial rape script that they analyze.

These examples have prompted me to ask several questions that I hope to answer in the pages that follow: first, why do critics represent the trauma of colonialism by citing one particular "rape script," identifying a triangulation of violence and desire? Why, for example, does Fanon substitute the colonizing for the colonized woman?[7] And, second, why do postcolonial critics return to Burke's earlier version that assigns the Indian woman to the place of rape victim? Finally, why do critics of colonial literature typically identify a single rape script that includes only three participants and why are alternatives to this narrative so often denied or obscured in studies of colonial discourse?

Whose Rape?

After reading more than fifty novels about India written between 1800 and 1947 by British men and women, I contend that Fanon is incorrect in arguing that the colonizing woman threatened with rape by a native man is the original rape narrative in British writing about India. Perhaps one reason why Fanon's claim has been so readily accepted by critics of colonial discourse is that there are so many popular novels about India written after 1857 that fictionalize events surrounding the Indian Uprising of 1857 and present narratives which hinge on Englishwomen threatened with rape by Indian men. Brijen Krishore Gupta, in his extensive bibliography of British and Anglo-Indian novels, lists more than eighty novels in English published in this period which allude to what British authors usually call the "Indian Mutiny of 1857."[8]

Some of the reasons for the obsessive repetition of narratives about the Indian Uprising of 1857 are suggested by a brief survey of the events themselves. Nineteenth-century British histories usually characterized the Indian Uprising of 1857 as a military uprising, initiated when Indian soldiers, or sepoys, in the Bengal Native Army refused to handle cartridges for the new Enfield rifle that were rumored to have been greased with a mixture of pig and cow fat, which would be defiling to Muslim and Hindu soldiers alike. The mutiny began on May 10, 1857, when a group of Indian sepoys shot their

British commanding officers and attacked the garrison of the East India Company in Meerut in order to free compatriots who had been imprisoned for openly defying their orders. The rebels then marched to Delhi, where they joined forces with sepoys from the local garrison, overwhelmed the small British community, and drove the survivors from the city. The uprising subsequently spread to major garrisons of the East India Company to the south and east, including Lucknow, Agra, and Cawnpore. When important Indian leaders joined the uprising, including Bahadur Shah II, the Moghul emperor whose court was in Delhi, Nana Sahib of Cawnpore, the Rani of Jhansi, and the hereditary rulers of the province of Oude, which had been taken over by the British in 1855, popular support for the rebellion increased significantly throughout this region. Fighting was savage on both sides, but British control was eventually restored by the time that Gwalior was retaken by British forces on June 20, 1858. The official British explanation of this uprising was that "the Bengal Native Army alone had mutinied and that any civil disturbances were the natural by-products of the breakdown of law and order" (Stokes, *Peasant*, 40), but the policies that the British adopted after 1857 indicate their recognition of more widespread discontent. They not only reorganized the Indian army and dramatically increased the proportion of British to Indian troops, but they also significantly revised the administrative structure of colonial government in India, abolished the East India Company, and imposed a new legal code on the colonized.[9]

Popular British imperial histories of the Uprising of 1857 not only documented the successful battles won by small, isolated groups of British heroes during this war, they also sensationalized the deaths of innocent English civilians, including approximately 200 Englishwomen and children who survived of the siege of Lucknow but were imprisoned and killed at Cawnpore on July 16, 1857. Because "mutiny" novels capitalized on both these themes, they helped to circulate a new rape script involving Englishwomen threatened with rape by Indian men. One of the purposes of this study is to show how and why the actors in Burke's scenario had, by 1857, changed both places and races, so that Englishwomen replaced Indian women as the victims of abduction, imprisonment, intimidation, and rape by violent and lawless Indian men.

Though British histories, melodramas, memoirs, letters, and other material about the Indian Mutiny no doubt played an important part in disseminating this particular version of the colonial rape script, as Patrick Brantlinger and others have argued, these novels performed much more significant ideological and symbolic work than can be summarized simply by reference to the historical events centered on the well at Cawnpore. Certainly, it is no accident that the dominance of this particular version of the colonial rape narrative which makes Englishwomen and their innocent children into a precious national sacrifice coincides with the most martial phase of British imperialism, between 1870 and 1914.[10] Imperial histories and novels alike were used to justify the extremely violent British military campaign of retaliation following the 1857 uprising and to legitimize more authoritarian, forceful, and racist policies in British colonial strategies of control after these events.[11] Because of the taboos and confusions that surround rape, this particular narrative helped mask the inherent contradictions in nineteenth-century English notions of nationality, and the conceptions about sex, gender, race, and class that underlie them, contradictions that have become more transparent to postcolonial readers.

In fact, nineteenth-century mutiny novels that represent the actual rape of white women as an accomplished fact are very rare, though more recent historical novels such as John Masters's *Nightrunners of Bengal* and Paul Scott's *Raj Quartet* perhaps cast a backward shadow.[12] A more typical treatment of this new rape scene can be found in one of the first mutiny novels, Edward Money's *The Wife and the Ward; or, A Life's Error*, published in 1859. In his preface, Money identifies himself as a lieutenant-colonel in the Indian army during the Uprising of 1857 and dedicates his novel to Lord Stanley, secretary of state for India at that time. He writes that his narrative dramatizing the valor of English forces at Cawnpore is "a tale of fiction founded on fact" (iii), a claim repeated in many British and Anglo-Indian mutiny novels.

In *The Wife and the Ward*, Money assigns the role of the rape victim to Marion Paris, the hero's "ward," who is a pure, beautiful, defenseless young English heroine "just bursting into womanhood" (216–217). With her "wondrously perfect Grecian profile," ivory skin, and massy blond hair, Marion fears she will be taken as a "prize" by Nana Sahib, the hereditary ruler of Cawnpore, or abducted and raped by one of his soldiers. Her fears are inspired by what her Indian ayah has told her about "all the horrors perpetuated at Delhi" on the English "ladies." The English matrons in the novel reinforce Marion's terror by refusing to discuss any of the details of the defeat of British forces at Delhi in May of 1857, saying only "it was not a fit subject for an unmarried girl" (386).

The climax of Money's novel occurs when the British forces gathered at Cawnpore can hold out no longer against the army of Nana Sahib and prepare for retreat. At this point, Marion asks the hero, Captain Edgington, to perform the ultimate chivalrous act: "If the rebels beat us; if they should storm the entrenchments, will you promise me, that under no circumstances I shall fall into their hands?" (371). He reluctantly agrees, saying, "I will do what you ask Marion; but remember, I will do it at the last moment. I have given you the promise, let me judge when the act is necessary" (371). Edgington's curious proviso indicates that this imagined rape scenario, like all the rape stories I will analyze in the pages that follow, is fundamentally about power and control, issues that cannot be separated from the "technologies of gender"[13] that work to constitute a British national identity founded upon traditional gender roles and presumptions about (hetero)sexuality.

Since Money is working within the constraints of what he insists are historical "facts" about the defeat of British forces at Cawnpore in 1857, his hero is eventually compelled to deliver on his promise when Nana Sahib's forces attack the English survivors as they climb into the boats at the ghat near Cawnpore. In the confusion of the battle, Marion appears beside one of the wounded soldiers, like "an angel of light amidst the dark scenes. . . . still beautiful, with a wild light in her eyes, and her partly untrammeled golden hair, blown out by the hot blasts, brushing against his cheek" (403). A few pages later, realizing that they are about to be overrun, Edgington shoots Marion. Money includes some unique, eroticized, and gruesome details, describing, for instance, how "the brains of Marion Paris bespattered the chest of her guardian" (403), but he dramatizes a new and more violent response to the threat of rape that is repeated endlessly in subsequent mutiny novels when the English hero kills, or promises to kill, the heroine in order to save her from rape by Indian men.

Money's *Wife and Ward* differs in one small but significant respect from many subsequent mutiny novels in that the hero committed his "life's error" earlier in the novel by falling in love and marrying the wrong woman, the tall, statuesque, egocentric and "strong-minded" Beatrice Plane (101). Edgington has already separated from his wife when he meets the blond, beautiful, and more docile Marion Paris. Though both the hero and heroine die at Cawnpore, Beatrice apparently survives, presumably enriched by the inheritance of her husband's wealth. Edgington's ill-fated marriage to the willful and selfish Beatrice thus suggests how the rape script in this novel also expresses the displacement of British domestic concerns about marriage, divorce, consent, male competition, and military honor, as well as male anxieties about losing patriarchal power and control.

Though Money's paradigmatic narrative about Englishwomen threatened with rape during the Indian Uprising of 1857 is repeated in dozens of popular British and Anglo-Indian novels for at least eight decades after this colonial war, this particular version of the colonial rape script is riddled with odd contradictions.[14] The imagined scenes of rape repeated in the name of history in these texts refer to and depend upon unverifiable, undecidable, and ambiguous events in the historical record. Given the social construction of nineteenth-century British notions of gender and sex roles and the newly re-invented conventions of chivalry in the 1850s and 1860s, the rape of an Englishwoman under these circumstances could have no reliable witnesses since Englishmen who see Englishwomen threatened by rape must die trying to save them. Likewise, Englishwomen who do not die while trying to protect their "virtue," or kill themselves afterward, became morally suspect and hence identify themselves as unreliable informants. Finally, after 1857, Indian ob-servers of either sex were categorically defined as constitutionally untruth-ful, as these novels show, so they also could not verify reports about the rape of Englishwomen by Indian men. Thus, there could be no reliable witness of Englishwomen raped, and indeed no verifiable historical accounting of the numbers of Englishwomen raped during the mutiny. Consequently, there was, and is, no easy way to answer questions about whether these novels accu-rately represent the historical experiences of actual Englishwomen during the Indian Uprising of 1857.

Rape and the Historical Archive

The difficulties that scholars face in assessing the accuracy of histori-cal or fictional representations of Englishwomen raped during the Indian Up-rising of 1857 is further compounded by larger ideological and social contradictions surrounding rape in both British and Anglo-Indian cultures in this period. While I recognize that researchers must be cautious about pro-jecting contemporary assumptions about rape into historical contexts where they are inappropriate, I would argue that there is much historical evidence to suggest that rape would have been vastly underreported by both British and Indian women in India throughout the nineteenth and early twentieth centuries.[15]

First of all, rape is notoriously difficult to define and describe. The word "rape" in English initially referred to the theft of goods or the abduction of a woman when it began to circulate in the early 1400s, and it only gradually acquired its most common modern meaning denoting a woman's sexual vio-lation in the 1580s, usages that Shakespeare employed in "The Rape of Lucrece" and *Titus Andronicus*. Early English legal traditions defining rape retained these associations, so that, until the early eighteenth century, rape was generally conceptualized as the theft of male property rather than as sexual violence against a woman, as Susan Brownmiller has documented (16–17, 25–30). By 1768, Blackstone's legal commentaries referred to rape as sexual assault in noting that "an attempt to rob, ravish, or to kill is far less penal than the actual robbery, rape, or murder."[16]

Though Englishwomen throughout the eighteenth century slowly gained more recognition for the personal damages that they suffered as a result of rape, some of these gains were reversed in the last two decades of the eighteenth century, when, as Anna Clark has documented, Great Britain witnessed a general silencing of women's reports about rape. Beginning around 1795, transcripts of London rape trials, for example, were no longer printed because they were considered "too 'indecent' to expose to the eyes of the public" (Clark, *Women's*, 75). By 1830, legal reforms made rape charges somewhat easier to prove in England, and, in 1841, the penalty for rape was changed from death to transportation (60). Nonetheless, middle-class women who were raped in the Victorian period faced many more social obstacles in reporting and gaining prosecution for the crime. Clark describes how "the dichotomy of chastity and unchastity" began to structure public discourses about rape in the early decades of the nineteenth century, transforming Englishwomen's perceptions about rape in at least three ways: "First, they robbed women of their ability to articulate their own experiences of rape, and imported a sense of shame to women who had lost their honour. Second, these discourses magnified a thousand-fold individual men's power to terrify women through rape, for fear served to warn women to behave according to restrictive middle-class standards. Third, they concealed the reality of violence against women. No matter how a woman behaved, men—lovers, masters, fathers, strangers, neighbours—could rape her with near impunity" (128). For many reasons, these social inhibitions were further amplified by the colonial culture of British India.

There is, to my knowledge, no archival study of reported rape cases in British India for any period in the nineteenth century that can be compared with Pamela Scully's scrupulous and brilliant analysis of the transcripts of rape trials in South Africa between 1831 and 1865. Scully's research suggests, however, that when rape occurs in British colonial contexts, it is even more deeply implicated in the power relations that enforced gender and class subordination as well as racial difference. At the same time, it is also important not to underestimate the contentiousness of colonial cultures. Anne McClintock characterizes these unstable dynamics when she observes that the British imperial project in India was "a contradictory and ambiguous project, shaped as much by tensions within metropolitan policy and conflicts with colonial administrations—at best, ad hoc and opportunistic affairs—as by the varied cultures and circumstances into which colonials intruded and the conflicting responses and resistances with which they were met" (15).[17] Rape in nineteenth-century England was already redolent with ambiguities, but when it took place in British India under the power regimes that characterized early nineteenth-century colonialism, it was loaded with additional ideological and symbolic meanings, and when it occurred under late nineteenth-century imperialism, it became dangerously overdetermined.

Moreover, when rape is imagined as involving a colonizing woman and a colonized man, it becomes even more ideologically fraught because of the history of how the colonizers exploited reports of rape for political purposes throughout the nineteenth and early twentieth centuries. Ann L. Stoler has compared reports about white women threatened with rape by native men during the Indian Uprising of 1857 with similar documents written in the 1920s and 1930s expressing concerns about the "protection" of white women in Southern Rhodesia, Kenya, and Papua. She concludes that "the rhetoric of sexual assault and the measures used to prevent it had virtually no correlation with actual incidences of rape of European women by men of color. Just the contrary: there was often no ex post facto evidence, nor any at the time, that rapes were committed or that rape attempts were made. . . . This is not to suggest that sexual assaults never occurred, but that their incidence had little to do with the fluctuations in anxiety about them" ("Carnal Knowledge," 68). Instead, as Stoler argues, this "concern over protection of white women intensified during real and perceived crisis of control—provoked by threats to the internal cohesion of the European communities or by infringement on its borders" (68). Thus, though the Indian Uprising of 1857 occurred "nearly half a century earlier than in colonies elsewhere," she contends that it provides a "template" for "an entire restructuring of colonial morality in which political subversion was tied to sexual impropriety and was met with calls for middle-class respectability, domesticity, and increased segregation—all focusing on European women" (87).

Three more specific historical problems should be kept in mind when considering the ideological work performed by reports about Indian men threatening Englishwomen with rape during and after the Indian Uprising of 1857. First, while mutiny novels busily circulated these narratives in the name of history, professional historians increasingly disputed their claims. As early as 1868, in his book entitled *Cawnpore*, the distinguished historian George Trevelyan confirmed that 206 Englishwomen and children died of sickness or were killed at Cawnpore on July 16, 1857, but he insists that there was no evidence to support rumors that Englishwomen had been raped before their bodies were thrown into the notorious well at Cawnpore. Instead, he claimed that these heroic Englishwomen died "without apprehension of dishonour."[18]

Second, these new rape narratives were deeply implicated in and marked by the increasing "racialization of gender norms" in British and colonial culture in India in the latter half of the nineteenth century. Trevelyan's history provides a telling illustration. In surveying the evidence concerning Eliza Wheeler, the only surviving rape victim whose case he could substantiate at Cawnpore, Trevelyan inadvertently reveals how Victorian notions about sexuality and race insinuated themselves into his narrative. Trevelyan verified that the youngest daughter of Sir Hugh Wheeler was abducted at Cawnpore, but he disputes the accuracy of several popular London melodramas that represent her as killing her Indian attacker in order to save her honor. On the contrary, Trevelyan reports that she and her attacker survived the fighting at Cawnpore and that she was discovered, several years later, living quietly with her "master under a Mohammedan name" (255). Indicating how rape, as early as 1868, became entangled with emerging ideas about racial purity, later authorized by social Darwinism, Trevelyan assumes that Miss Wheeler's survival proves either that she had consented to sex and so was not raped or that she was not a true Englishwoman, since a racially "pure" woman would have died trying to protect her honor or would have committed suicide immediately afterward. Trevelyan thus concludes that Miss Wheeler "was by no means of pure English blood" (255). His censorious treatment of Eliza Wheeler's example demonstrates why Englishwomen who were raped during the mutiny and survived would probably never tell their stories.

Our current understanding of the history and uses of rape in British India between 1880 and 1900 is much more complete, thanks to the meticulous scholarship of Mrinalini Sinha, Tanika Sarkar, and others who have recently analyzed colonial responses to the Ilbert Bill.[19] In 1883, Anglo-Indians organized large mass protests, objecting to this reform measure offered by the Gladstone government that proposed to remove the restrictions preventing qualified Indian judges from trying cases involving European and British subjects living outside the chief presidency towns (Sinha, *Colonial*, 38). Sinha notes that the most incendiary objections to the Ilbert Bill concerned the prospect of Indian judges trying cases that touched on "such 'delicate' subjects as rape, marriage, or divorce among Europeans where the 'damage to the prestige of the white race would be unimaginable'" (48). During this debate, an unprecedented number of Anglo-Indian women defied strong colonial taboos, which usually confined them to silence on public issues and prevented them from speaking about sex in general and rape in particular, when they organized protests and letter-writing campaigns in order to express their vehement objections to these judicial reforms.

Sinha's research also exposes one final ambiguity in official British reports about the rape of British women by Indian men. In a case widely publicized by the Anglo-Indian press, the wife of James Hume was reported as charging one of the servants in her household, a sweeper named Greedhare Mehter, with attempted sexual assault. Mehter maintained his innocence throughout the trial, but the jury nonetheless convicted him. Two years later in a private communication, it was revealed that Mrs. Hume and her husband had deliberately perjured themselves. She and Greedhare "had been involved in an intimate relationship for some six months prior to the case. Mr. Hume's discovery of this liaison had led to the charge against the native of attempted sexual assault" (*Colonial*, 53). This case suggests some of the dangerous instabilities created in the late nineteenth-century when sexuality was "racialized" and when rape laws were used to police errant desires among the colonizers as well as the colonized. While Mrs. Hume's case displays the violence directed toward individuals whose desire for connection and love prompted them to cross racial and cultural divides, it also shows the relative privilege that British women could claim at the expense of Indian men and women under the Raj.

In dramatic contrast to Englishwomen like Mrs. Hume who successfully filed charges of rape against an Indian man and fraudulently obtained a conviction, Indian women who were raped during the nineteenth and early twentieth centuries not only had to overcome the strong sex and gender norms of their own cultures, but they also had to contend with all the linguistic, legal, cultural, and economic obstacles faced by the "subaltern" in India.[20] On the most basic linguistic and cultural level, Indian women who did not speak English had to cope, first of all, with the cultural barriers imposed by the colonizers' language. For example, the Urdu word for rape, "*balāt*," conveys many of the same connotations as the English term since it is derived from the verb "to take" and carries associations invoking strength and force. Like the English word "rape," the word "*balāt*" can also be used in the metaphorical sense to mean, for instance, the "taking" of a city. However, the Bengali word for rape, "*dharṣan*," may be used as a synonym for the English verbs "to ravish," "to assault," or "to oppress," but it does not carry any of the associations conveyed by the English word which link rape with abduction and theft. The words for "rape" in several of the languages used in South India pose similar translation problems.[21]

Moreover, even if an Indian woman overcame these linguistic obstacles and persisted in seeking damages from an English or Indian man who had raped her, she would often have to persuade her father or brother to speak on her behalf in court during the period between 1830 and the adoption of Macaulay's uniform Indian Penal Code in 1861. Moreover, in the unlikely event that she or her representative actually obtained a hearing, she, like her English counterpart, would face severe social ostracism, especially if her complaint were legally dismissed. Finally, her case would be judged according to capricious and often ill-informed English interpretations of Hindu or Muslim laws and customs. Whether they were civilians employed by the East India Company who were trained in Indian languages and culture at Fort William in Calcutta or British military officers in the Indian army who were assigned to civil duty, most British men serving as colonial magistrates would have studied at least two of the most familiar texts defining relevant Hindu and Muslim legal traditions: *The Laws of Manu*, translated into English by Sir William Jones in 1794 (Schwab, 52), and *The Koran*, translated into English by George Sale in 1734 (Said, *Orientalism*, 63). Since both these texts consider rape in the context of marriage, they would prompt British magistrates who consulted them to regard rape as a matter of "personal" rather than "general" law. As Wendy Doniger and Brian K. Smith explain, in British India before the adoption of Macaulay's legal code in 1861, *The Laws of Manu* were "instrumental in the construction of a complex system of jurisprudence in which 'general law' was supplemented by a 'personal law' determined by one's religious affiliations. 'Hindu law' or *dharmashastra*, was applied to nearly eighty percent of the population of colonial India in matters of marriage, and divorce, legitimacy, guardianship, adoption, inheritance, religious endowments and so on" (Doniger and Smith, *Laws*, lx).

Both *The Laws of Manu* and the *Koran* discuss rape in ways that were, to some degree, compatible with British rape law as well as with Victorian social conventions defining rape, since both texts estimate the severity of the crime and set the requisite punishments by considering the victim's marital and family status. *The Laws of Manu*, for example, considers rape in relation to other acts of violence and regards the incidence of rape as an important indicator of social order (Doniger and Smith, *Laws*, 8:344), asserting that righteous men are duty bound to protect women and priests (8:348). The largest fines and most severe punishments are assigned to men who rape "unwilling virgins" who are above them in caste, while only a "very small fine" is set for men who have unwanted sexual relations with the wives of "strolling actors," "menial servant girls," or "female ascetics" (8:362–363).

At the same time, both these texts also pose serious challenges to English legal definitions of rape. *The Laws of Manu*, for instance, offers a complex system to determine the degree of a woman's sexual "consent" by assessing, among other things, her willingness to accept social practices concerning her seclusion (Doniger and Smith, *Laws*, 3:8–11, 8:382). At the same time, *The Laws of Manu* clearly recognizes the sexual agency of all women regardless of age or sexual experience. It declares, for example, that "if a man in his arrogance overpowers a virgin and does it to her, two of his fingers should immediately be cut off and he should pay a fine of six hundred (pennies)," but they also set much smaller fines for a man who "corrupts a willing virgin" when "he is her equal" (8:367–368).

Though many colonial magistrates were aware that the traditions defining Indian women's position and claims under the "personal" laws of Islam were more contested, they would find, if they consulted *The Koran*, that women's rape was discussed in relation to divorce. One famous passage, for example, elaborates on social practices that were much more liberal than English laws concerning marriage and divorce: "When you divorce women, and they have reached / their term, then retain them honourably / or set them free honourably; do not retain them / by force, to transgress; whoever does that / has wronged himself" (Arberry, 1:60).

Though the definition for and punishment of rape were more uniformly applied, regardless of the complainant's religion, after the Indian Penal Code was adopted in 1861, Indian women who charged Englishmen with rape still had to contend with laws that remained deeply engraved by the political power and epistemological privileges of the colonizer. English army officers, for example, could and did use the term "outrage" rather than "rape" when unruly soldiers raped Indian women. Conversely, British judges could, and occasionally did, redefine an incident involving an Indian man who touched an Englishwoman, as "sexual assault."[22] Moreover, when rape did occur under the colonial conditions in force in British India between 1861 and 1947, there were many other reasons why English judges might refuse to acknowledge the complaint, since rape charges exposed the failure of the presumedly benign paternalism that male colonizers were supposed to extend to the Indian women they were assigned to protect.

In short, because the incidence and verifiability of rape are so elusive—in other words, because rape's relation to the historical "real" is so difficult to ascertain, especially in this colonial context—uncertainties constitute rape's most powerful significance. Since my academic background is in British literature and critical theory, I will leave it to others to untangle rape's complex relation to the "historical real" in British India. What I offer, instead, in the pages that follow, is a "genealogy of the sexual imaginary" that produced various scripts about rape in British and Anglo-Indian novels about India written between 1830 and 1947.[23]

Contextualizing Rape

Though rape was legally defined in English law throughout the nineteenth century and, after 1861, in Indian jurisprudence as sexual intercourse without a woman's consent, rape nonetheless continued to be conceptualized, both inside and outside the courtroom, according to Sylvia Tomaselli, as "crime, vice, sin, ritual, physical violence, perversion or just another word for sex" (Tomaselli and Porter, 10). For all of these reasons, an adequately nuanced analysis of rape requires a multidisciplinary perspective that incorporates historical, political, ethical, economic, psychological, and cultural perspectives.

Like Shani D'Cruze, I regard rape, in literature or in life, not as the invariable consequence of sexual frustration or biologically determined male aggression but rather as the consequence of a complex process which prompts particular men to interpret the meaning of their gender, sexuality, desire, and bodily impulses in order to act in this particularly violent way. As D'Cruze explains, "The occurrence of sexual violence depends on the availability of scripts and the immediate and more general social environment, including the interaction of rapist and victim" (384). She notes that "scripts exist in the plural, they can be changed. . . . Scripts include moral prescriptions that define 'normal' behaviour and allow 'escape clauses' or neutralisations justifying behaviour in particular situations that may otherwise be seen as immoral. This does not necessarily mean that rape is defined in terms of sex, if scripts are available that define sex in terms of power" (384). In the following analysis of literature written in and about British India, I consider all the scripts related to rape that were in wide circulation between 1830 and 1947 in order to account for the dominance, after 1857, of the particular rape script of white women threatened with rape by Indian men. In this way, I hope to illustrate the ideological and symbolic work that these scripts performed.

Legal definitions of rape do not adequately comprehend its significance in nineteenth-century England because the laws defining it expose fundamental paradoxes in British women's legal and social relation to the nation-state, a relation that was opened to question particularly by the French Revolution. In the late eighteenth century, as Michel Foucault argues in *Discipline and*

Punish, "the human body was entering a machinery of power that explores it, breaks it down and rearranges it" in order to create "subjected and practiced bodies, 'docile' bodies," not only so "that they may do what one wishes, but so that they may operate as one wishes, with the techniques, the speed and the efficiency that one determines" (138). Foucault is silent here and elsewhere about how gender, class, race, and other hierarchies further determined the modern subject's relative power and relation to the nation-state. More recently, however, feminist theorists have elaborated many of the ways that "docile bodies" were "gendered" and "sexed" in the nineteenth century so that women remained legally invisible and subordinated to fathers and husbands, and to the state.

For example, Carole Pateman's *The Sexual Contract* documents how male bodies were designated as the "artificial" body that defined the "social contract" in place throughout the nineteenth and early twentieth centuries in Great Britain, so that women remained excluded from the full rights of citizenship. She offers a trenchant analysis of how English formulations of the "social contract" depended upon the primordial and unspoken "sexual contract" that organized the social arrangements of men's and women's lives in earlier periods. Pateman argues that this implicit "sexual contract" works to disguise contradictions in the writings of the "classic theorists" of English contract theory in the eighteenth and nineteenth centuries, and she enumerates some of these contradictions: "Women are not party to the original contract through which men transform their natural freedom into the security of civil freedom. Women are the subject of the contract. The (sexual) contract is the vehicle through which men transform their natural right over women into the security of civil patriarchal right. But if women have no part in the original contract, if they can have no part, why do the classic social contract theorists . . . make marriage and the marriage contract part of the natural condition? How can beings who lack the capacities to make contracts nevertheless be supposed always to enter into the contract?" (6). Because rape is an act that displays women's lack of consent to the sexual contract, either inside or outside marriage, it highlights British women's exclusion from the "social contract."

After the French Revolution, British feminists began to protest various inconsistencies in the sexual contract that defined women's place in marriage and attempted, at the same time, to renegotiate the social contract in order to gain greater recognition of women's rights as citizens. Mary Wollstonecraft, for example, reveals her legacy as an Enlightenment thinker when she identifies the centrality of women's consent in the sexual contract and notes that

Englishwomen's lack of education prevents them from exercising informed consent in their choice of marriage partners. She also challenges the sentimentality that mystified British marriage arrangements by arguing that women were "slaves" to their fathers and husbands (167). Moreover, as Anne Mellor has noted, Wollstonecraft's focus on the egalitarian family as "the prototype of a genuine democracy, a family in which husband and wife not only regard each other as equals in intelligence, sensitivity, and power, but also participate equally in childcare and decision making," offered a "truly revolutionary political program, one in which gender and class differences could be erased" (38).

Of course, the problem of women's consent to the social contract remained a point of contention in Great Britain throughout the nineteenth and early twentieth centuries.[24] Moderate nineteenth-century feminists supported various efforts to improve women's education and, later in the century, to open higher education and the medical and legal professions to women. Others campaigned for legal reforms in marriage, divorce, and property laws that disadvantaged women, and succeeded in obtaining reforms in the Custody Act of 1839, the Matrimonial Causes Acts of 1857 and 1878, and in the Married Women's Property Acts of 1870 and 1882, among other legal reforms. From the 1860s on, feminists were involved in various efforts to secure the vote for women, suffering a major defeat in 1867, and again gaining considerable support, and notoriety, during the suffragette campaign in first two decades of the twentieth century, winning the vote for middle-class Englishwomen in 1918, and for all Englishwomen by 1928.

In some ways, though, it was the campaign led by Josephine Butler to repeal the Contagious Disease Acts that had the most powerful effect in changing the social scripts concerning sexuality, prostitution, and rape, both in England and in British India, especially after 1886. Butler's domestic campaign gained force in the 1870s and succeeded in obtaining the repeal of the Contagious Diseases Acts in 1886 in England. Her campaign to repeal the Contagious Diseases Acts in India capitalized on the agitations around the Ilbert Bill in 1883. A fully contextualized account of rape in British India must consider how these various feminist campaigns restructured notions about gender, sex, and power, as well as the meaning of women's "consent" to the changing social and sexual contract.[25]

Moreover, an adequate analysis of rape also requires an ethics and model of citizenship that recognize the consequences of women's historical exclusion from the social contract. According to Moira Gatens, liberal individualist and contractual models of citizenship alike have failed to recognize how men and women inhabit their various bodies, experience their passions, and exercise their imaginations, and these exclusions are particularly relevant in the evaluation of rape cases (129, 137–139). Gatens points out that since the social contract was originally "entered into by men only, one must surmise that it is a contract designed to secure the needs of male bodies and desires" (51). She then offers the following corrective model of social ethics: "In so far as the political realm is concerned with the governance of ourselves and others, the organization of our needs and resources, our rights and obligations, it is quintessentially concerned with the passions and the imagination" (129). A more complete understanding of all citizens' relation to the state and community requires an ethics that considers how love relations between the sexes are shaped by "the fact that these take place in a patriarchal society that has a history of excluding women from political participation," since this history predetermines the ability "to love from a freedom of mind" and to reach "an agreement in power" that allows for trust and intimacy between men and women (133).

Finally, a fully contextualized analysis of rape in British India requires reference to a psychology that recognizes the historically changing social constructions of the body, the psychological tensions specific to colonial life in this particular time and place, and the larger economic world system that predetermined the trends in British colonial policy in India. In her excellent study *Bodies That Matter*, Judith Butler develops a sophisticated model of modern subjectivity that encompasses gender, sexual identity, and perceptions of the body and so is particularly useful for my analysis of rape in the pages that follow. Butler presents a paradigm that explains how an individual's inner experiences of the body find expression in the "performativity of gender" which enacts the historical and material forces that shape the "regulatory ideals" defining sexuality and gender identity. She explains that modern gendered subjects are thus constituted by the "imaginary logic" that allows them to apprehend the historical and social "real," a logic that is determined by the "domain of the symbolic." Since Butler's model acknowledges the mediation of symbolic language, it can be used to refute the simple biological determinism of many earlier writers on rape because it recognizes how psychological processes remain open to the prevailing "rape scripts" that are dominant in a particular time and place.

Moreover, when Butler's analysis of the interactive psychological processes that create modern gendered subjects is applied to describe the formation of colonial subjects in British India, it also helps to reveal more of the "imaginary logic" by which colonial subjects apprehend the historical and social "real" of life under the Raj. According to Butler, modern gendered identities are "installed" in children by reference to an "exclusionary matrix" that "requires the simultaneous production of a domain of abject beings, those who are not yet 'subjects,' but who form the constitutive outside to the domain of the subject" (3). Sexual identity is forged at the "site of dreaded identification against which—and by virtue of which—the domain of the subject will circumscribe its own claim to autonomy and life" (3). Thus, she explains, "the subject is constituted through the force of exclusion and abjection, one which produces a constitutive outside to the subject, an abjected outside which is, after all, 'inside' the subject as its own founding repudiation" (3).

Likewise, when we consider how these internal and interactive psychological processes worked to establish not only the gender but also the racial identities of colonial children in British India and how they operated eventually to produce the ambivalent heterosexual desires of colonizing men and women, we can see why the construction of colonial subjects depended, both literally and psychologically, upon a constant reiteration of the abject otherness of the colonized men and women who surrounded them. Moreover, when colonized men and women who were already racially categorized as abject assumed the roles of domestic servants, they were constantly forced to transgress those physical boundaries that initially defined abjection, since they were assigned to prepare food and dispose of bodily waste, though, at least under the Raj, they were ostensibly excluded from participation in the third domain of abjection: sexuality. Butler's analysis of the central importance of the processes and consequences of "abjection" in the creation of "docile bodies" thus suggests why interracial rape was such a powerful trope in British India, especially after 1857.

Butler's analysis of the "imaginary logic" that creates the modern subject helps to explain the psychological and symbolic significance of the many phantoms of "abjection" that haunt numerous Anglo-Indian novels written in the late nineteenth century. In *Mr. Jervis* (1894), a popular novel by Bithia Mary Croker, for example, one of the lost "mutiny ladies" makes a fleeting appearance, and to both the heroine and the hero of the novel, this fictional cousin of Eliza Wheeler appears more as a nightmare than an actual woman. This ghostly figure discloses the "abjection" that rape victims typically embodied since she is a fantastic projection of all the colonial taboos defining gender, race, and sexuality that anchored the identities of colonizing men and women, especially in the post-mutiny period.

When Croker's heroine, Honour Gordon, is traveling through Northern India, she is forced to share a room in a "dak bungalow" with a woman dressed in native clothing; she has been told that this woman is a "Persian lady." She is awakened in the night by this "handsome" (226) older woman, who explains that when she heard Honour play her violin a few hours before, something in her heart "melted": "I felt I must see you—for though I had never seen you face to face, I loved you! I asked you to share my room that I might gaze at you secretly and carry away the remembrance of your features in my heart" (226). Honour asks her what is troubling her, and she says, "I have not looked on the face of an innocent English girl for thirty-five years. I was once like you" (227). When Honour asks her name, she begins her story with, "Aye, who am I, that is the question, a question that will never be answered. For its own works lieth every soul in pledge; my soul is pledged to silence. You have heard . . . of—the—mutiny—ladies?" (227). When Honor responds with a conventionally patriotic, "Yes, poor souls; and proud I am of my countrywomen" (227), the mysterious woman replies: "I doubt if you would be proud of me. You speak of those who stood up, aye, as I have seen them, and offered themselves to the sword; those who were butchered and slaughtered like oxen; I speak of—of—of—others—how can I tell this child?—who were carried away and lost forever in native life. I . . . I am one of those. Lost honour, lost life, lost soul! God help me!" (227). She explains that she was once the "belle" of a station that she refuses to name. She was married to an English officer when the eruption of the mutiny separated them. When she and a group of other English survivors met two native regiments that had mutinied, she explains, "we were ordered out in turn just as we drove up, and as each man or woman or child alighted, unarmed and quite defenseless, they were shot or cut down" (228). Left for dead, she recovered and tried to escape but was discovered by an Indian soldier who spared her because of her beauty. "When the stars came out," she continues, "he swung me up on the crupper of his troop horse, and I rode behind him into Lucknow" (229). There, she explains, she eluded him only to fall into the hands of an old Indian man who "dressed me in native clothes, called me his kinsman, and gave me to his son as a wife,—a half-witted, feeble creature, who died, and I was left a widow, a native widow. . . . I never crossed that fatal postern; I was, as my people believed, in my grave" (229). *Mr. Jervis* serves to remind us that most British and Anglo-Indian novels that include the familiar rape scenario of the white woman threatened with rape by an Indian man are designed to assign not only the Indian man who rapes but also any Englishwoman who survives such a rape to the zone of abjection.

However, as Judith Butler contends, when violence, including the violence of rape, is reassigned to a foreign domain of abjection, the boundaries between self and the foreign abjected other must be constantly reinforced.

As Butler explains, the prevailing "imperative to be or get 'sexed' requires a differentiated production and regulation of masculine and feminine identification that does not fully hold and cannot be fully exhaustive" (187). This injunction "works not only through reiteration, but through exclusion as well. And in the case of bodies, those exclusions haunt signification as its abject borders or as that which is strictly foreclosed; the unlivable, the non-narrativizable, the traumatic" (*Bodies*, 187–188). In other words, when racial as well as (homo)sexual others are "abjected" by this process, the phantoms of "otherness" multiply and threaten even the mature colonizing subject. By tracing the shadowy career of this wraith, this ambiguous victim, this melodramatic survivor in *Mr. Jervis* and novels like it, we can gain deeper insight into the psychological dynamics and impact of the racialization of sex on colonial rape narratives after 1857.

Many of the British and Anglo-Indian novels in this study show how nineteenth-century feminist discourse about gender contested prevailing definitions of race, class, and desire that were produced by economic and political systems at work in nineteenth-century England, and forced redefinitions of "sexuality" and the bodies named and regulated by these codes. In analyzing the many examples of interracial rape and other preliminary acts of sexualized violence, I will show, to borrow Butler's words, how the "convergent set of historical formations of racialized gender . . . makes up both the social regulation of sexuality and its psychic articulations" (182).

Because these colonial subjects lived and wrote under the British Raj, the range of identities they could claim was limited by reference to a domain of abjection, the contours of which changed in response to each new phase of capitalism. This model of abjection provides a means to illustrate how colonial subjects were created to meet the changing political and social requirements in British India and how the sex, gender, and racial identities they embodied, performed, and reproduced were created by a particular set of psychological needs. Thus we can see the proliferation of rape narratives in the 1870s as a reflex of the increasingly more imperative need to create "docile bodies" that were responsive to the demands of emerging monopoly capitalism, a need met by reconfiguring the domain of abjection by reference to race and sexuality as well as to gender.

"Worlding" Rape

In analyzing the rape scripts at work in the colonial context of British India, I want to show how these narratives about rape are related to the changing global and economic contexts that produced them. While I have organized the chapters in this book thematically, I also want to highlight how these novels supported or challenged the prevailing capitalist relations of the period. I have borrowed the global systems analysis of L. S. Stavrianos as a frame for my discussion in order to illustrate how the colonial policies and ideologies in circulation in British India between 1830 and 1947 changed in response to metropolitan economic interests and how they acted to reproduce the requisite national identities. In following Gayatri Spivak's admonition to provide a more "worlded" perspective in my survey of representations of rape in these novels,[26] I also hope to suggest why particular rape scripts occurred at the same time in different cultures; why, for instance, narratives about the rape of white women by Indian men emerged in British India at approximately the same time as similar themes in American literature after the Civil War.[27]

I begin my analysis by considering British and Anglo-Indian novels that were, for the most part, written after 1830, because, as L. S. Stavrianos explains, this is the period that consolidated India's subordination as a "third world country" (244).[28] He identifies the 1770s as a time when new forms of mercantile capitalism emerged which fundamentally restructured the economic relationship between England and colonial India. Between 1757 and 1830, England took several decisive steps to undermine India's preeminence in the production of beautiful cloth and other luxury items and to "open" markets in India to "a capitalist economy capable of generating a mass trade in necessities against the traditional restricted trade in luxuries" (167). Pitt's India Act of 1784, placing more controls on the political activities of the agents of the East India Company (234), and the Permanent Settlement in Bengal in 1793, redefining land tenure and tax collection (244), restructured both the terms of international trade and the Indian economy to benefit the British. With the renewal of the charter of the East India Company in 1813, and the opening of India to free trade and to British missionary activity, India began to be remapped by new competing discourses defining and justifying the British colonial presence there. As the novels discussed in chapters 1 and 2 show, liberal reformers and Christian evangelicals struggled in the period between 1830 and 1857 to define colonial policies and practices in India, and the traces of this struggle find expression in both British and Anglo-Indian novels.

The 1860s, Stavrianos explains, marked the beginning of a transition from mercantile capitalism to a more global monopoly capitalism. His analysis allows us to see the Indian Uprising of 1857 in a larger economic context which depended upon imperial expansion. Between 1871 and 1900, Britain "added 4.25 million square miles and 66 million people to her empire" in

India (260), and the intense international competition fostered by monopoly capitalism prompted shifts in British colonial policy and ideology in this period. Stavrianos notes that between 1880 and 1914, the cost of supporting the empire often produced deficits in public revenues, so that the maintenance of the empire could be read as a sacrificial act, as the "white man's burden." This does not prove that imperialism was unprofitable; simply that the profits of imperial trade "went to private individuals" rather than to the government (261), as many of the British and Anglo-Indian novels of this period recognize.

Finally, Stavrianos identifies the decade following World War I as initiating the period when nationalist revolutionary movements begin to make their powers felt in India and many other colonial contexts. Anglo-Indian writers, including E. M. Forster, barely acknowledged the existence or mounting influence of Indian nationalism in their novels. Nonetheless this was a period that witnessed the founding of the Indian National Congress in 1885, the Swadeshi movement of the 1890s, the Home Rule agitations of 1916, and Gandhi's successful organization of the Non-Cooperation movement, which led to his arrest in 1922.[29] It is against the background of these revolutionary stirrings in India that I propose to read three novels by E. M. Forster, Sara Jeannette Duncan, and George Orwell.

Rape and British Literary History

A final reason, I contend, why it is so difficult to think straight about rape is that rape marks one of the great confused zones in literary histories of British Romantic and post-Romantic literature and in the literary theory that is currently used to interpret it. Conventional literary histories of British eighteenth- and nineteenth-century literature have failed, until recently, to account for the disappearance of rape as an organizing symbol in both literature and public discourse in the 1780s and 1790s.[30] Rape was, of course, one of the major organizing metaphors in eighteenth-century British literature. Samuel Richardson's *Pamela* (1740) and *Clarissa* (1748) are certainly the most famous examples, and Henry Fielding's play *Rape on Rape* (1730) provides perhaps the best proof that rape was an event that could be explicitly named.

Rape also held a central place in the English Gothic tradition between 1780 and 1830, but in Gothic novels written by women it was usually an unspeakable danger that threatened the heroine, a danger posed by a villain who was almost always a foreigner. As Kate Ellis observes: "One of the real achievements of the Gothic tradition is that it conjures up, in its undefined representation of heroinely terror, an omnipresent sense of impending rape without ever mentioning the word. A young girl pure enough to be a heroine cannot have the forbidden knowledge that would lead her to suspect the presence of ideas of that nature in the minds of men. . . . Pamela's terror came from knowing what her pursuer was after, but the terror of the Gothic heroine is simply that of being confined and then abandoned, and beyond that, of being, in an unspecified yet absolute way, completely surrounded by superior male power" (46). In English Gothic novels by male writers, however, rape is typically described from the rapist's point of view, so that sexual coercion and violent domination are presented as expressions of erotic desire or even love. This confusion is very clearly illustrated in Matthew Lewis's *The Monk* (1796), when Antonia's rape is presented in pornographic detail, ostensibly to evoke sublime sentiments aroused by the horror of this violation of an innocent. Lewis's prurient descriptions of sexual ravishment shocked many contemporary reviewers and readers. Coleridge, for instance, complained that "*The Monk* is a romance, which if a parent saw it in the hands of a son or daughter, he might reasonably turn pale" (Varma, 147). By the 1830s paternalistic canon makers had generally succeeded in wresting such books from impressionable young (and especially female) readers.

By the time that Queen Victoria was crowned in 1837, the subject of rape was banished from polite British literature about English domestic life. In literature that aspired in any way to meet the high literary standards of the period, rape—along with other scenes of sexualized violence—was consigned to the domain of the abject and the unspeakable. Rape was not represented again in serious literature until the 1890s. Elizabeth Barrett Browning, for example, elides Marian Erle's rape in *Aurora Leigh* (1857), though she does differ from most other writers of the period by allowing her protagonist to insist that she was raped rather than seduced. Thus, many of the deep desires and fears evoked by references to rape in Romantic Gothic novels were projected elsewhere.

Since the fantasy world of India offered a domain where the female body and its desires could be more fully represented, Indian women often appear in Romantic poetry as embodiments or symbols of femininity, spirituality, exoticism, and luxurious sensuality.[31] Hence when British and Anglo-Indian novels in the first half of the century take India as their subject, they often focus on the embodied experiences of secluded women of the zenana or the *devadasi*, and they typically describe these women as threatened by rape or sexualized violence, as I argue in chapters 1 and 2. Because Gothic conventions restructured British novels in such a way that Oriental men were usually assigned the role of the villain-rapist, Indian women were typically assigned to the victim's position, as is evident in many of the novels I will discuss. In short, well before the Indian Uprising of 1857, the positions assigned to both the rapist and the rape victim had become "Orientalized." Thus, British novels about India written in the first half of the nineteenth century often feature narratives that, to borrow Gayatri Spivak's succinct formulation, focused on "white men . . . saving brown women from brown men" ("Can," 296), though Anglo-Indian novels introduced some interesting variations on this theme.

While the novels about the Indian Uprising of 1857 popularized and circulated a new rape script, which assigned Englishwomen to the place of rape victims, rape in novels about English domestic life did not reemerge until the 1890s. Though Thomas Hardy blurs the line between seduction and rape in *Tess of the D'Urbervilles* (1891) and takes a less than entirely sympathetic view of Sue Bridehead's marital rape in *Jude the Obscure* (1895), he nonetheless reintroduced the subject of rape into British novels about domestic life.[32] The theme of rape was subsequently explored by several realist writers in the first two decades of the twentieth century, including John Galsworthy in *The Man of Property* (1906), H. G. Wells in *Ann Veronica* (1909), Wyndham Lewis in *Tarr* (1918), and Rebecca West in *The Judge* (1922). Perhaps it is the weight of these antecedents that caused George Orwell to present rape as a boring modern banality in *Burmese Days* (1934).

Because contemporary scholars tend to privilege modernist aesthetics, they are often more familiar with Forster's ambiguous treatment of Adela's possibly real, or possibly imagined, rape in *A Passage to India* than with these other modern though realist treatments of rape. Since Forster's novel is rarely compared with other contemporary representations of rape, this reading of Adela's experience uncannily repeats the process of Orientalizing rape that occurred in the early nineteenth century. This perspective is reinforced by other trends in the 1920s, and especially by the increasing acceptance of new psychoanalytic theories which questioned the reliability of women's testimony about "erotic" experience and which threatened to make heterosexual rape disappear entirely. As early as 1895, Freud declared that virginity itself was infused with an atmosphere of nervousness and of fear.[33] As a result of pronouncements like these, rape as an act that defined the abject limit of sexual desire was—and still is—in danger of being erased altogether in public discourse and in the courtrooms of the metropole. In modernist works like Forster's, rape is thus folded back into the cultural "imaginary" that relies on theories about female sexual hysteria to obscure differences between men's and women's experiences of violence and desire.

Rape is perhaps even more mystified when it is treated by psychoanalytically inclined literary critics more recently. René Girard, for example, in
his magisterial study *Violence and the Sacred* argues that ritualized violence
helps to define the fundamental boundaries of "civilization" and the sacred
by containing "internal" violence within a community. But rape is almost
completely obscured in his analysis, since his view of heterosexuality is so
male centered and essentialized that male violence against women is often
assumed as a physiological given. Girard asserts, for example, that thwarted
male sexuality leads "naturally to violence" and that "sexual desire" is liable
to "fasten upon surrogate objects if the object to which it was originally attracted remains inaccessible" (35). Despite his claim that "unappeased, violence seeks and always finds a surrogate" (2), Girard unaccountably contends
that women "are never, or rarely, selected as sacrificial victims" (12–13). In
making this assertion, Girard not only ignores how rape victims are represented in the classical Greek texts that he discusses, but he also overlooks
one of the most spectacular examples of human ritual sacrifice that emerged
as a popular theme in both British and European Romantic texts in the early
nineteenth century: the Hindu widow's sacrificial death by sati.

Patricia Klindienst Joplin brilliantly critiques Girard's *Violence and the
Sacred* by offering an explication of how rape narratives, from Euripides'
Iphigenia in Aulis to Ovid's version of the Procne and Philomel myth, invoke cultural boundaries in order to delimit the civilized from the barbarian:
"Like the ground beneath the walls of Athens (or Rome), the woman's chastity is surrounded by prohibitions and precautions. Both are protected by political and ritual sanctions; both are sacred. But female chastity is not sacred
out of respect for the integrity of the woman as person; rather, it is sacred
out of respect for violence" (43). All these violent acts display how "the political hierarchy built upon male sexual dominance requires the violent appropriation of the woman's power to speak" (41). Joplin's analysis thus
illuminates the symbolic logic that prompted Romantic poets to find a common denominator that equated rape with sati and other violent and ritualized
"sacrifices" involving women.

Writing in the Colonial Contact Zone

In organizing this study, I have attempted to represent the diversity of
voices audible in the "colonial contact zone" of British India.[34] I have selected a varied sample of more than thirty canonized and uncanonized novels written by British and Anglo-Indian men and women, by Liberals and

Conservatives, metropolitan writers and colonials, by the monolingual and the multilingual. Two-thirds of the novels I discuss were written by men and women who lived in, or at least visited, India for an extended period of time, between 1830 and 1947. This literature is characterized by something new in Orientalist discourse, since it is potentially informed by the personal experiences of the colonizer rather than the traveler or the scholar who stayed at home.[35] Once the East India Company's trade monopoly was abolished in 1813 and India was open to greater colonization by both English merchants and Christian missionaries, many more middle-class Englishmen, and increasingly more Englishwomen, deeply influenced by British Romanticism, actually went out to India. The novels they wrote indicate some of the intellectual baggage they brought with them, which included competing versions of Orientalized violence and desire.

My basic objective in this study is to analyze what happened to ideas about gender and sexuality, love and violence, consent and resistance, seduction and rape, when the writers' bodies, as well as their minds, were transported to India. How did the structure of these texts change when writers confronted the gritty and complicated reality of colonial life in India, when they felt the heat and dust, smelled the champack and the stench, heard the clash of dancing girls' jewelry and the clang of temple bells, and gazed on the bodies of one another? In short, which visions of the erotic possibilities of the Orient could be articulated in this colonial contact zone and why? What configurations of Oriental desire could be reproduced for novel readers in England and British India?

In order to highlight the ideological and symbolic work performed by these texts, I will focus on novels rather than on poetry or drama. As Mikhail Bakhtin has argued, the novel differs from, for example, the epic or the romance because it possesses dialogical capacities which allow it more fully to accommodate competing contemporary voices.[36] Anglo-Indian novels written by British men and women who actually lived in India in the colonial contact zone were potentially more open to what Bakhtin has called "polyglossia," to a wider range of voices than was evident to novelists who never ventured off English soil (12). Anglo-Indian fiction had somehow to contain this babble of voices, and so most of these novels bear the traces of the struggle to reconcile metropolitan and colonial discourses about India. In other words, the Anglo-Indian novel, unlike its metropolitan counterpart, commanded more authority to contest the official descriptions of India constructed by English parliamentarians, historians, journalists, artists, and writers who never left home.[37]

The Anglo-Indian novelists included in this study typically represent India as deeply divided, first of all, by mutually unintelligible languages. Many Anglo-Indian novels representing colonial life in British India, especially novels written by colonizing women, often represent characters bewildered by colonial polyglossia, characters who simply cannot understand, speak, read, or write the languages of the Indian peoples with whom they lived and over whom they presumably ruled. This tendency in Anglo-Indian women's fiction is hardly surprising since Englishmen in colonial service were usually required to learn at least one Indian language, while Englishwomen were excluded from the educational institutions that taught these languages until at least the 1880s.[38]

Anglo-Indian novels written by men and women often illustrate, nonetheless, the interesting linguistic possibilities of colonial life. Kipling's *Kim* provides a supreme example displaying the magic of colonial heteroglossia even as it demonstrates the imperial advantages enjoyed by an Indian-born "sahib and son of a sahib." Kim is able to understand, speak, and even dream in several Indian "vernaculars" with the fluency of a native, although he also enjoys the advantages of "thinking in English." *Kim* similarly displays the multilingual richness of Indian culture because it contrasts the fluid beauty of oral culture with the power conveyed by written speech, though the novel also shows the confusions created by native letter writers who imperfectly translate the spoken into the written word. Finally, *Kim* suggests the semantic possibilities offered by shape-shifting disguises, equivocal languages, and codes as Kim gradually masters not only written English but also the secret language used by the agents of the Great Game. Yet, for all his openness to colonial polyglossia, Kipling, like most Anglo-Indian novelists, insists that the colonizer can master the language and ways of the colonized, while the colonized are denied this power.

As *Kim* and many other texts in this study will show, Anglo-Indian novels differ from metropolitan examples since they include voices speaking an English dialect that some metropolitan readers could hardly understand, even with the aid of a dictionary like Yule and Burnell's *Hobson-Jobson*, which formally documented the linguistic features of this dialect. Whereas a novel as mainstream as Thackeray's *Vanity Fair* includes exotic Anglo-Indian vocabulary in order to enhance the comic possibilities of Jos Sedley's characterization, most Anglo-Indian novels include this vocabulary as a matter of course, often appending glossaries as an aid for the uninitiated English reader.

Anglo-Indian novels, especially those written after 1857, generally represent worlds that are more immediately constituted by imperial rhetoric and more invested in its reproduction. Thus, these novels often bear the traces of specific political causes endorsed by colonial administrations in India, but less well understood at home. Nearly all Anglo-Indian novels in this sample show a vehement resistance to colonial reforms proposed by Liberal metropolitan reformers, and often repress altogether the rhetoric and material evidence of the power of Indian nationalism. Thus, Anglo-Indian novels are deeply marked by complicity, even when the author considers him- or herself free from the more obvious bureaucratic agents of censorship and colonial consolidation.

Finally, these novels betray the deep divides created by gender, class, and sexuality, divisions intensified by Victorian notions of men's and women's separate spheres and by nineteenth-century feminist critiques of existing gender arrangements both in Great Britain and, increasingly, in India. In *Kim* and countless other novels by Anglo-Indian male writers, women of both races are marginalized even though Englishwomen are frequently identified as the cause of the Empire's "ruin." Scholars working in older critical traditions often relied upon genre hierarchies to screen out these gender differences, valorizing male "adventure" novels and dismissing the large corpus of novels by Anglo-Indian women by labeling them inferior "romances."[39] One of my objectives in rereading this fiction is to reassess the representations of British and Indian women in Anglo-Indian fiction and to reconsider the relationships between male adventure stories and these once-popular female romances.

Gender as Location

In order to demonstrate the diversity of Anglo-Indian writing and to highlight the variables of gender, race, and class, I want to begin by specifying the range of locations and positions in the colonial hierarchy of British India that these writers occupied in writing under the Raj. The literary choices they made to reiterate metropolitan models or to exploit the "ethnographic real," to stereotype the Indian peoples they observed and worked with, or to write with greater openness about the multiple cultures and languages of India were clearly determined by their personal choices and by their places in the complex, interlocking prestige hierarchies of British India.[40] These hierarchies were, in turn, constantly transformed by larger historical, economic, and political realities, most notably, of course, by the Indian Uprising of 1857, which prompted a restructuring of the entire colonial bureaucracy.

Most of the Anglo-Indian men who wrote fiction came to India because they worked in the Indian army or in a regiment of the British army assigned to Indian duty, as was the case, for example, with Edward Money, Robert Armitage Sterndale, and J. E. Muddock. Some were military men who were assigned to "civil duty" or, after 1857, who worked in the Indian Civil Service, like Philip Oliphant. A few, like Meadows Taylor, were members of the less prestigious and more racially integrated "uncovenanted" branch of what became the civil service. Still others, like George Orwell, served stints with the colonial police. Many of these men were amateur writers who began writing only after their retirement.

The two most famous and familiar male authors in this study, however, Rudyard Kipling and E. M. Forster, held positions that were anomalous, since they were professional writers and were able to take positions "outside" the most powerful institutions defining colonial life in British India. Although Kipling's father held official positions in several important cultural institutions in India, including a curatorship at the museum in Lahore, Kipling himself was less constrained during the early years of his career in India, because he began by working as a journalist.[41] Forster held a position even further outside the institutional structures of British India, because he worked as a private secretary for the Maharajah of Dewas Senior, and he knew that his appointment was only temporary. Others, like G. A. Henty and Hume Nisbet, were professional writers who capitalized on their experiences as "globe-trotters" and took advantage of the opportunities for cheaper travel to India that became available in the late nineteenth century.

The conditions defining the lives and writing of female Anglo-Indian authors were more complex than those for male writers since their status was usually determined by the men they married.[42] Moreover, whether they married or not, the situation of colonizing women was characterized by what Anne McClintock has usefully described as their "ambiguous complicity" in colonial culture:

> Barred from the corridors of formal power, they experienced the privileges and social contradictions of imperialism very differently from colonial men. Whether they were shipped out as convicts or conscripted into sexual and domestic servitude; whether they served discreetly at the elbow of power as colonial officers' wives, upholding the boundaries of empire and bearing its sons and daughters; whether they ran missionary schools or hospital wards in remote outposts or worked their husbands' shops and farms, colonial women made none of the direct economic or military decisions of empire and very few reaped its vast profits. Marital laws, property laws, land

laws and the intractable violence of male decree bound them in gendered patterns of disadvantage and frustration. The vast, fissured architecture of imperialism was gendered throughout by the fact that it was white men who made and enforced laws and policies in their own interests. (6)

The Anglo-Indian women writers included in this sample represent all the major sectors of British colonial life in India. Mrs. Fanny Farr Penny was married to a famous Christian missionary active around Madras. Several prolific writers, including Bithia Mary Croker and Maud Diver, were married to army officers. Others were married to men who worked in the Indian Civil Service, like Flora Annie Steel, or to officers in the Indian Public Works Program, like Alice Perrin. Still others, like Ethel Winifred Savi, were married to planters or, like Sara Jeannette Duncan, were married to men who worked outside official colonial bureaucracies; Duncan's husband, for example, was the manager of the Eastern News Agency in Calcutta. Finally, there was at least one woman, Vivian Cory, who escaped entirely from the constraints of life as a "incorporated wife" by remaining single. Cory, who wrote under the pseudonym of Victoria Cross, was born into a famous Anglo-Indian military family and lived for many years in India.

Most Anglo-Indian novels by women were published in the 1890s or later, and several of the women were prolific popular writers who were regarded as direct competitors with now-famous male authors like Kipling. Writing in the later years of the nineteenth century, many of these authors were able to exploit new markets created by the reorganization of the publishing industry in the 1880s and 1890s in England.[43] In short, all of these novels, whether they were written by metropolitan or colonial writers, illustrate the multifarious ways that the technologies of gender worked in concert with sex, class, race, religion, culture and "nationality" in service to the Raj.

Though my focus is on the novels of colonizers rather than the colonized, I have, in chapters 4, 5, and 6, included for purposes of contrast, a handful of poems by anonymous popular Indian poets and several important Indian novels, focusing particularly on Swarnakumari Devi's *The Unfinished Song* (1898), which she translated into English in 1913, and Rabindanath Tagore's *Gora* (1907), translated into English in 1924. Because these texts were widely recognized as important literary works and were easily available in English, they demonstrate some of the alternate perspectives that became increasingly available in the colonial contact zone. Since these novels were written by two Bengali intellectuals, in fact by a brother and sister, they only gesture toward the wider range of Indian literature written or translated into English that, by the 1880s, was in circulation in British India and, increasingly, in England as well.[44]

I have chosen to focus on *The Unfinished Song* and *Gora* because they address relevant issues concerning gender, sexuality, marriage, and consent at a time when these issues were being reconceptualized by Indian nationalists. Though the proper role of women in modern India remained as profoundly contested among Indian nationalists as it was in the decade before World War I in England, a few Indian groups had begun to call for the wider participation of Indian women in political activities and to endorse particular gender-related reforms. In 1919, for example, when the Government of India Act offered the vote to a mere 3 percent of Indian adults, it allowed provincial assemblies to drop exclusions in order to enfranchise a few Indian women who met the property requirements (Liddle and Joshi, 35). Thus, as one provincial delegate observed, "It is gratifying to find that in a country where men are accused of treating women as chattels the political progress of women has been more rapid than in England" (35).

Other gender-related reforms concerning Indian women's education, their age of consent, their rights in marriage and divorce, and widow remarriage were far more compelling concerns for Indian nationalists in this period than women's suffrage. Both Rabindranath Tagore and Swarnakumari Devi took what might be called feminist positions on many of these issues. Rabindranath Tagore's criticism of Hindu customs concerning child marriage and widow remarriage, as well as his support for women's education is well known (Thompson, *Rabindranath Tagore*, 81–83), but Swarnakumari Devi's participation may need some articulation. Devi edited the literary journal *Bharati* between 1885 and 1905, which was a pioneer in publishing women's writing and in offering commentaries on women's education and other aspects of Bengali life and culture (Tharu and Lalit, 237). In 1887, she helped form the Sakhti Samiti, an organization to assist Hindu widows, and in 1889 and 1890 she attended the Indian National Congress. Written at a time when many Hindu nationalists tried to transform "the entire system of nonconsensual, indissoluble, infant marriage" into a "love story with a happy ending" in order to prove that Hindu marriage was superior to "the utilitarian, materialist and narrowly contractual western arrangements" (Sarkar, "Hindu Wife," 226), Devi's *The Unfinished Song*, like Rabindranath Tagore's *Gora*, resists this nationalist impulse to reinscribe traditional gender orthodoxies. Both novels chart a space in the colonial "in between" by identifying alternatives to the sex and gender arrangements of the colonizers.

Reimagining Rape

In arranging the following seven chapters in this study, I have also adopted a historical periodization that recognizes the major shifts in British colonial policy in India, including the outlawing of sati in 1828, the Indian Uprising of 1857, the rise of Joseph Chamberlain and the "New Imperialism" of the 1890s, the outbreak of World War I, and the Jallianwallah Bagh Massacre in 1919. My main objective is to examine the rape scripts circulating in this specific colonial contact zone in order to disclose how these British and Anglo-Indian novels deployed the technologies of gender in order to reposition the English female and male body, to redefine the permissible sexual expressions for each, and to defend traditional gender arrangements against the increasing resistance expressed by feminists and other revolutionary thinkers. These tensions find different expression in novels written by British men and women in the hybrid culture of colonial India, and by feminists and antifeminists in these groups.

There are at least three sites in Anglo-Indian novels written between 1800 and 1857 where the woman's body "troubles" or ruptures the colonizers' texts. In chapters 1–2, I look more closely at these sites in order to illustrate why the representation of interracial rape carries such explosive power in British novels about India written after 1857. Chapter 1 charts a prehistory for this work by illustrating the Orientalizing of rape in poetry by Lord Byron, Robert Southey, and Percy Bysshe Shelley and by summarizing some of the effects of the new English translations of Indian literature on the representation of the sublime in these works. This chapter shows how the Indian sublime invited British Romantic poets and novelists to find parallels between rape and sati.[45] This chapter concludes with a short analysis of three novels that represent variations on captivity tales about "white slaves" in the harem, showing how all these texts circle around the problem of women's consent. While James Lawrence's and Mrs. Mainwaring's novels primarily define sexual slavery as an expression of the erotic excesses of the Muslim conquerors of India, Meadows Taylor presents a more complicated exploration of the themes of slavery and freedom which shows his liberal Reformist perspective as well as his Anglo-Indian investments.

All the novels discussed in chapter 2 consider other aspects of the Indian sublime that are embodied by the figure of the Hindu temple dancer. Sydney Owenson's *The Missionary* (1811) and Meadows Taylor's *Tara* (1863) show the lingering effects of a feminist Orientalism that recognized the highest ethical and spiritual ideals that promoted the *devadasi* to adopt this vocation.

Mrs. Penny's *The Romance of the Nautch Girl* (1898), on the other hand, expresses the dominant imperial view which endorses and institutionalizes evangelical objections to the sexual freedom traditionally allowed to the *devadasi*.

Four so-called mutiny novels centering on Englishwomen threatened with rape by Indian men are the focus for chapter 3. In contrasting two British versions of this rape script with novels by Meadows Taylor and Flora Annie Steel, this chapter explores why Anglo-Indian writers treat rape in the context of colonial marriage practices. All the British and Anglo-Indian novels about the Indian Mutiny of 1857 discussed in this chapter present themselves as "national epics" and register the epistemological crisis that emerged because Hindu and Muslim insurgents collaborated in this revolt and thus called into question the basic dualities that had previously organized colonial discourse about India by reference to religious difference. All these novels illustrate, instead, how "race" became the dominant marker distinguishing the colonizers from the colonized after 1857. This chapter explores why Social Darwinist notions of the colonizers' racial superiority required the valorization of the asexual "purity" of Englishwomen.[46]

One surprising effect of the colonial psychology of "splitting" is the subject of chapter 4.[47] This chapter analyzes novels that invert the usual mutiny rape script by describing Englishmen who are threatened with murder, and occasionally with rape, by the famous warrior queen, the Rani of Jhansi, who played an important part in the Indian Uprising of 1857. While the British novelists who treat this theme usually ignore the erotic appeal of this powerful racial other, Anglo-Indian writers present a more ambivalent story that inadvertently liberates new homosexual possibilities, either by overemphasizing the abjection of this racialized and sexualized Indian woman or by envisioning the possibility of heterosexual rape for men that, as a consequence, brings homosexual rape closer to view.

The next two chapters explore the contradictions posed when colonizing men indoctrinated with the "New Imperialism" of the 1890s collided with the "New Women" of the period. Chapter 5 examines the impact of the "racialization of sex" on the structure of the colonial family by considering English children who were lost during the Indian Mutiny of 1857. This chapter illustrates why the production of a mixed-race child became the most dangerous consequence of interracial rape in this period. While Sara Jeannette Duncan and Rudyard Kipling, in his famous *Kim*, develop plots about "lost children" that expose the dangers of losing the privileges of "whiteness," Philip Oliphant and Rabindranath Tagore show, instead, how gender completely redefines the limits of the "freedom" and power that colonizing and colonized women can claim, showing how gender supersedes race in British India.

Chapter 6 focuses on the problems created by the emphasis on British masculine force in the New Imperialism, since when this force is sexually enacted, particularly in relationships involving Indian women, it sets the stage for interracial rape. While Alice Perrin and Flora Annie Steel express more typical Anglo-Indian perspectives on interracial marriage, sidestepping any hint of rape and emphasizing, instead, the abjection of colonizing women who marry colonized men, Victoria Cross and Swarnakumari Devi describe "New Women" who marry Indian men who embody new challenges to colonial models of racialized abjection.

Finally, chapter 7 illustrates how literary modernism re-Orientalizes rape, even as it opens up more radical sexual and political possibilities. Once homosexual desire was acknowledged to exist in England and not in the Orient alone, the borders of abjection were challenged, as Forster's *Passage to India* shows.[48] This chapter compares Forster's novel with Sara Jeannette Duncan's *Burnt Offering* (1910) in order to illustrate the new revolutionary social and political potential of mixed marriages between colonizer and colonized that emerged in the modern period. It also shows how rape is erased in *A Passage to India* and why it is rendered politically insignificant in George Orwell's *Burmese Days* (1934). By analyzing the aesthetic practices of British modernism, with its emphasis on the body, sexual self-expression, and alienation, this chapter demonstrates how the destabilizing erotic power of the politicized New Woman, represented in more realistic novels of the period, is recontained during the last years of the Raj.

In defining this project, I see myself as engaged in a "complicity study"; that is, I have focused my analysis on the writings of the colonizers, though this analysis would not have been possible without the excellent new scholarship on Indian colonialism and nationalism by many important postcolonial critics and by scholars in India, Europe, the United States, and elsewhere. My intent is to describe the fantastic "simulacrum" of India that was constructed and reiterated by Anglo-Indian writers. The "real India" that Adela Quested hopes to find remains stubbornly beyond the limits of language and imagination in these texts. By focusing on writers who were forced to confront the reality of India as well as the phantoms of otherness that colonial discourse created, I hope to expose how these texts reflect their authors' complicity and investment in the colonial system that they lived, internalized, and represented, but I also hope to illustrate the space for resistance and transformation that imaginative and symbolic language allows.

In taking a position critical of the British imperial project in India, I assume a posture that is also informed by important neo-Marxist and postmodern literary theory and by cultural studies. But I do not assume that because I am an American academic, I have no investment in British colonialism in India in the past. I am mindful that I enjoy the advantages of a global economic system that fosters, among other pernicious effects, an economic and cultural imperialism that continues to work itself out not only in the material reality of the so-called Third World but in my own classroom. In fact, these novels suggest the pleasures that Englishwomen as well as Englishmen enjoyed by imagining India as a stage and themselves as actors licensed to exercise an unusual degree of personal power and authority over the colonized, pleasures to which I am not immune. India itself remains at least as mysterious to me as it apparently did to most of the writers in this sample. Visiting India briefly as a Fulbright fellow in the summer of 1986 provided only a small window on India's complex culture and history. In exposing the fantasies and absurdities of these fictions, I am warned to avoid underestimating my own ethnocentricity or overestimating my knowledge about Indian society under colonial rule.

At the same time, this study has been directed by my desire to understand American as well as British imperialism more fully, since I live in Arizona, one of the few places in the United States where the damaging effects of American colonialism remain a visible part of daily life. By reclaiming the lost novels I describe in this study, novels that tried to imagine life in British India in different terms, and by entering into a Bakhtinian dialogue with these dissonant as well as complicit voices echoing from and through the colonial contact zone, I hope to initiate a larger and wider conversation that moves beyond the self-reinforcing dualities and predictable plots about rape in these novels about the vexed relationships between colonizer and the colonized.

CHAPTER 1

Rape, the Body, and the Sacrifices of Desire

BRITISH ROMANTIC POETRY AND REPRESENTATIONS OF THE COLONIAL HAREM

※9②〇ꞓ※

> *Arrayed in the brilliant colors of exoticism and exuding a full-blown yet uncertain sensuality, the Orient, where unfathomable mysteries dwell and cruel barbaric scenes are staged, has fascinated and disturbed Europe for a long time. It has been its glittering imaginary but also its mirage. . . . There is no phantasm, though, without sex, and in this Orientalism, a confection of the best and of the worst—a central figure emerges, the very embodiment of the obsession: the harem.*
>
> Malek Alloula, *The Colonial Harem*[1]

$\mathcal{T}$here are many reasons why Edmund Burke's magnificent perorations about the rape of India by Warren Hasting and his men became one of the most important articulations of the "Indian Sublime" for nineteenth-century British writers, as Sara Sulieri and others have argued.[2] The context of Burke's speeches should remind us, however, that his identification of India as the new locus of the Oriental sublime was much more contested than many recent postcolonial critics have acknowledged. Moreover, Burke's representation of the Indian sublime was profoundly shaped by his anticolonial sentiments, and though this critique is consonant with current postmodern orthodoxies, his perspective was certainly a minority opinion at the time. While Burke's rhetoric impressed his audiences, then and now, he failed to convince his listeners about Hastings's guilt or to initiate a wider interrogatation of the basic economic assumptions that provided the foundation for the British imperial project in India.

Burke's speeches about India gained much of their power to shock not only because they reversed more familiar eighteenth-century conventions about the lawless sexuality of Oriental men and women that found expression in popular harem tales like *The Arabian Nights* but also because they were informed by his reading of some of the earliest new translations of Sanskrit texts, like Charles Wilkins's *Bhagavadgita* (1784) and Nathaniel Brassey Halhed's *Code of Gentoo Laws* (1776).[3] At the same time, Burke's perspective on the Indian sublime was predetermined and remained limited by his political conservatism and by the gendered formulation of his influential theory of the sublime. By representing a specifically Indian sublime that incorporated these new perspectives on Indian culture and religion but that were aesthetically and ideologically freighted, Burke multiplied the alternatives to the Oriental sublime that were already in circulation in late eighteenth-century England.

By 1800, English Romantic poets could draw from an even wider array of new translations of Sanskrit texts, including Sir William Jones's *Gita Govinda* (1792) and *Sacontala* (1789). Jones later argued that these translations introduced English readers to a "new world" of "sacred history & literature" (Rocher, 233), though he joined his Orientalist colleagues in expressing a "divided judgement" about Hinduism overall, seeing these texts as "arrayed on either side of a temporal divide: in the hallowed past, the sublime pristine deist Hinduism of the *Bhagavadgita* and the *Upanishads*, and now, in this cursed age, the corrupt, debased, and polytheistic practices they found repulsive" (226). While all of these new translations were, of course, deeply implicated in the British colonial enterprise in India, translations of Sanskrit works nonetheless offered partial access to a domain of Eastern religious thought previously unavailable to educated English readers, texts which could provide deeper insights into India's complex culture and history.

These new Sanskrit translations, and especially Sir William Jones's popular *Sacontala*, helped to create a cultural climate in England in the first three decades of the nineteenth century in which "a reappraisal of the erotic was taking place, which was intimately connected with a re-examination of the sexual imagery in Hinduism and ancient mystery cults, and also an investigation into the relationship between sacred and profane love" as Javeed Majeed has shown (117). When British Romantic poets evoked the symbolic constellation of ideas associated with the Indian sublime, they did so at a time not only when Hindu culture was suddenly more accessible to their readers but also when changes in English national identity made these texts, and especially new perspectives on spirituality, love, and sexuality in them, seem more relevant to public debate. At a time when feminists, abolitionists, and other liberal reformers began to challenge the social and sexual contract that prevailed in Regency England, India offered an imaginative space where women's ideal place in the nation could be envisioned and where vexing problems concerning women's freedom, consent, sacrifice, and desire could be reconsidered.

Byron's Oriental Tales

For many recent commentators, Byron's *Oriental Tales* epitomizes the basic patterns and essential themes of Orientalism in British Romantic poetry. Eric Meyer, for example, in his useful essay, "'I Know Thee Not, I Loathe Thy Race': Romantic Orientalism in the Eye of the Other," argues that Byron's *Oriental Tales* provide "an allegory of the conflicting cultural and political interests that intersect in the contested terrain of Orientalism, which here are tangibly focused in the need to lay claim to the bodies of Asian women, to penetrate and possess the oriental harem, and to assert control over its compliant subjects" (659).[4] Though Meyer acknowledges here that British Orientalism was "contested," he nonetheless follows Edward Said in reducing the varieties of British Romantic Orientalism to an allegory of rape that defines all Western desires to know the Orient and its people as revealing a universal lust for domination.[5]

It should be more widely noted, however, that Byron's Oriental poems are more conventional than many other Romantic poems about the East, since they typically focus on harem life among Muslim elites and reiterate a familiar literary geography in representing Oriental desires. Moreover, because these tales compare the culture of Islam with that of Greece, they conform to what is, according to Ronald Inden, a long tradition in Western discourse which casts the Muslim in the role of the self-consolidating Other: "The Ottoman was a potentially dangerous Alter Ego of the European. His religion, Islam, was a false, fanatical cousin of Christianity and he continued to rule over parts of Eastern Europe. But the Chinaman and Hindoo were the true Others. Both China and India were, thus, the opposites of the West" (424). Though his own travels in Turkey and Albania may have allowed Byron to see through many stereotypes about Muslim domestic life, he stayed within long-established conventions in his representations of the Middle East as a dreamy domain where beautiful, indolent Eastern women languish in the luxurious harems of Oriental despots.

In "The Bride of Abydos" (1813), for example, Byron presents the harem as a seemingly timeless paradise where "the flowers ever blossom" and "where the virgins are soft as the roses they twine, / and all, save the

spirit of man, is divine" (1:6–8, 14–15). Like many of his other Oriental poems, this work offers an appealingly simple allegory of a struggle for freedom that is envisioned as a male contest between the father as oriental despot
and his adopted son.[6] Zuleika, the ostensible heroine of this poem, by contrast, does not wish to escape from the harem; she, like countless other heroines in English novels of the period, simply wants the freedom to choose her
own husband. Like them, Zuleika resists the marriage her father has arranged
and hopes instead to find her life's fulfillment by eloping with the man she
loves. In the end, though, Zuleika's quest for erotic freedom proves to be "fatal" (l. 641) since she dies of a broken heart shortly after she sees her lover
killed by her father's guards. All of Byron's Eastern women, except perhaps
Gulbeyaz in *Don Juan*, learn similar lessons about the fatal consequences of
romantic love.

Since Byron was writing at a time when new scholarly translations made
the Indian sublime—and especially a more idealized Vedantan Hinduism—
more readily available, the implications of his decision to work within the
parameters of eighteenth-century harem tales should be more carefully
weighed. Since Byron's popular *Oriental Tales* and *Don Juan* present harems exclusively defined by the customs of Islam, they lend themselves particularly well to Saidian analysis since Byron does not pretend to represent
alternative social practices that characterized the zenana, the nearest Indian
equivalent of the harem,[7] nor does he attempt to describe the religious customs or philosophy of Hinduism. Instead, though the harems in Byron's *Oriental Tales* are exoticized, they reproduce basic assumptions in the British
social and sexual contract of the period. Byron typically envisions the harem
as a private, domestic, secular space absolutely controlled by an Oriental despot and characterizes it as a social world where women, whether wives, concubines, or daughters, are all defined as the property of the harem master.
Because Byron represents only the most privileged Eastern women living in
extensive harems, he imagines worlds where multiple wives and concubines
are a measure of wealth and where all the women in the harem are closely
associated with other luxury possessions.

In Byronic harems, then, rape is reconceptualized as one of the male
rights of ownership, and abduction is transformed into theft. The women who
inhabit the harems in Byron's *Oriental Tales* are typically defined as unable
to consent to or refuse any sexual act, so women's rape in the harem is indis-
tinguishable from other modes of intercourse. Rape can mark the consummation of lawful arranged marriages or simply display the despot's absolute
right to bend the will of his wife or concubine in accordance with his erotic

desires. The irony that Byron delights in showing in his *Oriental Tales* and in *Don Juan* is, of course, that the despot has lost all desire or capacity for enjoying such absolute erotic mastery, making room for interlopers like Selim and Don Juan who steal the hearts and more properly enjoy the bodies of the harem's inmates.

In these poems, Byron represents "sentimental," or what we now more often call romantic love, in terms that differ dramatically from those employed by Percy Bysshe Shelley, Robert Southey, and other Romantic writers. In one of his letters, Byron uses an imperial metaphor when he criticizes the "wish of all women to exalt the sentiment of the passions—& keep up the illusion which is their empire."[8] This remark indicates how Byron's particular brand of Orientalism could be used to reclaim the power that new Romantic conventions redefining heterosexual love otherwise gave to women (if only temporarily in courtship). In embracing Byron's peculiarly fatal definition of romantic love, his Eastern heroines also differ from popular Oriental heroines like Scheherazade in eighteenth- and nineteenth-century English translations of *The Arabian Nights* who survived rape because of her self-assertion, wit, courage, and skill in storytelling.[9]

Byron's treatment of love in the harem became popular, moreover, not only because it traded on the familiarity of eighteenth-century Oriental tales but also because it countered what Joyce Zonana has called the "feminist Orientalism" of writers like Mary Wollstonecraft and Percy Bysshe Shelley (602). Unlike Shelley, who represented harem life in "Laon and Cythna" in order to envision ways to liberate women from the literal harems of the East and the figurative harems of the West, Byron saw the harem, as he sardonically told his friend Thomas Medwin, as the preferable place for all women. European women live in "an unnatural state" he complained, "the Turks and Eastern people manage their matters better than we do. They lock them up, and they are much happier. Give a woman a looking-glass and a few sugar-plums, and she will be satisfied."[10] The jocular antifeminism that Byron expresses in this letter, like the antifeminism that directs his representations of harem life in his closet drama "Sardanapalus," was countered by many poems and novels of the period. In short, Byron's Oriental tales reiterate some of the most conservative, sexist, and racist elements of Burke's theory of the sublime, even as they elide those features of the Indian sublime that Burke, however sensationally, identified as unique to Indian culture. As a consequence, Byron's tales popularized a more generalized version of the Oriental sublime that was less disruptive of and more compatible with the status quo in Regency England.

Reconsidering the Indian Sublime

Readings which group the complex and contested strands of thought about India and the Near East, or about Hindu and Muslim cultures, under the deceptively simple monovocal rubric of Romantic Orientalism also ignore many of the ways that lesser-known works like, for example, Robert Southey's Indian epic, "The Curse of Kehama" (1810), acted to define and perpetuate alternatives to more popular Byronic versions of the Oriental sublime. Written primarily in 1801 and published in 1810, Southey's epic was one of the earliest popular Romantic poems to re-represent Hindu culture in light of the new translations by Sir William Jones and others (Carnall, *Southey* [1964], 163). The annotations for "The Curse of Kehama" fill more than one hundred pages and present a "Mythologic mine" that purported to offer English readers new insights into the "complexities of Indian mythology," drawn largely, though not too accurately, from Jones's poetry and translations, as well as from recent missionary accounts (Curran, *Poetic Form*, 134). For Robert Southey, and other writers who shared similar affiliations, "India" provided a screen for the projection of the most threatening and abjected aspects of the revolutionary desires that poets like Byron and Shelley celebrated. At the same time, poems like "The Curse of Kehama" illustrate how these new translations challenged emerging British evangelical views of women's body, sexuality, chastity, and reproduction, especially in relation to rape and other private and public acts of violence against women. As such, Southey's poem provides a useful summary of major elements of the Indian sublime that reoccur with predictable regularity in many British and Anglo-Indian novels about India for at least the next hundred and twenty years.

Shelley's letters present ample evidence that he read and admired Southey's "The Curse of Kehama," which includes extensive citations from Jones's *Sacontala* and *Gita Govinda*, as well as from Jones's original poetry in the appended notes. In 1811, Shelley declared that "The Curse of Kehama" was his "most favorite poem" and effusively praised Southey's heroine, calling her the "divine Kailyal" (*Letters*, 1:101). In another letter, Shelley commended Sydney Owenson's *The Missionary*, another text clearly influenced by Jones's *Sacontala*, saying, "Since I have read this book I have read no other" (*Letters*, 8:117). In this letter, he also calls Luxima, the Hindu heroine of Owenson's novel, a "perfect" and "divine thing" (*Letters*, 8: 112). Both Kailyal and Luxima embody and explore various dimensions in the "mystical conception of sexual imagery in ancient fertility and sexual rites" evident in the new translations of Sanskrit texts (Majeed, 116).[11]

Ambivalent and solipsistic though it is, Shelley's "Alastor" (1816) recognizes the revolutionary appeal of these two Hindu heroines, who were imagined, in some respects, as enjoying greater sexual freedom than their Western
counterparts. In describing Alastor's journey, Shelley contrasts the poet's bored
response to the submissive "Arab maiden," a typically Byronic figure who
selflessly feeds and tends him, with his powerful attraction to the more mysterious and independent veiled woman who appears in his dreams when the
poet arrives in the vale of Cashmire, a place traditionally associated with
Sacontala's sacred grove (Miller, *Theater*, 334). Alastor's dream maiden is,
like Sacontala, a poet, dancer, and beautiful, sensuously embodied young
woman, who speaks about "knowledge and truth and virtue," sings a song of
"divine liberty," and acts spontaneously on her erotic desires. As a figure of
female emancipation and sexual agency, Alastor's Indian dream maiden reveals aspects of Jones's Sacontala that made her particularly attractive to feminist Romantics. In sum, *Sacontala* offered one graceful model which could
be used to synthesize the rational Enlightenment ideals of feminists like Mary
Wollstonecraft with the more visionary beliefs about the power of romantic
love and the value of freedom that were more characteristic of Shelley's generation of writers.

As Southey's and Shelley's poetry suggests, Sir William Jones's translation of Kalidasa's play *Sacontala*, published in 1789, was instrumental in
prompting many British Romantics to consider new perspectives on the Indian sublime.[12] The play was originally composed in India during the Gupta
period, about A.D. 375 –415 (Miller, *Theater*, 9), and Indian pundits had long
considered it "among the best, if not the best Sanskrit drama" (Schwab, 51).
When Jones's translation of *Sacontala* was published in England in 1789, it
was an immediate success and was reprinted five times between 1790 and
1807 (51). By the end of the nineteenth century, it had been published in no
fewer than forty-six translations in twelve different languages (Figueria, 12).
According to Dorothy Figueria, Sakuntala, the young, beautiful, spiritual, cultured, independent, and sexually responsive Hindu heroine in this play, was
endearing to most of her British and European readers partly because of their
relative "ignorance of Indian cultural, linguistic, aesthetic, and historical contexts, combined with the virtual absence of a Sanskrit canon to which the
reader might refer," which made it more difficult to assess the motives of the
hero and other characters in the play (11–12). Of Sakuntala, Goethe, for example, wrote, "If you want the bloom of youth and fruit of later years, / If you
want what enchants, fulfills, and nourishes, / If you want heaven and earth contained in one name— / I say Sakuntala and all is spoken" (Miller, *Theater*, ix).

Sakuntala dramatized sublime, and ancient, solutions to conflicts Romantics found in "sacred" and "profane" love, and provided alternative perspectives on women's agency in marriage and in reproduction, as a brief summary of the plot of this play makes clear. Sakuntala is semidivine by birth; she is the daughter of the celestial nymph, Menaka, and Visvamitra, a royal sage in a court in Northern India during the Gupta period. When her father and mother abandon her, Sakuntala is adopted by a Brahmin ascetic and taken to his religious retreat in the foothills of the Himalayas, where she lovingly tends the sacred grove that surrounds the temple. By the time the play begins, Sakuntala has matured into a beautiful young woman. While her adoptive father is away, she meets King Dusyanta, who is hunting in the region, and they fall immediately and deeply in love. Already impressed by her grace and beauty, King Dusyanta, after hearing Sakuntala sing a lyric that she has written to expresses her longing for him, declares his love. Having learned that Sakuntala is of the appropriate caste and heritage, he proposes that they marry in a private sacred ceremony. According to ancient Hindu practice, the *gandharva* marriage rite that unites the couple allowed legal marriages to be celebrated by mutual consent alone, without the permission of parents or the consecrating authority of a priest. After they perform the ritual and the king gives Sakuntala a ring, the lovers consummate their marriage. Shortly afterward, Dusyanta is called back to his court, leaving Sakuntala behind. When her adoptive father returns and hears a mysterious disembodied voice in the temple chanting the news of Sakuntala's marriage and pregnancy, he rejoices. After invoking the blessings of nature on his daughter, he sends Sakuntala to Dusyanta's court. When she appears and announces her pregnancy, however, Dusyanta does not recognize her because a curse has blocked his memory. Since she has lost the ring that he once gave her, Sakuntala cannot prove the legitimacy of their marriage and leaves the court, overcome with grief and anger. Calling on the earth to open and receive her, Sakuntala is instead rescued by a female spirit and carried off to a celestial world where she gives birth to a son. Later, when Sakuntala's ring is recovered and brought to his court, dispelling the curse, Dusyanta is able to remember their marriage and mourns his loss of Sakuntala. In the final act of the play, Indra's chariot transports Dusyanta to the celestial realm, where he is reunited with Sakuntala and their young son, who subsequently becomes a great ruler of Dusyanta's kingdom.

When Sir William Jones translated *Sacontala*, however, he recognized that, like other poetry he translated, it straddled what were highly contested aesthetic, political, and social boundaries in British culture at the time. In his essay "On the Mystical Poetry of the Persians and Hindus," which first appeared in volume three of the *Asiatick Researches* in 1792, Jones anticipated his English readers' critical reaction to the blending of erotic imagery and religious truth in these texts and explained that they presented "a singular species of poetry, which consists almost wholly of a mystical religious allegory, though it seems on a transient view to contain only the sentiments of a wild and voluptuous libertinism; now, admitting the dangers of a poetical style, in which the limits between vice and enthusiasm are so minute as to be hardly distinguishable, we must beware of censuring it severely, and must allow it to be natural, though a warm imagination may carry it to a culpable excess" (Jones, "Mystical Poetry," 165). Before publishing his translation of *Sacontala*, Jones recognized that some aspects of the heroine's frank assertiveness about her sexual desires and pregnancy would be unacceptable to English readers. He censored several passages, especially in the court episode when Sakuntala unveils, unashamedly avows her pregnancy, and names King Dusyanta as the father of their child. Jones's translation emphasizes, instead, his heroine's "innocence," childishness, and "purity."

Romantic Epics, Rape, and the Indian Sublime

For Romantic poets like Lord Byron and Percy Bysshe Shelley who wished to counter increasingly more restrictive bourgeois concepts about the body, sexual identity, individual freedom, and civic responsibility, the Orient provided an imaginative domain where contradictions in contemporary British sexual and social contracts could be more fully represented and criticized. Because of their radical politics, avowed atheism, and philosophical skepticism, Byron and Shelley were less inhibited in their explorations of the relation between "sacred and profane" love than were most of their contemporaries. In their more ambitious epic works treating the Orient, Shelley and Byron exploited this setting as a means to envision some of the most "poetic" extremes of love and desire and to imagine the consequences of revolutionary changes in the social and sexual contracts of their day.

A comparison of Southey's "The Curse of Kehama" with Shelley's uncanonized masterpiece "Laon and Cyntha" (1817) and Byron's closet drama "Sardanapalus" (1821) shows that British Romantics differed profoundly in their assessment of women's proper relation to the prevailing sexual contract, especially as defined by what might be called the "sacrifices" of desire.[13] As we shall see, Southey's and Shelley's poems sharply contrast love with rape, consent with force, and men's freedom with women's enslavement, while

Byron's "Sardanapalus" erases these distinctions and offers, instead, a "captivity" tale that normalizes women's subordination inside and outside marriage. Readings of British colonial discourse that locate a single Orientalism at work in Burke's writing or in subsequent British Romantic texts thus obscure the specific ideological work that Byron's *Oriental Tales* and "Sardanapalus" performed in neutralizing the challenges to the "sexual" and "social" contract that otherwise found expression in poems like Shelley's "Laon and Cythna" and, as we shall see, in a number of Romantic novels of the period as well.

Though Southey's, Shelley's, and Byron's Oriental epics all display different assessments of the sublimity of revolutionary desires, they nonetheless all center on the female body, a spectacle they could describe more explicitly because of their Oriental settings. In all three works, the strong female heroes of these texts are threatened with rape by the Oriental despots who pursue them, and in the end their only escape from such suffering is suicide by fire. Why do these texts, written by authors whose political views and sexual politics otherwise range across the spectrum, texts shaped by such diverse responses to the new translations of ancient Sanskrit texts, center on the rape of their heroines and why do they end with their heroines' suicide? What is the textual logic that prompts all three poets to assign their female heroes to their role as sacrificial victims? Moreover, why is it ideologically and symbolically necessary that the female heroes in these Romantic works perform their ultimate self-sacrifice voluntarily? Answers to these difficult questions will help to explain why rape is the keystone in British Romantic reformulations of the Indian sublime.

Robert Southey's "The Curse of Kehama" shows some of the effects of this rediscovery of Sanskrit texts, though it emphasizes the more negative side of the "divided judgement" that Jones and other British scholars expressed toward Hinduism. While the "sublime, pristine deist Hinduism" that found expression in *Sacontala* as well as in more serious works like *Bhagavadgita* clearly informs Southey's characterization of Kailyal, his poem focuses primarily on the "corrupt, debased and polytheistic practices" that he, too, regarded as "repulsive" in more modern Hinduism (Rocher, 226). In his 1810 preface to "The Curse of Kehama," Southey asserts that his "story is original," but he claims that his poem accurately represents "one remarkable peculiarity" of Hinduism in its treatment of the power of "sacrifice": "Prayers, penances, and sacrifices, are supposed to possess an inherent and actual value, in no degree depending upon the disposition or motive of the person who performs them. They are drafts upon Heaven for which the Gods cannot refuse payment" (vii).[14] This remark helps explain why female "sac-rifice" is one of the organizing themes of this and other Romantic poems and why rape is thus an important crux of the Indian sublime.

Kehama, the "Almighty man" who is the protagonist in Southey's epic, is certainly not the effeminate lord of the harem later popularized by Byron; rather, he is a specifically Hindu rajah who is emphatically masculine and extravagantly oversexed. Kehama commands extraordinary supernatural pow-ers, over men and gods alike, because crafty Brahmin priests have performed occult "sacrifices" on his behalf. Likewise, Kailyal, the heroine of Southey's poem, is not the indolent inmate of some Byronic harem, since her Brahmin father is far too poor to provide either the servants that female seclusion re-quired or the luxurious splendor that Byron's Oriental tales displayed. Instead, when Kailyal claims the same freedom of movement as her English sisters and enters the public domain, she suffers the same threats and constraints since she is constantly threatened by a male sexuality that is invariably char-acterized as predatory and violent.[15]

While the hectic plot of "The Curse of Kehama" involves curses, floods, ruin, leprosy, sudden death, and the unexpected intervention of many super-natural beings, the narrative is impelled forward by the repeated attempts by Kehama's son, Arvalan, and later by Kehama himself, to rape the beautiful Kailyal because she steadfastly refuses to consent to marry either the son or the father. Kailyal displays her "sublime" nature throughout this poem by her patient endurance of her continual suffering. After she has escaped from sev-eral unsuccessful rape attempts, Kehama curses the beautiful Kailyal with leprosy, and she welcomes the deforming disease. Like Tess of the D'Urber-villes, who disfigures herself to escape the threat of rape,[16] Kailyal sees the effacement of her beauty as the only means of protection she can claim short of suicide in the threatening material world, saying to Kehama: "Shall I not thank thee for this scurf and scale / Of dire deformity, whose loathsomeness, / Surer than panoply of strongest mail, / Arms me against all foes? Oh, better so, / Better such foul disgrace, / Than that this innocent face / Should tempt thy wooing" (203). Even after her death, Kehama is confident that he will prevail by forcing Kailyal to become his consort and reign as queen of the dead.

In describing these double binds created by Kailyal's physical beauty, Southey reveals his debts to Burke's gendered theory of the sublime. Nowhere in the poem does Southey find it necessary to explain why Kailyal's pious daily sacrifice to the "spirits of the virtuous dead" (136) fails to give her any of the powers that Kehama enjoys. Kailyal's unornamented body itself illustrates the extent of her sacrifices as a "pure" and innocent woman, sacrifices that correspond to those that early nineteenth-century evangelicalism would demand of "pure" Englishwomen: "No idle ornaments deface / Her natural grace, / Musk-spot, nor sandal-streak, nor scarlet stain, / Ear-drop nor chain, nor arm nor ankle-ring, / Nor trinketry on front, or neck, or breast / Marring the perfect form" (140). In imagining Kailyal, Southey erases the innocent sensuality of Jones's Sakuntala as well as the active sexual agency of Radha in the *Gita Govinda* and the Hindu wife represented in Jones's original poem included in Southey's notes (346–348).

Having announced "sacrifice" as its theme, Southey's "The Curse of Kehama" presents a partial catalogue of the corrupt sacrificial practices, including human sacrifices, that he considered unique to Hinduism. Thus, Southey plots to bring his heroine to the great Hindu temple at Jaga-Naut (*sic*), which, he explains in his notes, "is to the Hindoos what Mecca is to the Mahommedans," making it "the chief seat of Brahminical power, and a strong-hold of superstition" (349). Kailyal is forced to ride in the car of the Juggernaut "as through the gate / A thousand Brahmins drag the enormous load" (146). Separated from the "frantic votaries" by physical distance and by her disgust over this ritual, Kailyal watches, powerless as "in a dream," while zealots throw themselves beneath the "ponderous Car" which rolls on, and "crushes all. / Through flesh and bones it ploughs its dreadful path" (147).[17]

Southey's poem is more concerned, however, with dramatizing the specific female sacrifices that he found particularly abhorrent in Hinduism. In the opening canto of the poem, Southey presents a sensationalized comparison of the ritual sacrifice of two Hindu women who perform sati, after Kehama's son, Arvalan, is killed, making them widows. Arvalan's first wife, Azla, is represented as seating herself "calmly" upon the "funeral pyre," voluntarily submitting to the ritual, like the heroic women described in François Bernier's *Voyages* (1699), excerpted in Southey's notes (271, 273–277). Though Azla faces death by fire bravely, Arvalan's second wife, Nealliny, resists, canceling out the "difference" that would otherwise categorically define high-caste Hindu wives as more heroic—and sublime—than Englishwomen.

In describing how the priests prepare the second wife, Nealliny, for the rite of sati, Southey rather unaccountably underlines parallels between sati and rape, suggesting the physical violence in both acts that prevent women from freely exercising their consent. Southey details how attendants "strip her ornaments away, / Bracelet and anklet, ring and chain, and zone," but they leave "the marriage knot alone" as a sign of her perpetual and indissoluble marriage (1:8). Echoing missionary accounts of sati from the period, Southey describes how Hindu priests force the younger second wife to mount the pyre and then "bind her to the dead" (1:7). Nealliny's death by sati is one of the most memorable, and pathetic, episodes in "The Curse of Kehama," and similar scenes are repeated frequently in British and Anglo-Indian novels. Southey writes:

> You cannot hear her cries, . . . all other sound
> In that wild dissonance is drown'd; . . .
> But in her face you see
> The supplication and the agony, . . .
> See in her swelling throat the desperate strength
> That with vain effort struggles yet for life. (1:8–9)

Yet the slippage between sati and rape in this narrative inadvertently admits the unresolved problems surrounding the legal concept of female "consent" not only in India but in England as well.[18] Before the outlawing of sati in 1828, British colonial officials attempted to discriminate "legal" from "illegal" forms of sati by assessing whether the widow "consented" to participate in the ritual. This reliance on the British concept of female consent carried with it some of the most contested elements defining British marriage law and social practices throughout the Romantic period.

Some of these problems surrounding female consent reappear later in "The Curse of Kehama" when Southey focuses on another sacrifice of desire that exclusively involved Hindu women who were temple "prostitutes." In this episode Southey sharply distinguishes Kailyal from the *devadasi*s in the "harlot-band" attached to the temple at Jaga-Naut. The notes to Southey's poem reveal that he knew that *devadasi*s were not ordinary prostitutes, since he writes that they were "not considered in a dishonorable light; they are considered wedded to the idol, and they partake in the veneration paid to him" (353). But in describing how the *devadasi*s prepare Kailyal for her temple marriage, Southey notes "the sweet music of their girdle bells, / Armlets, and anklets, that, with cheerful sound, / Symphonious tinkled as they wheel'd around" (150) in order to call attention to the jeweled bodies which indicate how these women have been enriched by their temple service. Because these dancers have accepted their ritual temple marriage, they have, in Southey's view, "consented" to their prostitution, and, having subsequently profited from it, they are moved to help prostitute innocent women like Kailyal. After they sing "a bridal measure," "a song of pleasure / A hymn of joyance and gratulation" (150), the *devadasi*s lead "the astonish'd" Kailyal to the "inner fane" of the temple, lay her on "the bridal bed," and then leave the "wretched Kailyal to her fate" (150). In his efforts to translate this ritual into terms his readers will understand, Southey, no doubt inadvertently, invites comparison between the forced sacrifice of Kailyal's virginity, which would seal her temple marriage, and a similar sacrifice demanded of pure Englishwomen as part of Christian marriage practices.

Moreover, in narrating Kailyal's resistance to this forced temple marriage, Southey identifies further links in the chain of English logic that ultimately connected the violence of sati with the violence of rape as well as with the more ordinary forms of violence that women routinely suffered in courtship and marriage, and in prostitution as it was practiced in Regency England or in colonial India. When Kailyal refuses to consent to this "temple marriage," she is again subject to rape. Just when the temple priest is about to "seize his prey" and rape Kailyal, the avenging spirit of Arvalan appears and tries to assume the priest's place. Though Kailyal's rape is momentarily averted when a good spirit tries to rescue her, the forces of good are defeated finally, and the only escape Kailyal can imagine from this assault, from both the living and the dead, is to stage her own suicide by fire. So, Kailyal, in spite of her implausibly Christian scruples about suicide, seizes a torch and lights "the bridal bed" (153). This fire, then, marks the burning link—consent—that united Hindu widows who performed sati with English wives who were subject to more familiar domestic violence and rape, either outside or within the context of forced marriage.[19]

After her escape from the evil priests and spirits in the world of the living, Kailyal again confronts Kehama in the world of the dead, and when he demands that Kailyal assume the throne beside him and drink of the "Amreeta cup," she is powerless to resist. When she drinks of the cup of immortality, Kailyal finally and permanently escapes Kehama's sexual threats because the draft makes her body "melt / Till all but what was heavenly pass'd away" (266). Given the evangelical strictures on female desire that Southey would impose on his Indian story, Kailyal cannot find peace until she is freed from her mortal body; only then is she united in spirit with her beloved. The strategies reflected in Southey's text thus suggest some of the ways that legal and social problems surrounding the notion of women's "consent" to the sexual and social contract that prevailed in Great Britain after the French Revolution were projected in this and other Romantic "epics" purporting to represent Indian culture.

Furthermore, rape becomes the engine of the plot in Southey's epic not only because he (mis)represents what he regarded as the abjected sexual side of Indian or Hindu culture but also because he frames the contest between Kehama and Kailyal by reference to Burke's gendered model of the sublime.[20] In his celebrated essay *Philosophical Enquiry into the Origin of Our Ideas of the Sublime and Beautiful* (1757), Burke defines the sublime as masculine and contrasts it to the beautiful, which he defines as feminine.[21] In "The Curse of Kehama," Southey closely follows Burke by defining his heroine's beauty as provoking an uncontrollable male response, putting the feminine and the beautiful under the constant threat of man's animal "lust" (66).

Since, according to Burke, the sublime operated by the same physics that defined sexual attraction, both impulses generated their power because of their impact on the body. For Burke, the sublime excites the impulse of self-preservation and activates feelings of pain: "Whatever is fitted in any sort to excite the ideas of pain, and danger, that is to say, whatever is in any sort terrible . . . is a source of the sublime; that is, it is productive of the strongest emotion which the mind is capable of feeling. . . . When danger or pain press too nearly, they are incapable of giving any delight and are simply terrible; but at certain distances, and with certain modifications, they may be, and they are delightful, as we everyday experience" (59–60). Thus, by Burke's chain of reasoning, rape becomes an event that trembles on the brink between the beautiful and the sublime.

It is the daughter's troubled relation to the sublime, as Burke defined it, that organizes Kailyal's experiences in both worldly and heavenly realms. On earth, Kailyal's desperate flight from Arvalan, and later from Kehama himself, makes her life a sublime contest, but one she is, by her gender, destined to lose. Kailyal's beauty constantly incites powerful and unscrupulous men to pursue her, and she, acting out of the purity and innocent belief in the paramount value of consent in love, resists them, even though marriage to either of them would clearly solve most of her problems. In short, the female body in Southey's text, as in Burke's essay on the sublime, cannot rest; feminine beauty, even when it is purged of most of the taints of female sexuality, remained a perpetual cause of violence in the earthly and supernatural worlds of Southey's epic. Of course, the conclusion of Southey's poem illustrates the Western solipsism that Said identified as one of the basic traits of Orientalism. Indeed, Southey clearly imposes a Christian cosmology upon his ostensibly Hindu subjects when Kehama is defeated by "Fate" and his "own wicked heart's device" (263).[22] Likewise, Kailyal is revealed to be a Christian heroine in disguise, when she is finally freed from her body as the ultimate reward for her innocence and allowed to experience the pure joys of a disembodied, heavenly love. Shelley's and Byron's epic treatments of similar themes show, by contrast, how the Indian sublime opened up new metaphysical perspectives on the body, erotic love, violence, and the sacrifices of desire.

"Laon and Cythna"

Shelley's "Laon and Cythna" (1817), like Byron's "Sardanapalus" (1821), moves outside the Christian framework that Southey provides for his Indian epic, although both works represent a less specifically Indian sublime. The traces of the Indian sublime in "Laon and Cythna" were further effaced when his publishers forced Shelley to retitle his poem and call it, instead, "The Revolt of Islam." The impact of the Indian sublime can still be seen throughout this poem, particularly in Shelley's deep exploration of the problems of women's consent that circle around rape. The "sublime, pristine, deist" elements that Jones and others located in Vendantan Hinduism are most obvious in Shelley's heroic characterization of Cythna and in his explicit, joyful, and spiritualized descriptions of the erotic passion that joins the lovers in this poem.

On the most literal level, "Laon and Cythna" presents a critique of Byron's *Oriental Tales*, since one of its central concerns is summed up in the rhetorical question, "Can man be free if woman be a slave?" (2:1045).[23] In turning his critique of harem life back on the West, Shelley echoes the "feminist Orientalism" of Mary Wollstonecraft (Zonana, 602) and presents an unusually outspoken critique of English hypocrisies about rape, and its relation to violence, freedom, female sexuality, pregnancy, and legitimacy.

Challenging Byron's more familiar treatment of the harem as a voyeuristic site of male pleasure, Shelley presents the harem in this poem as a place of female imprisonment, where sex often becomes rape. It is not the Tyrant Othman's religion or his "race," however, that drives him to overextend his empire but rather his more ordinary capitalistic desires for money and power. When the same destructive possessiveness impels him to abduct and rape Cythna, Shelley characterizes both these acts as violent crimes against Cythna's body and spirit rather than as damage to her as a male possession.

Moreover, in dramatizing Cythna's experience of rape and her "strange endurance" of its consequences, Shelley breaks the silence that began to restrict British women's ability to discriminate between seduction and rape, and in so doing he reveals deep sympathetic insight into the psychological damage that women often experience as a result of rape. When Cythna is imprisoned in Othman's harem and her "wondrous loveliness" inflames his lust, she refuses to submit to his embraces and is "borne, a loveless victim," to the tyrant's quarters. In describing the events that follow, Shelley characterizes her rape as an abuse of Othman's power, calling him "a king, a heartless beast, a pageant and a name" (7:5). Later when Laon retells Cythna's story, he asserts the "loathsome agony" of rape: "when selfishness mocks love's delight, / Foul as in dream's most fearful imagery / To dally with the mowing dead— that night / All torture, fear, or horror made seem light / Which the soul dreams or knows" (7:2875–2280).

In making Laon the spokesman for Cythna's suffering, Shelley partly complies with conventions about female modesty that increasingly silenced women's own testimony about rape, both in the courtrooms of nineteenth-century England and in the serious literature of the period. But Laon avoids the dismissiveness of Richardson's Lovelace, who reduces Clarissa's long, agonizing rape to the two little words, "Clarissa lives," and also the repetitive, predictable melodrama of Kailyal's endless flight from male lust in Southey's "The Curse of Kehama." Moreover, by elaborating on the terror and horror of rape, Shelley challenges the gendered hierarchy that provides the foundation for Burke's theory of the beautiful and the sublime.

Shelley's treatment of Cythna's rape is unusual, then, even among the second generation of Romantic poets, in at least three ways. First, Shelley details how Cythna's testimony about her rape prompts a revolution among the women of the harem. Cythna's rage over her violation acts as a "beam of light" which arouses the anger of all the women of the harem, so that "fearless and free . . . They began to breathe / Deep curses, like the voice of flames" (7:2890–2892). Later, Cythna notes that it was hearing the "truth" about her rape that created the shift in consciousness that prompted these secluded women to awaken from "their cold, careless, willing slavery" and join in the revolution. Though they were once complicit in the process of sexual enslavement, now nothing, "nor fear, nor gain / Could tempt one captive now to lock another's chain" (9:3550–3558). Cythna's rape story thus demonstrates Shelley's belief that the "misery" of "half of humankind," those who are "victims of lust and hate, the slaves of slaves" (2:982–987), must be addressed before "free and equal man and woman" may "greet domestic peace" (2:995).

Second, though Othman acts to suppress this harem revolt by separating Cythna from the other women in his household and by imprisoning her in an underwater cavern, she escapes the self-punishing obsessions with purity and guilt that kill Clarissa in her solitude. During her captivity, Cythna realizes that Othman has impregnated her, but Shelley insists that her pregnancy does not cancel her violation. In making this point, Shelley defies the assumptions that prevailed in legal and medical British discourse in the period that presumed that the victim of rape must have consented if she became pregnant as a consequence of her rape (Lacquer, *Making Sex*, 161–162). Though Cythna fearlessly contemplates "the dread bound of life and death" (7:3150) after her rape, she ultimately finds "recompense" and "hope" when she delivers and cares for her "divine" daughter (7:2983–2985). This recovery allows Cythna to recognize the measure of her own "greatness" and wisdom.[24]

Third, Shelley not only counters Byron's erasure of rape when he describes Cythna's violation and the revolution it inspires, he also inverts Southey's solution to the problem of female desire in representing all the joyful details of Laon and Cythna's physical love and sexual delight. Shelley's epic is much closer to Jones's *Sacontala* in its evocation of his lovers' mutual passion and its sublime consummation, when he describes how "the faint eyes swim / Through tears of a wide mist boundless and dim," and how sexual union finally blends "two restless frames in one reposing soul" (6:2650–2658). Shelley's description of Cythna's embodied sensuality, her "glowing arms," her "dark and deepening eyes," her "marble brow," and "eager lips" (6:2630), recalls Sacontala's pure sensuality much more vividly than Southey's or Owenson's pale imitations.

Shelley departs most markedly from Southey when he describes how his lovers meet in a ruined Greek temple, reaffirm their love, and celebrate their sexual union. Declaring that "to the pure all things are pure" (6:2596), Shelley characterizes Laon and Cythna's passion as a "rite of faith most sweet and sacred" that recalls the very ancient and ever-new "rite" that united Sakuntala and King Dusyanta. Like these sublime Indian lovers, Laon and Cythna do not need a minister or priest to consecrate their union. In thus assigning sexual love to a "sacred" realm beyond the authority of priests of any religious persuasion, Shelley rewrites the sexual as well as the social contracts of his day. Reimagining Southey's celebration of Kailyal's chaste and disembodied love, as well as rejecting Burke's notion of the natural subordination of woman to man, Shelley instead evokes the fire of mutual passion, the "quick dying gasps" of his lovers' "life meeting," as a revolutionary image of the union of the beautiful and the sublime.

While Shelley's epic envisions the glorious "dream" of a social and sexual revolution, it also expresses the political despair that radicals like himself faced after the defeat of their hopes for revolutionary political and social change. Though Othman and his forces fall, he isn't permanently dislodged from power, and the "nightmare" of the counterrevolution begins when the "Priests and Kings, custom, domestic sway, ay all that brings / Man's freeborn soul beneath the oppressor's heel" (8:3256–3259) unite to restore the tyrant to power. In orchestrating this turn of events, Shelley explores another aspect of the Indian sublime, when his female hero, like many Hindu queens, demonstrates her sublime physical courage by riding into battle on her beautiful black horse.

What remains puzzling about this poem is that after Shelley has reversed nearly all the prevailing English literary conventions characterizing rape and after he has overturned so many persistent gender assumptions that restricted women's contact with war and violence, he elects to end his poem, much as Southey ends his, by describing his heroine's voluntary self-sacrifice and death by fire. In her final act, Cythna unaccountably does not intervene to free her beloved; instead, she pleads for the right to die on the pyre with Laon when he is burnt at the stake as one of the leaders of the failed revolution. Again, Shelley gives us Laon's perspective on their final sacrifice:

> She smiled on me, and nothing then we said,
> But each upon the other's countenance fed
> Looks of insatiate love; the mighty veil
> Which doth divide the living and the dead
> Was almost rent, the world grew dim and pale,—
> All light in Heaven or Earth beside our love did fail.—
>   (12:4579–4584)

By concluding with this immolation of both the lovers, Shelley implicitly compares Cythna's voluntary sacrifice for love to the sacrifice of the sati. This strange visionary ending, apparently designed to show the moral as well as the physical courage of Shelley's male and female heroes, indicates how the Indian sublime invited Romantic poets like Shelley to reconceptualize the metaphysical foundation of the sexual and social contract in place in English culture.

Traces of the "sublime, pristine, deist Hinduism" of texts like the *Bhagavadgita* and *Sacontala* (Rocher, 226) also can be found in the sensuous paradise that Shelley envisions for Laon and Cythna after their deaths. The lovers are transported to this mysterious celestial world in a boat of "one curved shell of hollow pearl," recalling the chariot that carried Sacontala to the world of the immortals, and in this afterworld, Laon and Cythna are similarly reunited with Cythna's lost child. Unlike Southey, though, Shelley imagines an afterlife that is a sensual paradise, where his lovers recline, shaded by "strange and star-bright flowers," in an embodied world full of goodness and light. Finally, outside the reach of the political and religious authorities that persecute them, Laon and Cythna are able to establish a new family that transcends patriarchal laws and limits that defined marriage and child-bearing in terms of legitimacy and ownership.

"Sardanapalus" and the Reinvention of the Captivity Tale

Like Southey's "The Curse of Kehama" and Shelley's "Laon and Cythna," Byron's closet drama, "Sardanapalus" (1821) also ends with a fiery double suicide, though Byron swerves from the Indian sublime by evoking the world of ancient Assyria rather than India. While Shelley in "Laon and Cythna" represents the harem as a site of sexual coercion, conflict, and violence, Byron in "Sardanapalus," as in his earlier Oriental tales, imagines it primarily as a private domain where moral codes disciplining sexuality can be overthrown and sexual pleasures can be more fully enjoyed. Byron's arguably more "epic" treatment of harem life finds expression in this play in the form of a "captivity tale" about the relationship between a decadent Oriental tyrant and a "white slave." As such, "Sardanapalus" appropriates elements in popular narratives about "white slavery" that were written to advance the causes of abolitionism and British feminism at this time, but Byron's play brings them into conformity with the gendered politics of Burke's theory of the sublime.

Sardanapalus, the Oriental tyrant in this play, uses the harem to explore alternatives to the increasingly more restrictive sex and gender roles of early nineteenth-century England through his cross-dressing, gender impersonations, and sexual excess.[25] Though Sardanapalus has absolute power, including the power to redraw the boundaries between private and public life in his world, he precipitates the collapse of his empire because he ignores the personal and political imperatives that define his duties as ruler. Despite Byron's special pleading, Sardanapalus's career illustrates "the despotism of vice, / The weakness and the wickedness of luxury / The negligence, the apathy, the evils / Of sensual sloth" (1.2:67–70).[26]

Myrrah, the beautiful Greek woman who is the "harem favorite" in this play, is doubly enslaved since she is first a captive of war and then a "white slave" in Sardanapalus's royal harem. Although Myrrah exercises more influence over Sardanapalus than does Zarina, the despot's wife, her power arises from the fact that Sardanapalus finds her more attractive because she is more fully subdued by his power.[27] In the course of the play, Byron charts how Myrrah grows to love her captivity for the sake of her king. By showing how romantic love transforms Myrrah into a willing slave and Sardanapalus into an "energetic master" (1.2:72), Byron disputes the "feminist Orientalism" in

Shelley's epic and in other Romantic novels. At first, Myrrah feels dishonored by her captivity and by the "fatal weakness" that makes her love Sardanapalus in spite of herself, when she says, "King, I am your subject! / Master, I am your slave!" and protests that she is more "degraded by that passion than by chains" (496–502). Later, after Myrrah successfully intervenes to restore traditional gender roles by persuading Sardanapalus to take his proper place as leader in the final battles against an invading army, she revises her view of her master, saying, "'Tis no dishonour to have loved this man" (3.1:216). This resolution confirms the traditional sexual contract by showing that male domination is essential to guarantee order in the family and in the state.

Moreover, by dramatizing Myrrah's gradual "consent" to her enslavement, this play reveals how Byron's version of romantic love could be used to counter feminist arguments like those of Wollstonecraft and Shelley that England could not call itself an egalitarian society until women were granted the same legal rights as men and given the same education to insure that their "consent" was both voluntary and adequately informed. When Sardanapalus realizes he will lose his empire, he decides he would rather die than live beyond the collapse of his power, a resolve reinforced when he dreams repeatedly about his grandmother, Semiramis, the abject "man-queen" who once conquered India.

Resolved to destroy all his possessions, Sardanapalus invites Myrrah to join him in his final act of suicide by fire, and Myrrah, by declaring that she is willing to die with her "master," demonstrates the fatal consequences of her conversion to romantic love. Facing the fire, standing in the space of the sublime, on the brink between life and death, Sardanapalus reminds Myrrah that she may save herself, but she, like Kailyal and Cythna, heroically refuses to accept the "natural" double standard that Sardanapalus enumerates when he says, "For we now are on / The brink—thou feel'st an inward shrinking from / This leap through flame into the future, say it: / I shall not love thee less; nay, perhaps more, / For yielding to thy nature" (5.1:413–417). Rejecting this argument, Myrrah, like Kailyal and Cythna, refuses to accept this naturalized moral "double standard" and heroically reasserts that she is his equal in physical and moral courage: "And dost thou think / A Greek girl dare not do for love, that which / An Indian widow braves for custom?" (465–467). In Myrrah's last words, we can see how sati provided a spectacular means in English Romantic poetry and later in Anglo-Indian novels to mystify the contradictions in the English sexual and social contract that surrounded the problem of women's consent.[28]

Myrrah's spectacular death by fire is more Western than it seems, since, unlike sati, where the widow performs this ritual voluntarily after the death of her husband, Myrrah throws herself on the pyre to avoid another episode of rape and enslavement. As such, her death is more properly compared with the North Indian wartime ritual of "*jauhar*," made famous by the aristocratic royal consorts and concubines of Chitor who committed mass suicide in order to avoid becoming the spoils of war and so to escape torture and rape (Spivak, "Can," 303).

Likewise, Myrrah's suicide does not have the same material or spiritual consequences as sati since Sardanapalus is not Myrrah's legal husband; he has already ensured the preservation of his dynastic line by fathering sons and sending them to safety, along with his wife. This conclusion thus displays Byron's rhetorical skill at playing it both ways, for by this double suicide and immolation, the Assyrian kingdom is purified and space is made for the restoration of the principles of patriarchal hierarchy, authority, marriage, and legitimacy that Sardanapalus pretended to renounce.

The most important ideological work performed by Romantic texts like "Sardanapalus" is that they dramatized what Jerome Christensen identifies as the powerful appeal of modern hedonistic fantasies about male power offered to a growing market of middle-class readers (289–290). In order to argue, as Christensen does, that Byron's Oriental tales and plays invited all readers to enjoy the despot's posture and prerogatives as lord of the harem, one must forget all the forces that police gender differences and teach women, as "Sardanapalus" clearly shows, to love the conditions of their romantic subordination to men.[28] One must also assume that all consumers have the same buying power. Further, in redefining the source of power in the Orient as located in the fatally misguided and self-indulgent "Oriental despot," who exercises his power primarily in the harem, Byron reproduces stereotypes that obscured other kinds of power and agency, including, for instance, those successful Eastern entrepreneurs who once commanded the labor and markets that posed the greatest threats to British commercial ambitions in the East.

Byron's Oriental poetry, of course, was more successful in the literary marketplace of his day than were these poems by Southey and Shelley, and the appreciation for Byron's texts endured, especially after the brief flurry of interest in Southey's "Thabala" and his less-successful "The Curse of Kehama" died down. Byron's Oriental tales, then, were more often found among the intellectual baggage of the colonial servants and their wives who came out to India after 1830, especially those interested in writing novels. This matters more than it might seem, for, as David Knopf has noted, the popularity of Byron's poetry, and especially *Don Juan*, reinforced a profound change in Anglo-Indians' perceptions of the proper relationship between England and India, and between colonizer and colonized. As the students preparing for jobs as colonial administrators at the College of Fort William in Calcutta assumed more Byronic poses, their respect for the scholarship of men like Sir William Jones and his circle evaporated, as did their enthusiasm for learning Sanskrit, Bengali, and other Indian languages which might have led to better understandings of Hindu and Muslim culture.[29]

Romantic Novels and Representations of the Indian Zenana

When British Romantic poets wrote about "harem life," they were frequently preoccupied with redefining Eastern and Western women's relation to the sublime, often in direct or indirect response to newly translated Sanskrit literary and sacred texts. When Romantic novelists wrote about India, they were able to draw on a far wider range of variations on the Indian sublime than is usually recognized. Whether these novels were written by metropolitan writers with no direct experience of India, like James H. Lawrence in *Empire of the Nairs* (1811), Mrs. Mainwaring in *The Suttee; or, The Hindu Converts* (1830), or Sydney Owenson in *The Missionary* (1811), or by experienced Anglo-Indian writers like Meadows Taylor in *Ralph Darnell* (1864) and *Tara* (1863) or Mrs. Fanny Farr Penny in *The Romance of the Nautch Girl* (1898), these texts illustrate the persistence of contested alternatives to the Oriental sublime that was reinvented in Byron's poetry and plays. For several reasons, rape remained one of the central organizing metaphors in the majority of early novels about India, as the Romantic novels treating harem "captivity" tales discussed in this chapter, and those centering on the Hindu temple dancer, or *devadasi*, analyzed in the next chapter will show.

Many British and Anglo-Indian novelists in the early nineteenth-century wrote about life in the Indian zenana, partly because they hoped to capitalize on the popularity of Byron's harem tales. Of the more than 350 novels about India written in English between 1800 and 1900, many of the earliest and most significant Anglo-Indian novels offered descriptions of life in the zenana; William Hockley Browne's *Tales of the Zenana* (1827) and Meadows Taylor's *Confessions of a Thug* (1839) are perhaps the best known examples.[30] British and Anglo-Indians authors rarely wrote novels that represented the zenana simply as Malek Alloula describes it, as a "universe of generalized perversion and of absolute limitlessness of pleasure," as "the ideal locus of the phantasm in all its contagious splendour" (95).[31] This is not to suggest that in avoiding the "phantasm" of the colonial harem, British or Anglo-Indian novelists actually depicted zenana life accurately. On the contrary, most of these novels indicate how ill-informed the writers were about the multiplicity of traditions that shaped the cultural practices defining women's seclusion and veiling among various Hindu and Muslim communities in India.[32]

Like Byron's "Sardanapalus," many early nineteenth-century novels incorporate versions of the "captivity" plot, by focusing on Englishwomen who are, at some point, imprisoned in the zenana of a wealthy man. By analyzing three of these novels in more detail, James H. Lawrence's *Empire of the Nairs*, Mrs. Mainwaring's *The Suttee; or, The Hindu Converts* (1830), and Meadows Taylor's *Ralph Darnell*, we can see how the form of the novel proliferated and circulated a number of variations on the captivity tale. Further, by comparing novels by Lawrence and Mainwaring, who had no direct experience of India, with a novel written by Taylor, who lived for many years in India, we can begin to estimate how the ideological conflicts of the colonial contact zone further multiplied these variations. This brief survey of the variations and commonalities evident in these novels will help to explain why the rape of white women by Indian men became such an explosive and persistent trope in metropolitan and colonial writing about India after 1857.

In her influential study of travel literature about the Americas, Mary Louise Pratt has argued that narratives about the "captivity" of colonizing men and women appeared frequently in eighteenth- and nineteenth-century texts. Outlining the long history of the themes of "sex and slavery" in what she calls "survival literature," Pratt observes, "Many were the captives (and runaways) who became husbands, wives, or concubines of their captors. Throughout the history of early Eurocolonialism and the slave trade, survival literature furnished a 'safe' context for staging alternative, relativizing, and taboo configurations of intercultural contact: Europeans enslaved by non-Europeans, Europeans assimilating to non-European societies, and Europeans confounding new transracial social orders" (87). Early nineteenth-century captivity plots provided an occasion for writers to explore the meaning of slavery and oppression, though, in the end, they reaffirmed Eurocentric values that defined individual freedom and its limits under nineteenth-century capitalism since "the very existence of a text presupposed the imperially correct outcome: the survivor survived, and sought reintegration into the home society. The tale was always told from the viewpoint of the European who returned" (87). While all of the novels discussed in this chapter include versions of this "captivity" plot, they all avoid the "imperially correct" resolution that Pratt describes, suggesting that the representation of sex and gender in early novels about British India needs further consideration.[33]

Moreover, all of these novels about captivity in the zenana focus, in strange and unexpected ways, on the body of the mother, and one of my objectives in this chapter is to unveil the patterns in the "symbolic imaginary" that prompt this repetition. Read as a group, these novels suggest why "white" women in the harem continued to mark a "site of contradiction,"[34] as the concepts of freedom, consent, privacy, and legitimacy became more central to the definition of British national identity while it was being renegotiated throughout the nineteenth century in response to the changing regimes of capitalism and imperialism. More specifically, these novels expose how the Indian zenana provided a space for the projection of unresolved domestic concerns about the regulation of Englishwomen's sexuality, her relation to English marriage, property, and inheritance laws, and to reproduction. These texts, like many similar novels written by Anglo-Indians later in the century, show that these ideological conflicts concerning gender, sexuality, and agency could not be resolved simply by this process of imaginative export.

Many British and Anglo-Indian novels of this period which pretend to represent Muslim culture, including these three novels, describe an Englishwoman who is inserted into the zenana and reduced to the status of a "white slave" because she refuses a sexual alliance with the harem master and rejects the opportunity to barter sex for greater privilege. In contrast to Byronic poems about the harem, these novels allow more space for the expression of certain strands of the "feminist Orientalism" evident in the writings of Mary Wollstonecraft and the poetry of Percy Bysshe Shelley.[35] In charting the persistence of this theme, I hope to call attention to the ways that British and Anglo-Indian novels permitted more latitude for the expression of antihegemonic voices than Romantic poetry allowed.

These and many similar novels about Englishwomen's enclosure in the zenana kept alive, sometimes deliberately but more often not, feminist arguments about the legal and social bondage that colonizing women shared with the colonized. Until 1886, the married Englishwoman, like the imaginary white harem slave in these texts, could not control the disposition of the property she inherited, could not claim the profits of her labor, could not protect herself from unwanted sex, and could not claim the children she produced as her own.[36] Tales about the Indian zenana allowed metropolitan writers to displace these concerns onto a fantasy realm called "India."

Lawrence's and Mainwaring's novels present narratives about Englishwomen who, through their encounters in the harem, discover new aspects of their own economic, legal, and social subordination. Taylor's novel, as well as many other works by writers who actually lived in the colonial contact zone of British India, reveal even more complicated effects. Though it is unconventional in many respects, Taylor's *Ralph Darnell* shows how many of the contradictions in these themes were exacerbated because defenses of the British colonial empire in India, in the first half of the nineteenth century, were premised, as Thomas Metcalf has demonstrated, upon the assumed superiority of English practices concerning private property, the rule of law, the liberty of the [male] individual, and the value of an English classical education (*Ideologies*, 35).[37] Because all these novels explore the boundaries between the free and unfree woman, inside and outside marriage, inside and outside the home, they reveal why women's sexual consent remained a subtext in nineteenth-century novels about India. When these novels are read outside a Byronic frame, they present stories about rape and captivity that express the deepest fears and anxieties produced by the changing social and sexual contracts of nineteenth-century England.

Libertine Fantasies and the Indian Sublime

Like Byron and Shelley, James H. Lawrence offers an explicit catalogue of all the erotic pleasures that the Orient offered, but in his wildly improbable and somewhat adolescent novel *The Empire of the Nairs* (1811), he describes an Indian utopia where unlimited sensual pleasure, bodily freedom, and sexual abandon can be fully enjoyed without the danger and retribution that are part of Byron's and Shelley's epic formulas. Like many of Byron's later works, Lawrence's novel was written in exile, originally in German and loosely translated into English by the author. Unlike Byron's *Oriental Tales*, this novel was written without the benefit of any direct experience of India and makes no pretense of being historically or socially accurate.

Lawrence's novel shows that there were more radical Godwinian alternatives to Byron's Orientalist fantasies in circulation in the Romantic period that challenged the essentially Victorian separation of public and private life that Byronic harem tales later helped to normalize. In his introduction, Lawrence explicitly endorses Mary Wollstonecraft's program for the emancipation of Englishwomen as set forth in *A Vindication of the Rights of Woman* (1792), and throughout the novel he echoes her "feminist Orientalism" by similarly turning his critique of harem life back on English culture.

In his preface, Lawrence argues that greater sexual freedom for Englishmen and -women would effectively eliminate all the signs of the depravity created by English laws concerning courtship, marriage, and legitimacy: "In a country where there are no wives, there would be no courtesans; where every child were born legitimate, none would be insultingly styled a bastard, but all would be considered children of love. So long as Hymen continues a monopolist, Love will continue a smuggler" (1:xvi). The empire of the Nairs is presented, then, as a utopian alternative to the organization of private and public life in England; Lawrence's "India" envisions a revolutionary, though utterly improbable, solution to some of the contradictions in the social contract for women, at a time when it was being actively renegotiated.

Moreover, Lawrence anticipates Shelley in "Laon and Cythna" by insisting on the distinction between seduction and rape, a distinction that the more middle-class conventions of the British novel helped to erase in subsequent decades of the nineteenth-century. Unlike the English, the Nairs see the difference between love and rape as utterly self-evident. As Lawrence's Indian heroine, Osva, declares, "Love is a free gift, a mark of good will, which should not be extorted" (1:186). Rape, by contrast, is "an act of violence which should be punished with all the rigor of the law" (1:186).

In Lawrence's novel, female consent, before and after marriage, is a test of women's freedom, and, like Wollstonecraft and Shelley, Lawrence shows that "consent" must be considered in relation to female education. In the empire of the Nairs, for example, boys and girls are educated together, as Wollstonecraft recommended, and women's intellectual curiosity is not sacrificed to preserve men's false sense of superiority. As Lawrence proclaims in his preface, "There are many things a woman need not study, but there is nothing that she should be hindered from knowing" (1:xxix). The adventures of Lawrence's Indian hero, Firnos, as well as those of his mother and sister, demonstrate how coeducation allows women to make more fully informed decisions about consent in courtship and marriage.

The double plot in this novel allows Lawrence to contrast the adventures of his English hero, Walter de Grey, an aristocrat who travels to Persia and later to India in search of his lost sister, Emma, with those of Firnos, the Nair's next emperor, who travels to England in search of his missing mother and sister. Lawrence uses this plot to compare Emma de Grey's captivity in the harems of the Muslim Middle East with the physical and sexual freedom enjoyed by men and women in the empire of the Nairs. The novel begins in England when Emma is "seduced" by a married man, and Walter fights a duel in order to avenge sister's lost honor. After he kills her lover, Walter and his sister are forced to flee abroad, but Emma de Grey's career as a free sexual agent is soon cut short when she is captured by pirates, raped, and sold into "white slavery."

In contemplating Emma's fate as she is passed from owner to owner and immured in various harems in Turkey, Egypt, and Persia, Walter mourns not only his sister's losses but those of countless other women "shut up within the walls of a harem, and destined for the pleasures of a single individual, perhaps a hoary dotard, or a decrepit invalid" (3:191). In other words, Walter objects to harems partly because they give one man a sexual monopoly over women who should be free agents in their own sexual adventures. Unlike Don Juan, Walter is appalled by harem life under Islam and sees it as the epitome of "Mohometan despotism and polygamy" (1:9).

In describing Emma's experiences in various harems of the Middle East, Lawrence focuses primarily on the imprisonment, intimidation, and sexual slavery of her life rather than the "delights" to be found in the "colonial harem." Likewise, when Walter enters the harem in disguise in an effort to free his sister, he is discovered and threatened with castration. Unlike Byron's Selim or Don Juan, Walter is immune to the erotic frisson that surrounds cross-dressing and the threat of male rape in the harem episodes in Byron's tales. He barely avoids literal castration and is freed when a palace rebellion provides the opportunity for his escape.

Emma, by contrast, repeatedly fails in her efforts to escape from these harems. For her, resistance is futile, and she is often raped. Emma gains her freedom, then, only when the Nairs mount a successful attack on the royal harem at Kandahar to free abducted Nair women. As the Nair army prepares for battle, Lawrence's narrator invites comparisons with the French Revolution, "Who could describe the indignation of the Nair army at the sight of the seraglio? The sight of the bastille would not have filled a Briton with greater wrath" (10:8).

Unlike Richardson's Clarissa and countless other heroines in Anglo-Indian novels written later, Emma De Grey survives her harem captivity, though not without a sense of injury and loss. But when Emma is finally free, she complains about the undue emphasis placed on virginity and chastity in England and protests against the punishing shame directed at women who fail to conform to these ideas of purity. As she later tells her brother, "I can never return to England to render our name infamous. If formerly I was a disgrace to the family, what am I now, after all the indignities that I have suffered in the East" (5:131). Happily, Emma and Walter do not have to return to England; they are able to find their rightful (and elevated) place among the Nairs.

By comparing Walter's search for Emma with Firnos's efforts to locate his sister, who has traveled to England, Lawrence draws parallels between the visible, though imaginary, harems of Islam and the invisible harems of the West, where English fathers and husbands similarly tyrannize over their daughters and wives. In his preface, Lawrence argues that England is in need of profound social reform, especially in the private domain of the family, since the laws and customs of monogamous and indissoluble marriage do not follow "the system of nature." By sending Firnos's sister to England, Lawrence sets the stage for her outsider's critique of English courtship customs and laws of marriage, inheritance, and legitimacy. Both Osva and her mother recognize how these laws and practices profane the most sacred aspects of erotic love. During her visit, Osva observes, for example, that Englishwomen are "slaves indeed . . . but the days of courtship are their saturnalia, during which they are permitted to insult their masters" (3:70). She also notes the economic and social pressures that force Englishwomen to barter sex for social advance and asserts the power she would claim by exercising her sexual freedom, "To make a worthy man happy no good natured woman would refuse; her compliance is a trifle; but no threats or persuasions should ever have induced me to sacrifice myself . . . in order to wear a coronet, or to walk at the coronation" (3:29). In other words, Lawrence suggests that it is unnatural, and even immoral, to make a fetish of chastity as the English do or to use courtship customs and marriage laws to limit women's free expression of sexual desires in exchange for economic security. Under these conditions, Englishwomen cannot freely exercise their right to "consent" to sex. By these and other ongoing comparisons invited by his double plot, Lawrence challenges the self-congratulatory definitions of "freedom" that typically made nineteenth-century Englishwomen consider themselves as more privileged than Indian women (Melman, 104).

While the English episodes in the novel allow Lawrence to expose the patriarchal bias of English marriage practices and laws defining inheritance and primogeniture, the description of life among the Nairs provides the opportunity to imagine a matrilineal society ruled by the sons and heirs of Semiramis, a figure Lawrence idealizes rather than reviles. *The Empire of the Nairs* describes a blissful world where men and women can fully enjoy their sexual and physical freedom. All unmarried women over the age of eighteen are entirely free to enter into any erotic alliance they choose, for as long as they choose, with the blessing of their mothers and their queen. Lawrence discloses how the sex and gender arrangements in England are enforced by a larger economic as well as a legal system when he notes that among the Nairs, women are not coerced to marry to obtain economic security, to improve their class position, or to provide for their children.

Likewise, in the empire of the Nairs, women are granted the right to inherit property and to enjoy all the civil rights that the French Revolution opened to question.[38] In order to illustrate "the possibility of a nation's reaching the highest civilization without marriage" (1:ii), Lawrence enumerates the attitudes toward motherhood, fatherhood, and inheritance that prevail among the Nairs. In sum, like Shelley, Lawrence represents "India" as an idealized world where women are free to enjoy much greater sexual and physical freedom than their counterparts in England, though Lawrence's obsessive concern with sexuality, its role as the basic motivating force for most of the action in the novel, and his male and female characters' unusual frankness about sexuality also reveals his debts to eighteenth-century French and English translations of *The Arabian Nights* and to more extravagant Gothic works like Beckford's *Vathek* (1786) as well.[39]

The Empire of the Nairs represents a social order where the law of the father is literally unrecognized and where marriage, paternity, and illegitimacy do not have any cultural significance. Since monogamous marriage does not exist among the Nairs, all children are born outside the bounds of a legitimizing law and live with their mothers alone, financially supported by the state. There is no word for "father," and paternity is not formally acknowledged or enforced by either civil or religious law. Firnos, for example, can repeat the "succession of his own mothers for centuries back" but does not know the name of the man who fathered him. As he explains to Walter: "The relation between what ye call a father and the child is very doubtful, as it is always in the power of the mother to deceive her husband" (1:18).

Ultimately, Lawrence's celebration of the free love and sexual emancipation enjoyed by the Nairs exceeds Mary Wollstonecraft's feminist description of a utopian state in several scandalous ways. First, it identifies nakedness as the ultimate sign of freedom. Among the Nairs, "both men and women enjoyed the perfect use of their limbs; no restraint proceeded either from the materials or fashions of their habits . . . no unnatural ligatures repressed the agility of the men; no whalebone imprisoned the shapes of the women" (1:36). In fact, Lawrence places the naked body of the mother at the center of the ritual life in Calicut. In one of the strangest episodes in this bizarre novel, Lawrence describes the ceremony of the bath which sanctions the Nair's customs of free love and tolerance for sexual and physical openness. The Queen Mother instituted this yearly ritual after she saw "the state of slavery in which their neighboring nations held their women, whom they obliged to veil themselves from head to foot, and whose bodies they considered private property, which they were entitled to conceal as a miser would hide his treasures"

(2:101). Recognizing that this "false modesty was the first pretext toward the humiliation of her sex, and being herself revered as a prophetess," the queen wisely guaranteed women's "liberties" by "ordering the first woman in the empire to appear naked before the eyes of the whole nation" (2:101).

Lawrence details Walter de Grey's astonishment when he sees the aging queen disrobe. Expressing the incorrigible ageism of the West, Walter observes: "Perhaps a man of pleasure, who might have expected to have seen the figure of Venus rising from the water, would have been disappointed. The respectable Samorina, though of a dignified deportment, was old enough to be a great grandmother, and consequently no object of desire" (2:105). This ritual promoting a tolerance for nakedness is then linked to public rites of sexual initiation, when, shortly after she dries off, the queen recognizes the "happy moment of emancipation" when the virgins and youths in the Nair community are presented to her and declared "masters and mistresses of their own persons" (2:108).

However, the law of the father insinuates itself into the symbolic structure of this novel, nonetheless, when Lawrence acknowledges the threats that brother-sister and father-daughter incest pose to the Nairs' social order. Lawrence deflects the threat of brother-sister incest, a possibility that Byron and Shelley would make so notorious, by characterizing his Indian hero, Firnos, as immune to the sexual attractions of his sister, Osva, when he meets but does not recognize her in England. Father-daughter incest, on the other hand, poses a more profound threat to the social organization of the Nairs. When Osva returns incognito to the Nairs' capital city, many men, including her father, are attracted to her. Only the chance discovery of her true identity prevents Osva from casually obliging her father's erotic invitations. It turns out, then, that paternity matters after all in this sexual utopia, since Osva must learn the secret of her paternity in order to realize that she has come home, that she is "no longer a wretched exile, seeking asylum from the persecutions of her own [English] family" but rather is "a member of a free country, a princess of imperial birth, the pride of her family, and the idol of her people, a descendant of Semiramis, and a daughter of that very Agalva who [*sic*] she ever considered a superior being" (9:205).

Finally, though Lawrence repeatedly dramatizes the oppression of Emma de Grey and the other "white slaves" in the harems of Islam, he ends his novel by reasserting his opposition to the abolition of African slavery (5:201) and by defining miscegenation as the natural limit to women's promiscuity. The resolution of his plot makes it evident that while Lawrence happily imagined a revision of the sexual contract, he was unwilling to renegotiate the economic structures that defined the social contract and the class hierarchy that it upheld. When Emma de Grey is a prisoner in the royal harem at Kandahar, she is protected by a black eunuch named Ibraham (3:217), and she promises, in gratitude, to marry him should they ever escape. Though Ibraham shows a generosity that the narrator asserts is "uncommon among this despicable race of beings" (3:213), Emma is easily persuaded to break her promise to marry him as soon as she is freed from the harem and re-united with her brother.[40]

Walter soon persuades Emma that it is her primary duty to become a mother by reiterating a Malthusian argument. He tells her, "Population is the end of marriage—and every connection contrary to that end is criminal; but, while we detest these unnatural marriages that are usual in Persia, can we absolve our own country from blame? Our own laws permit the blooming victim of vanity or ambition to bury herself alive in the arms of decrepit age and is not such a union equally useless to the state?—equally contrary to nature? . . . Emma, you must become a mother" (9:182). Upon learning of Emma's change of heart, Ibraham commits suicide, and no one mourns his loss. In other words, though Lawrence draws his tale of "white slavery" at a time when it became a vehicle for antislavery propaganda, he reverses the abolitionists' message and reassigns the black man to the zone of abjection when he characterizes him as a eunuch.

In the end, then, *The Empire of the Nairs* betrays Lawrence's nostalgia for the "libertine" values of eighteenth-century English culture, evident in his efforts to preserve the race, gender, and class hierarchies that organize this text. While Lawrence's novel ostensibly illustrates the advantages of sexual freedom and recommends the reform of customs and laws that convert marriage into "sexual slavery," it does not endorse limitless freedom for women because Lawrence wants to preserve the power that male elites enjoy in the public sphere. In his introduction to the novel, he writes, "Let the males be their own masters, and employ themselves in public affairs; let the females be their own mistresses, and manage their own domestic concerns" (1:xxvii). It is the spectacle of pregnant women as warriors or statesmen that, in Lawrence's view, makes women's claim to a more equal share of public life appear to be "ridiculous."

At the same time, Lawrence's novel disputes the "imperially correct" ending for survival tales that Mary Louise Pratt described because Walter and his sister, once their status as aristocrats is assured, are happy to remain in the empire of the Nairs, in a community that shares their ideals of free love and their tolerance for illegitimacy. Likewise, with the return of his lost mother and sister, Firnos's claim as the next emperor is confirmed, as is Osva's and her mother's status as aristocrats and mothers. With this resolution, Lawrence reveals the hierarchies he would retain in his Indian paradise of free love, which makes his utopia differ profoundly from the egalitarian, though far more disciplined, republic that Mary Wollstonecraft described in *A Vindication of the Rights of Woman*.[41] Thus, though Lawrence imagined a sexual utopia where mothers held a greater place of honor in the social and symbolic domain, he also defined the limits of women's freedom by reference to their biological reproductive function and their "utility" to men and to the state.

In the Zenana of the "Gentle Hindoo"

Mrs. Mainwaring's *The Suttee; or, The Hindu Converts* (1830), like Lawrence's *Empire of the Nairs*, disputes Byronic formulas that playfully idealize life in the "colonial harem" under Islam and offers an alternative vision of the Indian sublime in her admittedly overly idealized representation of zenana life among the "gentle Hindoos." As such, Mainwaring's novel illustrates the complex afterlife of the feminist Orientalism that finds expression in Wollstonecraft's essays and Shelley's poetry, though it also avoids Lawrence's vision of India as a utopian site of sexual freedom. Simply put, *The Suttee* shows how, as late as 1830, Enlightenment appreciations of Vedantan Hinduism could continue to coexist with the Christian evangelicalism that Mainwaring explicitly endorses in her novel.

In the preface to *The Suttee*, Mrs. Mainwaring identifies Christian conversion as the ultimate goal of British colonialism in India and tenders a somewhat disingenuous apology for endowing the Hindu family described in her novel with "so many virtues previous to their conversion" (vi). She notes that "it is painful to reflect, that while Britain has made vast exertions to establish a mighty Empire in the East, little has been done to emancipate the Hindoos from the bondage of superstition, under which they have been so long kept by a sanguinary priesthood" (vi). In devising a preface that counters many of the details of her novel, Mrs. Mainwaring manifests the ambivalence she shared with many others of her generation concerning the expansion of the British colonies in India (Rocher, 222–223).

Mainwaring reverses the dualities that organize the Byronic Oriental tale by idealizing the "mild and quiescent morality" (ii) of her Hindu hero, Nuradda, and by demonizing the political and sexual practices of Timor, the Muslim leader and harem master in this tale. Mainwaring's novel presents two contrasting versions of the "colonial harem": one Hindu and the other Muslim. Nuradda is a wealthy Hindu rajah who presides over a well-populated zenana but one that is characterized as a sanctuary rather than a prison. In addition to sheltering his wife and their son, Nuradda also provides a home for his divorced sister, Azuma, and for "many a beauty" from his and his wife's extended families, "who unprovided and unprotected sought and received a brother's care" (11). A wise, generous, and enlightened ruler, Nuradda offers several contrasts with Southey's Kehama. Nuradda is content with only one wife, whom he treats with utmost love and respect. He has taught his wife to read and write since he realizes that "by improving the mind, he ensured the love of Temora, not making her a slave" (1:118). His wife's letters subsequently provide Nuradda with an "exquisite pleasure" and assurance of her "perfect love" (1:118); they also provide Mainwaring with a convenient plot device.

The feminist Orientalism in Mainwaring's novel combines with a more limited appreciation for the "sublime, pristine" features of Vedantan Hinduism than was evident in Shelley's Oriental poetry. Nuradda, for example, practices vegetarianism, and unlike "The Curse of Kehama," Mainwaring's novel describes no horrifying animal sacrifices and consistently emphasizes the "mildness" of the Hindus (2:106). Similarly, Nuradda and his wife espouse pacifism, as is shown when Temora naively asks her husband, "Oh, dearest Nuradda, why do men destroy each other, when our pious bramin [sic] thinks it a sin to shed the blood of animals?" (1:119). Though these principles make Nuradda reluctant to join Sultan Tipoo's campaign against the British, his honor and hereditary obligations require that he follow Timor into battle; as he explains to his wife, "I am a Hindoo and incapable of betraying any one" (1:135).

Mainwaring's novel presents a captivity tale, of a sort, since she focuses on the experiences of Lady Augusta, an Englishwoman, who lives for some time in Nuradda's zenana, but the feminist Orientalism in this text reverses the power relations and reorganizes the lessons that her heroine learns during her sojourn in the zenana. When Lady Augusta is suddenly widowed and finds herself homeless and unprotected in the unfamiliar world of India, Nuradda offers her shelter and, sometime later, an intellectual companionship that excludes any threat (or promise) of erotic attention. When one of the household priests questions whether Nuradda "intends to make this beautiful stranger a sharer in your affections, as well as your benevolence," he responds, "Is it not possible . . . to act with kindness, without entertaining an idea of becoming the master of her person?" (2:115). After many serious intellectual conversations, Nuradda tells Lady Augusta that she has taught him to value English customs that allow a "refined friendship with the softer sex. Here we are only lovers, but there, I understand, we may enjoy an attachment equally disinterested and pure—such as, I flatter myself, I may be permitted to say I feel for my admirable and interesting guest" (2:130). Nuradda's admiration for Lady Augusta deepens as he learns about her Christian faith and begins to study the Bible.

Still, Mainwaring's novel differs from most evangelically influenced novels written later in the century because it makes intellectual conversation and Christian tolerance the basis for this East-West friendship rather than the heroine's beauty or white skin. In fact, when Nuradda praises her "fairness," Lady Augusta defuses the compliment, saying it is "perhaps only pleasing in your eyes because it is uncommon in this country" (2:126). Unlike the Oriental wives and mothers represented in later novels, Temora is not jealous of her husband's interest in Lady Augusta. Instead, there exists a "perfect spirit of sisterhood" between Temora, Azuma, and Lady Augusta (2:123) that allows the heroine to remain content in the Rajah's zenana for several years.

The feminist Orientalism of Mainwaring's novel is also evident in her characterization of the brutalities of domestic life in Timor's harem, which challenges more Byronic fantasies of the blissful eroticism available in the "colonial harem." Azuma, Timor's divorced wife, ostensibly provides an "insider's" view of the terrors of her life in Timor's harem after she returns to her brother's home. Characterizing her experiences as one of Timor's several wives as "ostentatious slavery" (1:45), Azuma tells her sister-in-law about the murderous female competition in Timor's harem: "Thou, Temora, canst not have a thought of the miseries of a Mussulman harem, where uncontrolled desire throws among the inmates the torch of discord, instead of diffusing the lambent light of harmonious friendship and faithful love. Oh! it is the place where wicked spirits only ought to dwell. . . . The proud lord turns from the pale or grief-worn visage with painful feelings, though the object might once have been as dear as such wandering affections will possibly allow " (1:59–60). In Mainwaring's novel, then, it is the brutal and selfish harem master who exercises the ultimate power of life and death over all the women in his harem and not, as in "Sardanapalus" or in later Anglo-Indian novels, the harem favorite or the mother.

One stereotypical tableau epitomizes Azuma's complete subordination in the harem of this Oriental despot. When Azuma bears Timor a son and the child is subsequently poisoned by another harem inmate who wants to protect her child's prior claims as heir, Timor brutally reminds both mothers of his absolute power over them. When the remorseful murderer kneels naked before Timor and asks for his forgiveness, "with her beauties exposed to view shaded only by her long black tresses," Timor twists her hair around his arm and kills her, saying, "Thus let me punish my own rash judgment, warped by the glitter of a fair outside!" (1:84). Because she is implicated in this humiliation, Timor then divorces and banishes Azuma.

Like Mary Wollstonecraft, however, Mainwaring also compares the harem master's absolute power over the women of his household with the power that Englishmen exercise at their wives' expense because of the patriarchal bias of English marriage and property laws. Lady Augusta came to India because her husband was employed by the East India Company. After his unexpected death, she is imprisoned in the home of her brother-in-law, Charles Belmour, until she agrees to sign a document that grants him complete control of her late husband's estate. Not content with her money and property, Charles Belmour wants to force Lady Augusta to marry him, and her only escape is to flee. In detailing this struggle, Mainwaring characterizes colonial India as a world where unscrupulous Englishmen can claim the license to exploit or oppress women of any race, including their own.

The most threatening villain in Mainwaring's novel, then, is the devious and violent Englishman Charles Belmour rather than a "mighty" Hindu rajah like Southey's Kehama. Belmour's superior knowledge of English law increases his authority over colonizing women like Lady Augusta just as his role in commanding a superior military force amplifies the power he, and other Englishmen, exert over the colonized in this text. With an irony that cuts both ways, Lady Augusta recalls her brother-in-law's perfidy when she says to Nuradda, "Heaven has thrown me on the tender mercies of idolators, to save me from the machinations of those who are called Christians, but who are unworthy of that sacred appellation" (2:103).

The English concept of consent makes rape and sati twins in this text. Despite Mainwaring's efforts to display the "gentleness" of her Hindu characters, the crisis of this novel, as in Southey's "The Curse of Kehama," centers on sati, showing how the notion of female "sacrifice" organizes both works, revealing the Christian evangelicalism that informs them and many subsequent novels. Yet, unlike Southey, Mainwaring ingeniously stages this attempt at sati to display Temora's unworldly nobility of spirit and Lady Augusta's physical and moral courage. Earlier, when she learned that Lady Augusta was a widow, Temora explained the appeal of sati: "With us, it is a duty, and a happiness, to die with the lords of our life; and the widowed spirit that ascends in the pure flame of the funeral pile, aspires to everlasting bliss; the gates of Paradise open for such, without further probation on this earth"

(2:109). In this exchange, and elsewhere in the text, Mainwaring emphasizes the cultural conditioning that calls into question Temora's "consent" to this ritual.

Later, Temora receives mistaken news of her husband's death in battle and begins to prepare for sati, and in narrating this episode, Mainwaring echoes Christian missionary accounts that identify brahmin priests as the instigators of this "dreadful sacrifice."[42] Reiterating what, by 1830, had become a cliché in writing about India, Mainwaring describes how these priests prevent Lady Augusta from trying to persuade Temora to give up sati (3:40) and describes how they drug Temora and carry her "insensible" body up the steps overlooking the pyre.

By setting the stage for this spectacular public sacrifice, however, Mainwaring also provides the occasion for British soldiers to stop it, bringing the unscrupulous Charles Belmour and his troops onto the scene. Defying Christian missionary and British nationalist scripts that usually cast Englishmen in the heroic role of saving "brown women from brown men" (Spivak, "Can," 305), Mainwaring shows, instead, how this military intervention puts both colonized and colonizing women at risk by demonstrating that British soldiers in India were not above robbing and raping both Indian and English women. Temora is threatened with rape, for example, when Belmour's subordinate officer notices the "profusion of jewels" that she wears and asserts that he "knows what to do with the pretty Hindoo" (3:64). Likewise, Lady Augusta is also defenseless against Belmour, who wants to reassert his plans to force her to marry him. Mainwaring reveals further parallels between sati and rape when Belmour deploys his epistemological power as well as his military force to challenge Lady Augusta's credibility when she describes her experiences in the zenana. Before the assembled company of his troops, Belmour casts doubt on Lady Augusta's chastity when he says: "I am only surprised you did not apprize me of your captivity. Surely you did not remain a willing captive in the zezenah [*sic*] of a Hindoo chief, although you might wish to evade my just and legal rights over your person and your fortune" (3:86). In other words, Belmour claims the power to transform Lady Augusta's story into a "captivity" tale that ends, as Byron's "Sardanapalus" does, with her willing sexual surrender to the harem master, and she is powerless to dispute Belmour's revision.

In dramatizing this conflict, Mainwaring exposes the common patriarchal privileges that united English and Muslim men. When Lady Augusta's word was called into question, some men "pitied her but all believed the reports that had been made against her" (3:93). Timor calls Lady Augusta a "faithless wife" and advises her to return to Charles Belmour, who has promised to forgive her and accept her as wife, though "death," he tells her, would be the punishment she would face among Muslims. Even her one-time friend, Harley, advises Lady Augusta to submit to Belmour, declaring that he has "no authority" to protect her or even to "claim her person" in marriage (3:118).

In the end, Temora's failed attempt at sati proves providential when Nuradda unexpectedly appears on the scene, reunites joyfully with his wife, and corroborates Lady Augusta's testimony, helping her win an unlikely triumph in her war of words with Belmour. Nuradda confirms that Lady Augusta was "an angel of purity" (3:131) while she resided in his zenana. What clinches his argument and proves his truthfulness, though, is Nuradda's declaration: "I am more than half a Christian, and it is to her pure example, her mild and well-directed observations, that I am indebted'" (3:131). Nuradda confesses that though he is moved to learn that Temora attempted sati, he has, in the meantime, come to see it as a "cruel duty that condemns a Hindoo widow to a dreadful sacrifice, repugnant to the feelings of all but those devoted to superstitions and degrading idolatry" (2:269). In short, Nuradda now sees the ultimate sacrifice of sati in the light of Christian "reason."

Indicating one of several ways that Romantic idealism could meld with feminist Orientalism, as well as evangelicalism with the utilitarian liberalism of the 1830s, Mainwaring's novel ends with her Hindu hero's and heroine's conversion to Christianity, which brings it into line with her endorsement of the Christian evangelicalism announced in her preface. At the same time, the conclusion emphasizes her English heroine's decidedly "unfree" legal and economic status. By thus staging Lady Augusta's vindication after her "captivity" in terms that resemble a rape trial, Mainwaring illustrates how Englishwomen remain disadvantaged under the law in British India and England alike. Perhaps this is why Mainwaring allows Lady Augusta to avoid the "imperially correct" outcome for survival tales when she remains unmarried upon her return to England. In choosing perpetual widowhood, Lady Augusta also refuses the burden of reproduction that Lawrence's novel insists women must assume, even in an ideal state like the empire of the Nairs.

Writing Zenana Tales in the Colonial Contact Zone

Meadows Taylor's novels suggest how representations of the "colonial harem" could be reshaped by the experiences of life in this colonial contact zone. All Taylor's works illustrate how an Enlightenment appreciation of Indian culture similar to that of Sir William Jones could continue to coexist

with a feminist Orientalism reminiscent of Shelley and Mainwaring well after the Romantic period. Taylor's novels also express the pragmatic liberal
humanism of a man who lived and worked in India from 1824 to 1860, serving for many years as a military advisor at the pleasure of several Indian
nawabs.

The various representations of zenana life in Taylor's novels are more
intimate than in most British or Anglo-Indian texts, and many details suggest his familiarity with this "inner" domain of Indian society, gained through
his family connections and friendships with elite Indian men and women.[43]
Taylor was related by marriage to one of the princesses of Delhi, and he befriended many Indian men and women, including the Rani of Shorapur. All
Taylor's novels reflect his fairly well-informed understanding of the ways that
history, economic exigencies, social stability, caste and economic status, religious affiliations, and family structure all determine Indian women's experiences in the zenana.

In his first and most famous novel, *Confessions of a Thug* (1839), as
well as in his second work, *Tippoo Sultaun: A Tale of the Mysore War* (1840),
Taylor specifically counters Byronic fantasies about the zenana as a domain
of absolute male power. Both novels show that the customs of the Indian
zenana cannot entirely control or contain women's sexual energies unless
women consent to their seclusion. These novels include Indian women who
are unmarried virgins, married women, and widows who live in seclusion but
find ways to offer themselves to Taylor's attractive heroes. Thus, Taylor suggests that the zenana is not just a physical place but a way of life, and that
traditions of purdah, or veiling, do not necessarily restrict Indian women's
access to the "public realm," as Byronic Oriental tales imply. In *Tippoo
Sultaun*, for example, all three wives of Abdool Rhyman Khan follow him
into battle. When Khan tries to convince his youngest wife to remain behind,
she replies, "If the Mahratta women have done this many a time, thinkest
thou that a Moghul of the old and proud blood of Delhi dares not?" (329).

Only one of Taylor's novels, *Ralph Darnell*, includes all the ingredi-
ents of the captivity tale that I have been tracing since it presents the story
of a young Englishwoman, Julia Wharton, who, at one point in the plot, is
confined in the royal harem of the Nawab of Bengal. *Ralph Darnell* shows
Taylor's debts to Sir Walter Scott since he imbeds Julia's captivity tale in a
narrative that treats one of the most famous episodes in British imperial history, the colonial struggle for the control of Bengal in 1756–1757.[44] This
frame allows Taylor to compare the Indian adventures of Ralph Darnell, the
illegitimate son of a wealthy British family whose ancestral seat is in

Northumberland, with those of Julia Wharton. It also allows Taylor to compare his heroine's "captivity" in the zenana with that "resonant metonym for colonial horror" (Teltscher, "Fearful," 30), the imprisonment of the English survivors of the battle of Fort William on the night of June 20, 1758, in the infamous "black hole of Calcutta."

Taylor's feminist Orientalism clearly directs the comparisons he draws between Ralph Darnell's and Julia Wharton's lives, first in London and later in Calcutta, for he underlines inconsistencies in the social and sexual contracts that define their respective places in metropolitan and colonial culture. Ralph Darnell's life illustrates how the "social contract" stigmatizes him because of his illegitimate birth. When he is working as a clerk for his uncle in the East India office in London, for example, Ralph consorts with other hard-drinking, gambling, wild young men who enjoy the rollicking company of English prostitutes until they inherit sufficient property to marry suitably within their class. But when Ralph professes his love for his aristocratic cousin, he is rejected because his illegitimacy makes his claim on his father's property uncertain.

Taylor similarly calls attention to the sexual contract that organizes life in British India when Ralph is sent to Calcutta to work in the East India offices and observes that many of his fellow countrymen in the employ of the company "passed their time in the society of Mahomedan dancing women or their native mistresses" (219), since "money was abundant and freely squandered upon these parasites" (219). In showing that erotic pleasures could be easily bought from this group of Indian women whose status had been altered by contact with British colonizers, Taylor's novel explodes Byronic fantasies by suggesting that there was no need to break into the "harem" in order to enjoy the erotic spectacles and pleasures exhibited there. In this way, Taylor challenges one of the most pervasive myths of the Victorian period, that English colonizers were more "pure" than the colonized.

Likewise, in his frank characterization of Julia Wharton, the English heroine of this text, Taylor demonstrates his resistance to Byronic formulas that made the "white slave" in the harem such a "site of contradiction." Unlike most nineteenth-century heroines, Julia Wharton is beautiful but she is not "pure"; she has been sent to India, Taylor explains, to cloak a past sexual "indiscretion" (223) in London. Taylor gives Julia more agency than most Victorian heroines since she willingly and skillfully participates in the process of catching a husband. Julia is "very fair, with a plump figure and tiny waist," and knows "how to dress herself so as to display her charms to the best advantage" (222).

In describing the terms of Julia's subsequent marriage contract with Mr. Wharton, Taylor underlines the patriarchal bias of English marriage and inheritance laws, and he enumerates the economic exigencies that prompt Julia to marry him. Mr. Wharton is a wealthy, older English merchant who has offered "to settle a lac of rupees upon her" and who presents "her with a gorgeous necklace of pearls" (223). Taylor also provides a structural explanation for the jealousy and guilt that separates Julia from her husband's unofficial Indian "wife" by noting that part of their agreement specifies that Mr. Wharton will "put away her native predecessor" and disinherit their children after he has married her (223).

Like Cythna and Myrrah, Julia Wharton plays the part of a "national heroine," but of a more modest sort, when she and her husband are trapped in Fort William during the famous siege. Julia inspires the English troops by reading them psalms (278) and later shows her courage and fortitude when she is imprisoned along with other English survivors in the notorious "black hole," one of the cells in the fort. That night Julia is saved from suffocation by the heroic efforts of Ralph Darnell, but her husband expires. Shortly after her release, Julia is abducted and confined to the zenana in Suraj-oo-Dulah's palace.[45]

Unlike countless heroines after her, but like Emma de Grey, Julia accommodates to the sexual demands of her life in the zenana. As Taylor delicately puts it, "The English girl was not pure, but her impurity was as virgin snow before him into whose power her wayward fate had thrown her. She had lived—that was enough. She had sighed and prayed for death, but it did not come; and helpless, very helpless, she had resigned herself to her fate" (306). Although Julia is demoralized by her life in the zenana and her mind grows "into a kind of numb vacancy of submission" (364), her Christian faith gives her the strength to resist the nawab's efforts to force her to convert to Islam so that he can marry her in order to produce legitimate heirs. In other words, reproduction replaces rape as the central concern of this captivity plot. What makes Julia Wharton unusual is that she avoids the typical punishments delivered to nineteenth-century heroines who are immured in the harems of Eastern despots. She does not commit suicide, die, or otherwise destroy her own beauty, even after she is imprisoned in a subterranean cell along with the nawab's young wife. Instead, Julia comes to appreciate the gentle, patient, and loving disposition of the Indian woman with whom she shares her captivity.

Taylor further disputes the simple moral polarizing that characterizes most British imperial histories and Anglo-Indian novels about these events by adding a second "captivity" plot to his novel. In focusing on Suraj-oo-Dulah, one of the most vilified Muslim leaders in British histories of the struggle for control of Bengal, Taylor acknowledges that the Nawab of Bengal was a "cruel, rapacious, vindictive, insolent, and tyrannical" despot (2:120) and dramatizes this side of his character, for instance, by showing the absolute power he exercises over his guiltless wife. This second captivity plot, however, acts to humanize Suraj-oo-Dulah by describing his love for Sozun, a professional Afghani "dancing girl" who becomes his harem favorite during this crisis in his rule. Taylor presents a remarkably sympathetic portrait of Sozun, even though she later leads some of the Nawab's troops against the English during the siege of Fort William and subsequently plays a part in the lives of both Ralph Darnell and Julia Wharton. In departing from more conventional fantasies about white women who become harem favorites, Taylor shows all the reasons why Julia Wharton can't begin to compete with Sozun in the erotic and strategic power she commands in influencing and directing the Nawab.

Though Sozun's role is similar to Myrrah's in "Sardanapalus" in several respects, Taylor gives Sozun an unusual degree of self-consciousness, self-determination, and agency that expresses both his feminist Orientalism and his investments in liberal defenses of colonial policies in India. Like Myrrah, Sozun is brought to India as a captive of war, but Taylor invites more sympathy for her by describing how, as a motherless child of only eleven years old, she followed her father into battle and was captured after he was killed. When camp followers notice Sozun's beauty, they decide to capitalize on it. Sozun's "figure was tall, strong, and well formed, and her face gave promise of beauty. Her eyes were glorious—great brown flashing eyes, with long sweeping eyelashes, which seemed almost coarse," and, because "she appeared very fair" (203), they are able to sell her to a professional to be trained as a dancing girl, or "*tuwaif*."

Taylor does not represent Sozun, however, as a permanent victim of this system of sexual slavery. After her body and her art mature, Sozun is able to earn considerable fame and fortune: "From Delhi to Lucknow, at festivals, marriages, the durbars of princes, the merrymakings of rich bankers, even the sacred festivals of Hindu gods, and the anniversaries of Mahomedan saints, the Affghan [*sic*] girl danced and sang, and the gold of enraptured thousands was poured at her feet" (205). In keeping with the customs of her trade, Sozun cannot use this money to buy her freedom, but when Suraj-oo-Dulah notices her and offers to pay her "price" in order to bring her into his zenana, she agrees because she "felt her destiny was accomplished" (205), recognizing that it offered her the best opportunity to ensure her continued financial security. But by describing Sozun's relation to the Nawab in these contractual terms, by showing that the dancing girl must "consent" to them and that she may revoke their agreement at any time, Taylor suggests her complicity in what he defines as her "dishonour." In this way, Taylor shows his own investments in the more utilitarian and legalistic colonial ideologies that were typical of British Liberals in the 1830s and 1840s even though the novel was not published until 1865.

What gives Sozun her relative freedom and sets her apart from more stereotypical harem slaves, including Byron's Myrrah, is that she has been specifically trained to resist the "enslavement" of romantic love. Taylor writes, "Of all the cautions she had received from her instructress, the most constant was that she must shut her heart to love. She had to gain honour in her art, to gain wealth and power, but must harden her heart against all else; . . . Other women might marry, might have children to love them, might love themselves; but one like her, a Tuwaif, never!" (207). Though Taylor describes many scenes that show the Nawab's tender love for Sozun, he insists on her cool detachment. Watching over her sleeping lover, for example, Sozun echoes Myrrah when she declares "scornfully," "For this I am what I am, and but a slave after all" (206). Sozun's life does not follow the trajectory of Myrrah's conversion, however, which opens her to romantic love and to spectacular self-sacrifice. Instead, Sozun ruthlessly exploits the power that the Nawab's love gives her, though she has no illusions about the limits of her power and realizes that "he might some day turn on her unexpectedly and destroy her as he had destroyed others" (207). Later, Suraj-oo-Dulah does, indeed, reassert his power as absolute ruler when he imprisons Sozun with his wife and Julia Wharton.

Taylor's divided allegiances as colonizer are most evident in the ending he designs for Sozun's captivity plot. Taylor avoids the usual colonizers' script where Englishmen "save brown women from brown men" (Spivak, "Can," 305), but he also limits the power and agency Sozun can claim when she returns to the public sphere. Sozun arranges her own escape from the sexual slavery of zenana life, which, in her case, is also wage slavery, but the price of freedom for her, it turns out, is the sacrifice of all her sexual, maternal, and material desires. When Sozun asks to leave the Nawab's harem, it is so that she may help to lead his troops against the English. After she takes off her dancing girl's costume and puts on the "blue tunic" of her people, Sozun effectively undergoes a conversion experience when she recognizes "a sense of freedom and exhilaration to which she had long been a stranger" (242). After winning "admiration for her bravery" upon the battlefield (250) and recovering a measure of self-respect, Sozun decides not to return to her "dishonourable" life as the Nawab's favorite.

In other words, Taylor allows Sozun to remain in the "public sphere," but he requires that she conform to a British model of civility that was historically designed to "enhance and intensify the powers of specifically male bodies" (Gatens, 71). Sozun breaks the sexual contract that defined her relationship to men in the past, but she must then accept the only other role available to her, as defined by the English social contract. Having lost her parents and refused motherhood, Sozun must then accept the role of "saint" and "sister." Remembering the "women who had changed their life of sin to one of good works in the love of God and the Prophet—women who were honoured as they lived" (238), Sozun decides to renounce erotic love entirely, telling the Nawab, "I have vowed that man's love can never exist within me again" (311).

It is as a saint, then, that Sozun claims a rough equality in the world outside the zenana when she again joins the soldiers who storm Fort William, on June 18, 1756. As she crosses the ramparts, Ralph Darnell tries to stop her, but, seeing that she is a woman, he cannot kill her. Later, Sozun returns this debt of honor by tenderly nursing Ralph back to health, after the battle is done. When Ralph responds by professing his love for her, Sozun reiterates her vow of chastity, refusing marriage and motherhood, by declaring: "I am thy sister, sir, now, and I have many brethren since I made my vow, and put on these holy garments. . . . So it is merciful not to tempt one whose love is dead. I think I see thy heart, loving and generous; but, brother, it cannot be. Mine hath been a hard, shameless life; and such as thou shouldst mate with must be pure as snow" (326). In the end, then, Sozun helps to arrange Ralph's marriage to the Nawab's widow and confirms the ethics of her own exclusion from the private sphere.[46] As a *tuwaif*, she explains that she can enjoy none of the rewards that make the "inner" world attractive to respectable Indian women, though she admits that her exclusion has been the source of her "freedom": "I have been free all my life—free to go, to come, to live in sin, and now to live to God. I could not stay within; life was dead to me, and all the petty cares and troubles of the zenana hateful to me" (*sic*, 435). Thus, Sozun shows the traces of the Malthusian solution to the problem of female desire which required that European women participate in the social contract by recognizing the power of shame and refusing unwed motherhood (Jacobus, *First Things*, 83–104).

Imperial history, of course, dictated the defeat and eventual death of the Nawab of Bengal and its consequences for Sozun and his wife, but Taylor had a freer hand in defining the fates of Julia Wharton and Ralph Darnell. Because both characters repeatedly resist the "imperially correct" solutions found in many nineteenth-century survivor tales, Taylor's novel dramatizes his responsiveness to the greater play of ideological tensions in this colonial contact zone. Shortly after Julia is released from the Nawab's prison, Ralph Darnell notices her beauty and asks her to marry him. In refusing him, Julia rejects the imperially correct conclusion usually reserved for the English heroine who remains "pure" and finally marries the hero, a pattern repeated endlessly in later Anglo-Indian novels. Instead, Julia returns to England, with the money her first husband settled upon her, and because she is a "rich" widow she is able to correct her past by wedding the Englishman who initially seduced her but was forbidden to marry her.

Ralph Darnell also resists the imperially correct resolution for survival tales in several interesting ways. First, he comes to recognize the abject not in the black man or the eunuch, as in Lawrence's novel, but rather in the Englishman as rake and irresponsible father. Through a series of miraculous coincidences, Ralph meets the sailor who piloted his mother and father to Scotland and so obtains the "marriage lines" that he hopes will prove his legitimacy and give him the right to claim his father's property in another colonial borderland, Northumberland. The providential discovery of the written evidence of his legitimacy is usually enough to allow the hero in most English novels to return to England, marry, and live happily ever after, but Taylor devises a more iconoclastic ending more in harmony with his feminist Orientalism.

Retracing his parents' journey to Scotland, Ralph visits the church where they ostensibly were married and discovers that his father deceived his mother by arranging for a friend to pose as a minister: "Before that altar my dear mother knelt, believing one true who knelt by her, but who was false—and a ruffian read God's words over her" (407). Ralph then recognizes that his mother did not, in fact, consent to her "seduction," as he had always been told, but was deceived into believing she had legally married his father, and this discovery allows Ralph to see that his mother was "pure." In this way, Taylor explores the problem of woman's consent beyond the limits set by Wollstonecraft's essay or Lawrence's novel when Ralph realizes how his father exercised his power to deceive the woman he claimed to love.

The discovery of his father's perfidy and betrayal prompts Ralph to renounce his dream of inheriting a "baronetcy" in England, and he returns to India instead. Refusing to "carry his father's name" (433) any longer, Ralph adopts instead the work ethic of the new middle-class colonial servant, vowing "to work out one's own lot in life, and never to flinch from it till it was fulfilled" (427). With no "English" family to restrain him, Ralph decides to cross over the legal, religious, and racial boundaries that typically separated colonizer and colonized shortly after he sees the beautiful Indian widow of Suraj-oo-Doulah. Upon her release from the Nawab's prison, Noor-al-Nissa was "scarcely eighteen perhaps, fair in face, and with a lithe gracefulness of figure . . . more lovely than he could have believed a native of India to be" (363), and after several turns of the plot, she becomes Ralph's beloved wife. Taylor's narrator cites the "facts" of history in defense of their marriage: "I do not argue for it or against it—I do not say whether it were right or wrong, advisable or inadvisable—I only accept as a fact that, in those early days of Indian life of Englishmen—Englishmen in power and high station—there were many marriages like those of Ralph Smithson's [Darnell], which grew out of circumstances like his perhaps, or other—what matter. They were, and they were often happy" (437).

Finally, while most British and Anglo-Indian novelists insist on the fatal consequences of mixed marriage and miscegenation, Taylor lends an air of sublimity to this union not only in life but also in death. Before Ralph retires from his work with the East India Company, his wife gives birth to their only daughter, and shortly afterward mother and child die. When he returns to England, Ralph brings with him his greatest treasure, the curiously embalmed body of his wife. Taylor treats Ralph's extravagant efforts to keep his wife's memory alive with idealizing sympathy, and describes the moment when he dies kneeling beside her body as marking his spiritual reunion with his wife: "On the bed lay a still female figure, dressed in gorgeous apparel of cloths of gold and silver, and the finest Indian Muslin, and a few fresh roses were strewn about it and placed near the face. A gleam of sunshine, resting upon the bed, flashed back from the glittering stuffs and jewels which were on the wrists, arms, and neck of what lay there, with a strange, unearthly lustre—a mockery of the pale, wax-like face above them, lying in its calm sleep of Death." (499).

This ending for Ralph's romance, I contend, does not mystify "exploitation out of the picture" in the ways that Mary Louise Pratt has described. Taylor's novel emphasizes throughout the exploitation that English and Indian women share because of patriarchal social and sexual contracts that organize both societies, though this theme certainly does eclipse the other ways that British colonizers exploited the colonized in both the eighteenth and the nineteenth centuries. Ralph's experience of romantic love in his marriage blocks any desire to be reincorporated into English society after his wife's death. Moreover, by describing the dead body of the mother of his child as dressed in such Oriental splendor, Taylor acknowledges the ambiguously valued power of the mother, even after it is stilled by death. This spectacle of the mother who is no longer a mother repeats Sir Walter Scott's evocation of Zilla Moncanda, the Oriental mother in *The Surgeon's Daughter*, and bring us closer to an understanding of why the mother's body became central in Anglo-Indian representations of the zenana, even when, or perhaps especially when, the mother was of another "race."[47]

In short, the peculiar ideological problems that Taylor and other Anglo-Indian writers tried to solve in their descriptions of rape inside and outside the harem had a long and various history. As all of these novels show, when nineteenth-century writers represented the Indian zenana, they responded to the shifting relative valuation of Muslim and Hindu culture dictated by the larger dynamics of the economic and colonial policies that protected English interests in India. By mid-century, Anglo-Indian fiction showed very little appreciation for the "sublime, pristine, deist" Hinduism that finds expression in these Romantic poems and novels. Anglo-Indian novelists writing after 1857 increasingly depicted the zenana as a place for the display of luxury goods instead of women's bodies, as a place of darkness and secret erotic danger, and as an "inner" world inhabited by Indian mothers and mistresses who conspire to consolidate their power, hidden behind the curtain that separated public from private life, a veil colonizers helped to maintain.[48]

Anglo-Indian novelists writing about the zenana after the passage of the Married Women's Property Act of 1882, including Rudyard Kipling in *Naulahka* (1893) and Mrs. Penny in *A Mixed Marriage* (1903), typically shifted their attention to Englishwomen who voluntarily entered the harem, prompted by love, marriage, or sisterly duty, usually defined in British emancipationist terms, but these harem visits teach them to better appreciate their relative "freedom" as Englishwomen before and after marriage.[49]

All of the novels examined in detail in this chapter, as well as later Anglo-Indian novels like Penny's, which include representations of the zenana under Islam, show an unacknowledged, but constant, preoccupation with the mother's reproductive power. As a group, they suggest that representations of the zenana were tied up with the Malthusian paradox embodied by the mother in this period, which was, to borrow Mary Jacobus's compact formulation, "the terror of too many and too few" (*First Things*, 84). As Social Darwinism amplified the threat of "unbearable multitudes and the fear of extinction" (84), and raised the stakes by making it imperative that colonial couples reproduce legally and racially "pure" children, the mother inside, or outside, the zenana became a figure of even greater ambivalence and fear.[50]

CHAPTER 2

The Temple Dancer

EROTICISM AND RELIGIOUS ECSTASY

The institution of devadasis *constitutes a limiting case for women, whose interest stems not so much from a dubious exotic appeal but precisely because limiting cases can throw light on the average, common life of women in the Hindu world.*
Frederique Margolin, *Wives of the God-King*[1]

*T*he "white slave" who appears in British and Anglo-Indian novels about zenana life not only embodies the projections of fundamental contradictions in the social and sexual contracts in place in the Romantic period, as we have seen, but she also acts, in some respects, as the fantasy twin of the Hindu widow, since both figures, in the colonial imagination, appear as problematic anomalies when compared with Indian or English women who are "legitimate" wives and mothers. Because the white slave is ambiguously placed "inside" the private domain but "outside" the protection usually offered by the husband, "unfree" in that she is constrained by the literal conditions of slavery but "free" in that she is outside the legal bounds of marriage, the white slave epitomizes basic unresolved conflicts in colonial ideologies about labor, marriage, and reproduction.[2]

Nineteenth-century British and Anglo-Indian novels also typically represent a second group of Indian women who live in the space of the in-between, the Hindu *devadasi*—or temple dancer—who is usually represented as living outside the private domain of the zenana, in a contested public space which displays the changing boundaries between the sacred and the profane in the colonial imagination. The *devadasi* disrupts prevailing nineteenth-century British perceptions about femininity, first of all, because she literally embodies what Sir William Jones identified as Shakti, or "divine feminine energy," the power generated when spiritual and sexual love are combined

(Jones, *Works*, 6:318; Majeed, 40). Because the *devadasi* lives outside the secluded domain of the family and outside the bounds of marriage, though she remains ritually pure, she demonstrates how Shakti could be enacted in what colonizers regarded as the public sphere.[3]

The *devadasi* remained a source of confounding fascination for British and Anglo-Indian novelists throughout the nineteenth century for many reasons. In the "historical real" of Indian culture, especially before the opening of British India to Christian missionaries in 1806, *devadasi*s could claim many privileges otherwise categorically denied to British and Indian women alike. *Devadasi*s could be well educated, highly literate, and culturally sophisticated, since they studied dance and music, and were well versed in both the oral and written sacred traditions. They were often trained to read Sanskrit and other languages, and sometimes they composed and performed their own poetry. *Devadasi*s served important ritual functions because they danced in Hindu temples and performed in other religious celebrations, weddings, and other auspicious public events. Unconstrained by the restrictions of purdah, *devadasi*s remained unmarried, but were not required to practice chastity. They were exempt from many caste restrictions and were free to engage in sexual relations with any man of the proper caste without public censure. They also escaped the ritual prohibitions defining widowhood. Finally, they were able to inherit property and bequeath it to their biological or adopted daughters. As such, *devadasi*s highlighted specific contradictions in the social and sexual contract in force in Great Britain until at least the 1880s concerning women's freedom, sexuality, spirituality, and purity. In other words, the *devadasi* marked the threshold of several of the most contested boundaries in the colonial imagination that separated the inner from the outer, the private from the public, and the sacred from the sexual.

Literary representations of the *devadasi*s in British and Anglo-Indian novels changed dramatically from the beginning to the end of the nineteenth century, and their transformation registers new contradictions that emerged as the public and private spheres were reorganized in Victorian England and imposed, in selective and strategic ways, on British India. Some of the earliest images of Indian women in European medieval art present *devadasi*s, though these figures also reflect the Christian biases of the missionaries who produced them (Mitter, 4). The *devadasi*s depicted in German, French, and British Romantic literature between 1790 and 1830, by contrast, show how new translations of important Sanskrit texts, and especially Sir William Jones's *Sacontala* (1789), acted to transform the images of the *devadasi*.

One feature that made Jones's "incomparable" heroine so memorable for European readers was Sacontala's proximity to the sacred. As the foster daughter of a Brahmin priest, as the protector of a sacred grove, and as a celebrant in Hindu rituals, Jones's Sacontala was closely associated with temple dancers, even though she was not actually presented as a *devadasi* in the original version of the play. As we have seen, Sacontala inspired a number of Romantic poems. She held a "unique place in Goethe's heart," for example, and remained an "important aesthetic and religious model" throughout his life (Figueria, 13). Several of Goethe's poems, including, "Der Gott und die Bajadère" (1794), present *devadasi*-like figures who recall Sacontala's passionate spirituality and innocent sexuality.

By the first decade of the nineteenth-century, the concept of Hindu temple dancing was so familiar to European readers that, in 1807, Madame de Staël, in *Corinne*, could refer, without comment, to the *devadasis*—translated here as *bayadères*—in order to describe her heroine's sublimely graceful dancing: "She began to dance, shaking her tambourine in the air, and in all her movements there was a graceful litheness, mixing modesty and sensual delight, that might suggest the power exercised over the imagination by the Bayadères—the temple dancing girls in India, when they are poets of the dance, if you will, when they express so many different feelings through the set steps and captivating tableau they present to the eye."[4] Although Romantic writers, from Goethe to Shelley, imagined *devadasi*s who were idealized embodiments of joyful physicality and sacred sexuality, British and Anglo-Indian novelists more often present them as embodying unresolved conflicts concerning gender, sex, and romantic love. In other words, because the *devadasi*s who appear in these later nineteenth-century novels are typically imagined as beautiful and sexual, sacred and taboo, mature free women who are not confined to the domestic space of the Indian zenana, they challenge many of the most important boundaries in colonial defenses of empire.

British and Anglo-Indian novels written between 1800 and 1900 that depict the *devadasi* illustrate how Romantic versions of this figure were contested by Christian evangelicalism, imperial medicine, and, ultimately, by the gradual reversal of the relative valuation of Hinduism and Islam in colonial ideologies after the Indian Uprising of 1857. Sydney Owenson in *The Missionary* (1811) and Meadows Taylor in *Tara* (1863), as we shall see, imagine *devadasi*s who exhibit the traces of Jones's *Sacontala* and other Romantic poems that idealize them in similar ways, but they also attempt to obscure ideological conflicts concerning love, sex, and purity by focusing on *devadasi*s who are high caste Brahmin "child widows" who cannot remarry and so have chosen this vocation as a result. Anglo-Indian novels written during the height of the Raj show, by contrast, how the "technologies of gender" at work in the colonial contact zone eventually transformed the *devadasi* into a figure of abjection, as Fanny Farr Penny's *Romance of the Nautch Girl* (1898) illustrates.

Because *devadasi*s sang and performed sacred dances that frankly displayed female erotic desire, enacting a connection between sexual and religious ecstasy, they were especially problematic figures for British and Anglo-Indian writers influenced by Christian evangelicalism. As evangelical Christianity began to exert a significant influence on Indian colonial policy in the period between 1820 and 1850, the *devadasi* became the focus of colonial criticism that addressed her religious practices and "free" sexuality. For example, Charles Grant, an influential director of the East India Company in this period, resisted even the ambivalent appreciation for Hinduism typical of Orientalists like Sir William Jones, and regarded Hinduism, instead, as exhibiting "internal principles of depravity" (Majeed, 80). Since Grant and colonizers with similar evangelical and Anglicanist sympathies thought that "the ultimate aim of British rule should be the 'moral improvement' of its subjects" (80), social reforms like the abolition of sati in 1828 or even more sweeping Utilitarian legal reforms proposed by Thomas Macaulay did not go far enough. As Majeed has explained, many Anglicanists thought "it was through the propagation of Christianity that the real root of the problem in India could be tackled, namely the 'internal principles of depravity' in Indian cultures themselves" (80). For many Anglo-Indians, then, the *devadasi* was the most visible feminine embodiment of Hindu depravity, and her body provided the ground for ideological contests between old school colonial administrators, who followed the Orientalism of Sir William Jones, and Christian evangelicals who, in the 1830s and 1840s, often joined forces with Utilitarians.[5]

After the Indian Uprising of 1857, *devadasi*s became the subject of new strategies of imperial domination, as the emerging practices of medicine and anthropology worked to normalize repressive Christian and conservative Victorian perspectives on female sexuality and erotic desire.[6] John Shortt's paper "The Bayadère; or, Dancing Girls of Southern India," presented to the Anthropological Society of London and later published in the proceedings for 1867–1869, suggests some of the most powerful ideological forces that redefined the *devadasi* as a figure of "abjection" by the end of the nineteenth century.

John Shortt's personal example reflects one way that medicine cooperated with colonial anthropology in support of the Raj since he authorizes his research on the *devadasi* by noting that he was the Surgeon-General Superintendent of Vaccination in the presidency of Madras. In dramatic contrast to Sydney Owenson or latter-day Romantics like Meadows Taylor, Shortt matter of factly identifies all *devadasi*s as prostitutes. Demonstrating the epistemological habits typical of many Victorian colonizers, Shortt begins by admitting that the *"thassee,"* or "dancing girl attached to a Pagoda" (182), should not be confused with the "nautch girl," who was a secular performer, sometimes attached to Moghul courts, and who was often a professional prostitute, but in his subsequent discussion these distinctions immediately collapse. Regarding Christian monogamy as one of the marks of a superior civilization, a view English anthropology helped normalize at the time, Shortt assigns mature Hindu women to one of only two categories, imagining them either as respectably married women or as prostitutes.

Echoing evangelical condemnations of Hinduism that, after 1857, became nearly hegemonic, Shortt asserts that temple dancing is one of "the worst institutions connected with Hinduism" (194). Shortt initially characterizes the *devadasi*s as agent-less victims, blaming "idol-worshipping" Hindu priests as the managers of this system and claiming that "these poor creatures are more sinned against than sinning themselves" (194). Though he admits that temple priests teach *devadasi*s "to read and write their own and other languages," he claims it is only so that they will be "better able to master their lewd and immoral songs" (194). While temple priests provide this depraved education for the *devadasi*s, "their own wives, the mothers of their children, are deprived of learning of any kind, and are carefully shut out from society, not even allowed to appear in public before any assembly of men and are allowed further to grow up in the greatest ignorance and superstition" (194).

Shortt's essay also shows the traces of unresolved legal problems surrounding women's consent when he notes that dancers begin performing at "about seven or eight years of age" and imports the notion of female consent from English jurisprudence when he assumes that these young dancers are not mature enough to make the decision to enter what he regarded as a permanent life of prostitution. Similarly, in recognizing that *devadasi*s were not constrained by British laws of inheritance and primogeniture, Shortt reports, with thinly disguised patriarchal disdain, that "a dancing girl can adopt a daughter with the permission of the authorities of the pagoda to which she belongs" and bequeath her property to her, but she cannot "adopt a son, for the transmission of property" since "among dancing girls property descends in the female line first, and then to males as in other castes" (185). The impact of prevailing British medical assumptions is likewise evident when Shortt assumes that frequent sex with different partners typically made prostitutes infertile; he observes, "As a rule, it is seldom that these women have children of their own, unless, perhaps, they had lived in continual concubinage with some single individual" (185). Thus, imperial medicine is called upon to discredit the morality of the *devadasi's* system of female inheritance when he reports that *devadasi*s often resorted to "kidnapping good-looking girls from large towns and remote villages" (185) in order to pass on their property, before British surveillance put a stop to this method of recruitment. Older retired *devadasi*s become, by Shortt's logic, procurers in this vicious system of prostitution (187).

Finally, Shortt's essay illustrates how "race" replaces religion as the most significant determinant of the "abjection" of *devadasi*s in the post-mutiny period. Shortt calls attention to the signs of racial difference when he recognizes that *devadasi*s were often "of a light pale colour, somewhat yellowish in tinge, with a softness of face and feature, a gentleness of manner, and a peculiar grace and ease, which one would little expect to find among them" (189). Admitting that European officers "frequently" became "infatuated by these women in days gone by" (192), Shortt asserts that the imperial servants who are his contemporaries only "occasionally" form unions with *devadasi*s, and he dismisses the few who cross the color line with the rhetorical question, "Who can account for taste?" (193).

By the last decades of the nineteenth century, then, because of the combined assault of evangelically engineered colonial policy, public medicine, and anthropology like Shortt's, *devadasi*s were effectively desacralized, as British colonizers imposed their own notions of the sacred and the sexual on colonizing and colonized alike in British India. The *devadasi*s who appear in Anglo-Indian novels written in the 1870s and later reproduce these more abject stereotypes that British anthropology and imperial medicine helped to promote and circulate.[7]

Moreover, in the last three decades of the nineteenth century, as Indian nationalists put more emphasis on the sacred inner domain of the home, with the pure and spiritualized Indian woman at its center, *devadasi*s became figures of "abjection" not only to colonizers but to many middle-class Indian reformers as well. As Partha Chatterjee has argued, British colonizers and Indian subjects struggled to redefine the boundaries between the public and private spheres throughout the century, but by the last two decades of the nineteenth century, most Indian reformers conceded "the domain of the outside, of the economy and of statecraft, of science and technology, a domain where the West had proved its superiority and the East succumbed. In this domain, then, Western superiority had to be acknowledged and its accomplishments carefully studied and replicated. The spiritual, on the other hand, is an 'inner' domain bearing the 'essential' marks of cultural identity" (*Nation*, 6). When Indian family life was designated as the locus of this sacred inner domain (9), the continued presence of *devadasi*s in the public sphere could be seen to undermine Indian nationalist claims about the "purity" of Hindu women. Evidence of the devadasis' wealth, likewise, called into question the "purity" of Indian domestic life since it proved that Indian men continued to patronize them. Finally, *devadasi*s provided a reminder of how feminine spiritual values associated with Hinduism were once much more central in the public realm. Many Indian reformers, then, came to accept the colonizers' characterization of temple dancers as common prostitutes and similarly assigned them to the domain of abjection. In other words, *devadasi*s were desacralized and their role in linking the "outer" and "inner" spiritual realms was repudiated.

These dramatic changes in British and Anglo-Indian representations of the *devadasi* also help to explain why attention shifted from Indian to British rape victims in novels about colonial life. By comparing Sydney Owenson's entirely imaginary evocation of the *devadasi* in *The Missionary* with the figures who appear in Meadows Taylor's *Tara* and Mrs. Fanny Farr Penny's *Romance of the Nautch Girl*, we can better assess some of the ideological pressures at work in the colonial contact zone that prompted writers to refashion this figure. Meadows Taylor and Fanny Farr Penny lived for many years in British India and experienced the stresses of colonial life firsthand. Taylor's *Tara* shows that a more idealized view of Hinduism, formed by the translations of Sir William Jones and by the Romantic feminism of writers like Shelley and Owenson, could survive transportation back to India and could persist well past mid-century. Fanny Farr Penny's *Romance of the Nautch Girl*, on the other hand, clearly expresses not only her personal commitments to Christian evangelicalism and her loyalties as the wife of a famous missionary but also the effects of the larger forces driving colonial anthropology and imperial medicine which worked in concert with evangelicalism and with the social purity movement to reshape the figure of the *devadasi* in the last two decades of the nineteenth century. More specifically, Penny's novel demonstrates how the aggressive desires and sexual violence of the colonizers were displaced onto the *devadasi*'s body in the demonized representation of Deva, the mature temple dancer in this text. It also reveals the discursive instability created by the alliance between "imperial feminism" and the English social purity movement of the 1880s, in the depiction of Deva's daughter, Menachee, who is envisioned not only as a helpless child victim but also as a seductive threat to colonizing men. Read together, Taylor's and Penny's novels demonstrate how the *devadasi* mirrored changes in the sex and gender norms that redefined the meaning of both British and Indian women's sexuality by reference to racialized notions of purity in the post-Mutiny period.

The Romantic **Devadasi** *and the Threat of Rape*

Sydney Owenson's *The Missionary* (1811), which was slightly revised and republished in 1859 as *Luxima: The Prophetess*, describes the celibate love story of Hilarion, a Franciscan missionary to India, and the beautiful Hindu woman Luxima. Owenson's narrator quickly reveals some of the ambitions that prompt Owenson to select India as the scene for this novel, when she observes, "In all the religions of the East, woman has held a decided influence, either as priestess or as victim" (49). Noting that "the women of India seem particularly adapted to the offices and influences of their faith," Owenson's narrator distinguishes two groups of women who serve in Hindu temples, "the Ramgannies, or officiating priestesses," who are of an "inferior rank and class, and are much more distinguished for their zeal than for their purity," and the "Brahmachira [*sic*]" who belong to "an order the most austere and venerated" since it can "only be professed by a woman who is at once a widow and a vestal" (49–50). Owenson's heroine, Luxima, is thus identified as doubly pure, since she is a high caste "Brahmachira" (51); that is, she is both a child widow and "vestal virgin."[8]

Although *Luxima* is structured by the familiar conventional dualities which contrast the "masculine" values of the West with the "feminine" values of the East, a pattern evident in Shelley's "Alastor" and countless other Romantic poems and novels, Owenson evokes the gendered polarities of Romantic Orientalism in order to reorganize and revalue them. Early in the novel, she compares Luxima with Hilarion: "She, like the East, lovely and luxuriant; he, like the West, lofty and commanding: the one, radiant in all the lustre, attractive in all the softness which distinguishes her native region; the other, towering in energy, imposing in all the vigour which marks his ruder latitudes; she, looking like a creature formed to feel and to submit; he, like a being created to resist and to command; while both appeared as the ministers and representatives of the two most powerful religions on earth; the one no less enthusiastic in her brilliant errors, than the other confident in his immutable truth" (74). Owenson's plot reverses these values by showing that Hilarion is a self-deluding, rigid, and intolerant Catholic zealot who illustrates many of the dangers of militant evangelizing, since his insistence on chastity destroys both lovers.

Throughout the novel, Owenson idealizes Luxima's Vedantan Hinduism, suggesting some of the appeals that Jones's Enlightenment view of Hinduism offered to more emancipated women readers and writers and to sympathetic men like Shelley (Leask, 102). Luxima thus reflects a synthesis of values that characterized the brief period between 1800 and 1830 when Eurocentric notions of sacred and profane love were influenced by Jones's poetry and translations, which affirmed, among other things, the power of romantic erotic love to unite East and West.[9] Setting her love story in the seventeenth century, before British imperialism had much disturbed the map of India, Owenson is able to sidestep any acknowledgment of the role that Christian missionaries subsequently played in establishing the Raj in India.

Hilarion, like Shelley's poet in "Alastor," first sees Luxima through a "transparent veil" (37), when she is carried in a religious procession along with her grandfather, who is a famous priest. This is when Hilarion first sees Luxima's "perfect form thus shrouded, caught, from the circumstance, a mysterious charm, and seemed, like one of the splendid illusions, which the enthusiasm of religion brightens the holy dream of its votarist, or like the spirit which descends amidst the shadows of night upon the slumbers of the blessed" (37–38). The *devadasi*s who accompany Luxima are similarly idealized; they are described as the beautiful "dancing-priestesses of the Temple, who sang, as they proceeded, the histories of their gods, while incarnate upon earth. Their movements were slow, languid, and graceful; their hymns, accompanied by the tamboora, the seringa, and other instruments, whose deep, soft, and solemn tones seemed consecrated to the purposes of a tender and fanciful religion, excited in their auditors inspiriting emotions which belonged not all to Heaven" (37).

Moved by the desires that this spectacle arouses, Hilarion develops a plan to "convert" Luxima to Christianity in order to further his evangelizing mission in India. Owenson suggests the perversity of his response, though, by noting how "the music, the perfumes, the women, the luxury, and the splendour of the extraordinary procession, offended his piety and almost disordered his imagination" (38). Hilarion dramatizes the imperializing habits of the male imagination when he recognizes Luxima as "the powerful rival of his own influence and the most fatal obstacle to the success of the enterprise" of converting Hindus to Catholicism. Persuaded by these instrumental self-delusions, Hilarion convinces himself that the "conversion of the prophetess" was a "task reserved for him alone" (69).

In following Luxima through the sublime landscapes of the deserts east of Lahore to the luxuriant valley of Cashmire, Owenson brings her hero to a site that recalls Sakuntala's sacred grove, and in describing Luxima's impassioned and joyful worship of Camdeo, she evokes the powers of Shakti that both heroines worship and embody.[10] Though Hilarion's feelings turn from righteous resistance to admiration as he secretly watches Luxima at prayer, as her "enthusiasm" is "kindled" by her worship, so that "she looked the divinity she fancied, and uttered rhapsodies in accents so impressive and so tender and with emotions so wild, and yet so touching, that the mind no longer struggled against the influence of the senses" (56). Entranced by her beauty, Hilarion begins to understand the principles of her devotion when she tells him, "The true object of glory is an union with our beloved; that object really exists; but, without it, both heart and soul would have no existence" (98).

Though Owenson transports her lovers to a setting that specifically recalls the garden where Sacontala's consummated her love with King Dushyanta, she dramatizes Hilarion's resistance and shows how his rigid sense of cultural superiority blocks the miraculous happy ending granted to Sakuntala and her king. Three specific features of Owenson's plot mark its departure from the basic pattern of Sakuntala's love story and indicate how Luxima's tragedy is shaped by the projection of central problems in the English sexual and social contract of this period. First of all, Owenson provides Hilarion with a rival for Luxima's affections, the Muslim Solyman Sheko, who, like King Dushyanta, is a "hero and a Prince" (120). Even though Hilarion's priestly vows prevent him from marrying Luxima, he is jealous of Sheko's interest and concludes that Luxima needs his presence since it alone "could afford safeguard and protection." In other words, Hilarion sees himself as the only one who can protect Luxima from being abducted and raped, assigning himself to the role that colonizing men typically assumed in this period, when they saw themselves as saving "brown women from brown men."

Second, in contrast to Sakuntala's father, who blesses the union of the lovers, when Luxima's grandfather learns that she has innocently touched a foreigner, he rejects her and performs a ritual that makes her a permanent outcast from her family and her entire religious community. Declaring that Luxima has "justly forfeited caste," he curses her by enumerating the conditions of her isolation: "with none to pray with her, none to sacrifice with her, none to read with her, and none to speak to her; none to be allied by friendship or by marriage to her, none to eat, none to drink, and none to pray with her. Abject let her live, excluded from all social duties let her wander over the earth, deserted by all, trusted by none, by none received with affection, by none treated with confidence—an apostate from her religion, and an alien to her country" (203). Both Catholic and Hindu priests, in other words, reject

Luxima's basic article of faith, that the Creator is the universal parent and the emanation of love, which she eloquently asserts when she tells Hilarion, "Children of different regions, we are yet children of the same parent, created by the same hand, and inheritors of the same immortality" (82).

Finally, Owenson shows that her heroine is sacrificed because Hilarion has mistakenly assumed that the celibacy of the priesthood is the highest expression of sacred love. After she becomes an outcast, Luxima seeks Hilarion's companionship, protection, and love, but he continues to resist a physical relationship, on principle, saying, for example, "In thee, it is no crime to love! In me, it is what I abhor no less than crime—it is sin, it is shame, it is weakness" (178). Hilarion plans, instead, to take Luxima to a convent in Goa in order to impose permanent celibacy upon them both, and to protect himself from further sexual temptation.

Before Hilarion and Luxima are able to complete their journey to Goa, however, the Jesuits excommunicate him for his apparent sexual transgressions with Luxima. Seeing him as the "seducer of the fugitive Indian" (257), they sentence Hilarion to death by fire in an *auto-da-fé*. By this twist in the plot, Owenson designs an episode that contrasts Hilarion's life-denying resistance to the powers of Shakti with the sublime dimensions of Luxima's love. When Hilarion is about to be consigned to the flames, Luxima throws herself on the pyre with him, reciting the "Gayatra, pronounced by Indian women before their voluntary immolation" (307). By staging this sacrifice, Owenson displays the more heroic proportions of Luxima's selfless love. Though both Hilarion and Luxima are saved when the surrounding crowd riots, Luxima suffers a knife wound that kills her shortly afterward (308). In the *liebestod* that is the climax of this novel, Luxima reveals the irony of Hilarion's efforts to convert her, when she dies declaring, "I die as Brahmin women die, a Hindu in my feelings and my faith—dying for him I loved, and believing as my fathers have believed" (324). As Nigel Leask has argued, this ending reveals Owenson's objections to Christian evangelicals' hopes for mass conversion that began to direct Indian colonial policy in the 1830s and 1840s, for "rather than 'making a Christian' Hilarion only succeeds in 'destroying a Hindu'" (128). At the same time, the gender critique that animates this novel reveals Owenson's belief in the power of Shakti to transcend the cultural barriers that otherwise divide these lovers from East and West, a theme Shelley repeats in "Alastor."

Reimagining the Devadasi

Though Meadows Taylor's popular novel *Tara* was published in 1863, it demonstrates how idealized Romantic notions of Hinduism similar to those of Sydney Owenson and Percy Bysshe Shelley could persist along with endorsements of some of the Liberal social reforms promoted by English colonizers in India in the 1830s and 1840s.[11] *Tara* focuses on a young Brahmin woman who was widowed as a child, and who subsequently decides to become a *devadasi* in the temple where her father, Shastree, officiates as chief priest. In developing the plot of this novel, Taylor, like Owenson, identifies two types of *devadasis*, contrasting the "pure" Tara with the "impure" Gunga, the lead temple dancer from the sexually active group of dancers that Taylor calls the "Morlees."

Unlike Owenson and other Romantic writers, Taylor presents Tara's father as a man of refinement whose nature has been "evidently elevated and purified in character by his intellectual pursuits" (8), but he also provides Shastree with a sinister double, a visiting priest, Moro Trimmul, who lusts after Tara and pursues her relentlessly throughout the novel. Trimmul tries to gain access to Tara by arranging a marriage between his beautiful sister, Radha, and Shastree, who is eager to oblige since his first wife has not given birth to a son. Trimmul later plots with Gunga to persuade Tara to undergo a "temple marriage," a ritual that would legitimize his sexual congress with her, but Tara refuses to consent. Because Taylor's novel is organized around three episodes where his *devadasi* heroine is threatened with rape but successfully escapes, *Tara* reveals a great deal about why rape became so central in the colonial imagination in this period. At the same time, *Tara* presents a story that resists the categorical imperatives evident in Owenson's novel which defined Hindu women as either as "priestesses or victims," and challenged basic colonial ideologies that depended upon polarized representations of Hindus and Muslims. Taylor describes, instead, how his Hindu heroine is finally rescued by Fazil Khan, a courtly young Muslim soldier, and his novel concludes with Tara's willing conversion to Islam and their happy marriage.

Like Owenson, Taylor distances his story from British imperial politics, placing his heroine in the city of Tooljapoor in 1657, the site of a crucial power struggle between Muslim colonizers and indigenous Hindu forces led by the great warrior Sivaji. Taylor's historical frame invites us to read *Tara* as an allegory that demonstrates how shifts in the colonial balance of power between Muslims and Hindus transformed the symbolic meaning of Hindu temple dancing, spirituality, and female sexuality, as it was manifest in the public sphere nearly a century before the British began to establish their empire in India. In this respect, *Tara* demonstrates how the Muslim conquest of India transformed the sacred Hindu dance traditions and restricted the artistic and practical freedoms previously enjoyed by *devadasis* in this region (Singha and Massey, 35). Taylor's novel ends, however, by recognizing the cultural ferment created when Sivaji and his soldiers introduce new dance traditions and sacred plays to the temple community where Tara once danced.

Taylor follows Jones, Owenson, and Shelley in his lovingly idealistic representation of his heroine, Tara, who performs as a temple dancer throughout most of this novel. Like Owenson and Shelley, Taylor imagines his heroine as a beautiful young woman who combines intelligence and grace, and whose belief in Vedantan Hinduism (45) gives her access to the spiritual power associated with Shakti, as Jones described it. By emphasizing Tara's physicality throughout the novel, Taylor defies what were, by 1863, well-established Victorian taboos restricting descriptions of the heroine's body, indicating how India remained a less limited imaginative space for the display of bodies of any gender. When Taylor depicts Tara bathing at the temple, for example, he notes her physical beauty as "she stepped forth from the basin, her silk garment clinging to her sweet form, and revealing its perfect proportions" (20). Later when she appears in the dress of the temple dancer, he observes the "rich crimson silk drapery, its heavy borders and ends of flowered gold, and the massive gold zone which confined it round her waist" and describes how "the attitude she had involuntarily assumed, as she turned towards the shrine, showed the graceful outlines of her figure to peculiar advantage. She had wreathed a long garland of white flowers into her hair, which fell about her neck and bosom; and another was twisted round her brows, so as to form a coronet. It was a fanciful but simple and beautiful decoration, which suited the character of her small graceful head, and added to the charm of her attire" (279).

Taylor's feminist and reformist sympathies find expression not only in his treatment of her physicality, but also in his evocation of her spiritual and intellectual ambitions. In her first appearance in the novel, Taylor dramatizes Tara's "reverent" spirituality and notes that her father has taught her to read Sanskrit. He also observes that Tara's literacy sets her apart from most other young women of her caste, since "it was unusual then, that Brahmun [*sic*] girls were taught to read or write—more so than it is now" (10).

In explaining how Tara becomes a temple dancer, Taylor notes that she was married as a child but was widowed before her marriage could be consummated. Unlike other writers of the period, Taylor does not foreground these motives when he dramatizes Tara's decision to join the *devadasis*. Instead, Taylor invites comparisons with Christian conversion experiences when he explains that the goddess Durga appears to Tara in a dream and requests her service at the temple, so that Tara is suddenly moved by "divine afflatus" (19) to join a group of *devadasis* when she worships in the temple the next day: "No one dared to stop her, or touch Tara. The height of excitement, or, as they thought, inspiration, was in her eye, and that sweet face was lifted up with a holy rapture. She seemed to fly rather than to walk, so completely had her feelings carried her forward" (20–21). Taylor not only universalizes Tara's spiritual motives and innocent spontaneity, but he also underscores how her gender determines her spiritual practices when he notes that Durga "is perhaps more fascinating to women than to men" (19). This episode also exposes the absence of a corresponding feminine presence in Anglican Christianity when Taylor notes that women like Tara "may most naturally perhaps apply to another woman, in whose power she believes, for sympathy and assistance" (19).

Throughout the novel, Taylor offers a complex perspective on temple dancing that shows the persistence of his feminist Orientalism and his efforts to counter more evangelical and medicalized descriptions of temple prostitution like, for example, John Shortt's. Like Owenson, Taylor does not identify Hinduism as the source of "depravity" in this text but rather focuses on the abuses of power in the patriarchal structures defining the husband's power in polygamous Hindu families and justifying the priest's privileges. Taylor illustrates, for example, how patriarchal alliances blind Tara's father to Trimmul's unholy interest in his daughter after Shastree's marriage to Radha makes the priest a member of Tara's extended family, giving him easy access to the private domain of Tara's family. Because Shastree remains "utterly unconscious of any disturbance in his quiet household" (313) and continues to offer Trimmul his hospitality, he acts to inflame the priest's passion for Tara (279). Likewise, after Tara moves outside the protection of her family when she begins to serve at the temple, she becomes even more vulnerable to Trimmul's intimidation. Though Tara invokes the protecting power of "the Mother," another aspect of the power of Shakti that she worships, Taylor's narrative shows that it is her father's high status in the temple hierarchy that actually protects her, for as soon as her father dies, Trimmul initiates the first in the series of his attempts to rape her.

Taylor repeats Owenson's strategy in *The Missionary* by separating the *devadasis* into two groups, the pure and the impure, but the contrasts that he draws between Tara and Gunga, the head dancer at the temple, also illustrate his concessions to Victorian views of women's purity and sexuality. While Tara's identity as a high caste Brahmin and her superior education create a deep gulf between herself and the "impure" temple dancers, it is her determined asexual purity that generates the plot in this novel. Taylor's idealization of Tara's purity shows how effectively British imperialism acted to repress Romantic celebrations of the *devadasi*'s erotic and spiritual power, even in a text as sympathetic as Taylor's. Unlike the other "Morlees," then, Tara does not enjoy dancing in public, and her worst fears are realized when she notices Trimmul's intrusive gaze, and felt "for the first time" what "she had long dreaded,—the shame, as it were, of her vocation—the unavoidable exposure to any libertine glance which might fall on her" (287). At the same time, by insisting on Tara's innocence, Taylor challenges Victorian social conventions that assumed that women who sang, danced, acted, or otherwise presented themselves before the public gaze could not be raped since they had already signaled their presumably voluntary participation in a libertine subculture and so sacrificed any credible moral ground for self-defense.

In contrasting Tara's high-minded sexual purity with Gunga's unbridled sexuality, material rapaciousness, and passionate obsessions, Taylor acknowledges some of the same qualities that John Shortt defined as signs of the *devadasis*' abjection, but, in contrast to Shortt, he describes the psychological motives that make Gunga's behavior more comprehensible. Like the *devadasis* that Shortt describes, Gunga participates enthusiastically in all the "ceremonies and orgies" at the temple and assists "the lower order of priests who officiated for the inferior castes of the people" (*Tara* 53). Gunga also colludes with Trimmul in his efforts to prostitute Tara by urging her to accept the "mystic marriage to the sword of the goddess, which the 'Morlees' performed in order to cloak their [sexual] profligacy" (53). Since Tara intends to remain sexually chaste, however, she resists Gunga's arguments that she should perform this ritual in order to participate more fully in the sexual rituals at the temple.

At the same time, Taylor avoids presenting either Tara or Gunga as an agencyless victim, and so he disputes the basic categories of imperializing discourse like Shortt's in ways that make his novel more interesting and more disruptive than it may at first appear. As Taylor's plot unfolds, he reveals that Gunga is jealous of Tara because she is in love with Trimmul and hopes to be the exclusive object of his love, or at least the exclusive focus of his erotic attention. One of the most interesting aspects of his novel is Taylor's careful description of the psychology that motivates Gunga to cooperate with a priest who repeatedly abuses her, physically and emotionally. In detailing Gunga's enmeshment in this cycle of violence and in showing how it prompts her to try to draw Tara into a similar relationship, Taylor critiques Victorian efforts to remystify female virginity and to define all "pure" women as asexual victims of male lust. Gunga thinks that Tara's power will be destroyed when she is sexually humiliated, and this is one reason for her collaboration with Trimmul. Apparently believing that pure women must be compelled, at least at first, to submit to male desire, Gunga tells Trimmul, "Take her hence for a day, and she will be thine for ever, and will become a Morlee like me" (299). Taylor describes several beatings that Trimmul inflicts on Gunga, and his narrator calls attention to the "strange passion which often impels women to endure more from men who ill-use them than from those who caress them" (374; see also 286). On more than one occasion, Trimmul draws a knife and threatens to kill Gunga when her jealousy prevents her from cooperating with him. This cycle of violence ends, melodramatically, when Trimmul fails for the third and last time to abduct and rape Tara, and he revenges himself by stabbing Gunga and throwing her body off a balcony, killing her.

The most striking expression of Taylor's defense of Romantic feminism, however, can be seen in his treatment of Tara's outspoken resistance to rape. First of all, in elaborating Trimmul's sexual obsession with Tara, Taylor presents a strong critique of the Byronic Orientalism. In unfolding the destructive progression of Trimmul's passion for Tara, Taylor makes it absolutely clear that these are not the acts of a man motivated by passionate love. In the heat of his sexual frustration, Trimmul imagines Tara as a "witch" and a "devil" who has set him on fire (294), but Taylor clearly identifies this delusion as the product of Trimmul's violent pornographic imagination, since even Gunga sees that the "devil" resides in him and not in Tara.

Instead of reinforcing Byronic or Victorian formulas that confused rape with seduction, Taylor's novel reiterates a more Shelleyan perspective on rape in his efforts to draw absolute distinctions between love and obsession, desire and domination, seduction and rape. By assigning Trimmul, a priest and upper caste man, to the role of rapist, Taylor challenges both libertine and Victorian assumptions about class, sexuality, and male gender identity. By dramatizing Tara's remarkably outspoken resistance to Trimmul's three attempts to rape her, Taylor likewise breaks the general silence about rape and sexual violence in Victorian fiction as well as in life.

Taylor frames Trimmul's first attempt to abduct and rape Tara by setting it in the context of a military skirmish between Hindu and Muslim forces. This episode allows Taylor to underline the violence, wanton destructiveness, and desecration that surround rape when it occurs in times of war. It also provides the first occasion to bring together his Hindu heroine with his Muslim hero, Fazil Khan, in a world that is otherwise profoundly divided by culture and religion. When Trimmul isolates Tara and prepares to rape her, she calls loudly for help, and Fazil chivalrously comes to her rescue. Though Fazil is deeply moved by Tara's beauty, he refuses to treat her as Sardanapalus regards Myrrah, as a captive of war, but he must resist the arguments of both his father and a powerful mullah, who urge him to send Tara to the king's harem or take her himself as his concubine or slave. Like Shelley's Laon, then, Fazil refutes the patriarchal interpretations of religious "law" that they cite and consistently refuses to reimagine Tara as a slave: "She is my captive, if captive at all, . . . my slave, taken in war, according to your own texts, Huzrut—and I can release her or ransome her, or keep her, as I will. . . . we will be her safeguard, honourably and truly. After that . . . she can act for herself" (370). Thus, Taylor explicitly refutes Byronic fantasies about how "white slaves" are acquired for the harem masters of Islam when Fazil asserts, instead, that captives like Tara should be extended the respect due to a sister.

In staging Trimmul's second rape attempt, Taylor creates a context that allows him not only to critique the patriarchal bias of Islam but also to indict similar trends in orthodox Hinduism, which find expression, for example, in the austerities prescribed for Hindu widows and the prohibition of widow remarriage. When Trimmul succeeds, sometime later, in separating Tara from Fazil, she must appeal to an elderly Brahmin for help when Trimmul pushes her to the ground and nearly overpowers her. Unlike English heroines who usually faint in similar circumstances, Tara again loudly demands protection by claiming that respectable men are honor bound to help her as if she were their mother or sister (334). Though she is given temporary asylum in this Hindu household, Tara has no means to resist when one "grim" (399) old widow in the family insists that she submit to all the austerities of Hindu widowhood. By acknowledging that Hindu widows sometimes enforce the social practices that limit their lives, and the lives of other widows, just as Gunga cooperates in the system of temple prostitution, Taylor identifies patriarchal ideology rather than individual Hindu priests or negligent fathers as the source of "depravity" in this text.

Finally, to escape the strictures of Hindu widowhood, Tara unwillingly resumes her role as *devadasi* at the temple Tooljapoor. Because she is no longer shielded by her father's power in the temple, Tara soon recognizes that she does not have sufficient physical strength or moral support to resist when Trimmul again demands her sexual surrender as his priestly privilege, and she decides, like Southey's Kailyal, that death by fire is her only recourse.

By demonstrating how caste restrictions operate to separate her from all that she loved in her earlier life as a *devadasi*, and by dramatizing the sexual violence inside and outside the home that eventually forces Tara to consider sati, Taylor reveals a feminist agenda throughout this novel that discloses the centrality of women's consent in several important liberal colonial reforms of the pre-Mutiny period.[12]

At the same time, Taylor alters the usual reformist script whereby Englishmen prove their moral superiority by saving Hindu women from Hindu priests, since he allows his Muslim hero to save Tara from the flames. Because of Tara and Fazil's prior acquaintance, this rescue is motivated by chivalry and love, but when Fazil announces that he wants to marry Tara, he must again counter the fundamentalist arguments raised by his father and mullah. Echoing Owenson's and Shelley's objections to the arbitrary patriarchal power exercised by fathers and priests, Taylor shows that Fazil's father and the holy man that he consults worship a more militant and masculine Allah, and they oppose Fazil's intercultural marriage because they think that true believers should be committed to exterminating the "infidels" (211). In the end, Fazil overcomes the zealous religious fundamentalism of his elders, declares his love for Tara, and argues that religious tolerance should be extended to all Hindus. By highlighting these and other cultural differences among as well as between the Hindus and Muslims represented in this novel, Taylor challenges the simple and self-serving categories of Victorian colonizers who imagined that only they could establish peace between these two groups.

By plotting this idealized, and somewhat sentimentalized, marriage between his Hindu heroine and his Muslim hero, Taylor asserts, finally, his Romantic and universalistic humanism, his faith that "the same motives exist there as here, the same deep ties of affection, the same interests, and the same hopes and fears" (496–497), a tolerance at odds with the colonial ideologies of his more evangelical or Anglicanist contemporaries as well as with the more frankly racist British imperial attitudes that shaped the policies that emerged after the Indian Uprising of 1857. At the same time, by asserting the historical persistence of traditions of tolerance that have long been a part of Indian culture and have allowed cross-cultural marriages like Tara and Fazil's, Taylor recognizes the potential that many Indian nationalists later tried to revive when they identified common elements in the spiritual "inner domain" of the Indian family and privatized Shakti. In this way, Taylor questions the exclusive right of English colonizers to claim the high moral ground even as he reveals the cultural superiority that allowed him to offer himself and his fiction in service to the Raj.

"Abjecting" the Devadasi

When Fanny Farr Penny, by contrast, focuses on *devadasi*s in *The Ro-mance of the Nautch Girl* (1898), it is in order to represent what are to her the most horrifying aspects of Hinduism. Her novel reveals, as a result, how drastically this figure, who once was seen to embody the divine spiritual energy of Shakti, could be refashioned into a figure of "abject" otherness during the height of the Raj. The aversion to Hinduism that writes itself into this novel can, of course, be read partly as an expression of Penny's personal faith in evangelical Christianity and her loyalties as the wife of an important Christian missionary. In selecting Tinnevelly as the scene of this novel, Mrs. Penny identifies one of the few regions in India where Christian missionaries succeeded in exploiting intercaste and intercultural conflicts to effect mass conversions in the 1830s and 1840s (D. A. Low, 138). By the time the novel begins in the 1890s, then, the presence of a native Christian subculture was well established in this region of South India. This novel reveals, however, how "race" usually operated along with religion in the imperial ideologies that shape this text.

While Taylor's *devadasi* shows the shaping force of his Romantic idealism, Penny's refiguring of the *devadasi* displays some of the ways that Christian evangelicalism acted in the 1880s and 1890s in collaboration with colonial medicine and anthropology to impose English notions about femininity, spirituality, and sexual identity on the Hindu *devadasi*. Though Penny presents the *devadasi* as the ultimate Indian "other," her novel nonetheless provides clues about how the colonizers could join forces with Indian reformers in the anti-Nautch campaign of the 1890s (Ballhatchet, 159), since both groups adopted perspectives authorized by anthropological and medical "research" of colonizers like John Shortt, which relegated the *devadasi*s' spiritual practice and ritual functions to the realm of the private and considered them, as a result, primarily as prostitutes, or "nautch," girls.[13]

In *The Romance of the Nautch Girl*, Penny does not offer any hope for the religious conversion of the *devadasi*s she describes; instead, her narrative dramatizes the colonizers' fears that the *devadasi*s' public displays of "Oriental passion" will be fatally attractive to colonizing men. Penny's story compares the careers of two half-brothers, Felix and William Manning, sons of Colonel Manning by his first and second wives. Though both brothers are Indian born, Felix Manning has been educated at a British public school and has successfully completed his medical training in England; he is characterized as the ideal imperial servant: calm, rational, and vigorously masculine, "a young giant in health and strength" (4). His brother, by contrast, was not educated in England but was kept in India by his wealthy and indulgent mother, and so, when the novel begins, William has no "profession or regular employment to develop the manhood in him" (13). William reveals himself to be a "silly and thoughtless" fellow; he is wealthy enough to satisfy any whim, but he envies his brother his profession, his skills in cricket and soccer, and his masculine habit of command. When William begins to court Beryl Holdsworth, "a young and pretty maiden" who has "English roses in her cheeks" (17), he acts out a typical pattern of this period by creating a relationship that displays the triangulation of homosocial desire since he is motivated, in part, by the "hero worship" he feels for Felix. At the same time, William is conducting a secret flirtation with Menachee, the beautiful young daughter of a powerful *devadasi* in the local Hindu temple, when the novel begins. In other words, Penny uses her three principal English characters' responses to temple dancers as a test of their loyalty to British norms defining gender identity and the limits of sexual freedom.

The plot is set in motion when William, Beryl, and Felix are caught in an act of surveillance, secretly watching what Penny calls a "devil dance," a dance of Dravidian origin which coexisted with other sacred dance traditions in Southern India (Singha and Massey, 81–86). Fascinated by the young and beautiful Menachee, William invites Beryl to hide with him in a hollow tree in order to watch her perform in a midnight ritual conducted in the sacred grove of a local temple. Startled by a snake, William slips out of his hiding place and disappears, leaving Beryl behind. Felix, who has followed the couple, makes sure that Beryl returns home safely, but when he is called to treat Beryl's nervous "hysteria" the next day, he tells her, somewhat roughly, that she must not surrender to "hysterics" over William's disappearance and must learn to "control herself" (7). Most of the novel recounts Felix's search for his missing brother, which ends when William's body is found buried near the temple. In the end, it is clear that William has been murdered by the head priest and the *devadasi* Deva, who were outraged when they discovered that William had desecrated their midnight ritual by his act of "espionage" (61).

Ironically, Penny's own act of espionage in imagining the details of Deva's and Menachee's lives as temple dancers was made possible by the "research" of colonial servants and self-styled experts like John Shortt. By the 1880s, relevant Sanskrit texts, including the *Kama Sutra* and the *Natya Shastra*, had been translated into English, making public the otherwise "secret" (oral) aspects of the *devadasi*'s training and dance techniques (Singha and Massey, 21). Penny could thus avoid the risk of contaminating her own "purity" as an Englishwoman and Christian minister's wife when she represents the licentious and superstition-ridden life of these Hindu temple dancers, for without these texts how could she know?

Penny's novel also invites her readers into a similar posture of surveillance by describing the "dark mysterious secrets" of temple life (25) and its impact on two generations of *devadasi*s, as she contrasts the life of Deva, a very accomplished *devadasi* who has used all her "arts" to become the head dancer of the temple, with that of her daughter, Menachee, who has "no ambition" or desire to exercise similar "power" in the temple. Unlike Owenson and Taylor, who divide the *devadasi*s into two groups, the "pure" and the "impure," Penny leaves no doubt that both mother and daughter are "impure," and uses them, instead, to compare the roles of the *devadasi* in the public and private domains.

In her first description of Deva, the older temple dancer, Penny identifies several of the signs on this beautiful Indian woman's body that identify her as a prostitute. Deva first appears, standing on the steps of the temple, with the sun glittering on her heavy gold jewelry, as "the spirit incarnate of the precious metal, newly risen from the secret crucible of Mother Earth" (38). Like Southey, Penny notes Deva's rich costume, jewelry, and use of cosmetics, and, like Shortt, she also calls attention to the color of the dancing girl's skin as the most obvious sign of her otherness: "The colours of the silk sari and the gold harmonized with the warm brown tones of her skin. Jasmin flowers adorned her hair, and her face was powdered with sandalwood and saffron. Native women age early, but Deva, to the European eye, would have been considered still in the summer of her beauty" (37–38).

In describing Deva's masterful dancing and singing, Penny removes all vestiges of the idealized Vedantan Hinduism evident in Jones's Sacontala, Owenson's Luxima, or Taylor's Tara. Though Penny's text describes the invocation that conventionally signals the opening of classical Indian dances (Singha and Massey, 44–47), it presents Deva's initial prayer as evidence of her "terrible superstition" (52). Though Deva's dance begins with a display of her "cultivated grace" (52), the "subtle pervading passion" of her performance soon degenerates into lewdness and ends by inciting her audience to join in a sexual orgy. Singing one of the songs of the *Gita Govinda*, Deva stirs the "inmost souls" of her audience: "The words of the song were of love, the bride's invitation to her husband and her god to come, and come quickly, to her bower" (52). Deva's dancing prompts a "wilder and weirder" response, and the climax of her performance occurs when two other dancers, a male and female, "shriek" and tear off their clothes in a "fit of fury" (53), until they appear naked before the crowd. In other words, Penny presents Deva as a spiritually dangerous and sexually threatening figure of abject otherness because she is so skillful in exploiting the erotic appeal of her song and dance to command power over her listeners.

Moreover, Penny reverses the power hierarchy that Taylor describes in *Tara*, when she indicates that Deva exercises power and influence over the priests in the temple not only because of her skill as a performer but also because of the money she brings to the temple. Penny explains that on feast days, Deva's "religious enthusiasm awoke, transforming her into a new creature. She entered into the arrangements, made suggestions, fired poojari [the priests]—and people alike—with fanaticism. She put forth all her powers of attraction to lure rich zemindars and chetties, who were not at all averse to treading in the footsteps of a rajah. She became the life and soul of each festival. The temple authorities were pleased that it was so for she brought them wealth" (42). By identifying the sexual power that Deva exercises in attracting wealthy patrons to the temple, Penny shows the same habits of mind that prevent John Shortt from imagining the *devadasi*s he describes as anything more than talented prostitutes. By the end of the novel, we learn that Deva's immorality extends beyond the sexual domain, since she also plots to kill two people, William and another *devadasi* who had interfered with the exercise of her power.

In describing the history of Deva's daughter, Menachee, Penny illustrates how the *devadasi* disturbs the private realm, and designs a tale that presents the traditional patronage system that supported the *devadasi*s in the worst possible light. Penny's narrator explains that Menachee is the daughter of a local rajah who, sixteen years earlier, accepted Deva as his favorite sexual "plaything" (41), making Menachee an "illegitimate" child by English definitions. In focusing her novel on the moment when Menachee is dismissed from her first patron's household and is allowed to return to her public role as a temple dancer, Penny suggests that this system not only sanctions adultery and polygamy but also promotes child molestation and sexual slavery. Though Menachee inherits Deva's vocation along with her caste, she dislikes the life into which she has been born. In other words, Penny indicates that Menachee does not give her full consent in her relationship with her patron, partly because she sees him as loathsome, decadent, passive, and effete; he is "fat and stolid," and wears effeminate clothing and lavish heavy gold jewelry with "uncut gems of great value" (95). Penny further underlines the degeneracy of this rich Indian landlord by describing how he dismisses the beautiful Menachee from his service just when she arrives at the point when the British would see her as sexually mature. Menachee's patron prefers the company and sexual services of a younger dancer "only just in her teens." In other words, in relating this voyeuristic tale about Menachee's sexual initiation as a *devadasi*, Penny reminds her readers that Menachee and the dancer who replaces her are both under the legal age of consent in Great Britain, which was raised from thirteen to sixteen in 1885.

Unlike her mother, however, Menachee is glad to "resign her coveted place" in the zenana to the younger *devadasi* and is happy to leave her first patron's household. Her final dance before him expresses "the gladness of her emancipation" and her hopes for the future: "She sang her song with passion and emotion to the absent, unconscious one who swayed her heart . . . and she threw into her actions that half-refined, half-savage passion which brooks no control" (96). In some ways, Menachee's "dream of bliss" displays the results of more than eighty years of collaboration between Christian evangelicalism and British imperialism since Menachee hopes to retire from her life as a *devadasi* in order to marry and establish a respectable family life. The trouble with Menachee's dream, as Penny sees it, is that her hopes center on Felix Manning (103). In other words, in Penny's view, the liberation of the *devadasi* from similar domestic sexual slavery poses a direct threat to the stability of the colonial hierarchy because women like Menachee do not necessarily confine their erotic attention to men of their own "kind."

Thus, in moving outside the framework of the "pure" and "impure" *devadasi*s that Taylor employs in *Tara,* Penny creates a plot that shows, no doubt against her intentions, the dangers posed by the late nineteenth-century ideology of individualism when it is unconstrained by Christian ethics or cultural loyalties. In searching for his brother, Felix meets Menachee and discovers his brother's secret "romance" with this "nautch girl." After William disappears, a second sexual triangle develops when Menachee, the *devadasi* who had previously entranced William, is attracted to his more manly brother, just when Beryl begins to recognize that she, too, has fallen in love with Felix. Although Felix is able to recognize the threats that Deva poses because he sees that Menachee's mother is not "an ordinary native, but one who was highly educated in an oriental sense of the word, and whose cunning it was not easy to fathom" (39), he fails to notice the powers that Menachee employs and is more susceptible to her sexual appeal because he regards her as a "silly child" (89). (It seems that Hindus are not the only men who find children attractive.)

Penny indicates Felix's mistaken judgment when she narrates Menachee's first meeting with him and describes a gesture that indicates how

Menachee came to exercise such power over his weaker brother, William. In fact, Menachee's body, glance, and playful touch express all that "pure" Victorian Englishwomen were required to surrender: "She was one of the loveliest of Hindustan's daughters, a dream of soft southern beauty. The girl's lips were parted with a saucy, defiant smile, and she showed a perfect set of nature's pearls in her pomegranate mouth. From her brown eyes, as they rested on his face, there blazed forth the woman's admiration for the man" (38). When Felix, evidently moved by her beauty, looks at her "wrathfully," she responds by "kissing the tips of her fingers" and lightly laying "the kiss on the foot that rested in the stirrup. The action was indescribably graceful. It was done with a mixture of the abandonment of the savage and the simplicity of the child, which bespoke the instinctive Circe" (31).

Moreover, Menachee shows no evidence of the spirituality that protects Tara's "purity" and "innocence," and she poses the greatest threat to Felix when she becomes a sexual free agent after her "dance of emancipation." Outside the control of patron, husband, and mother, and apparently undirected by temple priests as well, Menachee claims her right to speak about her desire, prefacing her declaration of love to Felix with: "Why should I not speak with whom I choose? I have no husband to beat me" (88). Menachee's "Oriental passion" prompts her to consider complete sexual surrender and personal abasement, evident when she tells Felix: "I would rather be the dust beneath your feet than sit on a throne with [William]" (89). In other words, in Penny's novel, Felix is the innocent one; he thinks Menachee is simply exaggerating. Willfully ignoring the obvious motive for her devoted service, Felix accepts Menachee as an unpaid nurse in his clinic.

After the news of William's death frees Felix to profess his love for Beryl, and she declines his proposal since she is jealous of his relationship with Menachee, Felix is then prompted to recognize the "dazzling" prospect of Oriental love that Menachee offers him: "Slowly but surely he learnt a truth that he had never faced before; the conviction borne in upon him with overwhelming force. What he had sought in vain from one woman was offered unasked by another. A passionate yearning love shone in the gaze that met his. The cold English girl with her barren friendship faced and was lost in the torrid colours of the Oriental passion which blazed before his dazzled vision" (315–316). In this moral crisis, however, Felix proves his loyalty to British culture when he turns his back on Menachee and prays to be saved "from the power of the devil" that he, like Trimmul in Taylor's Tara, projects onto the body of this lovely dancer (317).

While Penny's novel insists that the desires of Anglo-Indian men must be controlled, it displays as well how the body and desires of Anglo-Indian women are even more thoroughly colonized because the process is unconscious. In comparison with Menachee, Beryl Holdsworth is so stupefied by the repressive Anglo-Indian conventions that define her class and gender that she fails entirely to understand this "other" woman. Though she once watched the devil dancing along with William and Felix, Beryl remains incredibly oblivious to its sexual import, remaining in "ignorance of the strange customs of the Hindus living around her" (259). Later, when Menachee asks Beryl how the "English would receive an Indian wife" (268), Beryl assumes that Felix must be engaged to Menachee. In describing Beryl's reasoning, Penny indicates how female desire is rendered unspeakable for English women under the Raj: "Would she have given him that love, unasked, unsought, without one spark of encouragement? Her refined European mind was totally unfitted to grasp the idea of an immodest, unsought love. It was foreign to her nature, incomprehensible and unnatural" (270).

In the end, then, Penny's *Romance of the Nautch Girl* is a cautionary tale about a *devadasi* who conforms to the "moral" of John Shortt's essay "The Bayadère" by failing to establish the cross-cultural love that is celebrated in Shelley's "Alastor," Owenson's *Luxima*, and Taylor's *Tara*. Penny's narrator admits that she has described the "intertwining of a few Anglo-Indian lives with the lives of a few Hindus," but she insists that "the intertwining was but a touching—there was no intermingling" (348). After Felix refuses Menachee's offer of "Oriental passion," he retreats to the self-defined and self-justifying moral high ground usually claimed by the colonizing male and acts to perpetuate the racially determined hegemony of colonial life when he marries Beryl. This marriage is meant to prove that "the Hindu with his strange creed and code must ever be an inscrutable being to the Briton; and the Briton, with his strange philanthropy, is equally incomprehensible to the Hindu" (348).

Yet Penny's conclusion asserts, at the same time, the incorrigible passions that, though racialized and abjected, remained uncontained, passions allowed freest expression in the figure of the secularized dancing girl. Thus, after Felix marries Beryl, Menachee "took wing to other scenes, where the drumming of the tomtoms and the orgy of the heathen pooja filled her wild heart with a gladness that made her life complete" (359). With this ending, Penny acknowledges, however unwillingly, the continuing presence of those unbound passions that compelled Shelley's poet in his search for the beautiful "veiled maiden" of Cashmire and inspired Taylor to represent, and perhaps live out, the erotic promises of cross-cultural love.[14]

CHAPTER 3

Mobilizing Chivalry

RAPE IN NATIONAL EPICS ABOUT THE INDIAN UPRISING OF 1857

⁂

The Mutiny proper began with the rising at Meerut on 10 May 1857 and the seizure of Delhi the next day; it virtually ended with the fall of Gwalior on 20 June 1858. . . . The highlights were the siege of Delhi and its recovery in late September, the operations around Kanpur and Lucknow including their famous sieges, and the central Indian campaign in 1858 of Tantia Topi and the Rani of Jhansi.

Percival Spear, *A History of India*[1]

*C*onventional British histories of the Indian Uprising of 1857, including Percival Spear's *History of India*, excerpted above, rarely acknowledge the epistemological privilege that has, until recently, prompted most British writers to define this colonial war as a "mutiny" and to focus their narratives primarily on the military battles, especially those that reestablished British control. This same epistemological privilege writes itself into analyses of the causes of the uprising, which often accept the cliché that this rebellion began when Hindu and Muslim soldiers refused to handle the cartridges of the Enfield rifle because they were greased with beef tallow and pork fat.[2]

Two anomalies disrupt these familiar narratives about the Indian Uprising of 1857 that assume that the rebellion began in, and remained primarily confined to, the British Army of Bengal. These anomalies concern bread and blood, chapatis and rape, since the events that these resonant symbols evoke do not fit into narratives which depend upon such simple causes and effects. Both elements have often been set aside, relegated to the status of

rumors. First, these histories must somehow account for the mysterious circulation of chapatis, traditional Indian flat breads, that were handed on from
one village to another throughout Northern India for several months prior to
the rebellion. Many Indian historians in the past, as well as Ranajit Guha and
others in the Subaltern Studies group more recently, have read this phenomenon as evidence of an organized native insurgency that used the bread to
signal the beginnings of a rebellion that spread far beyond the limits of an
army "mutiny." In surveying various postcolonial efforts to redefine the complex terms of this colonial crisis, Homi K. Bhabha has argued that the chapatis
reveal an important fact about past and present efforts to describe India's history as it unfolded in this colonial space of the "in between." Of the chapatis,
he writes that whether we regard them "as historical 'myth' or treat them as
rumour, they represent the emergence of a form of social temporality that is
iterative and indeterminate" (*Location*, 200). In other words, as Bhabha goes
on to show, the colonial culture of British India depended upon the control
of information and so was profoundly susceptible to such frightening rumors.

Since the chapatis have already provided so much food for thought
about the Indian Uprising of 1857, my objective in this chapter is to explore
the other phenomenon concerning blood by considering the wide circulation
of similarly indeterminate rumors about the rape of Englishwomen by Indian
men that frequently appear in British and Anglo-Indian novels about the 1857
uprising. The circulation of these rumors about the rapes of Englishwomen
by Indian men was, I contend, an answering, and similarly anxiety-ridden,
"iterative" response. Most British and Anglo-Indian novels that refer to this
uprising assert, of course, the colonizers' overmastering power to rename the
victims in colonial rape scripts, to foreclose other readings of the panic and
sexual violence that were clearly part of this colonial crisis, and to censor
accounts of the savage British reprisals for these rumored rapes that generated such rage and self-righteousness during and after the uprising.[3]

Flora Annie Steel, who wrote one of the most interesting novels about
what she called the Indian Mutiny of 1857, acknowledges some of the anxiety that surrounds the reading of both these indeterminate signs concerning
bread and blood. In her autobiography, *The Garden of Fidelity* (1930), Steel
reports that in 1894 she was granted permission to examine the contents of
some of the "secret dispatch boxes" that the British used in 1857. Steel describes her research as characterized by a "breathless haste, an inevitable hurry
about it, almost as if the spirit of the times had been caught and prisoned in
the papers" (*Garden*, 214). Familiar with stories about the Indian chapatis
whose circulation and meaning remained opaque to many of her countrymen,

Steel explains that she found a chapati with a "tiny note" inserted in it in one of these boxes (214). The chapati, with writing attached, is a potent symbol of British desires for the certainty of facts about the meaning of this otherwise enigmatic circulation of bread. This episode in Steel's autobiography also hints at the self-censorship that surrounded rumors of rape and British reprisals. Steel refers to the "confidential reports from all quarters" (214) that were contained in these boxes, but she cryptically concludes, "I don't think I learned much that was absolutely new in them; only—on both sides—details which I felt must be suppressed; but I found that corroboration of my fiction by facts, on which I have all my life learned to rely" (214). It is from these equivocal "facts," censored in the name of patriotism, that Steel and all the other novelists featured in this chapter constructed their narratives about the Indian Uprising of 1857.

By looking in more detail at the historical, ideological, and symbolic contexts of four typical British and Anglo-Indian novels about the Indian Uprising of 1857, we can begin to understand why the figure of the Englishwoman threatened with rape by the Indian man emerged as such an important theme in these works. By comparing two texts about the mutiny written by metropolitan writers, James Grant's *First Love and Last Love: A Tale of the Indian Mutiny* (1868)[4] and G. A. Henty's *Rujub, the Juggler* (1893),[5] with the novels of two Anglo-Indian writers, Meadows Taylor's *Seeta* (1872),[6] and Flora Annie Steel's *On the Face of the Waters* (1897), we can observe the play of particular tensions generated in the colonial contact zone. Like most of the more than eighty novels written in English between 1857 and 1947 about this event, these particular novels illustrate the epistemological shifts that accompanied the uprising of 1857 since they conceptualize "difference" not in terms of religion but rather in terms of "race." Three of them fictionalize historical events at Delhi and Cawnpore (Kanpur) in 1857, two sites where Englishwomen did, in fact, die. Moreover, all of the novels discussed in this chapter can be read, to borrow Steel's words, as British "epics of the race" (*Garden*, 226). A closer analysis of these texts will help us gain a better understanding of why this particular rape script was so unstable, why it had to be repeated again and again.

At the same time, these four novels also demonstrate in their various ways that British India was contested ideological territory, where the technologies of gender worked to redefine Victorian notions of honor, identity, sexuality, marriage, parenthood, and duty in service to the Raj. All these novels show the ideological double duty that they performed as they attempted to reconcile contradictions in at least two conflicting ideologies about "race" in

British defenses of empire in the postmutiny period: one that asserted the racial superiority of British men and women in India, and the other that insisted on the necessity of male domination in both the public and private spheres, which, by definition, included Indian as well as English men. Mutiny novels which were organized around the rape of Englishwomen by Indian men thus worked to legitimize British colonizers' moral superiority by asserting the natural lawlessness of Indian men. At the same time, these national epics of the race were designed to shore up Victorian notions of gender by assigning British women to the role of agency-less victims, countering nineteenth-century feminists' demands for women's greater political equality and social participation. In short, novels which focused on the rape of Englishwomen by Indian men were used to mobilize epic and chivalric literary traditions to reconcile these contradictions.[7] Ultimately, these novels all show how narratives about rape act, as Patricia Klindienst Joplin has argued, to conceal the ways in which "political hierarchy built upon male sexual dominance requires the violent appropriation of woman's power to speak."[8]

Legal Pretexts

Although Thomas Macaulay and the law committee that he chaired originally drafted a criminal legal code for British India in 1837–1838, it wasn't until 1861, when the code was adopted, that a unified definition of rape and its corresponding punishments could be applied in courts throughout British India.[9] Javeed Majeed describes the adoption of Macaulay's legal code in 1861 as marking a seismic shift in colonial policy, defining the end of the era of negotiation between Orientalists who proposed to rule India through the codification of Hindu and Muslim law and Anglicanists, like Macaulay and his original sponsor James Mill, who would impose the colonizers' definition of more "universal" and utilitarian laws upon the colonized.

Macaulay's code replaced "the previous system of separate 'regulations' made by the governors-general of the three presidencies of Madras, Bombay, and Bengal" (Majeed, 192) and superseded Hindu and Muslim "personal" law concerning rape and related crimes. Furthermore, this code did not apply the patchwork of written laws and common practices that made up the traditions defining rape in English jurisprudence since it was, in James Mill's words, "drawn not from existing practices or from foreign law systems, but created *ex nihilo* by the disinterested philosophic intelligence" (Majeed, 193). This legal code, Mill thought, would make India "'the first country on earth to boast a system of law and judicature as near perfection as the circumstances of the people would admit'" (192). Macaulay's legal code was adopted only after the nightmare of the uprising and the retribution of 1857–1858.

In the original report to Parliament of 1838, prepared by the Indian Law Committee, of which Macaulay was the leading member, rape was defined simply as follows:

> A man is said to commit "rape" who, except in the case hereinafter excepted, has sexual intercourse with a woman under circumstances falling under any of the five following descriptions:
>
> First. Against her will.
>
> Secondly. Without her consent, while she is insensible.
>
> Thirdly. With her consent, when her consent has been obtained by putting her in fear of death or of hurt.
>
> Fourthly. With her consent, when the man knows that her consent is given because she believes that he is a different man to whom she is or believes herself to be married.
>
> Fifthly. With or without her consent, when she is under nine years of age.
>
> *Explanation.*—Penetration is sufficient to constitute the sexual intercourse necessary to the offence of rape.
>
> *Exception.*—Sexual intercourse by a man with his own wife is in no case rape.[10]

Because Macaulay's definition of rape depended upon age as a measure of women's consent and because it attempted to regulate male sexuality outside marriage but not inside it by explicitly excluding the possibility of marital rape, it did not go far enough in reconciling the discrepancies in the sexual and social contract that defined women's anomalous relation to the state in British India. Nonetheless, the Indian Penal Code established a simpler and more universal and utilitarian legal definition of rape and its punishments than existed in England at the same time. As Susan Edwards reports, in Victorian England, rape was still treated variously as a crime against property and as assault; its prosecution was subject to extreme and capricious variation because the presiding judge at a trial could cite various precedents from common law or from case law to justify his verdict, punishments, and awards (*Female Sexuality*, 123–194).

Before Macaulay's definition of rape could be adopted in British India as part of the Indian Penal Code in 1861, two seemingly small changes were made which acknowledged unresolved legal conflicts that reformers faced in devising laws that would apply to colonizing and colonized women alike.

In the aftermath of the Uprising of 1857, Indian reformers were inclined to accept a British proposal to raise the age at which a young Indian woman could lodge a complaint of rape from nine to ten years and to apply this provision to both married and unmarried girls. As Mrinalini Sinha and others have shown, it was only in the 1890s, when British liberal reformers again proposed to raise the age of consent for Indian women from ten to twelve, that there was a storm of protest because this change reopened the possibility that Indian men who attempted to consummate their marriage with legally underage wives could be charged with marital rape (*Colonial Masculinities*,162). During the consent debates of the 1890s in British India, conservative metropolitan and colonizing men were invited into an uneasy, covert patriarchal alliance with colonizing men in order to ensure that complaints about sexual abuse by underage wives would be impossible to prosecute (166). These usually unacknowledged legal discrepancies between the laws of the metropole and British India concerning women, rape, and the age of consent reveal some additional reasons, I would argue, why the rape of colonizing women became such an anxiety-ridden as well as ideologically resonant spectacle in novels about the mutiny.

Symbolic Pretexts

While British and Anglo-Indian novels about the mutiny typically claim the authority of history, they also contradict authoritative histories like, for example, George Trevelyan's *Cawnpore* (1868). Trevelyan reports that of the 206 Englishmen, -women, and children who survived the siege at Cawnpore and were imprisoned at the Beebeeghur (*sic*) under the protection of Nana Sahib, over twenty died of illnesses and the rest were killed on 16 July 1857 (298). After a review of all the official records and reports concerning these events, Trevelyan insists that the Englishwomen who died at Cawnpore were not raped and so died "without apprehension of dishonour" (305).[11] When novelists writing about the mutiny made the rape of Englishwomen by Indian men the keystone of their narratives, they exploited the "dialogical" qualities of the novel since they reiterated, and often plagiarized, rumors that appeared in sensationalized stage melodramas, and in private diaries, letters, and returning soldiers' tales, all of which expressed the deepest fears and fantasies of English colonizers in India even after these accounts about the rapes of Englishwomen were officially discredited.

In creating novels that fictionalize some of the most contested episodes of the mutiny, these authors tried to construct heroic national epics by projecting these equivocal "facts" into what Bakhtin calls a distant, "absolute" epic past. Mutiny novels present various efforts to create in Bakhtin's phrase, a "world of 'beginnings' and 'peak times' in the national history, a world of fathers and of founders of families, a world of 'firsts' and 'bests'" (14). These novels typically use two strategies to evoke a certain epic "timelessness." First, they depend upon static characterization and formulaic romance plots; they create a hectic series of adventures which test the hero's and heroine's "chastity and mutual fidelity," but, in the end, little or nothing is changed about the characters. The result of the "whole lengthy novel is that the hero marries his sweetheart.... The hammer of events shatters nothing and forges nothing— it merely tries the durability of an already finished product" (106–107).

Second, mutiny novelists frequently allude to classical epics, apparently to lend a certain dignity to their often preposterous plots. Latin literature provided at least two relevant narratives that linked rape with the founding of the Roman empire: the rape of the Sabine women and the rape of Lucrece.[12] In alluding to the rape of Lucrece rather than the rape of Sabine women, James Grant, and indeed all who follow his example, avoid referring to a model of civic participation which clearly, though embarrassingly, corresponded to eighteenth-century British colonial practices in India. Faced with a shortage of marriageable women in the early days of Rome, Romulus quelled outrage over the abduction of the Sabine women by allowing these alien women to become the legal wives of the Roman men who once captured them, thus solving a problem of how to reproduce a sufficient number of legitimate citizens for the new republic.

By alluding instead to the rape of Lucrece, Grant invokes a model of citizenship that justified women's seclusion in the private sphere and offered Victorian women a punishing example of civic virtue and self-sacrifice. Lucrece's story valorizes the absolute chastity of women and transforms rape from an assault on an individual family into an "affair of state" (Bryson, 164). While the rape of Lucrece similarly suggests parallels between the birth of the Roman Empire and the establishment of the British Raj, it relies on violence and sexual shame to police the color bar and idealizes women's submission to male definitions of "honor" and "integrity." Roman narratives about Lucrece also hinge on racial difference. Lucrece is compelled to submit to rape by Tarquin after he explains how he will destroy her reputation as a chaste wife and mother if she refuses to submit to sex. He tells her that if she commits suicide in order to avoid rape, he will kill one of her Negro slaves and place his body beside hers in her bed, saying he will then tell her husband that he has killed her after finding her in the adulterous embrace of her Negro slave. The morning after her rape, Lucrece summons her husband and her father to her quarters, denounces Tarquin as her rapist, and calls upon them to revenge her, saying, "If you are men and care for your children, avenge me, free yourselves, and show the tyrants what manner of men you are and what manner of woman of yours they have outraged" (Bryson, 163). Lucrece then takes Tarquin's sword and kills herself so that others may not cite her example to justify unchaste behavior or adultery (163). Mutiny novelists often refer to the rape of Lucrece not only to emphasize the flattering parallels between the establishment of the Roman Empire and the British Raj but also to justify women's confinement in the private sphere as well as to restrict her political agency to similar pleas to protect her chastity or to revenge lost "honor." In other words, by evoking the myth of Lucrece, Grant and subsequent novelists created a rape script that reiterated ancient Roman definitions of woman's relation to the state that "relied upon notions of 'capture' and 'utility' rather than one of 'combining' to form a 'sociability' or 'ethical community' between men and women" (Gatens, 120). These texts also confirm the myth that a woman's death or suicide is the only certain proof of her innocence in rape cases.

Yet the hero of a Victorian novel inhabits an imaginary world that is far more ideologically contested than the hero of an epic poem, and these novels would have no plot if they did not recognize alternatives to the ideology underlying the myth of Lucrece. As Bakhtin notes, "In the epic, there is one unitary and singular belief system. In the novel, there are many such systems, with the hero generally acting within his own system" (334). Thus, while some mutiny novelists like Grant and Henty tried to reassert conservative formulas preserving British gender, class, and race hierarchies, all of these texts present characters and situations that dramatize alternatives recommended by nineteenth-century liberals, social reformers, and feminists at home and in India.

When Anglo-Indian novels about the mutiny are compared with metropolitan texts, they reveal particular ambiguities that swirl around the family and its relation to the "nation," on one hand, and to the "sacred," on the other. British and Anglo-Indian writers alike participated in the project of creating an idealized image of the British Empire in order to resolve what Immanuel Wallerstein describes as "one of the basic contradictions of historical capitalism" after 1770—namely, "its simultaneous thrust for theoretical equality and practical inequality" (Balibar and Wallerstein, 84). Throughout the nineteenth century, one of the most compelling ways to create a viable and coherent definition of "national identity" was, according to

Etienne Balibar, to invoke metaphors that compare the nation to a family so that differences among individuals within the state are relativized and subordinated by an emphasis on symbolic differences between "ourselves" and "foreigners." As Balibar explains, "The 'external frontiers' of the state have to become 'internal frontiers' or—which amounts to the same thing—external frontiers have to be imagined constantly as a projection and protection of an internal collective personality, which each of us carries within ourselves and enables us to inhabit the space of the state as a place where we have always been—and always will be 'at home'" (95).

For Anglo-Indian novelists like Meadows Taylor and Flora Annie Steel, who were—and were not—"at home" in British India, this effort to confer a "sacred" status on the nation by reference to the family and its boundaries was called into question, in part, because colonial family practices differed so dramatically from those in England at the same time. For example, by the 1870s and 1880s, the number of Englishwomen in British India had increased, but, as transportation became less expensive, colonial children, from families who could afford it, were typically sent to England for their education, often at a very young age. Kipling's narrative about his childhood experience in the "house of desolation" is certainly the most famous account of the effects of this separation on the colonial child, but many autobiographies and novels by Anglo-Indian women and men describe similar experiences.

Texts by Anglo-Indian women suggest that this separation was also profoundly "wounding" for the married colonizing women who had to choose between honoring their obligations as wives by staying at their husbands' sides in India or acting on their duties as mothers by accompanying their children "home" to England. Many of Steel's novels show the consequences of her separation from her daughter, who was sent to England when she was only sixteen months old. Many other colonial novels, especially those written by women in this period, attest to the accuracy of Steel's observation that there is "something lacking" in the bonds between colonial mothers and their children (Paxton, "Disembodied Subjects," 403).

Because concepts of national identity depended increasingly in the late nineteenth century upon idealized notions of the family, changes in social mores defining sex and gender norms were often seen as threatening to "desacralize" it. Balibar writes that "the sense of the sacred and the affects of love, respect, sacrifice and fear which have cemented religious communities" declined in this period, so that "national identity, more or less completely integrating the forms of religious identity, ends up tending to replace it, and forcing it itself to become 'nationalized'" (Balibar and Wallerstein 95). The

result is that "as lineal kinship, solidarity between generations and the economic functions of the extended family dissolve, what takes their place is
neither a natural micro-society nor a purely 'individualistic' contractual relation, but the nationalization of the family, which has as its counterpart the
identification of the national community with a symbolic kinship, circum-
scribed by rules of pseudo-endogamy, and with a tendency not so much to
project itself into a sense of having common antecedents as a feeling of having common descendants" (102). Because it represents the destruction of the
sacred foundation of the family, rape can thus be seen as an attack on not
only the the family but also the nation, as my analysis of these novels will
show.

The political significance of rape in British India was amplified in the
1880s, when rape became the center of a bitter controversy concerning the
Ilbert Bill, which precipitated what many Anglo-Indians regarded as a "crisis of control."[13] In brief, this "white mutiny" erupted in 1883 when Gladstone's Liberal government introduced a reform measure which would have
allowed qualified Indian judges to exercise "jurisdiction over European British subjects living outside the chief Presidency towns" (Sinha, "Chattams,"
98). Three to five thousand Anglo-Indian civilians and governmental officials, planters, and soldiers joined in mass protests, which eventually forced
India's viceroy, the Marquis of Ripon, to modify the Ilbert Bill. Some of the
most hysterical objections to this bill concerned the imagined spectacle of
an Englishwoman who brought charges of rape or sexual assault against an
Indian man in a court with an Indian judge presiding (103).

One of the most striking features of this white mutiny was that colonizing women played an unusually outspoken part in it. Breaking strong social taboos which usually confined them to silence on public issues and on
rape in particular, many Anglo-Indian women organized letter campaigns and
spoke vehemently in public meetings protesting the Ilbert Bill. This "mobili-
zation of white women on their own initiative," as Mrinalini Sinha argues,
"threatened the edifice on which colonial society was built" ("Chattams,"
106). As these and many other mutiny novels demonstrate, the "image of the
pure and passionless white woman as the helpless victim of a lascivious native male" (105) performed its ideological work best when the victim remained passive and silent. In her "epic of the race," Flora Annie Steel tried
instead to imagine new, less fatal ways for colonial women to prove their "integrity" and loyalty to the British empire. By looking more closely at how
the representations of rape function in Grant's, Taylor's and Henty's mutiny
novels, we can better understand the ideological work it performed and iden-

tify some of the patterns that Flora Annie Steel tried to reimagine in *On the Face of the Waters*.

Reviving Lucrece

The most extraordinary feature of James Grant's *First Love and Last Love: A Tale of the Indian Mutiny*, one early British novel about the mutiny, is that it violates perhaps the most powerful literary taboo of the Victorian era, which otherwise prohibited the description of the naked (white) female body and generally censored mentions of rape in polite literature.[14] Writing about the mutiny from the safe distance of the mother country, Grant describes anonymous Englishwomen lost in the chaos that followed the retreat of the British forces from Delhi on May 11, 1857, and graphically details how they became the victims of "every indignity that the singularly fiendish invention of the Oriental mind could suggest" (133). Defenseless Englishwomen, he reports, were driven into the streets:

> always stripped of their clothing, treated with every indignity, and then slowly tortured to death, or hacked at once to pieces, according to the fancy of their captors. . . . No mercy was shown to age or sex. Delicate women were stripped to the skin, turned thus into the streets, beaten with bamboos, pelted with filth, and abandoned to the vile lusts of blood-stained miscreants, until death or madness terminated their unutterable woe. (157–158)

In assigning Englishwomen this spectacular place as victims of torture and rape during the mutiny, Grant inadvertently echoes Edmund Burke's descriptions of the rapes of Indian women, but he assigns Englishwomen to the place of the "delicate" victims, while the Indian rabble replace Hastings and his men.

Grant justifies this shocking violation of Victorian literary decorum and underscores the "epic" dimensions of these human sacrifices by alluding to the rape of Lucrece. Characterizing these anonymous women as rendered speechless by "unutterable woe," Grant also alludes glancingly to Shakespeare's famous poem cataloguing the suffering of Lucrece and the "speechless woe" of her husband (1674).

The gap Grant attempts to span in comparing Rome with Delhi is, needless to say, a wide one. The strain of drawing these parallels is suggested, for instance, by one surreal description of two Englishwomen caught in the streets of Delhi. Noting that they were first "stripped perfectly nude," he describes how they were "bound by their tender limbs with ropes to two nine-pounder gun-carriages, on which, with their dishevelled hair sweeping the streets, they were drawn away towards the market place, amid the jeers and mockery of the lowest ruffians in Delhi" (198). In this episode and elsewhere in the novel, Grant describes Englishwomen who suffer rape and torture in silence, imitating Lucrece's final sacrifice to the power of the phallus.

By alluding to the rape of Lucrece, Grant also attempts to create an epic frame for his narrative about love and war. Focusing on events following the rout of British forces from Delhi on May 11, 1857, and their eventual recapture of the city in late September, Grant's novel highlights the heroic efforts of two young British officers, Rowley Thompson and Jack Harrower, as they defend and protect two beautiful English sisters, Kate and Madelena Weston. This native insurrection interrupts Rowley and Kate's wedding ceremony, and nearly three hundred pages of heroic military self-sacrifice and hectic adventure stand between the ritual and its erotic consummation, a pattern which is typical of these novels.[15]

The violence faced by Kate, Madelena, and their younger sister, Polly, register the technologies of sex and gender at work in Victorian England. Though Grant alludes to Lucrece, it is important to note that the three Weston sisters do not claim Lucrece's power of speech or imitate her heroic resolve in killing herself. By the 1850s, Victorian social conventions restrained "pure" women from recognizing or speaking about rape, severely restricted their movement in public spaces by insisting they needed male protection outside the home, and blurred the distinctions between rape and seduction (Clark, *Women's Silence*, 128). The various fates of the three Weston sisters thus disclose Grant's allegiance to a conservative gender ideology that he projects onto colonial society in British India.

Madelena Weston, the oldest sister, has been courted by Jack Harrower but has rejected him, preferring a Byronic cavalry officer with more status and sex appeal. During the crisis caused by the mutiny, Madelena escapes from a fate worse than death by assuming native dress and hiding for several weeks in the "wilderness" outside Delhi, with Jack as her chivalrous protector (and a convenient witness to prove she is not dishonored by her move into undomesticated space). Chastened by her ordeal, Madelena abjures Byronic fantasies of passion and eventually agrees to marry Jack out of gratitude for his protection. This is one of the ways that rape policed female sexual desire in British novels about India.

Grant faces an even more difficult problem in representing Kate Weston's fate since he apparently wished to preserve his heroine's virginity so that she could be happily reunited with her husband. When Kate is abducted by one of the Indian insurgents and imprisoned in her own home, Grant must provide some plausible reason why her captor does not simply rape her, an outrage the typical Oriental villain should, almost by definition, attempt. Grant's narrator explains that her abductor is caught in a dispute with his superiors about who has the right to "possess" Kate, so he contents himself with humiliating her by forcing her to act as a maid servant before his "leering" male friends. In this way, Grant displays how rape threatens Englishwomen with a loss of class status as well as bodily violation. This scene also inadvertently suggests parallels between the sexual contract and the wage slavery that Victorian marriage arrangements imposed on Englishwomen.

The fate of Polly Weston, the youngest, sixteen-year-old, "immaculately blond" Weston sister, is perhaps the most illustrative of Grant's reiteration of the Victorian politics of rape in this tale about the Indian Mutiny. Polly is seized by one of the princes of Delhi and imprisoned in the royal harem. The aristocratic Muslim prince wants to enjoy her love before he possesses her body, but because she resists all his advances, he finally loses patience and sends her into the streets, where she is raped and tortured by the rabble. In this way Grant endorses Victorian presumptions that while upper-class men may seduce, only lower-class men rape (Clark, *Women's Silence*, 128). In describing Polly Weston's death, Grant allows his heroine to trump Lucrece because she does not surrender to the prince who captures her. In this way, Polly avoids the "dilemma" that St. Augustine and other Christian fathers located in this pagan epic, which defined Lucrece's suicide as her most heroic act. St. Augustine writes, "If Lucrece is adulterous, why is she praised; if chaste, why put to death?"[16] Setting aside the problem of Lucrece's consent under duress, Grant offers Polly's mute body as the ultimate female Christian sacrifice to purity. When the British retake Delhi, Jack Harrower discovers what the rabble has done to Polly Weston: "There against the palace wall, which was shattered by cannon shot, and thickly starred by rifle bullets, was the body of a girl, snowy white, sorely emaciated and nailed by her hands and feet against the masonry, with her golden hair—that mute ornament which God has given to woman—waving in ripples on the wind." (412) In representing the rape and murder of Englishwomen in such spectacular terms—and, in Polly's case, as a crucifixion—Grant insists that heroic Englishwomen were too pure to suffer rape and survive. In short, by valorizing Polly's ultimate sacrifice, Grant's novel indicates that the glory of the empire resides in the involuntary sacrifices of fair, golden-haired Englishwomen who preserve their innocence at all cost and are violently reduced to silence.

Refusing Rape

Meadows Taylor's *Seeta* (1872) is much more open to the heteroglossia of colonial life and more perceptive about the conflicts generated by the racist and sexist ideologies at work in the "contact zone" of British India than most other Anglo-Indian novels. Though Taylor's narrator occasionally mentions the historical events at Delhi, Cawnpore, Lucknow, and Jhansi in the "red year" of 1857, he presents a love story about colonial life elsewhere during the mutiny, fictionalizing his own experience as a district commissioner in West Berar in 1857–1858, where he maintained order by force of his personality alone, without the aid of any British troops.[17]

Taylor not only avoids the battle scenes that typify other mutiny novels, but he also refrains from reproducing the rape script in many popular mutiny novels which center on white women who are threatened with rape by Indian men. Instead, *Seeta* dramatizes how racial prejudices are inflamed by sensational rape narratives like Grant's, by describing the short life of an Indian woman who is threatened with rape and abduction by an Indian man, before and after her marriage to the English hero of the novel. Like a few other Anglo-Indian novelists who wrote about the mutiny before 1880, including George Chesney in *The Dilemma* (1876), Meadows Taylor creates an alternative to these national epics of the race that celebrate imperial values which require that "fathers and founders of families" conform to imperial ideals of racial purity.[18]

First of all, Taylor's novel differs dramatically from other epics of the race because it does not attempt to create an epic distance between the days of the mutiny and the present by referring, for example, to Roman myths like the rape of Lucrece, which help to project the recent historical past into a universe that is as "absolute and complete . . . as closed as a circle" (Bakhtin, 16). On the contrary, *Seeta* presents a colonial world which includes the possibilities of intraracial rape as well as interracial marriage. Though he avoids the self-aggrandizing allusions to the rape of Lucrece, Taylor does refer to Greek and Indian epics where daughters are exchanged in marriage to establish stronger and more peaceful political alliances between conquering and conquered warriors. By dramatizing Seeta's marriage with the Englishman, Cyril Brandon, Taylor recalls, instead, the narrative of the Sabine women, which defines marriage, rather than rape, as providing the sacred foundation for the family and the state.

Taylor's title also invites comparisons between his heroine and Sita, the female heroine of the popular Indian epic the *Ramayana*, and so invokes an alternative cultural frame for considering the meaning of rape in his text. In several versions of this Indian epic, Sita is herself a victim of rumors about rape rather than of rape itself, and she is, in the end, exonerated. Unlike Grant's *First Love and Last Love*, Taylor's *Seeta* thus recognizes the ambiguities that allow rape to be confused with seduction, making it what Patricia Joplin calls an "equivocal sign" (46). Taylor shows, however, that in colonial societies like British India, the indeterminacy that surrounds rape generates dangerous suspicions, for imperialism itself breeds mutual betrayal, suspicion, violence, and revenge, feelings that Taylor indicates are experienced by both the colonizer and the colonized. Taylor's *Seeta* disputes the certainties of British colonizers who regarded either their religion or their "race," rather than their personal ethics, as providing undisputed evidence of moral superiority.

In rejecting the simple racial imperatives in other epics of the race, Taylor presents a narrative that conforms in some ways to the script that Gayatri Spivak has identified as characterizing earlier nineteenth-century colonial texts, where "white men save brown women from brown men" ("Can," 297). Yet I would argue that by exploring of the meaning of interracial marriage in *Seeta* and demonstrating of how rumors of rape act to consolidate "racial" categories, Taylor discloses a world which reaches into "the present day with all its inconclusiveness, its indecision, its openness, its potential for re-thinking and re-evaluating" (Bakhtin, 16).

The autobiographical traces that appear in *Seeta* also mitigate the epic distancing found in most national epics about the mutiny. Cyril Brandon, the novel's hero, violates the unspoken racial premises of most mutiny novels when he falls in love and marries Seeta, a rich and beautiful Indian widow. Taylor's description of Seeta's physical appearance and personality suggests parallels with Mary Palmer, Taylor's beloved wife, whose grandfather was Warren Hastings's English secretary and whose grandmother was one of the princesses of Delhi.[19] During a visit to London in 1838–1840, one bigoted English matron disparaged Mary's "blackness" and ridiculed Taylor's apparent devotion to his "little Indian queen" (Taylor, *Letters*, x). Though Taylor's wife died in 1844, his sharp Romantic critique of British hierarchies of race and gender is evident in all his novels.

Seeta thus poses a question that most mutiny novels repress, a question that Taylor, in his autobiography, articulates more explicitly when he writes: "[English] people ask me what I found in the natives to like so much. Could I help loving them when they loved me so? Why should I not love them?" (*Story*, 445). Perhaps because it is infused by this sympathy, *Seeta* presents the least racist and most optimistic representation of interracial marriage in any Anglo-Indian novel that I know, which is not to say it escapes racism altogether.[20]

Second, Taylor's *Seeta* insists that the type of Romantic love that Shelley, for example, idealized in "Laon and Cyntha," provides the best "sacrament" for the foundation of a family. In representing the mutual love that Seeta and Brandon share, Taylor, like Shelley, asserts the power of enlightened education, sympathy, and sexual passion to overcome racial prejudice and accommodate cultural differences. Taylor recognizes no inherent racial differences in his assessment of the emotional and intellectual potential of Indian and English women. Believing in companionate marriage, Cyril Brandon wants a wife who is more intellectually and morally compatible than the poorly educated Englishwomen he meets in India. Dismayed by Brandon's Shelleyan desires, his more conventional male companion protests, "If all men in India were as aesthetic . . . as you we should have flights of blue stockings coming out by every mail" (74).

Third, Seeta differs dramatically from the silent and passive victims epitomized by a character like Polly Weston. Unlike most English heroines in mutiny novels, Seeta asserts Lucrece's eloquent power of speech and political agency early in the novel when she testifies in court about the details of her first husband's murder, her own near rape, and her other injuries. Brandon, who acts as magistrate in this hearing, marvels over "evidence given so clearly, so firmly . . . so minutely" (66) and promptly awards her damages. Thus, Brandon falls in love with Seeta not only because of her beauty and wealth but also because of her power with words. Unlike most Indian and English women, Seeta is "a good Sanscrit scholar" (86), with an inquiring mind, an expansive imagination, a high spirit, and a generous heart. Like the Sabine women, she uses these skills to reconcile insiders and outsiders in her society.

In contrast to most British and Anglo-Indian novelists of the post-mutiny period, Taylor does not represent this interracial union as biologically doomed. Married to a man who publicly espouses and privately practices his feminist principles, Seeta escapes from those Indian—and Victorian—proprieties that would keep her silent and confine her entirely to the domestic sphere. In contrast to those "delicate women who had never in their lives known hardships" (314), whose victimization Grant and others pornographically describe, Seeta displays extraordinary physical and moral courage during the uprising. Assuming the "simple boy's dress" (286) that allows her to ride astride and armed with a small revolver, Seeta takes a "strange delight" in sharing her husband's dangerous "duty" (318), as he travels around the district maintaining (English) law and order.

Fourth, Taylor does not depict the insurgents in the Uprising of 1857 as interchangeable "oriental fiends" who are driven mad by a racially determined lust to rape white women. Instead, he particularizes the individual motives of one man, Azrael Pande, a discharged and disillusioned Indian sepoy whose surname was later applied to all the rebels of 1857. In this novel, Pande is presented as a brilliant demagogue, a skillful politician, and a potential Indian nationalist, though he also confirms the significance of his given name by his irrationality and his fascination with Thuggee and witchcraft. Taylor insists, though, that Pande is ultimately driven mad not by his balked desire for Englishwomen but rather because he is obsessed with possessing the rich and beautiful Seeta. By describing how Pande continues to threaten Seeta with abduction and rape even after her marriage, Taylor discloses the ongoing sexual rivalry between English and Indian men as they vie for the attention of a beautiful Indian woman, a conflict that is nearly always obscured in English mutiny novels and histories. In the process, Taylor draws clear distinctions between the motives of the lover and those of the rapist in contrasting Brandon's love for Seeta with Pande's desire to abduct, humiliate, violate, and torture her. By emphasizing the distinctions between love and violence, and between the legitimate "sacred rites" of marriage and the trauma of rape, Taylor highlights distinctions that are elided in most Victorian literature.

To illustrate the incendiary power of rumors about interracial rape during the Indian Uprising of 1857, Taylor shows how by transforming the news of Seeta and Cyril's marriage into a story about Seeta's abduction and rape by a powerful Englishman (135), Azrael Pande is able to exploit this rumor to unite Hindus and Moslems in a common effort to take revenge against the English. Pande's retelling of Seeta's story is deliberately designed to arouse the anticolonial rage that Edmund Burke once tried to tap, though by 1856, Pande's Indian auditors had many more reasons to resent British domination. Taylor does not mention, let alone criticize, new colonial policies like the annexation of Oude in 1855, but he does show that Indians were more quickly enraged by Pande's version of this rape script because of the increasingly more exclusionary social practices and marriage arrangements of the British colonizers. Taylor also recognizes the intensified racism that characterized colonial administrations in the 1850s by noting that the Englishmen who are Brandon's superiors in the colonial bureaucracy see the politically dangerous consequences of interracial unions and refuse to recognize Cyril's marriage as genuine, legitimate, or permanent.

Taylor likewise dramatizes how gender influences the interpretation of these rumors about rape by showing how women from both the colonized and colonizing groups see Cyril and Seeta's marriage through the veil of their own fears. Before their marriage, Seeta's aunt concludes that Cyril has taken advantage of his superior position in the colonial hierarchy and has seduced her niece, since, as the representative of justice in this district, Cyril could rape Seeta without fear of reprisal (120). The English matrons in Cyril's home station of Noorpoor are affronted because he has chosen to marry an Indian woman rather than one of their daughters. Inflamed by envy, ignorant racial bigotry, sexual hunger, and boredom, they imagine Seeta as the agent and Cyril as the victim of her seduction (213). The Anglo-Indian women at Brandon's station later take revenge on Seeta and assert their moral superiority by explaining that the Church of England will not recognize her marriage as "sacred" since she has not converted to Christianity, nor will it recognize the children of their union as legitimate.

In the end, then, Seeta assumes the pose of one of the Sabine women when she tries unsuccessfully to intervene when insider and outsider, colonized and colonizers, meet in battle. Failing to persuade Pande to spare Brandon, Seeta repeats Lucrece's ultimate sacrifice, for she is fatally wounded as she interposes her body to protect Brandon and receives the sword thrust meant to kill her husband. Taylor apparently could not imagine how Seeta's union with Brandon could be sustained after the mutiny, when colonizers confused racial bigotry with patriotic zeal and when interracial children were increasingly assigned to the zone of "abjection," as many of these novels attest.[21]

 Ultimately, then, Taylor's novel shows his divided loyalties. He presents a narrative about the mutiny that disputes the civic model implicit in novels like Grant's that glorify the rapes of Englishwomen by comparing them with Lucrece's. Taylor's novel shows that he refused to regard women of any race as a species of property to be valued only for their "purity." However, by cutting short Seeta's marriage before she can produce an heir and hinting at her near conversion to Christianity when she is on her deathbed, Taylor reasserts familiar colonial desires that identify Christianity as providing the sacred and necessary foundation for the new "national" family. With Seeta conveniently eliminated, Brandon returns to England, claims his estate, marries a liberal, well-educated Englishwoman who also knew and loved Seeta, and produces a male heir who will be more easily accepted in English society. Brandon's second marriage thus admits Taylor's investment in notions of national identity which defined British laws concerning legitimacy, inheritance, land tenure, and most of all social order based on the rule of (English) law as the marks of a superior civilization which Taylor labored all his life to bring to British India. By assigning this heroic death to Seeta, Taylor thus avoids the deeper psychological issues that Flora Annie Steel explores, as we shall soon see, in her treatment of the "mystery" of fatherhood and its relation to the sacred foundations of family and state in *On the Face of the Waters*.

Recalling Lucrece

Two of the most extraordinary features of novels about the Indian Uprising of 1857 are their sameness and persistence. The 1890s witnessed a new wave of novels about the mutiny which invites us to ask what prompted the repetition of this particular rape script? With the mutiny more than thirty years in the past, epic distance became easier to create, and many British novelists continued to produce novels like Grant's which imagine Englishwomen's rapes in order to justify and glorify their exclusion from the political process, especially in reaction to the revived campaign for women's suffrage as it began to gather new support in this decade.

By the 1890s, then, as a result of increasing political activity surrounding women's suffrage and as a reaction to it, there was considerable debate about the continuing viability of Victorian sex and gender arrangements, both inside and outside the family, both at home and in British India. The "New Imperialism" of the 1890s intensified the tensions surrounding Victorian gender arrangements because of the emphasis on male aggressiveness as one of the racial signs of Englishness.[22] In a letter published in the London *Times* in 1883, for example, James Fitzjames Stephen, a former law member of the Viceroy's Council and an important judge in this period, bluntly sums up many of the changes in the colonial attitudes and policies in the years following the introduction of the Ilbert Bill:

> The Government of India is essentially an absolute Government founded not on consent, but on conquest. It does not represent the native principles of life or government, and it can never do so until it represents heathenism and barbarism. It presents a belligerent civilization, and no anomaly can be so striking and dangerous as its administration by men who, being at the Head of a Government founded on conquest, implying at every point the superiority of the conquering race, of their ideas, their institutions, their opinions and their principles, and having no justification for its existence except that superiority, shrink from the open, uncompromising straight forward assertion of it, seek to apologize for their own position in it.[23]

At the same time, a return to a model of civility like the one that Lucrece represented was foreclosed by many legal and social changes successfully promoted by feminists and other liberal reformers in this period. The passage of landmark laws like the Married Women's Property Act of 1882, as well as the emergence of the "New Woman" of the 1890s and the greater visibility of male homosexuality, contested efforts, like those expressed by Stephen, to appropriate biological determinism to authorize Englishmen's (hetero)sexual and racial superiority.[24]

British India, of course, responded to these changes as well. As middle-class women won access to better education and some prepared for careers outside the home, India often provided opportunities for them to work in professions that remained closed to them "at home," as Antoinette Burton has shown (7–8). Likewise, as Anglo-Indian women began publishing novels about colonial life, especially in the 1880s and 1890s, they directly challenged Victorian social conventions which equated domestic seclusion with modesty and female honor with silence. While some female novelists in this period published their work under sexually ambiguous names like Maxwell Grey, others signed their texts with frankly feminine names like Hilda Gregg and Flora Annie Steel. The presence of significant numbers of British and Anglo-Indian women writing in the 1880s and 1890s suggests, in itself, how traditional gender roles were unraveling by the end of the nineteenth century. By the time that Henty and Kipling began to write, there were many prolific Anglo-Indian women who competed directly with them, and several women in this generation wrote novels about the mutiny.[25]

G. A. Henty's *Rujub, the Juggler* (1893) and Flora Annie Steel's *On the Face of the Waters* (1897) register some of the legal and social changes that were transforming life in England and British India, making the New Imperialism of the 1890s attractive to them both. Nonetheless, the "epics of the race" that Henty and Steel composed present radically different ways for their heroines to display their "integrity" and "loyalty" during the mutiny. While Grant's novel ignores, and Henty's novel counters, feminist challenges to the social contract and attempts to dignify conservative gender arrangements, Steel's mutiny novel, like Taylor's, shows how nineteenth-century feminism was redirected in service to the Raj. At the same time, Steel's novel also suggests how uniquely feminine anxieties about the body, sexuality, and motherhood proved instrumental in this process.

Like most mutiny novels, *Rujub, the Juggler* combines a story about love with a story about war, and one sign that Henty's narrative is addressed to "adult" readers is that it hinges on the near rape of the heroine. Henty's hero, Ralph Bathurst, plunges "headfirst into adventures" (Bakhtin, 151), but his heroine, Isobel Hanney, participates more fully in his adventures. The threat of rape functions in this text, then, as a check and reminder of the import of her sexual difference and as a powerful force prompting Ralph to come to Isobel's defense.

Henty's plot is set in motion when the orphaned Isobel Hanney comes to India to act as hostess for her uncle who is stationed at Cawnpore, the historical site where Englishwomen were, in fact, killed, and the point of origin for the most notorious and persistent rumors of their rapes. Predictably, because of her beauty and grace, Isobel attracts the unwanted attentions of the Indian leader, Nana Sahib. During the mutiny, she is captured by his soldiers and imprisoned in Nana Sahib's harem, where he repeatedly threatens to rape her.

Isobel averts rape, and the necessity of Lucrece's heroic suicide, when she enacts Ralph's bizarre strategy to "save" her, which identifies self-mutilation as her only defense against rape. Isobel apparently does not ask the hero to bring her a sword to defend herself or poison to kill Nana Sahib. Instead, she wordlessly acquiesces to his plan and follows his scientifically precise directions to spread acid all over her face and shoulders to blister her skin, making herself so unattractive to Nana Sahib that he releases her from the harem because he thinks she is diseased. When Isobel rejoins the other captured Englishwomen, one matron laments her defacement but applauds her courage, saying: "'Bravely done, girl! Bravely and nobly done'" (3:135). In this exchange Henty indicates how by the 1890s Victorian women could be relied upon to police their own sexuality through such self-destructive responses to the threat of rape.[26]

The sex and gender crisis of the 1890s is most evident in Henty's characterization of the hero, since Ralph Bathurst questions his own manhood when he cannot actively participate in battle. Ralph suffers from a "nervous" complaint that causes him to tremble and shake "like a girl at the sound of firearms" (1:33). When the mutiny erupts, Bathurst's secret is forced into the open, and he is humiliated because he cannot take his place with the other marksmen shooting at the mutineers and is forced to "play the part of a woman rather than a man" (3:25).

In this novel, Rujub—the father of an Indian woman Ralph once saved—is presented as the embodiment of all the mystical secrets of Eastern philosophy; and it is he who cures Bathurst and helps him finally to perform adequately on the battlefield (and as it turns out in the bedroom). Only a hack like Henty could disclose the powerful secrets of Rujub's "magic" with such symbolic—and hilarious—naïveté, for Rujub's most marvelous and unexplained trick involves a telescoping pole that extends itself more than one hundred feet into the air, bearing his daughter aloft, and then slowly deflates, causing her to vanish magically. The trick of the monumental telescoping phallus is performed twice, and confounds even the most scientific Englishmen in this novel, who subsequently show a studied respect for Rujub's inexplicable prowess. In describing this magic trick, Henty inadvertently suggests the heterosexual rivalry that colonizing Englishmen were expected to repress.

Like many servants in Anglo-Indian novels about the mutiny, Rujub and his daughter prove their loyalty to the Raj when they later cooperate with Bathurst to help Isobel escape from Nana Sahib. When Isobel and Ralph reach safety many pages later, they declare their love and their desire to marry, but Bathurst must first prove his manhood by surviving in battle. Their marriage ceremony is conducted just minutes before Bathurst's volunteer company departs, so the consummation of this marriage, like Kate Weston's in *First Love and Last Love*, is delayed by a long wartime campaign. In most novels of the 1890s, this is how mutiny stories dramatizing the threat of interracial rape served the new imperialism.

Revising the Epic of the Race

Flora Annie Steel's *On the Face of the Waters* presents an "epic of the race" that demonstrates an alternative to Henty's conservative—and glib—resolution of the new tensions surrounding gender, sexuality, and the British family in the 1890s. Like Taylor's *Seeta*, Steel's novel is more open to the heteroglossia of colonial life than the novels of Grant or Henty. In fact, Steel emphasizes the multiplicity of voices in the colonial contact zone by contrasting, for example, the mutinous sepoy with the Indian soldier who remained true to his salt, the treacherous household servant with the loyal Indian ayah, and the duplicitous wife of the king of Delhi with the devout Moghul princess who remained aloof from the plotting against the English. Moreover, as these polarities suggest, Steel saw gender as a determining factor in the experiences of both the Indians and British caught up in the drama of the mutiny. While English characters remain at the center of her novel, Steel challenges the gender paradigm of earlier epics about the Indian uprising by refusing, like Taylor, to write a narrative which hinges on the rape of an Englishwoman. Rejecting the civic model and the ethics represented by the rape of Lucrece, Steel attempted to create a national epic that allowed Englishwomen to be female heroes without becoming sacrificial victims. In order to satisfy this objective, however, Steel's novel naturalizes the racism that Taylor's *Seeta* contests.

Perhaps some of the reasons for Steel's refusal to repeat the rumors spread by other novels about the mutiny concerning the rapes of English-women can be found in her experience of life in British India and in her endorsement of some of the goals of British feminism. During her twenty-year stay in India, Steel studied several Indian languages and worked outside as well as inside the home, superintending several Indian girls' schools for a time. When she returned to live permanently in England in 1889, Steel defied the Victorian conventions that would keep her silent; she joined with the conservative branch of the "suffragette" movement to fight for the vote for Englishwomen and she wrote more than twenty popular novels before her death in 1929. Steel's life in India apparently convinced her that the colonizers should not separate the private realm of home and family from the public realm of work, not only in times of war but also in peace. Because English-men and -women were both called to work in service to the Raj, her novel proposes to judge them by the same code of honor and so rejects the gender-specific ethics that are exalted in Grant's and Henty's novels.

In *On the Face of the Waters*, Steel begins by acknowledging the "desacralization of the family" in pre-mutiny times by noting the sacrifices of desire that her heroine, Kate Erlton, must make in order to remain in a loveless marriage that lacks both "honour" and "glory."[27] While most mutiny novels insist on a sexual rapaciousness that is presented as specific to Indian men, Steel's novel discloses instead the sexual lawlessness and hypocrisy of British men who freely transgress the boundaries set by marriage and by the color bar. Major Erlton, the heroine's husband, suffers no censure from his military superiors even though he flaunts his adulterous relationship with the pretty, adventurous Englishwoman, Alice Gissing. Married to a man who fails to behave "like a gentleman" by showing proper sexual restraint and who, in fact, does not love or even respect her, Kate Erlton experiences sexual relations, even in marriage, as rape.

Likewise, even Jim Douglas, the man who proves, somewhat ambiguously, to be the hero of this novel, has been ostracized from polite colonial society because he was caught in an adulterous alliance with his superior officer's wife, resulting in his court-martial. Douglas subsequently places himself beyond the pale by "buying" and living for seven years with a Muslim woman. Like many feminists of her generation, Steel thought the best way to eliminate these sexual double standards was by subjecting British men to the same "repressive standard of sexual morality" that was applied to respectable British women.[28]

The most audacious and iconoclastic gesture in Steel's national epic is that Kate Erlton fakes her own rape during the Uprising of 1857. Flouting conventional definitions of female heroism that define rape and suicide as the ultimate test of an Englishwoman's virtue, Kate escapes rape by assuming the costume of a native woman and staging her own abduction. During the fall of Delhi, Kate is separated from her husband, and, as she runs through the streets, she recognizes Jim Douglas, who is also in disguise as a marauding Afghani. Douglas helps Kate escape to safety by throwing her across his saddlebow while she screams, as if she expects to be raped. Douglas then shelters Kate in his home in the native quarter of Delhi, where she must save herself from detection by passing as Douglas's new Indian paramour, wearing eastern veils and accepting life in seclusion. This is, indeed, imprisonment in the harem with a difference. Steel thus turns inside out the Orientalist conventions Grant and Henty invoke since her heroine uses this occasion to teach her morally rebellious hero, Jim Douglas, to appreciate the pleasures of a chaste and companionate English marriage, though Kate scrupulously avoids any sexual contact with him while living in his home.

Steel's national epic differs perhaps most of all from the other mutiny novels because it briefly imagines the revolutionary consequences of feminist critiques of male sexuality and violence in the 1880s and 1890s that held the potential to create an international and interracial sisterhood by uniting colonizing and colonized women. When Douglas is detained, Kate manages her own escape from Delhi by establishing sisterly bonds with Indian women. She is first protected by a Muslim princess who lives in a neighboring house and later by her Hindu servant, Tara, who helps her hide temporarily in an ashram. Kate remains in this religious retreat for nearly a week, and, for a brief time, she is able to see war as the "primitive art" of a "primitive people" (393) and to envision the possibility of a world without war, a paradoxical discovery when war is raging all around her.

In the end, though, this fragile sisterly alliance between British and Indian women is sabotaged by Kate's—and Steel's—unqualified belief in the racial superiority of the English and by her aggressive individualism and unacknowledged sexual competitiveness. Steel's characterization of Kate's relationship with Tara, in particular, exposes these tensions. Steel attempts to show that Tara is Kate's moral inferior when she describes how Jim Douglas, earlier in her life, prevented her from performing sati, and she, like countless other high caste Hindu widows in Anglo-Indian novels, immediately fell in love with her rescuer. Since Steel previously translated and published an English version of the *Ramayana* for children, she was well aware that this epic idealized sati as the ultimate test of an Indian wife's heroism.

Faced with this counterexample of Sita's courage, chastity, and devotion, Steel labored hard to show why Tara's failed attempt at sati proved her moral inferiority. Steel locates the moral differences between Kate and Tara when she notes that Tara was willing to abandon her religious vows because Douglas excited her passions and sexual desires. Tara's Hinduism is also defined as the reason why she is willing to abase herself later by acting as Douglas's domestic servant.

In reproducing this older script about how Englishmen saved "brown women from brown men," Steel creates a narrative problem for herself since she designs a plot that later requires Tara to sacrifice herself in order to help Kate escape from Delhi and return to her husband. Steel provides no plausible motive for Tara's generous sacrifices since Kate enters into only the most superficial and patronizing relationship with her, an implausibility evident in Henty's treatment of Rujub and in many other British novels featuring similarly self-sacrificing servants.

The most spectacular proof that Steel offers to demonstrate that Kate is Tara's moral and racial superior is Tara's public display of her nearly naked body when she prepares for a second time to perform sati. Simply put, in Steel's view, Tara unsexes herself when she displays her nearly naked body by joining a ritual procession through the streets of Delhi: "She was naked to the waist, and the scanty ochre-tinted cloth folded about her middle was raised so as to show the scars upon her lower limbs. The sunlight gleaming on the magnificent bronze curves showed a seam or two upon her breast also. . . . Her face, full of wild spiritual exaltation, was unmarred and, with the shaven head, stood out bold and clear as a cameo" (112). In willingly exposing her body to the public gaze, Tara betrays a lack of pride in her womanhood that, for Steel, condemns both her Hinduism and her "race."

These ideological conflicts between gender and race, and between the ideals of international feminism and the New Imperialism, also disrupt the conclusion of Steel's novel in several ways. First, Tara is made to sacrifice everything in the name of sisterhood in order to lead Kate out of the city to be reunited with her husband, who is encamped with the other English soldiers on the ridge above Delhi. Though Tara is still in love with Jim Douglas, she recognizes that Kate is a more worthy mate for him and so returns to her earlier plan to perform sati. Tara subsequently cuts herself off from her brother, defiles her caste, violates her religious integrity, and betrays what in another novel could be defined as the cause of Indian nationalism in order to save Kate. After completing this mission, Tara has nothing more to live for and voluntarily performs a suicide that is a sort of desacralized sati when she remains in a house that is burned as the British soldiers retake Delhi. Although Tara's death could also be seen to replicate the heroic sacrifices of Sita or the royal consorts of Chitor, Steel treats it instead as an expression of Hindu fanaticism rather than a laudable act of courage.

In the end, Steel gives in to the demands of the New Imperialism when she describes how and why her heroine renounces her earlier vision of peace and international sisterhood. Surrendering to colonial desires to imagine Englishmen as natural conquerors and Englishwomen as the best guardians of the purity of the race, Steel sends her heroine back to her husband, restores her to a place in the conqueror's history, and reunites her with the English soldiers preparing to retake Delhi. Forced to face the violence of war, Kate renounces her desire for "healing and atonement" and "forgets" her vision of a world beyond war that once united her with Indian women. In the British war camp, Kate realizes that she can "imagine a world without women . . . but not a world without men" (432). She consequently learns to see the causes of the mutiny in orthodox (and self-punishing) patriarchal terms: as one of Steel's characters puts it earlier, "Delhi had been lost to save women; the trouble begun to please them" (286). Back in her place in the familiar patriarchal and military world of British India, Kate learns to feel "a pride, almost a pleasure in the thought of the revenge which would surely be taken sooner or later . . . for every woman, every child killed, wounded,—even touched. She was conscious of it, even though she stood aghast before a vision of the years stretching away into an eternity of division and mutual hate" (460). In short, Kate's anger allows her to be quickly converted to promoting the heroics of revenge.

In recounting the "facts" of the English assault on Delhi, Steel also reveals her endorsement of the worship of force, revealing her allegiance to a New Imperialism which defined conquest as an expression of the racial superiority of the British. Steel glorifies John Nicholson, a famous and brutal British war hero who died of wounds sustained in the final attack on Delhi, characterizing him as a compelling figure "full of passion, energy, vitality" (440).[29] Restored to his natural male role as conquering soldier, Kate's husband recovers his lost honor by proving his courage on the battlefield, though he dies unheroically enough in the random gunfire before the final attack on the city. Major Erlton's death thus frees Kate to marry Jim Douglas, the man who has learned to love her during her captivity in his home in Delhi.

Thus, despite her earlier sharp criticism of the "fathers and founders of families," Steel allows her narrative to be "used to silence" the voice of the Other when she succumbs to that amnesia, that pressure to "not-see, to not-know, to not-name what is true" about the violence suffered by those whose bodies and minds are colonized by male notions of honor and desire (Joplin, 55). In this way, Steel reveals the privilege of the colonizing woman who, whether she writes or not, has many inducements to forget her own experience of colonialization and the insight it gave her into the lives of the multiply-colonized Indian men and women.

In designing this conclusion for her novel, Steel preserves the power that colonial family arrangements granted to Englishwomen by upholding their class and race prerogatives and by stressing their "purity" as memsahibs and mothers. Though Steel exposed the reality of violence that underlay the exchange of women in the marriages in this novel, she apparently felt compelled to endorse Social Darwinist theories of race which enhanced the power of white women as mothers. From her vantage point in the late 1890s, interracial marriages like Cyril and Seeta's seemed unpatriotic, and the fates of the children of such racially mixed marriages are envisioned as unavoidably tragic.

Despite its resistances, then, Steel's novel finally confirms the patriarchal bias of the New Imperialism of the 1890s, which assumed a hierarchy of racial difference that Steel legitimized in her representation of the "mystery of fatherhood and motherhood" (357) by making chastity the sign of the moral and racial superiority of the Englishman as well as the Englishwoman. Far from feeling grief over the death of his son by the Muslim woman he once bought, Jim Douglas feels relief when this "little morsel of flesh" (357) dies. Setting aside guilty memories about his Indian mistress and their son, Douglas goes to war hoping that battle will purify him and make him worthy of an Englishwoman like Kate. Only then can he imagine fathering a son he would be "proud of possessing," a boy who would go to school and be "fagged and flogged and inherit familiar virtues and vices instead of strange ones" (357).

In presenting this conclusion and this marriage, Steel's novel reflects two conflicts in the feminisms of her time that persist today. First, it suggests the power of cultural as well as political imperialism to redefine not only feminism but national identity itself through its representation of motherhood and fatherhood; that is, through its emphasis on the heterosexual couple. Steel's heroine is given a second chance in life because of an Indian woman's vision and self-sacrifice, but as a result, Kate's survivor's guilt makes her susceptible to the patriarchal logic of a nation-state that defines her body, her sexuality, and her gender role in terms of her "utility" to the empire.

Second, Steel's novel reveals the conflicts that are part of the history of nineteenth-century feminism by showing the difficulties she faced in reconciling emancipationist feminist discourse, which would justify elite women's participation in the public sphere, with late nineteenth-century British feminist discourse about female sexuality, which stressed women's sexual victimization by men. Thus, Steel authorized British women's emancipation at the cost of silencing their stories about rape and sexual desire. This gesture is not unexpected, as Patricia Klindienst Joplin reminds us, because writing about sexuality was—and is—profoundly threatening to the woman writer since "coming into language, especially into language about her body, has entailed the risk of a hidden but felt sexual anxiety, a premonition of violence" directed at women who try to tell unconventional truths about rape (39).

Steel achieves closure in her novel by invoking the authority not only of Social Darwinism but also of a triumphalist "national" history. As Bakhtin argues, however, such history "demands that we acknowledge it, that we make it our own" (342). In showing that her heroine's rape is just a ruse, Steel, like Taylor, avoids repeating rumors about the rapes of Englishwomen which were used to justify the limits imposed on Englishwomen under the Raj, in life as well as in fiction. Yet Steel's novel remains haunted by the ghost of Miss Wheeler, by the part of the story about rape that always threatens to break through the narratives which would deny it. In surrendering to the "authoritative word" of the conquerors' history, Steel knows that she is surrendering to "the word of the fathers" (Bakhtin, 14), but she has apparently so internalized the racial imperatives of colonial culture of the 1890s that she can see no other way to maintain her pride of womanhood and her pride of race.

Finally, even feminist efforts less conflicted than Steel's must fail if they require authorization by reference to unequivocal "facts" in the historical archives, since parts of women's history, like the "facts" about many rapes, especially during war, remain irretrievably lost.[30] Certainly, there were other Englishwomen whose stories were censored by historians like Trevelyan in order to shore up conflict-ridden interpretations of the honor and glory of a nation that defined rape in epic terms as women's unavoidable and fatal sacrifice. And though official British records may not acknowledge it, there certainly were accounts in circulation about Indian women raped by Englishmen drunk on power, violence, and revenge during this and subsequent colonial conflicts. In the end, Meadows Taylor's *Seeta* refuses to represent rape in the required way, though his love for India and Indians apparently blinds him to his complicity in enforcing those laws that worked to further subordinate the colonized under the Raj. Steel's *On the Face of the Waters*, in contrast, admits this self-betrayal. Steel, after all, promised not to disclose what she read in the "confidential reports" about the mutiny that she found in the British dispatch boxes that she opened.

CHAPTER 4

Hostage to History

THE RANI OF JHANSI IN ROMANCES
ABOUT THE INDIAN MUTINY

Splitting constitutes an intricate strategy of defense and differentiation in the colonial discourse. Two contradictory and independent attitudes inhabit the same place, one takes account of reality, the other is under the influence of instincts which detach the ego from reality. This results in the production of multiple and contradictory belief. The enunciatory moment of multiple belief is both a defense against the anxiety of difference, and itself productive of differentiation.

Homi K. Bhabha, *The Location of Culture*[1]

*W*hile many novels about the Indian Uprising of 1857 present this historical conflict as the foundation for national epics, with only partial success, as we have seen in chapter 3, many other British and Anglo-Indian novels written in the 1880s and later shape this history to conform to an alternate literary form that these writers began to call "romance." Mutiny romances illustrate at least two aspects of what Homi K. Bhabha has defined as the "splitting" he sees as endemic to colonial discourse, both producing an "anxiety of difference" and at the same time insisting on it. First, this splitting finds expression in the doubling of popular forms of the novel that occurred when British and Anglo-Indian male writers appropriated the term "romance" to describe adventure novels that focused on war and violence rather than on love and courtship.[2] Second, many of these "male" romances about the Indian Uprising of 1857 illustrate the colonial impulse to "splitting" in their inversion of the usual rape script in mutiny novels by including episodes of Englishmen threatened with murder, and occasionally with rape, by the most famous Indian warrior queen of the Indian Uprising of 1857, the Rani of Jhansi.[3] The purpose of this chapter is to explore why "national epics" about the Indian Uprising of 1857 were shadowed by these less serious romances, and to analyze how new ideological conflicts that emerged in the 1880s and 1890s were perhaps more easily "solved" by this turn to romance.

In the 1880s, prominent English writers, including G. A. Henty, Robert Louis Stevenson, Rider Haggard, Rudyard Kipling, and a host of imitators, began to characterize the novels that they were writing as offering "refreshment" to their readers by this return to the "pure" form of "romance." Updating Sir Walter Scott's definition of romance as a "tale of wild adventures in love and chivalry," these men wrote texts that focused primarily on a boy's preparation for maturity and on his performance of the rituals of male bonding, instead of on the erotic awakening, courtship, and marriage that are more often the subject of conventional Victorian "romances."[4] Moreover, late nineteenth-century adventure stories marketed for boys began to shade into "romances" written presumably for more adult male readers, as Rider Haggard indicated when he dedicated *King Solomon's Mines* to "all the big and little boys who read it."[5] These new adult romances, typically including more titillating subject matter, were particularly recommended for male readers who wanted an escape from the "more complicated kind of novel" written, for example, by George Eliot or, in the 1890s, by a growing number of "New Women."

Fredric Jameson in *The Political Unconscious* provides a starting point for a consideration of why these male romances provided "an imaginary solution" to the real historical, political, and social contradictions of colonial life in British India. In its "original strong form," Jameson writes, the romance offered a "symbolic answer to the perplexing question of how my enemy can be thought of as being evil (that is, as other than myself and marked by some absolute difference), when what is responsible for his being so characterized is quite simply the identity of his own conduct with mine, that which—points of honor, challenges, tests of strength—he reflects as in a mirror image" (118). Jameson does not acknowledge that his definition of "romance" presumes that both the hero and his "enemy" are male. Though he cites Emily Brontë's *Wuthering Heights* and Scott's *St. Rowan's Well* as famous nineteenth-century examples of the "art-romance," he does not discuss how the genre of romance was redefined and doubled in this period. While the "art romance" was reorganized to make more room for protagonists—and antagonists—who were women, an alternative literary form, also claiming the name of "romance," emerged in the 1880s that focused more and more exclusively on the male domain, purposefully excluding women.

An adequate history of British and Anglo-Indian fiction about India should include a fuller consideration of the impact of these shifts in the content and forms of romance and on the audiences that each genre addressed. As Doris Sommer and others have shown, many late nineteenth-century novels about colonial life in colonial contexts other than India were constructed as "national romances." In *Foundational Fictions*, for example, Sommer explains that the central contests in Latin American romances were organized around "the structural relations among the lovers and the antagonist who threatens to usurp the maiden from her legitimate partner. She is the object of desire. Whether she becomes rhetorically synonymous with the land, as she often does, or with the 'naturally' submissive and loving races and classes that the hero will elevate through his affection, woman is that which he must possess in order to achieve harmony and legitimacy" (85). Studies like Sommer's should make us ask why these male romances written by British and Anglo-Indian writers in the 1880s and 1890s almost always reject interracial marriage as a viable "solution" to the racial, religious, and cultural differences that divided the English colonizers from the colonized in British India.

By rejecting interracial marriage as a possible resolution for their "national romances," British and Anglo-Indians romance writers also reconfigured what Eve Sedgwick has called the "homosocial" structure typical of earlier novels about colonial life. In so doing, these writers risked seeming to recommend other even more tabooed solutions to the ideological conflicts evident in their "romances." After the Labouchère Amendment, with its legal prohibitions and medicalized definitions of homosexuality, was passed in Great Britain in 1885, the "homosocial" structure of novels about military life in British India suddenly became more suspect.[6] Thus, male adventure romances about the Indian Mutiny written in the 1880s and 1890s typically avoid representing, on one hand, the fervent, spiritualized, all-sufficient male friendships of earlier novels like William Delafield Arnold's *Oakfield* (1854) and, on the other, the excessive misogyny of novels like *Maurice Derring* (1864), which described the ostensible heroines of this text in the most contemptuous terms. In other words, these late nineteenth-century male romances about British India had to conform to newly narrowed limits on male heterosexual identity in representing male camaraderie in war and in courtship.

When writers created male romances based on the Indian Uprising of 1857, they faced another problem that G. A. Henty's famous boys' adventure novel, *In Times of Peril* (1881), serves to illustrate. Because these romances dramatize well-known events in imperial history, they cannot unequivocally evoke that "space of the degraded language of romance and daydream" that, in Joseph Conrad's fiction, for example, corresponds to the "non-place of the sea" or the "blank places" of the earth (Jameson, *Political Unconscious*, 213). Instead, these mutiny romances claim to represent a space more obviously populated and variously described, a place called India.

Henty, of course, developed one of the most influential formulas for the marketing of British history as the raw material for mass-produced adventures for boys.[7] Unlike *Rujub, the Juggler* (1893), which he claimed was written for more mature audiences, Henty's *In Times of Peril,* like most of his other boys' adventures, exhibits much greater freedom in his use of historical "facts," but, at the center of this extravagantly improbable historical romance, he places a hero who, paradoxically, claims that one of the most invariable signs of British national identity is the racially determined ability always to know and tell the truth. *In Times of Peril* presents a wildly unlikely plot that allows Henty's hero, Ned Warrener, or his younger brother, Dick Warrener, to take part in all the major battles of the Indian Uprising of 1857, even though they have to traverse long distances separating Delhi, Cawnpore, and Lucknow with impossible speed and extraordinary timing. Historical romances like Henty's can be seen, then, to reconcile contradictory Victorian desires for historical truth and for "story," and these inherent contradictions became even more difficult to resolve when romance writers turned to colonial worlds like British India, where notions of male gender identity were further restricted by prohibitions concerning sex and race.

Because he is writing a romance, Henty is able to represent many of the ideological conflicts posed by the Uprising of 1857 in very simple terms, characterizing this war as a "struggle for existence" (69) and reducing all its complexities to the racially determined dualities of "black" and "white." As one British soldier tells Ned, "If the mounted officers are white, it is all right; if not, they are mutineers" (66). In short, all the difficulties of discriminating friend from enemy in Henty's romance are solved simply by reference to race, and the political and ethical problems suggested by the rape of colonizing women in national epics about this uprising are virtually ignored. Though Nana Sahib, one of the most vilified Hindu leaders of the revolt, first appears as a "rollicking gentleman" in this text, he is soon revealed to be "in fact a human tiger" (177). Similarly, all the compromising "neutralizations" justifying the bloody campaign of British retaliation after Cawnpore are erased when Henty's narrator assures his readers: "To the credit of the British soldier be it said, that infuriated as they were by the thirst for vengeance, the thought of the murdered women, and the heat of the battle, not a single case occurred, so far as is known, of a woman being ill-treated, insulted, or fired upon" (311).

What marks *In Times of Peril* as a typical male romance of the 1880s is not only Henty's treatment of race but also his handling of gender and sexuality, although many of the problems associated with sexuality are ostensibly avoided because his heroes are so young. When the novel begins, Ned, who is training for a career in the Indian army, is sixteen and his brother, Dick, who has a "passion for the sea" (4), is fifteen. Ned and Dick travel to India with their sister, Kate, and cousin, Rose, just a few months before the uprising breaks out. Soon after their arrival, the brothers meet two sisters, Edith and Nelly Hargreaves, and become their "recognized lovers" (34), though the girls are just sixteen and fifteen years old. While Henty's novel is ostensibly presented as a romance, the age of his principals allows him to focus primarily on the boys' "courage, coolness and quickness of invention" (340) in their military adventures while giving only lip service in recognizing the "heroic fortitude" of the "English women in India during the awful period of the mutiny" (36).

Clearly the ruling desire at work in Henty's *In Times of Peril* is for military adventure rather than for mature love and erotic experience. When Ned and Dick meet the Rani of Oude, for example, she is charmed by them and offers them protection because she regards them as harmless "boys" rather than men (169). Henty transforms the brothers' meeting with the Rani, whose claims were overthrown when the British annexed Oude in 1855, into a comic interlude when she arranges for their escape by helping them dress as Indian women, disguises that the boys, in contrast to Kim, do not hesitate to assume.

In fact, the incestuous ending of Henty's novel makes it plain that this novel is not really about the achievement of sexual maturity. When Ned becomes a captain, though he is not yet eighteen, and Dick realizes he is about to become a "lieutenant," the brothers propose marriage to the Hargreaves sisters. Dick's "intended" evades his proposal, saying, "You know I like you, Dick, very, very much. It would be absurd to say more than that to each other now" (375). Three years and several promotions later, after their father, a widower, marries Nelly's mother, Ned, at twenty-one, having earned the rank of "commander," finally persuades Edith to consent to marriage. Because his brother has also won over Nelly, they make it a double ceremony, and keep all the wealth and honor that the brothers have acquired in their military adventures within the family. Writers of romances for more adult readers, however, could not reproduce such a tight and incestuous ending to set credible limits for their heroes' sexual adventures.

British and Anglo-Indians writing male romances for adults in the 1880s and 1890s further confounded the paradoxes associated with "historical

romances" like Henty's by designing plots that depended on coincidences far
in excess of the historical record, at a time when the historical record was
becoming more widely known. The 1880s and the 1890s witnessed the publication of a variety of British histories of the Indian Mutiny, from Sir John
William Kaye's *History of the Sepoy War in India* (1864–1880) and G. B.
Malleson's *History of the Indian Mutiny of 1857–58* (1896) to Lt. Col. T. Rice
Holmes's *History of the Indian Mutiny* (1883), and a host of memoirs and
autobiographies. These texts offered various arrangements of historical "facts"
so that the writers of these historical romances about the mutiny could select
the history that best matched their politics. Most novelists writing romances
about the mutiny typically named the historical study that they considered
most authoritative, though most agreed in presenting this war as a watershed
in Indian colonial history which exposed the dangers of interventions in Indian culture by the misguided servants of the East India Company or by overly
ambitious Christian missionaries. Mutiny romances usually characterized liberals and evangelicals alike as misguided by missionary zeal, impractical humanism, and overdeveloped feminine sympathy.

In the 1890s, Joseph Chamberlain's "New Imperialism" authorized a
redefinition of the proper relationship between colonizing men and "racially"
defined others. Echoes of Chamberlain's famous credo, "I believe in this race,
the greatest governing race, so proud, so tenacious, self-confident, and determined, this race which neither climate nor change can degenerate, which
will infallibly be the predominating force of future history and universal civilization,"[8] can be found everywhere in these romances. As James Fitzjames
Stephen's frequently quoted summary of colonial policy in India in the 1890s
makes clear, the New Imperialism put much more stress on British male gender roles because it did not depend upon the "consent" of the colonized but
rather on the virile masculine force of the colonizer.[9] By focusing on war
and military force rather than courtship, which presumably involved mutual
consent, these writers were better able to display their endorsement of the
New Imperialism.

Given the triumphalism of British histories and romances about the Indian Mutiny, it is difficult to account for the emergence of a series of Anglo-
Indian romances about the Rani of Jhansi, an historical figure who challenged
and disturbed all pronouncements about the natural sexual, racial, and military superiority of British men. The first British descriptions of the Rani of
Jhansi came from General Hugh Rose, who led the attack on the Rani's army
near Gwalior in 1858; he called her "the Indian Joan of Arc," the "best and
bravest of the rebel leaders" (Lebra-Chapman, 113–114). Rose provided an

eyewitness account of the Rani's valiant army and its defense of the insurgents' position, explaining how the Rani appeared frequently before her troops and rode into battle on the day she died, "dressed in a red jacket, red trousers, and white puggery," and wearing "the celebrated pearl necklace of Scindia which she had taken from his treasury and heavy gold anklets" (113–114). Rose also reported how her soldiers mourned when she was mortally wounded in a British charge on June 17, 1858. The British defeat of the insurgent forces gathered at Gwalior reestablished their control in this strategically important region and effectively marked the end of the organized military resistance during the uprising.

Subsequent accounts of the Rani's life offered by British historians dispute these appreciative reports by Rose and others in his regiment. They challenge the accuracy of these accounts by observing that this "perfect Amazon in bravery" was "just the sort of daredevil woman soldiers admire" (Fraser, 290). Other popular histories of the mutiny, including George W. Forrest's *History of the Indian Mutiny* (1904–1912), impugn the Rani's moral character, calling her "intemperate" and "licentious" (290). Because the Rani had family ties with Nana Sahib, and was thought by her detractors to have similarly ordered a massacre of English refugees at the fort at Jhansi, many English writers called her the "Indian Jezebel," or worse (290). Still others disputed the chronology and degree of the Rani's involvement in the final battles of the Indian Uprising, as well as the details of her death. None, however, disputed Malleson's conclusion that "her countrymen will ever remember that she was driven by ill-treatment into rebellion and that she lived and died for her country" (3:221).

So variously described, so troublesome to triumphal British histories, so challenging to simple narratives about "facts" and to new prescriptions for British male gender roles, the figure of the Rani of Jhansi who appears in these romances about the Indian Mutiny can help us chart the outer limits of the ethics of love and war in these texts. By analyzing three male romances by colonial writers which feature the Rani of Jhansi—J. E. Muddock's *The Star of Fortune: A Story of the Indian Mutiny* (1894), Robert Armitage Sterndale's *The Afghan Knife* (1879), and Hume Nisbet's *The Queen's Desire: A Romance of the Indian Mutiny* (1893)—I hope to disclose some of the changes in the "sexual imaginary" of the 1880s and 1890s that prompted this turn to the male romance. Although these novels suggest the new ideological work that the anomalous figure of the Rani of Jhansi was drafted to perform, they also expose the "contradictions" that these colonial romances could not reconcile.

More specifically, what I wish to discover by analyzing male romances that include the Rani of Jhansi is to identify those ideological and symbolic conflicts that could not be solved through references to the rape of English-women as the consolidating event of the British Raj. I also want to expose some of the ways that narratives written by Anglo-Indians differ from those of metropolitan authors like Henty. All three of these men may be considered Anglo-Indian writers since Muddock and Sterndale served in the Indian army during the mutiny and Hume Nisbet traveled widely in India and the Far East prior to writing *The Queen's Desire*.[10] The plots they create indicate how the technologies of gender worked in the contact zone of British India to shape the colonial writer's investments, sense of agency, and capacity for complicity with or resistance to metropolitan discourses of race as well as to the sex and gender roles prescribed by the New Imperialism.

There were many possibilities and patterns of resistance available in the colonial contact zone of British India that these Anglo-Indian romances failed to acknowledge, so I will turn briefly to indigenous folk songs about the Rani of Jhansi which were in circulation in the 1880s, many of which are still recited today. According to Joyce Lebra-Chapman, the first novel about the Rani of Jhansi by an Indian novelist appeared in 1888, written by a Bengali, Chandi Charan Sen. Since this novel was not translated into English in this period, it remained unavailable to writers like Muddock, Sterndale, and Nisbet, and indeed Henty himself, since they lacked the language skills and, to put it mildly, the scholarly inclinations to read or even consult fiction or histories by Indian writers. In turning to oral Indian sources about the Rani's history as a counterpoint to these romances, I want to suggest why the epic continued to flourish in Indian culture, though British epics of the race had to be written over and over again and generally failed to claim a respected place in British literary history. In this comparison, then, we will find some answers to why many British and Anglo-Indian novels about the mutiny failed to sustain their pretensions as epics of the race.

Gender as the Subtext of Colonial Romance

J. E. Muddock's *The Star of Fortune: A Story of the Indian Mutiny* (1894) provides one example of how adventure novels for adults usually converted more politically conservative histories of the Indian Mutiny into the materials for male romance, and it also illustrates some of the ideological and symbolic work that the Rani of Jhansi performed in these plots. Muddock prefaces his novel by asserting the authority of his personal experiences in India, explaining that he took part in the mutiny, that "tremendous struggle which nearly cost us our magnificent Indian Empire," when he was "exceedingly young": "Not a few of the scenes and incidents" presented in the novel, he claims, "came under my own personal observation" and are "still vivid in my memory" (v).[11]

Muddock's novel begins and ends in the metropole, as do many of these novels that roughly imitate Sir Walter Scott's definition of romance. In fact, Muddock underlines his literary debts to Scott by beginning in Scotland, describing how the innocent, pretty, and mawkishly sweet heroine, Hester Dellaby, meets the "singularly handsome" (1:31) young hero, Jack Hallet, on Princes Street in Edinburgh, and falls in love with him at first sight. In keeping with romance formulas, Hallet is described as physically attractive: he has a "patrician face, with clear, frank blue eyes, and a delicate chiselled nose" (1:31). Coming from a family that is "more than respectable," Hallet, in certain moods, reveals "the true soldierly nature, a nature stern, determined, defiant, unyielding, and full of courage and fire" (1:31). At twenty-five, he has "the vivacity of the boy, the laughter of the boy, the joyousness of the boy" (1:31), but he also displays a litany of soldier's virtues: he is "proud with the pride of independence; and brave he was with the courage and instinct of the true soldier; and reckless he was with all the recklessness of youth" (1:34).

What blocks the development of this love story on home grounds is Hester's controlling father, a retired civil servant who worked for the Old East India Company. Regarding his twenty-year-old daughter as too young to marry, Mr. Dellaby objects even more vehemently to the match when he learns that there was a "black page" in Hallet's past. During his college career at Oxford, Hallet had an "intrigue" with the proverbial farmer's daughter, promised marriage, and had to "pay over to the girl's friends a very liberal sum of money to hush the affair up" (1:23). One sign of the new gender prescriptions in circulation by the 1880s can be seen when the narrator describes Hester's accommodation to her lover's past. Hester, he notes, "had the good sense to understand that a young man could not be gauged and controlled by the same fixed standards by which a girl's conduct is judged" (1:38). The narrator continues, "the shrieking sisterhood, who talk glibly of 'woman's rights' will protest this doctrine, but, happily, they are in a very insignificant minority, and the generality of the fair sex, who prefer to remain women, will make no murmur" (1:38–39). In their last meeting in Edinburgh, Hester obligingly overlooks her lover's "peccadilloes," telling him she is "not so foolish to expect to find a saint in the incarnate garb of a man" (1:46), so she promises to trust Jack with her "life" and "woman's heart" (1:47).

Soon afterward, Muddock transfers his heroine to the proper territory for this impending military romance when Jack requests a transfer and Hester accepts her sister's invitation to visit her family in Meerut, where the Indian Mutiny officially began. Hearing Hester's profession of love, Jack declares that her "trust will keep me straight. It shall be my beacon star, and whatever my Fate may be, wherever I may wander, I will not be unmindful of what I owe to you first, and through you to myself" (1:47–48). After Mr. Dellaby violently separates the lovers, Jack sees his suit as hopeless and joins a regiment bound for the Middle East, where he hopes to "flesh his maiden sword in some benighted Persian" (1:90), but Jack's orders are changed and he is sent to India instead.

Upon their arrival in India, both lovers must learn to ask the basic question posed by romance: "Who is my enemy?" In Muddock's romance, as in Henty's, the answer is obvious and simple. Reading backward from his conservative historical sources, Muddock allows his most favored male characters to anticipate the coming colonial crisis and to distinguish enemies from friends along clear racial lines. Hester's brother-in-law professes confidence in the loyalty of the natives and laughs "scornfully" at the signs of possible danger, declaring that the "chapattis [*sic*] carried from village to village" have not the "slightest significance" (2:133). His commanding officer, Colonel Sandon, by contrast, "hates" the natives and predicts that the "whole country" will soon be ablaze. Sandon longs to avenge the death of his brother, who died during the mutiny at Vellore in 1806 (2:137), and the New Imperialism provides a convenient license. When an Indian civilian attacks Sandon, he kills the man and justifies himself by saying, "The English did not conquer India by the display of maudlin sympathy and rotten sentiment" (2:75).

The English and Anglo-Indian women in Muddock's romance generally fail to understand the dangers of colonial life. When Sandon hears about the mutineers, he declares that they should be hanged, while Hester thinks they should be jailed for a week. Women, however, are allowed to judge matters of the heart, for when Sandon declares he is in love with Hester, he proves he is a "gentleman" by accepting her refusal and giving her his friendship and protection instead.

The eruption of the mutiny allows Colonel Sandon to act out the dream logic that typically organizes these male romances, a logic which gives him the right to claim Hester eventually as his bride. Just before the rebellion begins in Meerut, Sandon reveals his own abduction fantasies when he tells

Hester that he has dreamed that "the natives had risen against us, and they were beleaguered in this place. My whole anxiety was about you. There was some desperate fighting, and I succeeded in cutting my way out, and carrying you off on horseback. In return for this you promised to become my wife" (2:54). Sandon's dream is quickly realized in the dream world called India in this text when Indian rebels attack the home of Hester and her sister, giving Sandon ample opportunity to kill uncounted "enemies" in order to protect Hester and her family. Sandon displays superhuman strength and courage in this battle because he knows that if Hester and her sister fall into "the hands of the rebels, they would meet a fate worse than death, while even the innocent children would be subjected to the most fiendish torture" (2:162). In other words, this contest is designed to reify Victorian sex and gender roles, for, as Sandon argues, "We want fighting men in India, not preachers of twaddle. This country must be ruled by soldiers, not old women" (1:263).

In keeping with these rigid gender prescriptions, all the enemies that Sandon overcomes in his battles are male and are clearly racial "others," so when Muddock introduces the anomalous Rani of Jhansi, the narrator must intervene to identify her unequivocally as the enemy. The narrator explains, "Amongst the high-caste natives throughout India no one had been more active in propagating sedition and inflaming the passions of the people than the Rannee of Jhansi, and the British had no more dangerous enemy than this remarkable woman" (1:219). Characterized in this novel as treacherous and cruel, Muddock's Rannee acts to keep the lovers apart by imprisoning Hallet, thus inadvertently helping to advance Sandon's suit with Hester. Already disposed to consider unconventional women as the enemy, Hallet recognizes the true nature of the Rannee shortly after he arrives in Jhansi, and he is outspoken in declaring that she has "heart of a devil" (2:192), though other soldiers in his company are deceived.

Confronted with the "facts" of British history, however, Muddock must recognize the Rannee as an important historical agent, so he describes her as animated by natural forces that are both unreflective and heartlessness. In Muddock's version of this history, the Rannee is obsessed with a "wild fantastic dream" of "freeing herself from the British yoke" (2:189), and she possesses the capacity to "murder and smile while she murdered" (2:190). Like Nana Sahib, she ruthlessly plans to destroy Hallet's company gathered at Jhansi. Having heard his insolent remarks about her, the Rannee decides to save Jack for a "bitterer death" (2:200) than the one she plans for the rest of the troops and has him brought to her quarters. Recognizing her for "the savage she was," as a "merciless, pitiless barbarian . . . thirsting for blood," Hallet draws his sword to kill her, but, outmaneuvered by history, he fails. The Rannee then declares she will cut his tongue out and will punish him in exactly the same way as were the nameless Englishwomen in James Grant's *First Love and Last Love*: "Every morning, so long as he shall live, let him be tied naked to the tail of a bullock cart, and scourged through the streets so that my faithful subjects may see that I know how to treat the enemies of my country" (2:208–209). After Hallet is imprisoned, however, he discovers that the bars of the window in his cell are loose, and he miraculously escapes, only to discover that he is too late to prevent the English who were sheltering at the fort at Jhansi from being killed. In Muddock's historical romance, the Rannee is directly responsible for this "butchery" since by her "order, not a man, not a woman, not a child was spared" (2:205).

Finally, Muddock's romance shows that its primary burden is to celebrate and mourn the death of boyish idealism, as is also evident in Henty's *In Times of Peril* when the heroine asks the hero not to grow up into a "great lumberin' man" but to "always remain as you are now" (354). After Hallet's escape, he begins his journey toward a more mature understanding of the hard facts of colonial life, as he wanders through the countryside until he finds Colonel Sandon's company. Shortly afterward he is mortally wounded by a sepoy and realizes "it was precious hard, after all he had gone through for Hester's dear sake, to die as it were on the threshold of her door. But no man can avoid his destiny" (2:243). Calling Sandon to his side, Hallet asks him to return Hester's portrait and tell her that his "last words were of her" (2:243). In this moment of extremity, Sandon is allowed to hold Hallet's hand until he dies. Later when Sandon tells Hester about Hallet's death, she feels that "Fate had been unduly cruel to her and him in bringing him through so many perils only to separate them for ever at last" (2:248).

By the end of Muddock's novel, Hester is saved from the fate of Kurtz's Intended in Conrad's *Heart of Darkness,* when, three years later, Sandon returns to Devonshire and asks her to marry him. Eschewing Marlow's fastidiousness, Sandon says, "Your face has been ever present before me. I have seen it through the cannon's smoke; and it has been like a vision of sweetness amidst the horrors of the battle-field. I have earned the right now to ask you to share the future with me" (2:257). Having recovered from her grief over the loss of her first love, Hester happily accepts. In other words, the conquest of the Rani of Jhansi, and the historical forces she represents, make Colonel Sandon's dream marriage possible.

Reimagining Race

Robert Armitage Sterndale's romance *The Afghan Knife*, published in 1879, presents a somewhat more complicated fantasy version of the Rani of Jhansi's role in the Indian Uprising of 1857 that reveals his liberal politics and greater linguistic and cultural familiarity with the diversity of Indian culture. The multiple frames that Sterndale provides for his story are one of several indications that this novel, like Conrad's more profound romances, is directed toward a more adult, though no less male, audience. The politics of black and white that characterized Muddock's vision of the mutiny are challenged throughout this novel by many characters who illustrate the hybridity and multiple allegiances of colonial life.

In Sterndale's *The Afghan Knife*, not all Indians are "enemies," and in dramatizing the difficult choices faced by Indian domestics, soldiers, and civil servants, Sterndale presents a tale that highlights the conflicting loyalties many experienced during the mutiny, a theme much more common in Anglo-Indian novels than in romances by metropolitan writers like Henty. Early in the novel, Sterndale demonstrates that neither race nor religion can be used as an infallible sign to predict the loyalty or disloyalty of Indian subjects when he describes how his heroine, Grace Lufton, nurses one of the Muslim servants in her household through an illness. Because of Grace's kindness, Hajii Sahib realizes, "He could not say to his heart, judge it as he might by written rule, that these were the enemies of his faith, against whom he might fight for the heavenly prize" (147). Hajii is secretly a member of the radical Wahabai sect, one of the infamous groups of Muslims that nineteenth-century histories identified as inciting the popular unrest that accompanied the Indian Mutiny, but he begins to question his participation in the conspiracy when he discovers that one of the leaders intends to take Grace Lufton as one of his wives. Hajii proves his loyalty when he subsequently helps to rescue Grace's father, and later both men work together to free her from Nana Sahib's control in order to reunite her with the novel's hero, Paul Stanford.

Sterndale's romance also dramatizes how gender further complicates religious identity as a predictor of disloyalty when he describes Grace's alliance with Fazilla, a beautiful Muslim woman, who is held captive, along with Grace, in the fort controlled by Indian insurgents. Fazilla articulates the basic enigma obscured by many other mutiny romances, when she tells Grace her history and concludes: "I have been torn away from my home and from my betrothed, for what reason I know not, and am kept here, for how long I know not. Who is my enemy, I cannot tell" (247). Shortly afterward, Fazilla

realizes that she faces the same threats that Grace confronts, the choice between "death and dishonour" (259), and she elects to join Grace in fleeing
from the rebel's stronghold. In other words, in the imaginary world of India
in Sterndale's romance, personal loyalty can override race and religion.

In *The Afghan Knife*, Sterndale not only contests the simple polarities
of enemy and friend presented in other mutiny romances like Henty's and
Muddock's, he also challenges the newly narrowed definition of the male hero
in them. Sterndale's hero, Paul Stanford, is not a career soldier but rather a
wealthy, cosmopolitan intellectual who aspires to become an artist, and he is
traveling in Italy to study painting when the novel opens. In Florence, Paul
meets and falls in love at first sight with Grace Lufton, a "slight and graceful" seventeen-year-old woman with a "small, beautifully rounded head and
oval face, a mass of auburn hair" and "irregular" features (51). In this beautiful city, Paul also meets a mysterious Muslim prince and asks him to sit for
a portrait, showing, as Sterndale's narrator notes, that Paul is free of "that
prejudice" against the Indians that, according to the Prince, is typical of the
English in India (58). In Sterndale's romance, the heroine's father encour-
ages rather than prohibits the heroine's romantic interest in the hero, since
he prefers that she marry an "intellectual" rather than a soldier (328), so it is
the mutiny rather than the obstructing father that operates to keep the lovers
apart.

In spinning out his plot, Sterndale further complicates the main question of romance, "Who is my enemy?" by allowing several Muslim characters to help the hero and heroine during the Uprising of 1857. After Paul
Stanford arrives in Calcutta and hears "fresh accounts of tragedy upon tragedy" (114), he volunteers for military service. On his journey up country to
join his company, he is saved from drowning by Abdul, an attractive young
Muslim man, who offers to fight along with the British when Stanford tells
him he will buy him a sword and horse. Sterndale calls attention to some of
the ways that Abdul challenges the narrowing sex and gender prescriptions
for British men evident in so many mutiny romances when he notes that
Abdul's face is "almost femininely soft, almost girlish," though there is a masculine "fire and animation in his eyes," "determination in the curves of his
mouth and chin," and virile strength in his "well-knit and athletic" physique
(205). Later, Abdul performs an essential service for the hero by passing un-
detected into the Rani's fort and discovering where Grace is imprisoned.

Sterndale's romance also challenges the conventional patterns of extreme race and gender segregation that characterize Henty's and Muddock's
adventures. In Sterndale's romance, both his heroine, Grace Lufton, and the

Rani of "Asalgurh" act with intelligence and self-direction, far beyond that shown by either Nelly Hargreaves in Henty's *In Times of Peril* or Hester Dellaby in *The Star of Fortune*. By bringing Grace Lufton to the fictionalized Indian kingdom of "Asalgurh," where her father is an acting judge, Sterndale creates an Indian world where he can exercise more latitude in appropriating details from various histories of the Rani of Jhansi's role during the uprising. When Judge Lufton tells Grace that they are in danger because of this unrest, she shows her "real character" when she bravely sets to work "to make a small bundle of her jewelry, her mother's miniature and diamonds, and Paul's picture of the Madonna" (168). As she loads her gun, she is compared to "Judith preparing to go forth to the camp of Holofernes" (168). One of the levers of Sterndale's plot, as a result, is the female competition between these two high caste women. When the Nawab Sahib offers the survivors of the English garrison safe passage and refuge in the Rani's fort, Grace proudly steels herself so the Rani can see "how the daughter of an Englishman could bear herself" (192). Once in the fort, Grace and her father are separated so that the Nawab Sahib can carry out his plan to persuade Grace to become his "white queen."

Though Sterndale identifies the Rani as responsible for the murder of the Englishwomen and children who were given refuge in her fort, he makes her appear less inhuman in several ways. Initially characterizing the "Rani of Asalgurh" as "a woman of about five-and-twenty, reputed to be of great beauty, indifferent moral character, and vast energy" (76), Sterndale later details her physical beauty, noting she had a "Grecian profile, her forehead was broad, her nose straight and well chiselled, her mouth small and chin well rounded" (103). Unlike Muddock, Sterndale also legitimizes the Rani's motives for resisting English domination when he explains that she is the "regent for a young son" (76) and indicates that she is prompted to join with other Indian leaders in their campaign against the British because she was angered and threatened by the exploitative policy of "lapse," that authorized their takeover of the government of Oude (103).

Although Sterndale ultimately conforms to the typical pattern in these romances when he identifies the Rani's "furious" sexual jealousy (249) as the cause of the breakdown of the alliance between the male leaders of the rebellion and herself, he makes her reaction more understandable by noting how the Nawab Sahib has dishonored her by arranging to shelter Grace in the Rani's own fort, without her permission. In contrast to Muddock, who portrays the Rani as prompted by diabolical wickedness to spare Jack Hallet only in order to exploit further her opportunity to torture him, Sterndale's

Rani rescues and treats kindly one young English soldier, Wigley, whom he describes, oddly enough, as a "fair-haired, pretty faced lad, one of those who make up in private theatricals as a very pretty girl" (250). Upon his release, Wigley, like Hugh Rose and his soldiers, becomes partly responsible for introducing an alternative version of the Rani's character into the historical record, since he always "declared throughout his after-life, that she was all that was good and kind to him, and he firmly believed that she was goaded on to the course she took by many injustices on the part of the British government" (307–308).

Finally, *The Afghan Knife* provides a powerful illustration of the "splitting" that Homi K. Bhabha claims is typical of colonial discourse when he divides Nana Sahib, one of the most famous Indian leaders of the Uprising of 1857, into two figures, one Hindu and one Muslim. It turns out that the mysterious Muslim prince that Paul met in Florence later takes over some of the political and military activities usually assigned to the rebel Hindu leader that the British called Nana Sahib. Moreover, Sterndale's Muslim prince is allowed to articulate an unusually sharp criticism of British colonial policies and economic assumptions, criticism nearly always excluded from these romances, when he tells Paul, "It is the old story, necessity hath no law; it was necessary for your ambitious views to absorb state after state, province after province, vows were pledged and broken, solemn treaties made and set aside; like the coils of a huge Python, the British power enfolded tract after tract of the fairest country, and what are we now, a nation of helots; the noblest prince among us subservient to the nod of any English stripling, who goes out, à la Clive, to make his fortune out of the gorgeous East" (57).

This splitting allows Sterndale to reassign the usual compelling desire to acquire the heroine as his "white queen" (257) to Paul's Westernized friend, the Muslim prince, Nawab Sahib. Though the Nawab Sahib later abducts Grace Lufton and keeps her in luxurious captivity in the Rani's fort, he is too much of a gentleman to rape her and tries, instead, to persuade her to accept marriage, by flattering her, saying, "He could find no companionship among the ignorant and debased daughters of his own race. For one such as he was, there should be a mate who could understand the loftiness of his aspirations. Let her think well over this, and decide between an ignominious death or slavery, and a brilliant destiny" (257).

While Muddock omits entirely any reference to the famous battles where the Rani displayed her courage and bravery in combat, Sterndale dramatizes one battle only, the one that ended the Rani's life. In Sterndale's romance, the Rani leads her troops into battle because she is enraged by the failure and cowardice of her male confederates. Sterndale invents an episode where the Rani offers a "petticoat and a shawl" to Nana Sahib and clinches the scene by declaring that "princesses of her race knew how to die, but not how to turn their backs on the foe" (305). However, in contrast to Rose's account, in Sterndale's novel the Rani disguises her gender by assuming a costume that makes her unrecognizable as a woman to the British troops. When the Rani rides into battle, she is dressed as a boy, and because of this masquerade, the Irishman who notices her "great skill" with her sword is able to kill her, unencumbered by chivalrous scruples about being "haunted" by the knowledge that he deliberately killed a woman. Later, considering the "fierce look on the rigid features, the clenched teeth and knitted brows," the trooper reconsiders his assumptions about gender and race when he says, "Who would have thought that little tigress had so much spirit in her?" (306–307).

In designing the conclusion of his romance, Sterndale emphasizes the reconciliation between the conqueror and the conquered rather than the demarcation of permanent, deep racial separations reified in Henty's and Muddock's romances. In *The Afghan Knife*, Englishwomen do not simply become the prizes for the most courageous military heroes, as in Henty's and Muddock's tales. While others arrange for Grace's rescue, Paul retains his hold on her heart. After the British forces complete their bloody campaign against the insurgents, Paul resigns from his company, and after he learns that he has inherited a "baronetcy" because his cousin has been killed at Cawnpore, he and Grace marry. Unlike the heroes and heroines in many other mutiny romances, Paul and Grace spend their honeymoon in Asalgurh, admiring "the Lalla Rookh Style" of this "thoroughly oriental retreat" (333), before they retire to England.

The final meeting between Judge Lufton and Hajii, his one-time servant, displays Sterndale's conciliatory politics, as well as the political reorganization after 1857 that brought the British conquerors into closer alliances with the Muslim elite whom they displaced. When Hajii kills one of his fellow insurgents with his "Afghan knife," and is condemned to die, Judge Lufton visits him in prison. When his old servant laments that Lufton is not "one of the chosen," the judge reassures him, saying, "We are both men of the Book. . . . We believe in the same God, have the same prophets, excepting that we choose Hazrut Isa, the spirit of God, as you yourselves call him, in preference to your Hazrut Mahommed" (386).

The epilogue of the novel further dramatizes the rich benefits of Sterndale's conciliatory plot when, years later, Grace's cousin, Fred Scamperby, meets the dying Nawab Sahib after a battle with the British in Turkey.

In this final episode, Sterndale identifies the Nawab as a "gallant" soldier (444) and explains the moral basis of his resistance to the British, when he notes that he joined the insurgents because of his loyalties to the King of Delhi. Declaring his undying love for Grace Lufton, the Nawab bequeaths her a string of pearls, sends Paul a diamond ring, and gives his sword to Fred, insisting that there was no blood of either "Englishwoman or child on it" since "it has been drawn against you, but always in a fair fight" (443). In other words, in Sterndale's novel, gender-specific codes of honor among upper-class Englishmen and aristocratic Muslims bridge other differences of race and culture.

Eroticizing the Rani as Racial Other

Both Muddock's and Sterndale's romances can be usefully contrasted with one of the most flamboyant colonial novels about the Rani of Jhansi, Hume Nisbet's *The Queen's Desire* (1893). Nisbet explicitly identifies his novel as a romance "in the most literal sense" (v) and asserts his dubious claims to authority in his descriptions of Indian colonial life by referring to his reading of G. B. Malleson's history of the Indian Mutiny, Meadows Taylor's *Confessions of a Thug*, and William Hockley Browne's *Pandurang Hugi* (*sic*). Nisbet claims that his reading is supplemented by his acquaintances with many Hindus and Buddhists whom he met while traveling in the East and while living for six years in Australia, when he was a young man (vi). Despite these claims of informed reporting, Nisbet slyly admits that his romance about the Rani of Jhansi may challenge his Anglo-Indian readers' preconceptions about the mutiny, noting with ironic understatement, "I fear many Anglo-Indians will not quite accept my version of this most awful tragedy" (v).

Certainly one of the most iconoclastic features of Nisbet's narrative is that he describes his hero, George Jackson, as a half-hearted renegade who is literally captivated by the Rani of Jhansi. By describing in detail the development of Jackson's illicit sexual relationship with the Rani and by opening up the possibility of male rape in this relationship, Nisbet reveals new complications in the basic question organizing these male romances, "Who is my enemy?" While he is in captivity, Jackson enjoys being tempted to join the Rani's rebel army, but when his military self-discipline eventually reasserts itself, he successfully persuades the Rani to release him. After he returns to his regiment, Jackson atones for his sexual and patriotic transgressions by killing the woman who was once his lover when he meets her on the battlefield.

Nisbet's novel begins by violating one of the most honored taboos of male mutiny romances when he describes off-duty English soldiers who do, indeed, exercise undisciplined power over the colonized, gratuitously beating Indian civilians and attempting to rape Indian women. In an unusual and vivid scene, Nisbet describes the "sport" of "wild" young English recruits "as they run amuck" through the streets of old Delhi: "Tommy Atkins and his friends are behaving like wild beasts to-night, as they run amuck through the moonlit streets, with their belts swinging round their heads and making ugly cuts where the buckle falls on the dodging skulls of Mahometan and Hindoo, upsetting the religious processions, chasing shrieking females into dark places, and hustling even the cavalcades of the maharajahs and princes who are going to the palace" (7–8). When these boisterous English "boys," who have "tasted too much of blood and rum to have any reverence left for king or priest" (9), meet a procession of native women who are carried in covered palanquins through the streets of Delhi, they display the violence that is almost always tactfully omitted in British and Anglo-Indian novels about the mutiny or about army life in India after 1857.

Far from protecting these defenseless Indian women, the English soldiers assume that the women are prostitutes and gleefully plan sexual assault. The women scream, cower, "huddle together," and try to keep their faces covered, but their effort is in vain, "for the ravishing hands are tearing the gauzy material to shreds as they drag them from their places and handle the dancers as only Tommy can handle when he is on the frolic and his spirits are up" (9). One woman in the group, who later proves to be the Rani of Jhansi, resists this attack and threatens the soldiers with a *tulwar* which looks "sharp and wicked" (9): "A striking figure she is in her rich nautch-dress with its flashing jewels and the gold-spangled gauze veil which floats about her on the night air; tall, lithe, rounded and youthful, with perfect symmetry of outline, and majestic even in her rapid motions, she does not speak a word as she stands in the centre of that admiring circle, who are men, even if rude ones, and cannot use their belts and buckles on such an adversary" (9–10). When one of the soldiers dives forward, declaring his intention to "have that woman in spite of her sword" (10), she decapitates him without a word. At this critical juncture, the hero of the novel, the handsome young Sergeant Jackson, intervenes to prevent the soldiers from raping or killing the Rani in retaliation. In gratitude, she offers Jackson a gorgeous jewel and promises that she will never forget him (11).

Although this carelessly violent act of self-defense reveals the Rani's cool aristocratic pride, romantic love soon reduces her to a more conventional posture. Unlike Muddock and Sterndale, Nisbet describes the Rani's experience of love in order to emphasize the commonalties she shares with Englishwomen rather than her racially or religiously defined differences. After Jackson learns that the Eastern beauty whom he saved is the Rani of Jhansi, he waits in the moonlight in the gardens of the Delhi Palace, hoping to see her again, displaying his "shapely figure" and his "semi-poetic and sentimental" looks to her unseen gaze:

> He was handsome in the truest and most manly sense of the term . . . a man who could talk gently and persuasively to the woman he loved, and yet rise up like a young lion in her defence when the need came, such a man as women, either pale-faced or tawny, would like to look upon and be flattered to hear love from, warm-blooded, powerfully-built, and with all the fascination of youth and strength, aided by a tight-fitting costume, which revealed the contour and sweep of the shapely limbs; a soldier, therefore the conqueror of weak woman, and in his most dangerous mood of waiting for an adventure, with the blue smoke eddying up from his lips and his eyes watching the floating circles dreamily. (34–35)

After the Rani appears and converses for a few minutes with him, she, like one of many heroines in the *Arabian Nights*, precipitously confesses that she is in love with him. What especially attracts her is Jackson's claim that he would not countenance his wife's flirtatiousness nor would he willingly "share" her with another man, as his commanding officers seem willing to do. Professing a more "Oriental view" of woman's place in marriage and outside it, Jackson asserts that he would keep his wife "to himself" and "take good care that no one else shared her" (37). In other words, Jackson's bourgeois view of the proper role of husband and wife is offered as a corrective to the decadent mores of his English social superiors in the days before the mutiny.

Hoping to see her unveiled, Jackson carefully calculates the progress of his seduction and professes, at just the right moment, to be in love with her, saying: "Can you doubt my desire, my queen, to be yours, and yours only, all the days of my life? for my heart is all your own—I love you" (38). Jackson's masterfulness and possessiveness, rather than any sincere expression of romantic love, prompt the Rani to declare, "Until to-night I hated your people with a bitter hatred, for they have wronged me deeply, so that blood alone can wipe out the insult" (38). Because Jackson has saved her life, she explains that in her eyes he is "no longer Faringhee, but blood of my blood," and she promises, "I will save you alone of all your race" (38).

Thus, romance, in both senses of the word, reshapes history when the

Rani conspires with Nana Sahib, the king of Delhi and his princes, and the Maulavi of Faizabad to kill all the British, though she declares her intention to save Sergeant Jackson. Soon after the mutiny erupts in Meerut, the Rani kidnaps Jackson and keeps him in an underground "paradise" which recalls the sumptuous underground retreats in *The Arabian Nights*. The apartment where the Rani confines Jackson "has been partitioned off as a bathing chamber, and lined with marble and mirrors for fully eighteen to twenty feet up, above which great open spaces yawned, by which the air entered cool and fresh" (177).[12] In detailing how Jackson accommodates himself to this life of love and leisure, Nisbet emphasizes Jackson's less exalted class position that apparently prompts him to consider the economic advantages of joining the "enemy." Unlike the heroes in other national epics and romances, George willingly surrenders the uniform that is a mark of his allegiance to the British cause, and when he is offered the English regimental dress of a captain, major, or general, he chooses instead to dress himself in a "very rich Oriental robe" (175). When the Rani offers Jackson the best French champagne, he asserts his middle-class male preferences for beer and brandy, and when she serves elegant Eastern repasts, he requests steak and potatoes (179).

Apparently immune to the class-defined sexual scruples that prevent British heroes from enjoying similar situations in other mutiny romances,[13] George Jackson submits cheerfully to his confinement and to the Rani's attentions and sexual desires. Unlike Englishwomen imprisoned in similar circumstances, he obligingly declares his love for the Rani, and, even though he has already pledged his heart earlier in the novel to an English sweetheart at Lucknow (184–185), he professes a desire to marry the Rani, "I am content with you, my Beauty, and shall be all my life, of course—for that is the English way" (211). Eventually, he begins to resent being "everlastingly pawed over" by the besotted Rani, even though "she was beautiful still in the Sergeant's eyes . . . when she posed and danced for his amusement" (208).

This is the point in Nisbet's novel where chivalry runs up against itself, when George Jackson recognizes that love and liberty are at odds, and when mutual seduction begins to reveal the threat of male heterosexual rape. After more than a month of "unwonted luxury and indulgence" (208), Jackson grows bored with the "infernal" monotony of his life underground. Tired of pretending that he liked love play "better than liberty and action" (209), Jackson becomes increasingly fearful of "the savage energy" of the Rani's lovemaking. Only then does Jackson begin to notice the stirring of conscience that recalls him to his military duty during the uprising.

Though Nisbet thus allows his hero to approach the threshold that separates mutual seduction from rape, he shows that his hero gains his release almost magically when he tells the Rani that his "manhood" is compromised by his failure to fight with his compatriots. Belatedly proving that his honor is above price, Jackson subsequently refuses all the Rani's bribes: "mohurs and ruppees by the lakh, with cut and uncut stones, besides rare pieces of jewellery, which fairly took away his breath" (212). No longer willing to consent to his seduction, Jackson easily obtains release when he says, "Listen, dear, . . . You are all that a man can wish for, when the trouble is over; but, to have you with this, and the drink galore, while the boys are starving and fighting for their lives, it ain't right; and—I must go to the front and take my chance with the others" (212–213). Why the Rani, who is otherwise characterized in this novel as an excellent battle strategist, would allow Jackson to return to his place in the British army rather than force him into the renegade's position by requiring that he join her own army, is never adequately addressed.

Nisbet covers this flight of fantasy by contending that the Rani's "Oriental" ideas about male heroism are "not very lofty," but his narrative reveals that this Oriental queen is finally, and improbably, defeated because she employs the same strategies in love that her "English" sisters use (207). Before the Rani agrees to release Jackson, she tries to set the terms of her sexual surrender, "All she asked from him was . . . to be the sole partner of his pleasures and keep him as her consort; it was her first real love affair, and she behaved herself much in the same way as one of her English sisters would have done, that is, she loved him intensely, yet did not intend to trust him altogether, like an inexperienced girl; she had been a wife once already, and that made all the difference" (207).

Despite the self-conscious and often ironic critique of Anglo-Indian hypocrisies about race and class that distinguishes *The Queen's Desire* from most male romances, it conforms with other romances in identifying gender as marking the great divide between colonizing men and all women, whether they are the colonizers or the colonized. When George is reunited with his countrymen, he describes his captivity in ways that conform to more patriotic romances, like Muddock's, which demonize the Rani; he says, vaguely, "A woman took me, a queen of somewhere got me into her clutches with some damned witchcraft, and kept me from my duty; but tell me, am I back in time to take my hand at fighting?" (236). When he recounts his adventures to the English ladies who have sought refuge with his company, Jackson censors his narrative further. Agreeing with his superior officer that the women "mightn't see it in the same delicate way that we men folks take it,"

Jackson "touches lightly" on the part about the Begum "for the sake of the ladies" (212).

Like many other mutiny romance writers, Nisbet denounces English efforts to convert Indians to Christianity and identifies evangelicalism as one of the contributing causes of the mutiny, but in *The Queen's Desire*, English ladies are its primary agents. Latitia Mortimer, the wife of one of the senior officers stationed at Meerut, has, for example, unwittingly contributed to the tensions between colonizer and colonized because of her "indefatigable attempts to convert the Hindoos and Mahomedans from their polygamous ways" (121). It is another evangelizing Englishwoman, Mrs. Eugenie Finch, who shows her true colors as the real "enemy" in this romance. Though she is similarly preoccupied with the "vapourings of religious mania," Mrs. Finch proves to be one of the most "dangerous sirens" (32) in British India because she uses her skills to trap an endless supply of men, married and otherwise. Like Kipling's Mrs. Hauksbee and Thackeray's Becky Sharpe, Mrs. Finch's real sin is that she behaves like a stereotypical Oriental potentate, ruling over "an orderly and well-conducted Zenana" (100) of men. In this way, Nisbet ironically explodes his culture's favorite myths about the disinterested self-sacrifice of Englishwomen during the mutiny.

In the final pages of this novel, George Jackson literalizes the undercurrent of misogyny evident in all these novels when war provides the opportunity for him to kill his former lover. When he meets the Rani of Jhansi in battle during the siege of Gwalior, Jackson does not recognize her because her face is hidden behind a "chain visor, her head covered with a golden helmet crowned with blazing jewels,"and her body is covered with "chain armor" (305). Coveting the golden ornaments that she wears, Jackson plunges his sword into her body, wounding her fatally. The Rani maintains consciousness just long enough to tell him that she was his "first wife": "She who . . . gave you her heart to split" (306). Like countless other Oriental women in these romances, the Rani, with her dying breath, thanks her "husband" for killing her since "all good husbands give this last favour to those they love best" (306), though Jackson is unmoved by this revelation. In converting the Rani's heroic sacrifice for the cause of Indian nationalism into this implausible love sacrifice, Nisbet reduces the Rani to fit the narrower gender conventions that prevail in these male romances, although he also acknowledges some of the powers that Hindu nationalists recognized in extraordinary women like the Rani.

Having killed the Rani and proven his bravery in battle, Jackson is promoted to captain and becomes financially able to marry his English sweetheart, Maggie Wilson, when he, along with Havelock's forces, arrives during the first relief of Lucknow. In dramatizing the reunion of his hero with his English sweetheart, Nisbet wickedly pokes fun at the ostensibly "chaste" morality of other British heroes by underscoring Jackson's sexual hypocrisy. He notes that "this accommodating hero felt no qualm or compunction about clasping that golden-haired girl to his heart . . . as if no word as inconstancy was to be found in the dictionary" (254). Their marriage, a few months later, is described, playfully, as a "grand sacrifice" for the hero (288), thus proving that the sacrifice that matters most in Nisbet's text is, apparently, the hero's sexual "liberty."

Nisbet's novel illustrates the effects of colonial splitting not only in his double-dealing treatment of the Rani, Mrs. Finch, and Maggie Wilson but also in his iconoclastic summary of the events at Cawnpore and his unusual treatment of Nana Sahib. Though Nisbet admits that "the terrible sufferings of these English ladies will never be known," he recognizes that English soldiers were equally brutal in their retaliation against the insurgents (144, 166–167). Likewise, in relating the events at Delhi, he asserts that British women caught up in this crisis were not universally heroic. "Mayhap one or two yielded under the terrorism of their conquerors and entered the zenanas; if so their record is lost, they may still be alive or their children, but the privacy of the Mohommedan's household is respected throughout India, and there has been no supervision, which perhaps is as well for the victims, if any, who yielded to purchase life on such conditions" (227).

Finally, having identified the Rani of Jhansi as the most powerful conspirator in the mutiny, and designated dominating women like her as the real "enemy" in his romance, Nisbet no longer needs to demonize Nana Sahib. In dramatic contrast to most Anglo-Indian epics of the race or to romances about the mutiny, Nisbet concludes his novel by disputing the conventional description of Nana Sahib as the chief villain of the Indian Uprising, presenting him instead as fired by pure Hindu nationalism. Discrediting the theory that Nana Sahib was driven to rebellion by his lust for Englishwomen, Nisbet insists instead that this leader was no "sybarite but rather a Brahmin of the highest caste; beef and wines were abominations in his eyes" (141). Already possessing a zenana that was "pretty well filled" with "many sealed wives appointed to him throughout the land" (142), he gave his favorite wife "no cause for jealousy" (142) and doted on their daughter. Though Nana Sahib joins Azim-Ullah (*sic*), Tantia Topi (*sic*), the Begum of Oude, and the Rani of Jhansi in planning the early stages of military campaign against the British, he simply loses interest in the rebellion and turns his attention to the ritual worship of Shiva and Kali (249).

Exploiting the mystery of Nana Sahib's final disappearance, Nisbet takes issue with most English histories and romances of the time, by inviting sympathy for the "butcher" of Cawnpore. Characterized as an impulsive patriot rather than a treacherous plotter, Nisbet's Nana Sahib orders the massacre at Cawnpore in a fit of pique which could have been prevented by better diplomacy on the part of the British. In imagining Nana Sahib's final days, as he flees from the vengeful British into the foothills of the Himalayas with his favorite wife and their daughter, Nisbet reasserts one of the most persistent conventions of Orientalist discourse when Nana Sahib's wife asks him to "raise up my pyre. . . . and let me die like a royal daughter of India" (309). Obligingly, though he is himself near death, Nana Sahib gathers wood for the pyre so that his wife and daughter may die before him.

It is hard to know whether it is Nisbet's ambivalent treatment of the Rani of Jhansi, his equivocations about the heroism of British women during the mutiny, or the cultural relativism he shows when he compares Nana Sahib with English "heroes" like Oliver Cromwell (166) that prompted Hilda Gregg, once a well-known Anglo-Indian writer, to criticize Nisbet for his "want of patriotism" (24). At any rate, Nisbet's *The Queen's Desire* clearly shows the double binds created when the sexual agency and desire of both colonized and colonizing women is recognized in these male romances.

The Rani of Jhansi Imagined Otherwise

All these male romances about the Indian Uprising of 1857 suggest various reasons why British and Anglo-Indian novelists preferred to write romances rather than more serious national epics. At the same time, they show, however inadvertently, that gender could work alone or in conjunction with religion or class to challenge the basis of British racial solidarity during and after the mutiny. Anglo-Indian romances in particular illustrate the psychological "splitting" that was generated by life in the colonial contact zone as well as by the infinite self-division engendered by the extreme ethics of individualism under the regime of monopolistic capitalism during this period.

In designing various imaginary solutions to the contradictions posed by the Rani of Jhansi in British accounts of the Indian Uprising of 1857, Anglo-Indian historical romances typically attempted to obscure these conflicts by discrediting the Rani's virtue or by disguising her gender, describing how she entered battle "dressed as a boy." In other words, these romances tried to prove that such heroism is actually an exclusive male (and usually British) attribute. Yet this gendered version of colonial history leaves a gap, leaves something to be desired, which even these "tales of wild adventures in love and chivalry" admit when they represent the Rani of Jhansi and women like her.

In the end, these historical romances about the Indian Uprising of 1857 reveal paradoxes beyond those that arise from their extravagant use of coincidence, which puts them at odds with more authoritative British historical narratives about the mutiny. When they are read alongside various British histories of the mutiny, these male romances recognize desires unmet by these historical records, for as Trinh Minh-ha has argued, when history "separated itself from story," and "started indulging in accumulation and facts," it began to imagine the past as "lying there in its entirety, waiting to be revealed and related." When mutiny historians repudiated the "magical (not factual) quality—inherited undoubtedly from 'primitive' storytelling—for the Past perceived as such is a well-organized past whose organization is already given," they simultaneously created the demand, and perhaps the psychological need, for these romances.[14]

One thing that these, and many other, historical novels about the mutiny try to deny is the powerful desire for independence that animated the Rani and prompted so many to sacrifice themselves to this cause. The traces of these dignified motives for resistance and sacrifice reappear in many "oral" Indian versions of the Rani's history like the following:

> We have to die one day, brother, and I shall choose today
> For our queen I shall lay down my life.
> I shall hack the Firinghi with my sword
> And the world will forever remember me![15]

The feminine power that is celebrated in these oral histories is allied with those powers that British histories and historical romances about the mutiny worked so relentlessly to discipline and contain. Even Nisbet's iconoclastic hero, George Jackson, realizes he must censor the Rani's story in order to diminish the power of her speech, her dance, and her "storytelling," for her narrative contained "at once magic, sorcery, and religion. It enchants. It animates, sets into motion, and rouses the forces that lie dormant in things, in beings" (Trinh, 129).

In many oral Indian versions of the Rani's history, these magical and animating powers are recognized and enumerated. In one poem, for example, the Rani's power to transform is specifically described:

> From clay and stones
> She molded her army.

From mere wood
She made swords.
And the mountain she transformed into a steed.
Thus she marched to Gwalior! (Joshi 278)

Failing to defeat this powerful conjunction of female energy and Indian nationalism, Anglo-Indian romances had to be written, and read, over and over again.

With the advantages of hindsight, we can see how, and perhaps why, these paradoxical British and Anglo-Indian male romances could not completely perform the ideological work that they assumed, for of all the hierarchies they tried to shore up, the gender hierarchies challenged by the Rani's history were perhaps the most difficult to defend and sustain.

Your name, Rani Lakshmibai, is so sacred
We remember it in the early hours of dawn,
The name of a woman worthy of retelling,
The name of a woman worthy of being followed by all . . .
Your image shall be in our minds forever,
Your legend repeated everywhere
Your memory fresh in mind eternally
Your ideals practiced by all for all time to come.[16]

Despite the closure that these male romance would impose on the history of the Uprising of 1857, despite the narratives about the Rani's death and all the little "deaths" of the Anglo-Indian marriages in these novels, the Rani evokes larger possibilities. Once the Rani's power was recognized and described, it could not be entirely erased because "once told, the story is bound to circulate; humanized, it may have a temporary end, but its effects linger on and its end is never truly an end" (Trinh, 133).

Finally, when we view these romances about the Rani of Jhansi in the "the mirror of representation," we can see how they reflect other colonial desires that Homi K. Bhabha has enumerated. The romances written in the 1890s reveal the Rani as colonialism's "uncanny 'double,'" because she is shadowed by her English sisters in these texts, and both "reveal things so profoundly familiar to the West that it cannot bear to remember them" ("Representation," 120). In the end, these male romances disclose the impossible consequences of the new restrictions on British male identity that were forged in the 1880s, when concepts of maleness depended upon the denial of female agency and the resistance to women's political and sexual desires. When these scripts about male power and identity were rewritten under the colonial regimes of the British Raj, when the surrender to sexual delight was redefined as a renegade pleasure and the color bar was raised so high that even Indian princesses were redefined as "abject," romance writers found themselves in an imaginary cul-de-sac where violence became the only measure of male enjoyment. Under these circumstances, the revenge of the repressed finds inevitable expression in the parallel fantasies about the abduction and rape of Englishwomen by Indian men, fantasies that underlie so many colonial romances about the mutiny.

CHAPTER 5

Lost Children

NATIONALISM AND THE REINSCRIPTION
OF THE GENDERED BODY

*Here then power is associated with the discourses that surround
the body and create "sex" and sexuality.*
Vikki Bell[1]

*I*n the 1890s, narratives about English
children lost to their colonial families and communities began to emerge as
a major theme in Anglo-Indian fiction, Kipling's *Kim* (1902) being certainly
the most famous example. Many of the cultural and psychological anxieties
that find expression in Kipling's *Kim* become more visible when this novel
is read in the context of two other Anglo-Indian novels, written in the same
fifteen-year period, about English children who were lost during the Indian
Uprising of 1857: Sara Jeannette Duncan's *The Story of Sonny Sahib* (1895)
and Philip Lawrence Oliphant's *Maya: A Tale of East and West* (1908). Since
it also focuses on an English child lost during the Indian Uprising of 1857,
Rabindranath Tagore's *Gora* (1910) provides an alternative version of this
story, but it charts a very different trajectory for an English child adopted by
Indian parents.[2] The novels in this chapter reveal why colonial anxieties concerning interracial rape found expression in narratives about English children lost during the Indian Uprising of 1857, and show how colonial fears
about identity, sex, reproduction, and miscegenation were amplified in the
1890s, when novelists imagined children who were temporarily assigned to
that intolerable space where mixed-race children were forced to live, in the
world between the colonizers and the colonized.

Interracial rape was most threatening to the foundations of nineteenth-
century colonial societies when the rape victim gave birth to a "mixed race

child," resulting in what colonial law defined as "illegal reproduction," as Pamela Scully has shown in her brilliant analysis of rape cases in Cape Colony South Africa between 1831 to 1865.[3] Since there is, to my knowledge, no comparable archival study of rape cases in British India, either for the earlier period that Scully surveys or for the postmutiny period, the following analysis of novels about lost children provides another perspective on the same colonial anxieties about race, class, gender, and sex. All of these novels consider the abjection produced by the favorite rape script of the period by imagining the life of an English child who is temporarily assigned to the place of a mixed-race child who is the product of interracial rape.

Drawing from her review of records of actual rape trials in South Africa, Scully concludes that the legal actions taken concerning interracial rape reveal how fixed notions of "race" challenged two other hierarchies that were central to the maintenance of colonial order: class hierarchies, on one hand, and gender subordination, on the other. Scully analyzes, for example, the case of Annie Stimpson, a married and seemingly "white" woman who reported in 1850 that she had been raped by one of her husband's employees. The rapist was tried, subsequently confessed, and was convicted, but when the English magistrate in charge of the case discovered that Stimpson was "coloured" rather than a woman of "pure" white heritage, he reduced the punishment for her rapist from death to a term of imprisonment with hard labor. Scully concludes from this and other cases in her study that "when race, class, sexuality, and gender were put up against one another, a woman's sexuality was determined by her 'race'; class and culture could not rescue her" (358). Scully's analysis suggests, ultimately, why race, as a biological given, could not adequately close the question "as to whether cultural practice alone could bring a person into the fold of European civilization," especially after mid-century, when "racial categorization based on the inevitability of biology became increasingly hegemonic in the British Empire and elsewhere" (359).

Most Anglo-Indian novels about lost children that were written between 1895 and 1910 present them as born during the Indian Uprising of 1857, when the children's fathers are honorably absent, and describe how these children, after losing the protection of their mothers, are subsequently adopted by Indian families who care for them for several years. Kipling's *Kim* differs in this respect from the other three novels discussed in this chapter because Kim is orphaned approximately thirty years after the Uprising of 1857. Kipling recalls the mutiny, nonetheless, by including an interpolated narrative offered by old Indian soldier who recalls his experiences during the mutiny. Echoing colonial narratives concerning Indian soldiers and servants who remained "true to their salt," he tells Kim, "In those days I rode seventy miles with an English mem-sahib and her babe on my saddle-bow. . . . I placed them in safety, and back came I to my officer—the one that was not killed of our five. 'Give me work,' I said, 'for I am an outcaste among my own kin, and my cousin's blood is wet on my sabre'" (47). In recognition of his loyalty, the soldier explains that he was awarded the land that he has since held, given as a "free gift," he says, "to me and mine" (48). What the old soldier's story encodes, then, is Kipling's defense of the Raj, for it signals his approval of the compact between the British and a new class of Indian landholders created in 1858 when they were awarded land confiscated from supposedly "disloyal" natives.[4]

Though Philip Oliphant's novel *Maya* is set fifteen years after the Uprising of 1857, it also includes a short narrative about it, inserted when an experienced soldier instructs the handsome hero, Francis D'Aguilar, about the significance of an historical event he is too young to remember. This mutiny story, however, contains something new: the soldier tells D'Aguilar, "You can't remember the Mutiny days; I can't forget them. My God! D'Aguilar, only those of us who went through it know what stuff our women are made of. But there are a few—a very few—whose courage failed them at the pinch, or who lacked the means of escape by death. They are behind the walls of the zenana to this day, and no power on earth would induce them to face the shame of it and come out. They prefer to stay where they are, and pray God that they may be forgotten" (235–236). Oliphant's brief narrative about the mutiny thus expresses growing suspicions about female sexuality that began to gather around the colonial mother and her children in the 1890s, suspicions which are displaced in these novels by projecting them backward onto the events of the mutiny, forty to fifty years in the past.

The novels of Oliphant, Duncan, and Tagore all demonstrate how the mutiny provided a convenient plot device to explain the honorable absence of the lost child's father, who is forced to leave his pregnant wife when he is mobilized or volunteers to fight during this colonial emergency. In Duncan's and Tagore's texts, as in *Kim*, the colonial mother dies soon after giving birth to a son who is then sheltered in an Indian home and subsequently lost to the English community. Written at a time when so many mutiny novels idealized suicide as the English heroine's best method of preserving her "honor," these novelists kill off the colonial mother in order to avoid describing the impossible moral dilemmas that she would face if she were forced to choose between protecting her reputation for racial purity by killing herself or protecting her child by surviving. This double bind was further heightened by the ferocious judgments expressed, for example, by the old soldier in *Maya*, who excoriates any Englishwoman who allowed herself to be raped or forced into concubinage and compelled, by these same survival instincts, to deliver and nurture mixed-race children. In contrast to *Kim*, *The Story of Sonny Sahib*, and *Gora*, Oliphant's *Maya* represents the dangerous compromises made by just such a colonial mother who seeks refuge in the home of an Indian man, who was categorically defined by his race and gender as a sexual predator. *Maya* thus tells the often-suppressed story of a colonial mother who elected to tolerate life in the Indian zenana for her daughter's sake.

Read as a group, these novels about lost children display the unease that began to collect not only around the colonial mother's body but also around the body of the colonial child who was raised in British India in the 1880s or later, when colonial ideologies began to rely upon increasingly blunt assertions of the racial superiority of British colonizers as part of the defense of empire. In focusing on lost colonial children, these novels expose, first of all, some of the contradictions inherent in claims that the colonial child's "white" body was already indelibly marked by its racial superiority since these stories all admit that colonial children need to be nurtured by a properly English family and by a rigorous, disciplining education, preferably acquired in England rather than India, in order to appreciate the full significance of their "race." These novels also call attention to unacknowledged contradictions in colonial child-rearing practices since an Indian ayah or nurse, rather than an English mother, typically assumed the mundane tasks of tending to the young child's bodily needs, creating the necessity for the colonial child's linguistic and emotional re-education.

Second, although the Anglo-Indian novels in this group do not directly question the meanings assigned to "whiteness," they do recognize that neither the mastery of the English language nor the profession of a secure faith in Christianity provides adequate or secure signs of racial superiority. Since the children in these texts have been lost to their English parents, they live outside the cultural networks that teach them to read the meaning of their physical appearance, bodily processes, skin color, desires, and aversions according to the proper colonial script. These novels thus acknowledge the linguistic and cultural pathways that must be laid down in the psychic space inside the lost child, connecting him or her with British colonial values and, ultimately, with the "mother country." As such, they admit that proficiency in the English language could not be used as a reliable sign of national identity, or even loyalty, since such mastery of English was increasingly displayed by the colonized as well as the colonizers.[5] Philip Oliphant's *Maya* offers an important variation on this theme, for although Maya's mother survives the mutiny, albeit only for a few years, she fails entirely to establish her daughter's identity as a colonizing woman either by teaching her English or by offering her religious instruction that establishes a basic understanding of the principles of the Christian faith. Maya's example raises questions, then, about why Oliphant allowed the colonial mother to survive since she has so little permanent influence on her daughter's racial and national identity. Tagore's *Gora* identifies other challenges to race as a meaningful colonial category by dramatizing the life of a "white" child who learns to see himself as an high-caste, orthodox Hindu and later as an Indian nationalist.

Third, all these novels focus on the definitive moment when the lost "British" child, with its improperly inscribed body, approaches the age when it will act on the meaning of its gender and sexual desires. The Anglo-Indian novels in this group inadvertently expose contradictions that arose when colonizers relied upon Social Darwinist defenses of racial superiority that sometimes conflicted with late Victorian gender hierarchies. These novels recognize that the child-rearing practices which prevailed in British India could not only implant alternative meanings of "race" but could also foster multiracial desires.[6] The novels of Kipling, Duncan, and Oliphant all defend themselves against this knowledge by asserting, in their various ways, the spontaneous emergence of "innate" gender-specific signs of "English" identity in their heroes. Kipling's and Duncan's texts describe heroes who recognize their intellectual and/or physical superiority as a consequence of their gender when they compare themselves with their male Indian playmates. Philip Oliphant's *Maya*, the only novel I have found about a girl who is lost during the mutiny, makes this incongruity central to its plot because it shows that the seemingly inherent racial qualities of leadership, decisiveness, and loyalty do not emerge spontaneously in the case of a lost English girl, though Maya somehow still discovers a "pride" of womanhood that is characterized as racially specific. Before Maya can return to her assigned place in British India, however, her body and soul must be subjected to all the disciplines that create the distinctive gender differences that define the English colonial woman. Oliphant's novel shows with particular clarity, then, how Anglo-Indian authors were caught between the desire to assert the naturalness of racial identity and the need to maintain Victorian gender stereotypes.

Finally, novels about lost children show that "there is nothing natural or ahistorical about these modes of corporeal inscription" (Grosz, *Volatile*, 142) that install the meanings attached to race and gender that were essential to the colonial order in British India. Thus, while Anglo-Indian novels about lost children present the "white" body as a contested sign of the colonizing man's or woman's racial affiliation, they reluctantly reveal, at the same time, the contradictions evident in colonial practices that typically prescribed very different educations for colonial girls in contrast to boys. While these novels about lost colonial children employ various strategies to hide their inconsistencies, they shadow forth the fears that transformed the mixed-race child into a figure of abjection.

Creating the Body of a Sahib

Kipling's *Kim*, the most familiar novel about a lost English child, demonstrates the crisis in the colonial processes which apply "racial" significance to the child's body. Unlike most colonial children who are described as blond with very fair skin, Kim's skin, hair, and body present uncertain signs of his race. In the colonial world of British India, so dramatically divided by race, Kim's body, marked as it is by his poverty, produces uncertainty about his biological heritage and, as a consequence, his future place in the colonial order. Kipling begins by recognizing this incongruity, noting that Kim's "skin was burned black as any native" (49) but insisting that he was "a poor white of the very poorest" (49).[7] Initially, then, Kim's skin color allows him to pass easily for an Indian child, since he also knows what to wear and how to imitate the outward gestures that allow him to pass as a Hindu or Muslim, though he is restricted to imitating those indigenous children who were in public view: children unprotected by their families, street beggars, orphans, the outcast, the abandoned. Kim's recovery, education, and subsequent career in the Great Game reveals, of course, how, as a "sahib and son of a sahib," Kim's race and gender override his class identity and save him from the suffering experienced by the abandoned and often mixed-race children who serve as his models.

Because the human body is not marked with self-evident signs of race, gender, sexuality, or class, a large array of forces must inscribe the child's body with meanings that gradually become legible to the child, as Elizabeth Grosz has eloquently argued. Noting that the "child's body and its bodily experiences are not simply the product of its own endogenous sensations and its various experiments with its bodily capacities" (*Volatile*, 75), Grosz argues, instead, that the child's body is born into a world where the culture's fantasies of difference must be "etched" onto it. The child's body thus acts as "a screen onto which the mother's—and the culture's—desires, wishes, fears, and hopes are projected and internalized" (75). Grosz outlines both "involuntary" means whereby the body is assigned to "socially significant groups—male and female, black and white," as well as more "voluntary" means, evident in "life-styles, habits, and behaviors," including diet, clothing, and adornment. As a motherless child, who is fed but otherwise not much supervised by the "half-caste" Indian woman his father lives with, Kim demonstrates the potential dangers of a child who is not properly taught the meaning of his race.

The inscrutability of Kim's skin and body is most dramatically displayed when he is caught by the Reverend Arthur Bennett as he tries to escape from the military encampment where he has been lured by the prophetic magic of the regimental emblem of the red bull on the green field. Bennett is unable to read the ambivalent signs of Kim's racial identity, and so he summons the Catholic chaplain, Father Victor, to help him interpret the meaning of this child's enigmatic body. Because Bennett initially thinks that Kim is a thief, he assumes he is a native. When Father Victor opens Kim's shirt to expose his untanned, though dirty, skin, he observes "he's not very black" (134). This visual evidence, however, is not enough to convince either the English- or Irishman of Kim's race.

Neither Reverend Bennett nor Father Victor is convinced that Kim is "white," then, until they have both consulted the three documents he wears around his neck. Considered separately, none of these documents provides unequivocal proof of Kim's race. They first inspect his father's membership certificate as a Mason, but, as Kipling himself notes in his autobiography, the Masonic Lodge in Lahore admitted educated, middle-class Indians as well as Englishmen, so this evidence of affiliation acknowledges that class can sometimes override race even in British India. They look second at O'Hara's clearance certificate, documenting that he had been honorably discharged from the British Indian Army, but participation in the army did not provide unambiguous proof of race either since the army, of course, included Indians as well as British recruits, though the document itself would have indicated O'Hara's race. Finally, they survey Kim's baptismal certificate, which proves Kim's legitimacy if not, conclusively, his race since his mother could have been an Indian Christian. It is Father Victor's recollection of seeing Kim's father marry the English nursemaid, Annie Shott, that provides the most persuasive evidence in establishing Kim's biological identity as Anglo-Irish, and thus, in the context of British India at least, he is proven to be "white."

The significance of Kim's Irish heritage is still read differently by the Anglican and Catholic chaplains, and the future each projects for Kim reflects each man's class and cultural allegiances. Bennett concludes that Kim is from an inferior class and, being Irish, something of an embarrassment to upper-class Englishmen, so he would send Kim to an orphanage to be disciplined and trained for the army.[8] Father Victor imagines a more expansive future for Kim, though he, too, insists that because he is a "soldier's son," Kim must become "as good a man as your—as good a man as can be" (138), tactfully omitting a reference to the dubious morality of Kim's biological father. At this point in the narrative, Kim has yet to assent to the colonizers' legalistic view of the significance and value of his "whiteness." Kim mocks Bennett, for example, for his literal mindedness when he tells the lama in a language that Bennett doesn't understand: "He thinks that once a Sahib is always a Sahib" (136). In short, Kim's words as well as his body challenge simple certainties about the biological, racial, and moral inheritance that both Bennett and Victor assume.

In spite of the colonizers' claims about the indelible meaning attached to whiteness, Kipling's novel shows that Kim must be schooled to understand the full implications of being a "sahib and son of a sahib" in British India. As Sara Sulieri has convincingly argued, Kim's identity as a "sahib" must be installed by his schooling at St. Xavier's, a discipline that includes the narrowing of his desires to the proper objects of knowledge and power (124–131). Once Kim passes through the "gates of learning," he cannot turn back; for at St. Xavier's he learns that the "psychic price demanded by a repression of colonial desire" is the "necessary denial of intimacy" with colonized men and women (124). Ironically, the lama, the man who loves Kim most, pays for him to learn this insidious calibration of desire.

One of the essential transformations that Kim's education produces is his increased fluency and less distinctly Indian accent in his spoken English. While most Anglo-Indian novels represent grotesquely exaggerated differences between the spoken English of the colonizers and the colonized, Kipling initially defies this convention by admitting that Kim's mastery of English does not provide a reliable index of his race. Kim, Kipling writes, "spoke the vernacular by preference, and his mother-tongue in a clipped uncertain sing-song" (49). Though Kim possesses a multilingual fluency that he has acquired by living as a "friend of all the world," his "uncertain English" initially undermines his espoused racial and national identity as a "sahib and son of a sahib." Kim's accented and imperfect English, like that of most colonial children, thus demonstrates the dangers of using English fluency as the primary sign of ethnic identity and national affiliation at a time when more and more Indian intellectuals could display comparable proficiencies. Although Kim's English is, at first, demonstratively inferior to that of Westernized Indian intellectuals like Hurree Mukerjee, his subsequent verbal skill is inexplicably offered as evidence that Kim is linguistically, and so somehow racially, superior to Mukerjee, who is made to betray his grotesque hybridity by his frequent malaprops and florid syntax later in the novel.

Kim shows clearly that language is instrumental in making flesh into "a particular type of body," but the novel mystifies rather than illuminates how Kim's adolescent body is gendered and taught to recognize the pleasures and prohibitions of sexual desire in this particular colonial world. One reason for this void may perhaps be located in an ideological crisis outside the text, since in the 1890s in Great Britain, Europe, and the United States, new ideas about sexual identity, sexual variation, and Freudian psychology began to undermine the presumed fixity of gender identity. At any rate, there is a curious absence inside Kipling's text which suggests why lost children like Kim served to identify particularly vulnerable sites in the processes designed to implant the colonial child's gender and sexual identity. Elizabeth Grosz describes the mother's fundamental role in transcribing cultural desires onto the body of the child, establishing the child's body image and responsiveness to desire. Grosz's model suggests several reasons why Kipling avoids any direct exploration of Kim's emerging sexual identity:

> The biological processes or instincts seem to provide the ground or preconditions for the emergence of sexual impulses, but they must not be too closely identified with them: without these biological processes tracing a path through the body, the raw materials for sexuality would not exist. But these biological processes were not enough. What must be added to them is a set of meanings, a network of desires which, in the first instance, emanate from and are transmitted by the mother or nurturer. These desires and significances impose a set of (pliable and usually inarticulable) meanings on the child's bodily processes. In this sense, it is not surprising that in the case of so-called wild children, children raised outside the constraints and significances, there is neither sexual drive nor language. (*Volatile*, 55)

Because Kim's body has not been inscribed in this way, he is a particularly dangerous candidate for the sexual border crossings required of secret agents in the Great Game.

Although Kipling avoids representing Kim's sexual awakening, he does call attention to clothing and the ways that it hides the body and shapes its desires, even though this theme challenges assertions that the colonial child's racial identity is self-evident and secure. Once Kim is securely "caught" by

Father Victor and housed in the regiment, gender-laden English values begin to force themselves upon him from the outside. When he puts on the red drummer's uniform, he feels the first pressures of colonialism chaffing against his skin and recognizes how "trousers and jacket crippled body and mind alike" (154). By the time he has completed his first term at St. Xavier's, however, Kim is more comfortable in the summer "white drill" uniform of the school. Having earned greater freedom by learning to speak and write "proper" English, and having submitted to the discipline of St. Xavier in exchange for the anticipated pleasure of "commanding" the natives, Kim is ready to begin his apprenticeship as a double-agent in cross-cultural passing.

Gail Ching-Liang Low has argued persuasively that Kim's cross-cultural masquerade offers a key to the political meaning of Kipling's novel. Countering more sentimental or more postmodern estimations of the revolutionary potential of Kim's various acts of "passing," Low observes that in *Kim* "the primary attraction of the cross-cultural dress is, then, the promise of 'transgressive' pleasure without the penalties of actual change. Such metamorphosis does little to subvert existing hierarchies, since the cross-dresser may always reveal or revert to the white identity underneath the native clothes" (93).[9] While I agree that Kim's cross-cultural dressing reveals the pleasure he takes in claiming the powers of the colonizer in British India, I would also note that *Kim* is remarkable for its failure to display the heterosexual "release of libidinal energy which accompanies cross-dressing" (93). It is also important to recognize that nowhere in the text is Kim represented as crossdressing in the usual sense, by assuming the clothing of an Indian woman, though the customs of veiling would make it one of the easiest disguises to wear. This unnamed prohibition against transvestism thus reveals the prevailing homosocial structure of desire in British India. Moreover, if, as Foucault argues, the body bears the inscriptions of the circuits of power, knowledge, and desire, then Kim demonstrates a significant absence of erotic heterosexual desire, even in those few arenas where it was allowed expression under the Raj. What Kim's successful and repeated acts of cross-cultural masquerade dramatize, most of all, then, is the deformation of desire under a colonial regime where the promise of "power and knowledge" compensates for the severely restricted opportunities for the experience or expression of sexual pleasure.

More specifically, we should ask why Kim's teenaged cross-cultural passing does not seem to produce any "release" of genitally specific heterosexual desire, a theme Kipling disguised further when he revised Kim's age downward by ten months in the final edition of this novel, setting his hero's age at "fourteen years and ten months" when he graduated from St. Xavier's.[10] In addition to the formal education that Kim receives at St. Xavier's, he also undergoes extracurricular training that allows him to pass for a wider range of natives, but not without a curious change in his previous methods of passing.

After a few months at St. Xavier's, when Kim is about eleven years old, he looks forward to his first summer vacation, when cross-cultural dress will provide him with some relief from the stifling rules and prohibitions of the colonized. Before this holiday, Kim pays the first of two ritual visits to native prostitutes, which allow the reader to measure the changes in the consolidation of his gender and sexual identity and to recognize particular absences in the pattern of his sexual desires. In this initial visit, Kim seeks the assistance of a native prostitute to help him dye his skin and wrap his turban, procedures he has not needed help in accomplishing before. Kim enlists this woman's help by inventing a tale he imagines she will find credible, and perhaps endearing, when he pretends to be in love with a twelve-year-old English girl, the daughter of a schoolmaster in a "white" regiment. In other words, only after Kim's own identity as "white" is consolidated by his schooling, only after his loyalty as "a sahib and son of a sahib" is secured by the ligatures of language and the promises of power and knowledge, does he truly qualify for his first act of cross-cultural passing; earlier, he needed no assistance in what was simply child's play.

Three years of schooling at St. Xavier's amplify Kim's pleasure in his cross-cultural masquerades because he learns more about power and the significance of his boundary crossings. Impersonating adults whom he has learned to name as colonial others requires that Kim accept the elaborate colonial mores ostensibly prohibiting, among other things, sexual contact with colonized women and, though it is not named in this text, with colonized and colonizing men as well. In other words, Kim learns, rather later than usual, that "entering another's soul" (207) is safe only if it is not sexually enacted; that is, when all sexual activity with colonial others is accepted as "abject." When acts of cross-cultural passing are structured this way, Kim experiences a sense of freedom that awakens "a demon" in him (207).

As Kim's training with Sahib Lurigan makes clear, the greatest pleasure excited by his many performances in cross-cultural masquerade is produced when he is watched by a man whom he desires to impress. Kim is "annoyed" when Lurigan watches Mukerjee rather than himself during his last, most masterful performance, imitating an ash-smeared (and no doubt nearly naked) faquir. Later, Kim's desire to be watched nearly compromises him when he meets the terrified secret agent, E 23, on the train, begins to undress him, and only then realizes that he is being watched by two natives, the lama and the Jat, who should not be allowed to see the part Kim now plays in the Great Game. Throwing a cloth over the Jat's head, Kim threatens him, saying: "Dare so much as to think a wish to see, and—and—even I cannot save thee" (251), commanding him to be dumb as well as blind. The lama, who is characterized as being more interested in Kim's newly acquired skill in healing than in his talent for disguise, offers no comment about this performance and remains apparently oblivious to all subsequent evidence of Kim's compromising participation in the Great Game.

Kim's formal induction into the Great Game is marked by a second visit to a native prostitute, immediately after his graduation from St. Xavier's, when he is nearly fifteen. Though this is hardly Kipling's intention, Kim's visit to Huneefa exposes the weak links between his body, his race, his sense of manhood, and his sexual identity. Just before this visit, Mahbub Ali gives Kim an outfit of sensuous Pathan clothes and a small gun to celebrate his passage into manhood. Surveying Kim in his new attire, Mahbub Ali anticipates the presumably female "hearts to be broken," and, as he handles the gun, he prays to hasten the day when Kim will "kill a man" and father a child (219). Asserting his loyalty to the "laws" of the sahib, however, Kim renounces these illicit sexual pleasures, showing why he is more comfortable playing the part of the lama's chaste *chela* rather than, for example, the hypersexualized role of an imaginary Afghani prince. Immediately afterward, Mahbub Ali, who is, after all, a secret agent in the Great Game, brings Kim to the prostitute, Huneefa, and warns him, rather inconsistently, to avoid sexual contact with all women, saying "it is by means of woman that all plans come to ruin" (225).

In dramatizing this second visit to a prostitute, Kipling emphasizes Kim's corporeality, skin color, and nakedness in describing how Huneefa colors his skin, this time with a longer-lasting dye. Kipling takes pains to defuse any heterosexual charge that this ritual might otherwise have aroused since houses of prostitution correspond, of course, to common European sites and rites of sexual initiation. Kipling presents Huneefa, instead, as the "abject" female Other in its most unattractive aging corporeality: she is "a huge and shapeless woman clad in greenish gauzes," virtually wearing armor, since she is "decked, brow, nose, ear, neck, wrist, arm, waist, and ankle, with heavy native jewellery" (225). In fact, Huneefa displays the powers of the witch rather than the prostitute in this scene when she invokes the aid of supernatural beings to protect Kim. When Mahbub Ali tells Kim to "strip to the waist and look how thou art whitened," Kim hesitates to undress, until he realizes that Huneefa is blind. Kim's reluctance suggests that he has finally passed that adolescent sexual threshold whereby his genitals have become "definitive objects of consciousness" (Grosz, *Volatile*, 76). As this scene makes clear, Mahbub Ali's warnings that Kim avoid the most common heterosexual modes of "going native" seem unnecessary, since Kim has already been thoroughly trained in the erotics of "homosocial" desire. This ritual also ensures that Kim will continue to avoid sexual contact since his undyed skin between navel and knee would certainly serve as a deterrent to any sexual act to which undressing is a prelude.

In other words, *Kim* can be read as a novel about the sacrifices of desire required by the Raj, but this theme of erotic sacrifice is masked because Kipling presents his hero first as a "wild" child and later as a lingering adolescent. Nonetheless, Kim consistently acts out his part as a "friend of all the world," loved by many men who assume various paternal roles which promise differing degrees of intimacy, though Kipling carefully tries to desexualize these relationships. Given the prescribed strictures on homosexual desire, the colonizing men, Reverend Bennett and Father Victor and, most of all, Colonel Creighton are presented as more austere and remote than the other native father-substitutes, but because Mahbub Ali, Lurigan Sahib, and Hurree Mukerjee are secret agents in the Great Game, they too have been trained to uphold the erotic prohibitions of the Raj. This proliferation of fathers also disguises, and overcompensates for, the dereliction of duty shown by Kim's Irish father, who "loafed down the line," indulged in his opium habit, lived with a "half-caste" Indian woman, and, apparently, mostly ignored Kim.

Having learned the proper objects and disciplines of desire at St. Xavier's, Kim is handed on to the lama, a spiritual teacher who possesses deep insight and spiritual authority in the discipline of all desires, sexual and otherwise. It is the lama who teaches the final lessons that retard the development of Kim's body image and so prevent him from acting out his physical maturation in sexual ways. The lama tells Kim, for example, "There are many lies in this world, and not a few liars, but there are no liars like our bodies, except it be the sensations of our bodies" (245).

In the colonial world of British India at the turn of the century, when racial signs became more ambiguous, and when the mastery of English was no longer sufficient proof of racial identity or national allegiance, Kim must display his loyalty both by what he does and by what he avoids, by performing daring acts of courage on the Northwest Frontier and by avoiding sexual entanglements with Indian women.[11] Kim proves by his political espionage that he is a loyal player in the Great Game, but he also must prove that he is sexually and biologically "loyal to civilization" by rejecting the woman of

Shamlegh, who tempts him to relocate the objects of desire outside the homosocial orbit required under the Raj. Although Kim is attracted because she—unlike all the other native women in his experience, including the nameless prostitute at Lucknow, Huneefa, and Sahiba—does not "treat him like a child" (315), he engages in only the mildest acts of foreplay and leaves her with just a kiss.

By the end of the novel, Kipling seems to admit that Kim's efforts to prolong his adolescence and to renounce sexual desire entirely leads, inevitably, to a dead end. Thus, Kim's adventure on the frontier is followed by a physical collapse and his return to a native "mother," who performs a ritual which restores him to a more childish relation to his body. When Sahiba and her female helper lay Kim "east and west, that the mysterious earth-currents which thrill the clay of our bodies might help and not hinder," they "take him to pieces all one long afternoon—bone by bone, muscle by muscle, ligament by ligament, and lastly, nerve by nerve. Kneaded to irresponsible pulp, half hypnotized by the perpetual flick and readjustment of the uneasy chudders that veiled their eyes, Kim slid ten thousand miles into slumber—thirty-six hours of it—sleep that soaked like rain after drought" (324). Through this body ritual and, later, by feeding him all the food he wants, Kim's foster mother reduces him to a state comparable to that of the child who lies replete at the mother's breast. In this way, Kipling registers a nostalgia for the state of "wildness" that a multilingual colonial child like Kim experienced when he lived for a while "outside the constraints and significances" of his "own" culture.

Paralyzed by conflicting desires, Kim, at fifteen, experiences no compelling "sexual drive" moving him toward a rigorously prescribed and disciplined heterosexuality (Grosz, *Volatile*, 55). In this condition, reduced to tears, Kim can only ask that inevitable adolescent question, "And what is Kim?" (331). He finds the answer by remembering his more recent and utilitarian lessons in colonial mastery: "Roads were meant to be walked upon, houses to be lived in, cattle to be driven, fields to be tilled and men and women to be talked to. They were all real and true—solidly planted upon the feet—perfectly comprehensible—clay of his clay, neither more nor less" (331). But this ending also tacitly recognizes one question that most novels about lost colonial children are designed to deflect, a question Kim poses when he asks himself to which mother, and to which culture, does he belong?

Leaving Home

Sara Jeannette Duncan's novella *The Story of Sonny Sahib* (1895), like several other children's stories, exposes the underlying ideological conflicts around race, gender, and sex that are part of the cultural context shared by Kipling's Anglo-Indian readers. Duncan's story confirms the fixity of "race," suggesting an indelible correspondence between outside and inside that Kipling's novel in some ways dares to question.[12]

The circumstances of Sonny's birth to English parents and his separation from them are far less ambiguously presented in Duncan's novel than in *Kim.* Sonny is the first child of Captain John Starr and his young wife, Evelyn, and he is born during the British retreat from Cawnpore in 1857. Sonny's father is honorably absent, having been injured during the mutiny and hospitalized far from the scene when the story begins. Sonny's mother is near full-term in her pregnancy when the siege of Cawnpore begins, and she is saved from death because her Muslim ayah, Tooni, directs her to take refuge in a native bazaar. Duncan is very explicit about the time of Evelyn's death, inserting it into the historical narrative about the massacre of Englishwomen and children at the Bibighar in Cawnpore that her readers knew by heart: "As to Sonny Sahib's mother, she was neither shot in the boats with the soldiers that believed the written word of the Nana Sahib, nor stabbed with the women and children who went back to the palace afterwards. She died quietly in the ox-cart before it reached the ghat, and the pity of it was that Sonny Sahib's father, the captain, . . . never knew" (10).

Like Kim, then, Sonny is nurtured by a native woman, but unlike Kim, he grows up, until the age of six, in a poor, working-class Muslim household headed by his nurse, Tooni, and her husband, Abdul, completely outside the networks of British colonial culture. Sonny lives in the small village of Rubbulgurh, where "there was no fighting because there were no sahibs. The English had not yet come to teach the Maharajah how to govern his estate and spend his revenues" (12). Tooni, in contrast to the "half-caste" woman who looks after Kim, is a professional nurse who has worked for many years for British colonial families and has accepted their ways somewhat unthinkingly: "She crooned with patient smiles over many of the bablock in her day, but from beginning to end, never a baba like this. So strong he was, he could make old Abdul cry out, pulling at his beard, so sweet-tempered and healthy that he would sleep just where he was put down, like other babies of Rubbulgurh. Tooni grieved deeply that she could not give him a bottle, and a coral, and a perambulator" (12). Duncan repeats rather than penetrates the disguise of the servants' mentality that colonialism produced by noting that Tooni is "surprised" that Sonny hasn't "inherited his mother's language with his blue eyes and white skin" (15).

Evidence of Sonny's "race" and gender, nonetheless, spontaneously emerges, revealing his difference in both body and mind from the other boys in the village. Sonny likes meat and commands the largest share of sweets when he visits the bazaar. He is bored by the games and stories of his Muslim playmates because, as the narrator contends, "it was his birthright to pretend, in a large active way, and he couldn't carry it out. The other boys didn't care about making believe soldiers, and running and hiding and shouting and beating Sonny Sahib's tom-tom. . . . Sonny had to represent them all himself" (22). Unlike his friends, Sonny is unafraid when he is summoned to the palace in Lalpore in order to play with Moti, who is the son and heir of the local maharajah.

Though Sonny moves from a Muslim to a Hindu household and crosses the economic boundaries that widely separate Tooni from the Maharajah, there are no episodes of cross-cultural masquerade in this novel, perhaps because Sonny's identity as an English child is not as firmly consolidated as is Kim's. Instead, Duncan's narrative recognizes the collaboration between English education and late nineteenth-century medical practices which were called upon to discipline the desires of colonial children. When Sonny, prompted presumably by his racial instincts, asks permission to learn English, he is taught by an English doctor who works as a medical missionary in Lalpore under the maharajah's protection. In describing Sonny's slow progress in learning English, however, Duncan also acknowledges the subversive power of language to override the mental pathways already inscribed in the child's mind by its biological inheritance and bodily experiences. Learning English is difficult for Sonny; he "reads Urdu better than English" and asks "strange questions about his father's God" (60).

Duncan's novel, in contrast to *Kim*, dramatizes the double-binds of the colonial child who must recognize and act on his racial and gender superiority and show his allegiance to British culture while, at the same time, proving his superior moral integrity by honoring the ties of affection and loyalty that otherwise bind him to his Indian "parents." When British soldiers invade the maharajah's territory in order to avenge the death of the missionary who once taught him English, Sonny, like Kim, is attracted by the glamour and ritual of the British regiment and feels compelled to leave the palace to visit the English camp. But Sonny is allowed to articulate the double allegiance that Kim, and Kipling, ignore. Before he leaves the palace, Sonny proves his instinctive English sense of honor and duty by leaving behind all the gifts he has been given, promising the maharajah that he will "take your Honner in his hart to his oun country but the gifts are too heavie" (*sic*, 83). Likewise, Sonny leaves a note for Tooni that tells his nurse that he loves her and pledges, "When I find my own country I will come back and take you there too" (87). In this careful balancing of debts and promises, Sonny's story suggests why Kipling characterizes Sahiba as an independently wealthy woman, so Kim can assign her to the place of "mother" and still take what he needs from her without, as with a servant, incurring any obligation.

Finally, Sonny, in contrast to Kim, refuses the invitation to act as a spy when he visits the British encampment. In this episode, Sonny shows his racially determined "courage" when he asks to be taken to the commanding officer. When prompted to describe the maharajah's water supply, fortifications, and guns, though, Sonny refuses to play the part of the saboteur that Kim plays with such oblivious relish, when he responds, "I am English, but the Maharajah is my father and my mother. I cannot speak against the Maharajah, burra sahib" (103). In Duncan's narrative, it is the maharajah's failure to trust in Sonny's "word of honour"—in other words, his failure to recognize Sonny's inherently trustworthy English nature—that causes him to surrender because he assumes Sonny has told the British that his remaining ammunition is defective. In the ceremony arranging the terms of peace, the British officer assures the maharajah that Sonny did not betray him. Shortly afterward, the officer recognizes Tooni in the maharajah's entourage and discovers that Sonny is his long-lost son, born before his wife died at Cawnpore.

Thus, in *The Story of Sonny Sahib*, the colonial child is reunited with his English father but is not required, as in *Kim*, to betray his Indian foster parents, though he must consent to be permanently separated from them. In this way, Duncan's text exposes the losses as well as the contradictions that Kipling's novel covers up. The death of the colonial mother in this text relieves Sonny of any ambivalence in his relation to his Indian foster mother, whom he is able to love and later leave without significant conflict. After Sonny is reunited with his father, and returned to English cultural ways, there is no turning back. In this resolution, Duncan thus tacitly recognizes the conflicts surrounding the colonial mother and reiterates the importance of "consent" in the "social contract" that organizes colonial life, uniting father and son in the postmutiny colonial world described in this text.

The Making of a Memsahib

Philip Oliphant's *Maya* (1908) helps to expose more of the cultural ambivalence projected onto the colonial mother in this period by recounting the
experiences of a lost daughter rather than a son. As such, *Maya* reveals how
colonial gender hierarchies disrupt the structures of power and knowledge
that organize both Kipling's and Duncan's novels. More specifically, this text
makes us ask why colonizing women are excluded from the cross-cultural
passing that Kim enjoys and why they are denied even the limited pleasure
that Sonny Sahib experiences in the circuits of "knowledge and power."

Like Duncan's hero, Maya is lost during the Indian Uprising of 1857,
when her father is "murdered by the men of his regiment" but Maya's mother,
unlike most colonial mothers in these tales, escapes from Delhi only to fall
into the hands of the Rajah of Mandra. Maya's mother is taken as "a captive
to the palace on the rock, and there, in the season of rams, she gave birth to
a daughter" (8). Unlike Kim and Sonny, then, Maya is initially nurtured by
her English mother, and, after her mother's death, she is raised in the zenana
of a wealthy rajah, where she is protected by Subadra, a widow of the rajah's
dead brother. This adjustment in Oliphant's plot suggests that a servant like
Tooni would not have sufficient power to protect an alien girl in the zenana.
Like Anandamoyi in Tagore's *Gora*, Subadra is a high-caste Hindu woman
who ignores the caste restrictions that should separate her from Maya's mother.

In contrast to Kipling, who marks Kim's body with uncertain signs of
his race, Philip Oliphant identifies the signs of Maya's race immediately in
the opening pages of the novel. Maya's fair skin, blond hair, and body all
suggest she is "white": "She was not much more than fourteen, and the locks
of hair which had escaped from beneath the sari over her head were golden,
and the little hand that rested on the parapet was white" (6). What makes
Maya's identity "undecidable" is both her incongruous appearance as a white
woman in a native woman's clothes and her "soul-less" look: "Her features
were well defined; the little, straight nose, short, curving lip and rounded chin
seemed fully and perfectly developed, and gave no indication of her
age. . . . Nature had made her beautiful and no other intelligence had inter-
vened to set its mark upon her face. The knowledge of good and evil was
not written upon it, only the wonder-wide look which instinct imparts to all
young animals" (6). In other words, Oliphant locates Maya's unsettling challenges to the colonial system not in her skin color but in the undecidability
of her moral being, for her life in an upper-class Indian family has produced
an English girl who is "soul-less" (6).

Oliphant is explicit, and somewhat unconventional, in defining the conditions that produced this absence in Maya's identity. In contrast to more evangelical Anglo-Indian writers like Mrs. Penny, who in *The Romance of the Nautch Girl,* for example, identified Hindu beliefs as a sufficient cause of "soul-lessness," Oliphant is more attentive to the "ways in which the inside constitutes and accepts itself as an outside, how experience itself structures and gives meaning to the ways in which the body is occupied and lived" (Grosz, *Volatile,* 115). Maya's mother is identified as a Christian who rejected suicide and submitted to the presumed (but unspoken) sexual indignities of her life in the maharajah's zenana for her daughter's sake. Although Maya's mother lived long enough to teach her daughter to "speak English and to write," and to tell her "of a God who loves little children, and of Jesus Christ, the Son of God" (12), her mother's teachings do not reproduce a female subjectivity that is recognizably British or Christian in her daughter. Maya can recall the apartment where she lived with her mother, but her memory provides no sure pathways to transfer her mother's English identity to her. Like Adrienne Rich's "savage" child,[13] Maya remembers the heavy curtain that separated her "from the rest of the women . . . a heavy curtain of crimson felt embroidered with designs of men and animals and hideous deities in bewildering confusion. Her mother would never let her look closely at the pictures on the curtain, but would call her away and, holding her in her arms, cry softly over her and sob out, 'O God take pity on my child'" (9). Maya, like many colonial children separated prematurely from their mothers, cannot recall or reproduce the maternal language that would bridge the gaps between her mother and herself.[14]

Oliphant is also unusual in asserting that Maya is soul-less not because she has been raised since before the age of reason as a Hindu but because she has lived her life entirely in seclusion. As Elizabeth Grosz argues, "It is power which produces a 'soul' or interiority as a result of a certain type of etching of the subject's body" (149), and Oliphant shows how Romanticism continued to linger in the colonial imaginary in the late nineteenth century when he indicates that Maya is soul-less because she has not experienced the frustrations of spiritual and erotic desire that, according to Keats, transform the world into a "vale of soul-making."

In describing how Maya discovers her soul, Oliphant surprisingly echoes the final passage of *Kim*; the "click" that marks Kim's ultimate re-engagement with the material world corresponds to a similar moment in Maya's life, when her apprehension of her soul is created by friction with the material (and in fact commercial) world. Oliphant's narrator echoes Kipling's more matter-of-fact colonialist argument that roads were "meant to be walked upon" (254), when Maya wanders through a well-stocked bazaar for the first time in her life and has an epiphany: "This was the wonderland of Maya's dreams. . . . There were real people, with real aims and occupations. They spoke a language which she could understand. There was a purpose in their movements. They existed for themselves. . . . The feeling of aloofness with which she had regarded all that lay beneath the rock of Mandra was slipping away from her. She had come down to the world to realize she belonged to it, and that her pulses beat to the same measure that stirred theirs. She was beginning to be clothed with the mantle of humanity" (48). Having thus reoriented Maya to material (and consumer) reality, Oliphant allows his heroine to resist Christian conversion, though she also revises her Vendantan Hindu beliefs in "the universal soul, which alone exits, besides which there is nothing" (245). In other words, once Maya's identity has been consolidated by this contact with the marketplace, her remaining unorthodox religious practices do not pose a significant challenge to "white" colonial culture. In this way, Oliphant's novel conforms to the new pressures of late nineteenth-century monopoly capitalism that link gender identity with particular types of consumption, though the Indian bazaar also recognizes India's inferior position in this emerging world economy (Hennessy and Mohan, 351).

Like Kipling, Oliphant focuses his narrative on events that occur after Maya has reached her adolescence, but, unlike Kim, Maya recognizes that she is standing at the legal, psychological, and physical threshold that will subsequently determine her life as a woman. At this juncture, her resistance to sexual surrender prompts her to recognize an inherent "pride of race" in herself. Maya's body is literally and indelibly marked—indeed, it is overdetermined—to indicate her female "destiny." Because she was dedicated to temple service as a *devadasi* shortly after her birth, "the sacred hawk of Vishnu was branded on the white skin of her breast" (7). When one of Maya's friends in the zenana urges her to cross the sexual threshold and accept her position as *devadasi*, saying, "better a dancing girl than a widow" (30), Maya feels an "instinctive" reluctance to offer her body as a "sacrifice" in the initiation ritual of "Shaktipuja" wherein "Brahmin, Sudra, and pariah give themselves up to indiscriminate debauchery and lust" (23). The narrator explains: "Though she saw daily dancing girls and their like received without demur into the society of the highest of the land, yet she could not reconcile herself to their profession. There was no sense of moral repugnance in her prejudice against them, for Maya was strictly unmoral. It arose simply from inborn aversion, and pride of race. She could never consent to occupy the position which other women accepted as the right and inevitable status of womanhood. She was, as yet, too young to understand or analyze her feelings; but she was conscious of her superiority" (31). In this way, Oliphant links Maya's sense of womanhood to a "pride of race" that prompts her to withhold her "consent" in assuming her assigned role as a "public woman." Maya avoids becoming a sacrificial virgin and *devadasi* when the death of the rajah reorganizes the female power hierarchies in the zenana, and she escapes with Lakshmi, one of the rajah's wives who wishes to avoid the austerities of Hindu widowhood. Ironically, Maya must impersonate a dancing girl, identified as one of the most "abject" female Others in the colonial imaginary, as we have seen in chapter 2, in order to escape from the Rajah's domain.

Like Kim, Maya, upon her return to colonial society, is allowed to express her resistance to the harsh disciplining of the body and mind that is part of her reeducation as a colonial woman, but Maya's training offers her none of the consolations of knowledge and power that Kim and Sonny enjoy. Indeed, though Maya's body is re-coded as "white," she is compelled to accept a gender identity that diminishes her power. Like other lost children, Maya must learn to speak and write English properly, but the mastery of English alone is not enough to make her into an Englishwoman. Maya also has to pass through the grueling school of English ladyhood; she must don their uncomfortable clothes and learn everything from table manners to the oddities of the English diet (179). Moreover, as a colonial woman, she must also accept all the inhibitions restricting her free expression of sexual (and other) desires. Like Kim, Maya initially experiences this "education" as an assault on her physical being; she objects, for example, when the ayah in the English household where she has been sent, helps her put on English clothing: "She crushed my feet into little leather shoes, so that I could neither stand nor walk, and drew the strings of the corselet so tight that it seemed to squeeze the breath out of my body" (174). After two months of this torture, Maya is subdued, though Oliphant is ironic about the effects of such a "civilizing" process upon women. After her long apprenticeship, Maya concludes: "Among the sahibs the women were free to go where they pleased; but they were bound down by rigid formalities of speech, action, and dress, and were expected to fulfill certain requirements and responsibilities. Maya was still inclined to think that the women of the sahibs paid dearly for their emancipation" (280).

Oliphant's novel is unusual, then, because it frankly exposes the asymmetrical structure of colonial gender arrangements by noting that power and knowledge are withheld from Maya and other colonial girls. While Kim's schooling provides both power and knowledge as a compensation for the narrowing of the channels of desire in this colonial order, Maya's training offers neither compensation.[15] Instead, she submits to a disciplinary "education" because she has already learned the feminine ways of desire that apparently translate easily across racial lines. She has fallen in love at first sight with the novel's hero, Francis D'Aguilar, who is the first "man of her own race" that she sees after crossing into British territory (104). Thus Oliphant's novel demonstrates how colonial gender and sexual ideologies counter racial ones in colonial India, a display that Kipling neatly sidesteps by banishing any Englishwomen from *Kim*.

Oliphant's treatment of Maya's romance with D'Aguilar also exposes the painful consequences for colonial women in a colonial culture that prescribes a prolonged adolescence for its men by setting high economic standards for marriage and by rerouting heterosexual desire through homosocial networks while prohibiting homosexuality. In his first conversation with Maya, D'Aguilar is confused by her apparently white appearance and her unexpected fluency in "Hindustani," since colonial girls rarely had any opportunity for formal schooling in this language. When he asks Maya who her parents were, she shows a hybridity that is more than linguistic by repeating a variation on Sonny Sahib's native aphorism in describing her origins and identity: "Truth is our mother, justice our father—we have nothing to fear . . . ask me no more of my parents" (159).

D'Aguilar's response to Maya in this first meeting also indicates that cross-cultural passing is not a neutral act, open to colonizers of either gender; instead, it is usually considered safe for colonizing men alone. D'Aguilar reprimands Maya for assuming the disguise of a disreputable dancing girl: "It is unbecoming in a white woman to be wearing the garb of shame" (159). After he learns that Maya is a child lost during the mutiny, he asserts his patriarchal privilege and restores an unwanted patrimony to her: "Thou art the daughter of Leland Sahib. . . . He was a valiant soldier, who died doing his duty. He commanded a regiment of horse. There are many who will welcome the daughter of Leland Sahib among her own people. Wilt thou come with me to them?" (165). At this moment, Maya cannot find the words to tell him that "she loathed the men and women of her race" (165), but she submits to his direction because she has fallen in love with him.

Oliphant thus shows how the conventions of romantic love, as the colonizers practice them, keep the sexual contract in place. For most of the novel, D'Aguilar refuses to recognize Maya's erotic interest in him, a denial characteristic not only of Kim but of many other Anglo-Indian heroes as well.

D'Aguilar's resistance seems particularly willful since as a civil servant he has been educated in the "language and customs of the people" (156). When D'Aguilar persists in calling Maya a "child," her English guardian reminds him: "You seem to forget that Maya was brought up among women who are married at ten or eleven years old. She is positively an old maid in her own opinion" (213). This refusal to recognize Maya's sexual being seems hardly credible in this period, when the legal and social boundaries separating the girl from the marriageable woman were so contested in metropolitan and Indian cultures alike.[16]

Finally, what this novel ultimately displays is the force of colonial desires to preserve the Victorian sexual contract. Though D'Aguilar orchestrates Maya's education, it is not designed to promote her freedom or provide her with an autonomous vocation; it is simply organized to train her for the invisible harem of the Anglo-Indian household and to accept the deferred promises of monogamous erotic love confined to marriage. Only after D'Aguilar reluctantly confesses that he loves her, that is, only after Maya's allegiance to this Englishman is psychologically and legally secure, is she allowed to perform a single act of cross-cultural passing. D'Aguilar asks Maya to re-enter the zenana where she was raised in order to warn Lakshmi, who has been forced to return to the Maharajah's household, that she is in danger. This act, like Kim's adventures in cross-cultural passing, is designed to test Maya's courage and loyalty as a British subject. Now that Maya has a reason to want to stay in Anglo-India, she is positioned to see the danger of trespassing the boundaries separating the Indian from the colonial woman and to regard confinement in the Rajah's zenana as a threat.

Maya's act of cross-cultural passing fails entirely in its ostensible objective since Maya arrives only in time to see Lakshmi jump off the cliff at Mandra, having decided that suicide is her only escape from persecution inside the zenana, a plot detail that is apparently meant to reveal the "abjection" of secluded Hindu women. What Maya's ritual act of cross-cultural passing shows, then, is that Maya is now securely bound by British notions of romantic love and by the blindness it demands of all colonial women, for in consenting to return to her race, Maya must submit to be ruled by the "same laws" that govern Anglo-Indian men, though she is refused the access to all the "power and knowledge" that compensates for their sacrifices.

Calling India Home

Rabindranath Tagore's *Gora* (1910) also presents a story of an English child lost during the Indian Mutiny, but the radically different conflicts and resolution in this novel, as well as the ideologies that organize gender and nationality in it, help to further reveal the gaps and inconsistencies in Anglo-Indian novels about lost children. In short, *Gora* helps us see more clearly the culturally specific grids of power, regulation, and force that inscribe the male and female body in British India at the turn of the century. Tagore's novel dramatizes an appreciation for the preciousness of children that is curiously absent from Anglo-Indian novels about lost children, not only in the Indian servants who are prompted to try to return lost English children to their families in order to collect a reward but also in the English parents, and especially in the fathers, who seem so careless, and so easily resigned, to the loss of their children. There are three other orphans in *Gora* in addition to the hero: Gora's friend, Binoy; Sucharita, the woman Gora finally marries; and Santish, her younger brother. The ease with which Sucharita and her brother are adopted, the generosity extended to them and to Binoy, and the complexity they introduce in comparison with narrower English notions of the "family" all expose, by contrast, the legalistic narrowness, possessiveness, and exclusiveness of the colonial English family represented not only in the Anglo-Indian novels about lost children but in most British novels of the period as well.

Unlike Kim, Sonny, and Maya, Tagore's hero, Gourmohan, does not know he is an English child, though his nickname, which translates into English as "whitey," provides one clue that would be transparently obvious to characters and readers alike of Anglo-Indian novels (Spivak, "Burden," 285). Gora's unusually large physical stature provides another anomaly which in Anglo-Indian novels would serve as a self-evident demonstration of his "whiteness" and superior racial inheritance. Instead, Tagore's narrator notes simply that Gora "was not exactly good looking but it was impossible to overlook him, for he would have been conspicuous in any company" of Bengalis (6). Gora himself remains oblivious to the mismatch between the body he inhabits and the cultured, urban Brahmin subjectivity he has acquired.

It is the English colonial magistrate, that powerful judge of the meaning of "race" and "illegal reproduction" in colonial culture, who identifies the anomalies that mark Gora's body as racially undecidable, as neither clearly Bengali nor clearly white. When Gora comes before him, charged with instigating a "petty rebellion against the British Raj," the judge notes: "This kind of six-foot tall, big boned, stalwart figure he could not remember to have come across before in this province. Neither was his complexion like that of the ordinary Bengali" (140). The magistrate's uncertainty about whether Gora is of the "King's race" (143), however, does not prevent him from sentencing Gora to a term in prison.

The organization and alliances in Gora's family and the characterization of his foster parents also depart dramatically from the "feudal" patterns imposed on the Indian families represented in Anglo-Indian novels about lost children (Spivak, "Burden," 286). Both of Gora's adoptive parents reveal the consequences of their subordinate place in the colonial hierarchy, but their strategic hybridity exposes the implausible interior blankness projected onto the Indian "foster parents" in most Anglo-Indian novels, whether they are literally servants like Tooni or princely rulers like the nameless maharajahs who shelter Sonny and Maya. Tagore explains, for example, that Krishnadayal, the man Gora believes to be his father, was once a member of the Brahmo Samaj, and this episode in his personal history illuminates the ideological motives that justified his decision to accept an English child into his family, just as his return to a more "orthodox" form of Hinduism (21) provides a reason for his desire to hide the secret of Gora's birth from him. This shift in colonial allegiances also illuminates one of the causes of Krishnadayal's alienation from his second wife, Anandamoyi, who initially urged him to adopt Gora.

Anandamoyi, the woman who acts as Gora's mother, differs even more dramatically from the "foster mothers" in Kipling's, Duncan's, and Oliphant's novels, for she is an extraordinarily strong, intelligent, capable, politically astute, "modern" Indian woman who, by contrast, reveals the thinness of the stereotypes in Anglo-Indian texts where English mothers as well as Indian foster-mothers repeatedly demonstrate their powerlessness and incompetence. Gora's foster mother is more courageous, more resourceful, and better educated, being the daughter of a great Benares pandit, than any of the colonial mothers described in any of the Anglo-Indian texts I know. She displays her openheartedness by sheltering Gora's mother, who gave birth to him in her household, and her openmindedness in fully accepting and loving Gora as her "son" despite the color of his skin.

Maternal love prompts Anandamoyi to continue her principled refusal to comply with caste restrictions not only in her treatment of Gora but in all her associations, including her relations with her household servants. She is tolerant of the extreme Hindu orthodoxy that Gora has adopted as a young man, and she extends her care and affection to his orphaned friend, Binoy, even after he begins his slow drift toward the more liberal ideals of the Brahmo Samaj, which causes a rift in Gora's friendship with him. Anandamoyi's love and support are also offered to the younger generation of Indian women in this text, who embody alternatives to the English New Woman. Because Anandamoyi's example demonstrates the powerful desires that link mothers to daughters as well as to sons, it reveals a large range of desires and alternatives that are conspicuously absent in the Anglo-Indian versions of this story.

Second, in Tagore's novel the circuits of knowledge and power are located neither in the boys' school nor in the masters who teach English language and culture to colonial boys; instead, they are located in Hinduism and in the emerging political ideologies of Indian nationalism. Thus, Tagore's novel acknowledges that desire can be directed to the consolidation of communal as well as individual identity and can be defined as comprehending a wide range of feelings of affection and love as well as erotic attraction. Initially, Tagore charts this wide range of desires by contrasting Binoy's infatuation with the beautiful Sucharita with Gora's passionate "love" for "Mother India." When Binoy rapturously describes the radiant beauty of his beloved's eyes, Gora counters by describing the object of his equally rapturous patriotism: "When once my love of country becomes so overwhelmingly self-evident, there will be no escape for me,—it will draw out all my wealth and life, my blood, the very marrow of my bones; my sky, my light, in fact my all" (70). Tagore's novel shows, by contrast, then, how Anglo-Indian novels limit male maturity and collapse love of country into love of woman, and so assign an enormous symbolic burden to the pure unmarried English girl and to an erotic, heterosexual love that is otherwise frustrated by so many of the social and cultural arrangements of British India.

Gora also shows how Bengali elites were invited to display their mastery of English and their understanding of English ways for the approval of the colonizer, but in contrasting the acceptable and unacceptable modes of cross-cultural "passing" permitted for women as well as men, *Gora* reveals a third feature that Anglo-Indian texts often hide, that love and marriage are central in creating a sense of solidarity among the men in his cultural group and in cementing their loyalties to community and nation. Binoy and Gora repeatedly argue about the kind of "love" that should provide the proper foundation for Indian family life. Binoy challenges Gora to acknowledge the gender inequities in Hindu culture when he notes, "We look on India only as a country of men; we entirely ignore the women" (82–83). When Gora responds by charging Binoy with allowing English standards to colonize his desires, he identifies one of the greatest incongruities in colonial gender ideologies when he says, "Like the Englishman . . . you want to see women everywhere—in the home and in the world outside; on the land, the water, and in the sky; at our meals, our amusements and our work,—with the result that for you the women will eclipse the men" (83). Gora contends that Indian nationalists should adopt ideals that recognize the importance of the psychological and metaphorical resonances of "Mother India," but his remark ironically displays his ignorance about his own genealogy, desires, and identity as well as his egocentric failure to see truly the complexity of his adoptive mother's inner being or that of the country—and the women—he claims to know. By the end of the novel, Gora is forced to recognize how his misunderstandings about his identity and purity have projected themselves onto his notion of India.

Like other lost children positioned on the threshold of adulthood in Anglo-Indian novels, Gora eventually learns the secret of his birth, and his discoveries change the course and objects of his desire. Gora's revelation comes when his adoptive father, Krishnadayal, becomes gravely ill and realizes that Gora must be told that he does not have the right to perform the son's part in his funeral rites. The truth of his biological and paternal heritage is conveyed by Anandamoyi when Gora asks her, "Am I not then his son?" (402), and she tells him he is not. But when he asks if she is his mother, she says something that no English mother is permitted to say in Anglo-Indian novels: "You are the only son of mine. I am a childless woman, but you are more truly my son than a child born from my own body could have been" (402). When she explains that his father was an Irishman and that his English mother died during the mutiny after giving birth to him, Gora's first response is shock: "In a single moment, Gora's life seemed to him like some extraordinary dream. . . . He had no mother, no father, no country, no nationality, no lineage, no God even. Only one thing was left to him, and that was a vast negation" (402). Gora's complex reaction exposes the extraordinary lack of ambivalence in Kim's attitude toward his Irish father as well as the fatuous and psychologically improbable simplicity of Sonny's easy return to his English father and to English ways and loyalties.

Moreover, rather than renounce the allegiances that have shaped his inner as well as his outer identity, as do the lost children in Anglo-Indian novels, Gora realizes he is no more capable of casting off his country than he is his foster mother. In recognizing the religious and political realities that shaped his mother's choices, Gora accepts the real rather than the ideal mother that he has sought. Admiringly, he tells Anandamoyi: "You have no caste, you make no distinctions, and have no hatred—you are only the image of our welfare! It is you who are India" (407). In the end, then, Gora readjusts his ideas about India and the political identity and patriotic duties that arise from it; for him, a return to Anglo-Indian society is unthinkable: India is no longer "a creation of my own imagination—it is the actual field of welfare for the three hundred millions of India's children. To-day I am really an Indian. In me there is no longer any opposition between Hindu, Mussulman, and Christian. To-day every caste in India is my caste, the food of all is my food" (405–406). Having made this adjustment, Gora is able to accept the sexual aspects of his love by marrying Sucharita and reconciling himself to the unorthodox marriage that Binoy celebrates with Lolita.

Finally, *Gora* reveals by its absence the extraordinary obsession with skin, body, and the control of its desires that is the relentless message of comparable Anglo-Indian novels about English lost children. *Gora* forcefully demonstrates, instead, that "racial" and national identities are socially constructed; they are not, and cannot be, simply skin deep. Nor can models of national identity afford to deny the power of the mother, for without her cooperation the "racial purity" and gender identity of her children cannot be maintained or reproduced. Most of all, *Gora* shows what is missing when the "moral" codes that police love and desire are applied in gender-specific ways, since, as Anandamoyi shows, the highest and most altruistic acts of mother love could be enacted in ways that undermine entirely the race and gender hierarchies of the colonial order.

CHAPTER 6

Mixed Couples

THE NEW WOMAN AND INTERRACIAL MARRIAGE

We agreed in thinking that the question of mixed marriages—marriages between European women and Indian gentlemen—is growing in importance every year that passes. It is a problem which will have to be seriously dealt with in the near future.
Fanny Farr Penny, *A Question of Colour*[1]

*M*ale romances about the mutiny written by British and Anglo-Indian novelists in the 1880s and 1890s, including those about the Rani of Jhansi and about lost English children, nearly always exclude the possibilities offered by cross-racial marriage, suggesting how Social Darwinism, especially when it operated in concert with the New Imperialism, acted to redefine racial and gender differences and to valorize male aggression and extreme individualism. Anglo-Indian romances about courtship, usually written by and about women in this period, indicate, by contrast, a greater willingness to represent lovers who cross racial boundaries and establish legal marriages between colonizers and colonized. Though the mutiny romances considered in the previous chapters, like the romances discussed in this chapter, illustrate how racial differences gradually replaced religious identity as the dominant sign of difference in colonial epistemologies in the postmutiny period, this distinctive group of "female" romances about cross-cultural love written in the first decade of the twentieth century deserves closer attention because it demonstrates how the racialization of difference acted to eroticize Indian women and men in new ways, thus undermining the dominant rape script of the postmutiny period.[2]

As a group, these little-known Anglo-Indian novels about cross-cultural marriages reveal some of the ideological changes at the turn of the century that undermined basic assumptions about women's sexuality and gender identity, assumptions that made the colonial rape script involving a white woman threatened with rape by an Indian man so meaningful in the period between 1857 and 1900. Maud Diver, for example, in *Lilamani* (1909), explicitly recognizes how cross-cultural love and marriage challenge the very foundations of imperial discourse about India when she subtly revises Kipling's famous, and endlessly repeated tag line, "East is East and West is West, and never the twain shall meet," writing instead, "East and West are not antagonistic, but complementary: heart and head, thought and action, woman and man. Between all these 'pairs of opposites' fusion is rare, difficult, yet eminently possible. Why not, then, between East and West?" (194). In *Lilamani*, Diver describes the courtship of the Englishman, Nevil Sinclair, and the beautiful Rajput widow, Lilamani, and she charts the happy marriage of this interracial couple and their children in three subsequent novels, *Far to Seek: A Romance of England and India* (1921), *The Singer Passes: An Indian Tapestry* (1931), and *The Dream Prevails* (1934).

Most Anglo-Indian romances about interracial marriages written between 1900 and 1910 that focus on Englishmen who married Indian women do not end as happily as Diver's romance; most conclude, instead, as does Alice Perrin's *Waters of Destruction* (1909), with the misguided hero's belated recognition of the power and reasonableness of the social and moral codes prohibiting mixed marriage and miscegenation in Anglo-Indian culture.[3] Because defenses of the Raj continued to depend upon stable, mutually exclusive categories of East and West, women and men, "black" and white, higher and lower, romances about Englishwomen who willingly married Indian men are far more challenging to the colonial hierarchies of race, class, and gender than were love stories like *Lilamani*. Novels which include British women who fall in love and marry Indian men are less common and also less likely to conclude with pat and easy re-endorsements of the colonial ideologies that enforced the racial and gender subordination defining social life in British India.[4] Flora Annie Steel's *Voices in the Night* (1900) and Victoria Cross's *Life of My Heart* (1905) both represent New Women who marry Indian men, although their dramatically different treatments of these cross-racial unions illustrate some of the contradictions in notions about female agency and sexual desire in the colonial imaginary of this period. These novels thus display how the interplay between New Imperialism and "imperializing feminism" acted to undermine, and ultimately to transform, the sex and gender norms of colonizing women.

Some of the unspeakable dimensions of the prevailing Anglo-Indian taboos against interracial marriage become more visible when these romances are read in relation to Swarnakumari Devi's *Kahake* (1898), which she translated into English as *The Unfinished Song* in 1913.[5] Devi's novel provides an alternative perspective on the restrictiveness and arbitrariness of the sex, gender, and racial boundaries that colonizing women transgressed when they dared to cross the literal and figurative barriers that were supposed to separate the "races" in colonial culture. *The Unfinished Song* presents a Hindu heroine who, by contrast, refuses to accept the moral and sexual double standards that were embedded in the prevailing gender arrangements of Anglo-Indian life and in the symbolic economy that supported it. Thus, Devi's novel, like Tagore's later romance, *The Home and the World* (1916), engages with larger political forces in the historical real of British India, which were almost always either unrepresented or misrepresented in Anglo-Indian novels of this period.[6] Devi's novel identifies a third type of marriage, one that criticizes, on one hand, British imperial models of marriage and, on the other, resists the emerging Hindu nationalist model. Her book thus imagines an Indian alternative to the New Woman that challenges the idealization of the Hindu woman's subordination in the traditional nonconsensual and indissoluble Hindu marriage that nationalists began to recommend in the 1880s as exhibiting a "higher form of love" that transcended the "allegedly utilitarian, materialist and narrowly contractual western arrangements" (Sarkar, "Hindu," 226).

What made these cross-racial romances possible and, at the same time, intensified the crisis in the sexual imaginary was the emergence of the New Woman as a popular figure in romances of the 1890s. The English New Woman challenged Victorian gender norms by taking advantage of changes in Englishwomen's relation to the social contract, which was legally amended in the 1880s, and to adjustments in the sexual contract that feminists helped to renegotiate in the 1890s. As Ann Ardis argues, New Women outflanked antifeminists, who continued to endorse the separation of the private from the public sphere in order to justify women's exclusion from the latter. Ardis writes: "In this context, the New Woman was often contrasted not simply with the 'old' angel in the house but also with three other groups of women in late Victorian England who struggled to renegotiate the gender-based division of labor. These are, in order of their increasing 'deviancy' from the dominant Victorian ideal of femininity and as they have been labeled by recent critics: single-issue social reformers, 'Independent women,' and middle-class women who 'converted' to socialism in the 1880s and 1890s" (14–15). In other words, while New Women were a product of feminist reforms, they also often distanced themselves from important feminist causes in the 1890s, and especially single issues identified with the social purity movement. One way to understand the ideological work performed by the New Women in these Anglo-Indian romances, then, is to examine how they open up space for new configurations of social and erotic desire.

All the New Women who appear in these cross-racial romances can be seen as products of the changes in the social and sexual contract in the historical real of British metropolitan culture in the 1880s. One of the most important legal changes was initiated by the passage of the Married Women's Property Act of 1882, which overturned "the common law of coverture by which a wife forfeited all property upon marriage" and gave married women the same rights to own and dispose of their property as single women (Hennessy and Mohan, 331). This reform gave British women more direct control over their own money and property, and meant that mothers were sometimes able to pay for their daughters' educations and to bequeath some of their property to them. These legal reforms thus made it possible for more British women to choose not to marry and made divorce a more viable, though still socially tabooed, choice as well.

Rosemary Hennessy and Rajeswari Mohan have argued that the liberating effects of the Married Women's Property Act of 1882 were offset by the passage of the Criminal Law Amendment Act of 1885, which raised the legal age of sexual "consent" for girls in Great Britain from thirteen to sixteen and so fostered more surveillance of young women in the public sphere.[7] Moreover, as Hennessy and Mohan point out, changes in the laws concerning the age of sexual consent for Englishwomen also intensified the debate about raising the age of consent for Indian women. They explain, "Through legislation like the Criminal Law Amendment Act in Britain and the Age of Consent Act in India [1891], control of female sexuality was gradually moved out of the private space of the patriarchal family and into the domain of state regulation. In the process, woman as subject of the law was constituted as a sexualized body to be protected by the state when the respectable father or husband was absent or, as in the case of the colonies, when the uncontrolled sexuality of the colonial man rendered him unfit to protect the colonial woman" (348). Thus, according to Hennessy and Mohan, these two acts managed "complementary adjustments in the contradictory position of women in Great Britain as the relationship between public and private spheres and middle-class women's place in both was gradually shifting" in the 1890s (334). New Women typically resisted these new mechanisms of control by more frankly expressing female erotic desires and often by asserting their sexual independence.

The reforms that British feminists promoted in 1890s and 1900s in England found less support among colonizing men and women in British India, and generated somewhat contradictory effects, producing what Antoinette Burton has usefully called "imperial feminism" (1–2). Many newly trained professional women and some British feminist activists came to India in order to serve the Empire, accepting the invitation to regard Indian women as their "right and proper colonial clientele" (34). By the first decade of the new century, British India was particularly hostile territory for women's suffrage and for social purity activists. Some Anglo-Indian women supported women's suffrage, though often, like Flora Annie Steel, they joined the movement only after they returned to England. In the first decade of the twentieth century, many of the most powerful colonial officials, including Lord Curzon, who was viceroy from 1898 to 1905, and Lord Kitchener, who was the commander and chief of British forces in India from 1902 to 1909, were outspoken and tenacious opponents of British women's right to vote (Burton, 13).

Opposition to the feminist efforts to repeal the Contagious Diseases Acts and the related Cantonment Acts in British India had a longer and even more contentious history. In 1886, Josephine Butler began a campaign for the repeal of the Contagious Diseases Acts in India, and, in the 1890s, she and her supporters joined forces with the British social purity movement in order to advance their cause. The controversies they generated grew so heated that they nearly provoked a "constitutional crisis" in 1894 and, again, in 1897, as Philippa Levine has persuasively argued ("Rereading," 585–612). By creating alliances with the social purity movement in the 1890s, some feminists hoped not only to repeal legislation like the Contagious Diseases Acts in India, which authorized the compulsory examination of Indian women suspected of carrying venereal disease, but also to dismantle the entire system of "registered" brothels staffed by Indian prostitutes which served the British troops (127–169). The social purity campaign disrupted the daily life of many Anglo-Indians affiliated with the military and, in 1894, provoked a virtual stand-off between the ruling Liberal government and senior military officials in India who refused to comply with regulations abolishing mandatory medical examinations for prostitutes (600). While feminist antiregulationists succeeded, for example, in 1894, in closing the "lock hospitals" that confined diseased prostitutes in India (Ballhatchet, 160), they failed to achieve their overall goal of entirely eliminating state control of prostitution because of various defensive political strategies undertaken by political and military leaders in India and by the alternative measures they devised to arrest the spread of venereal disease. Two famous purity crusaders, Elizabeth Andrew and Katherine

Bushnell, further inflamed antifeminist sentiments in India, and provoked expressions of outrage from many Anglo-Indian men, inside and outside the military, when they published their exposé about the conditions that Indian prostitutes faced in these "registered" brothels, in their book, *The Queen's Daughters in India*, in 1898 (Burton, 157–164).

Although many Anglo-Indian leaders at the turn of the century resisted these feminist challenges, the prevailing colonial sex and gender ideologies were nonetheless transformed by these controversies and by a growing awareness of population trends. During and after the Boer War, for example, British men and women became keenly aware of the implications of the falling birth rate in Great Britain (Davin, 10), and these anxieties were amplified in British India because Anglo-Indians were such a small minority. In 1901, for example, they numbered approximately 170,000 in a total Indian population of 294,000,000, and the Eurasian population of 89,000 (Ballhatchet, 6) was more than half as large as the Anglo-Indian group. When considered in this context, novels like Perrin's *Waters of Destruction* and Steel's *Voices in the Night* can be seen to express deep colonial fears about the Malthusian threats posed by a rising mixed-race population.

Anglo-Indian men and women were deeply divided, however, about the best means to restrict and control the sexuality of colonizing men while at the same time encouraging colonizing women to marry and reproduce. As Philippa Levine observes, "Increasingly over the course of the nineteenth century, commercial sex between colonizing men and local women rather than concubinage or other more permanent or monogamous liaisons became the preferred colonial practice, more particularly in military circles" ("Rereading," 589). Some Anglo-Indian military officials in this period responded to the efforts to eradicate the registered brothels by trying to pressure their subordinates to marry, but this tactic sometimes meant that they seemed to condone mixed marriages, particularly in Burma, which came under British control in 1886 (Ballhatchet, 148–151). Mixed marriages between Englishwomen and Indian men were regarded as an affront to colonial prestige; Lord Landsdown, for example, officially expressed his "strongest disapproval" for one high profile cross-cultural marriage in 1893, between the Maharajah of Patiala and Florry Bryan, objecting particularly because this marriage involved a woman "far below" the prince in rank (Ballhatchet, 117). Given the double binds surrounding these and other efforts to control the sexuality of colonizing men and women, it is hardly surprising that Lord Kitchener, and many other Anglo-Indians in the Edwardian period, defined the sexual restraint of British men as essential to the maintenance of colonial rule (Wurgaft, 10–11).

The New Women who appear in these cross-cultural Anglo-Indian romances of the 1890s and later reflect many of these ambivalences. Because
they are often portrayed as working as teachers, governesses, and, increasingly, nurses and doctors rather than simply searching for suitable husbands,
the New Women in these romances demonstrate that independent women
posed particularly serious threats to Anglo-Indian society. Moreover, the
Anglo-Indian women who are the subject of this chapter dramatize their compliance with imperial imperatives to reproduce, but they do so with a man of
the "wrong" race. In assessing the careers of these sexual renegades, I will
focus on three more specific consequences of the introduction of New
Women, and the feminist causes that they embodied or opposed, defended
or denounced, in Anglo-Indian cross-cultural romances.

First of all, by representing New Women who passionately loved Indian men, these romance writers undermined the favorite rape script of the
postmutiny period by representing the erotic attraction across racial barriers
that colonial rape narratives had categorically denied (Sainsbury, 170).
Because New Women spoke frankly about sexual desire, they challenged colonial ideologies that celebrated colonizing women's innate "pride of womanhood," which had been linked to Englishwomen's pride in their own racial
"purity" and, more to the point, in the racial purity of their children. Second,
the New Women in these texts show, in various ways, how colonial prohibitions against interracial sex collided with those promoting respectable middle-
class marriage as a morally superior way to control and contain the sexual
desires of colonizing men and women. Third, the inclusion of New Women
in these romances prompted a re-envisioning of the private sphere that challenged the proxemics of colonial life that enforced the multifarious polarities of race and class.

All these romances about racial crossing display a curiously persistent
emphasis on the arrangements of domestic space, but since this thematic concern is often read as a typical womanly preoccupation, many critics in the
past have dismissed these novels as convention-bound romances, relegating
them to the dustbin of literary history, often without reading them.[8] These
novels about mixed marriages typically contrast the arrangements of domestic space in the households of the colonizers with those of the colonized in
order to dramatize the alienation of the heroines and heroes who, after being
ostracized by "their" culture, are forced to leave the domestic space where
they feel at home and to enter a "native" domain where intimacy, privacy,
and sexuality are organized differently. The treatment of domestic space in
these texts is not a trivial matter, then, for it reveals how marriage across racial

lines reopened what we might call the zones of "abjection" in the colonial imaginary.[9] This was the period, after all, when colonial planners and "sanitary" engineers in British India tried to stabilize the zones of abjection in the historical real by literally redesigning public and private space in many cities in British India.[10]

This emphasis on space allows us to read these cross-racial romances as demonstrating the psychodynamics that Judith Butler identifies in her analysis of the relation between sexual and racial abjection in *Bodies That Matter*. Butler's starting point is Julia Kristeva's categorical analysis in *Powers of Horror: An Essay on Abjection*. Kristeva writes: "We may call it a border; abjection is above all ambiguity. Because, while releasing a hold, it does not radically cut off the subject from what threatens it—on the contrary, abjection acknowledges it to be in perpetual danger. But also, abjection itself is a compromise of judgment and affect, of condemnation and yearning, of signs and drives. Abjection preserves what existed in the archaism of pre-objectal relationship, in the immemorial violence with which the body becomes separated from another body in order to be—maintaining that night in which the outline of the signified thing vanishes and where only the imponderable affect is carried out" (9–10).[11] Abjection, according to Kristeva, is established in three arenas, typically operating in relation to food, to waste, and to sexuality, shaping, in turn, the individual's defenses and enforcing larger social taboos. Because these romances bring British and Indian characters into intimate sexual contact, they offer new maps of the zones of abjection in Anglo-Indian life, when they compare their British and Indian characters' different relations to food and bodily waste, to disease and death, and, most of all, to sexuality and reproduction.

Butler historicizes Kristeva's concept of abjection in order to illustrate the psychic consequences of the repudiation of homosexual potentialities in men and women who defined themselves as heterosexuals under the regimes of early twentieth-century capitalism. The cross-racial romances discussed in this chapter, like the American novels that Butler analyzes from the 1920s, exemplify "the complex set of racial injunctions which operate in part through the taboo on miscegenation." As such, these novels suggest how we "might understand homosexuality and miscegenation to converge at and as the constitutive outside of a normative heterosexuality that is at once the regulation of a racially pure reproduction" (*Bodies*, 167). Butler's analysis of the formation of heterosexual male identity through the abjection of homosexual desire sheds a light backward on the construction of the sex and gender identities of colonizing men discussed in the last three chapters. Her analysis of miscegenation, and its relation to interracial desire and to motherhood, provides a particularly useful starting point for my analysis of female sexuality in the cross-racial romances that are the subject of this chapter.

Racial Crossing and the Abjection of Paternity

Alice Perrin's novel *The Waters of Destruction* illustrates some of the ways that racial difference was newly eroticized in early twentieth-century romances, though it also suggests why the sexual fulfillment offered by the newly eroticized Indian woman must be repudiated by colonizing men in order to protect the racial and gender hierarchies essential to colonial rule. Perrin's narrative also suggests why the rape of the Indian woman by the colonizing man remained under erasure in this period. Although Perrin's hero, Stephen Dare, is not technically guilty of raping Sunia, the young Hindu woman in this text, the author must work hard to clear her hero from any charges that he exercised power over her in ways that allowed him to exploit her vulnerability. Put another way, Stephen Dare illustrates the increasingly obvious double binds created by the presumed paternalism of the colonizing male's relation to the colonized woman at a time when the New Imperialism reimagined the colonial project in terms of conquest and (British) masculine force.

The geography of colonial space provides a crucial key to the larger meanings of Perrin's romance, first of all, since the plot is set in motion when the hero is transferred from a large military station (3) to a "lonely subdivision in a remote and unpopular district fifty miles from any railway" and thirty miles from a "little civil station" (4). Reassigned to a world outside the regimented colonial space of an Anglo-Indian military station, Dare grows desperate under the pressure of his self-imposed racial segregation. One sign of his sexual panic is evident when he welcomes the visit of Loo Larken, the New Woman he dismissed earlier in the novel, when she accompanies her brother-in-law on his inspection tour of the canals that Dare, as an irrigation engineer, oversees.

Perrin advertises her distaste for the New Woman by invoking class prejudice in her characterization of Loo Larken, identifying her initially as one of three "lively but vulgar" India-born English sisters (22). Shortly after meeting Dare, Loo Larken proclaims her identity as a New Woman by defining marriage as a choice rather than her natural vocation, prefacing her comments about marriage with the qualification "If ever I can persuade myself to marry . . ." (26). Loo also embodies that sexual inflammability that is typical of many New Women in these and other romances, when she proves that she is "fast" by deciding almost immediately after meeting Dare that she has fallen in love with him (19). In describing Loo and her family, Perrin's narrator acknowledges a slippage in Anglo-Indian racial categories when she notes that as a newcomer, Dare "was ignorant of the quick emotions and readily stirred impulses which are so curiously combined with the easy nature and indolence of those who are born and bred in India, and who have consequently assimilated many racial characteristics of the country, though their descent may be, as with the Larkens, purely European" (59).

The New Woman's disruptive impact on the organization of the public and private spheres in Anglo-Indian society is suggested by Loo Larken's first visit to Stephen's home, when she picks up Dare's photographs and asks intrusive personal questions. Moreover, when Stephen attempts to escape from the relentless Miss Larken, he accidentally meets Sunia, who lives nearby. Stephen finds Sunia much more erotically appealing than the voluble Miss Larken, especially when she kneels before him and tearfully requests his protection after being turned out of her home because she refused to assume the costume and austerities that Hindu orthodoxy prescribed for widows. Stephen eventually finds himself tempted, in turn, to test one of the most important boundaries separating the public from the private sphere in Anglo-Indian society when he encounters Sunia again and lets her see his appreciation for her beauty, youthfulness, and passivity. Thus, Perrin's plot makes the New Woman partly responsible for Stephen's transgression by emphasizing his nostalgic appreciation for all the Victorian "feminine" qualities that Miss Larken, and other New Women, repudiated: "He saw that her slender limbs were finely modelled, her skin of a delicate golden brown, and her eyes deep and lustrous as those of an antelope. He pitied the pretty little thing sincerely. He had a vague notion of the miseries of Hindu widowhood, and it seemed to him deplorable that this helpless, graceful child who lay at his feet should be condemned to an existence of slavery and repression" (30). What is striking about Stephen's assessment of Sunia's charms is that he both objectifies and eroticizes the signs of her racial difference. He admires the "golden brown" of her skin, for example, rather than responding with the prescribed abjection which should warn him to keep his distance and confine her to her proper place in the power hierarchies of the Raj. Later, noting "the delicate nose and chin, curved lips, tiny ears, and the silkiness of her fine hair" (63), Stephen tries to rationalize his erotic interest by equivocating about Sunia's race, observing that "she was completely unlike the ordinary village girl of the plains" and noting that it was "very obvious that she favoured the Northern race to which her mother had belonged" (63).

Kristeva's theory of abjection is literalized in Perrin's novel because it is Sunia's transgressive act against the mother goddess, Kali, that causes her final expulsion from Hindu society and prompts her to seek Stephen's protection and help in converting to Christianity.[12] Though he has resolved to keep aloof in order to avoid further sexual temptations, Stephen later agrees to shelter Sunia temporarily until he can find a companion to travel with her to the missionaries' school to "learn to sew, and read and write, and sing" (105). Stephen confronts one of the double binds faced by social conservatives like himself when she resists his plan to send her to school, saying, "Why should I want to read and write? What is the use of such wisdom to a woman" (105). Indeed, Sunia is shrewd enough to recognize that Stephen finds her attractive precisely because she has no ambition to acquire such "wisdom."

Moreover, in agreeing to allow Sunia to remain in his compound, though she is neither servant nor kin, Stephen violates one of the basic rules of colonial segregation and later multiplies his error by allowing her to serve as his nurse when he becomes ill, inviting her into an intimate relation more like that of a wife than a casual servant. In other words, in describing the moral slippery slope that Stephen traverses before he actually marries Sunia, Perrin comes dangerously close to recognizing fundamental contradictions in the sexual double standards that characterized British and Anglo-Indian marriage arrangements (as well as their relationships with domestic servants).

Perrin's staging of the cross-cultural marriage in this text also reveals some of the conflicts created when the discourse of New Imperialism collided with moralizing notions about the sexual and racial "purity" of British colonizers in India. Although Stephen could easily satisfy his sexual desire for this young Indian woman without the benefit of marriage, since she is both poor and unprotected, Perrin apparently feels obliged to design a plot that requires her hero to remain chaste until he is married; otherwise, Stephen would compromise the moral superiority that is the most meaningful sign of his race. At the same time, Perrin insists on the inauthenticity of this marriage, since it improperly sanctions sexual relations between a man and woman who, in her view, should not be united.

The character who solves this plot problem for Perrin is the overly zealous evangelical Christian missionary, Mr. Tod, who recognizes the force of Stephen's desire and wrongly pressures him to marry Sunia so he can recruit another soul for Christianity. Just as Loo Larken is portrayed as a threat to the private order of colonial life, so Mr. Tod is defined as a threat to public order because, in his efforts to convert Hindus to Christianity, he lives too close to them and transgresses the supposedly natural racial boundaries that should, in Perrin's view, separate the colonizer from colonized. Mr. Tod's tattered clothes and inelegant speech, indicating his lower-class origins, mark him as doubly objectionable, if not abject. When Mr. Tod, who has agreed to accompany Sunia to his school, suddenly falls ill, Stephen's plans to keep Sunia at a distance collapse.

Perrin brings Mr. Tod and Stephen into the zone of abjection when she describes how the missionary falls ill and Stephen comes to the dying man's bedside. Pressured by his urgent requests, Stephen witnesses Sunia's specious conversion and baptism to Christianity, and then, compelled by guilt and sexual desire, he agrees to marry Sunia. Perrin indicates how he rationalizes this decision when he asks himself, "Why deny himself a pleasure, a solace, even perhaps a comfort? He realized with a vague reluctance that such a death-bed ceremony would bind him to the native girl morally, if not legally, for ever" (143–144). In other words, Perrin brings Stephen to this scene of disease and death in order to signal his parallel contamination when he crosses that most important border defining sexual abjection in Anglo-Indian society and marries Sunia.

Because Sunia's conversion to Christianity ostensibly removes the religious barriers that partly defined her difference, "race" becomes the name for all that remains separating the partners. But in describing the chain of logic that allows Stephen belatedly to see the moral correctness of the colonizer's thinking about the value of sexual restraint and British racial purity, Perrin inadvertently shows how and why paternity under these conditions reveals the colonial father's "abjection." In briefly summarizing the effects of the first two years of their marriage, Perrin's narrator declares that all Stephen's efforts to "Europeanize" Sunia fail. Stephen's union with Sunia is meant to confirm the narrator's view that the "gulf between black and white" should remain "unbridgeable": though some Europeans "may succeed in throwing a plank across the chasm, it is the Westerner who has to venture over to the other side, for there is never a meeting half way" (115).

Having crossed over, Stephen comes to hate not only himself and his wife but also their son, who offers living proof that the racial dualities of British India can be physically reconciled and embodied. While Dare is initially touched by Sunia's "pretty pride and delight in her motherhood," the "first sight" of his child, that "little black and yellow creature had stabbed him with dismay" (158). Later, in a psychological example of colonial "splitting," Stephen decides that the child's nature is "all of its mother and nothing of himself" (158). As Kristeva's theory of abjection predicts, Stephen's abhorrence is stirred most because his son is racially uncategorizeable. Thus, though Perrin's romance shows how the race and gender hierarchies of the period can collude with each other, it also suggests that the control of male sexuality and paternity is a central problem of contemporary Anglo-Indian life.

Stephen's response to his domestic space illustrates another aspect of abjection in this novel. Though he has provided this home space for his wife and child and, presumably, has the power to arrange it more to his liking, he blames his discomfort on his wife. Watching her play with their son, he concludes: "It was all so essentially native; the badly-lighted, untidy room, the musky atmosphere, the woman seated on the bed, looking like an illustration from a Hindu story-book, and the black-eyed child making awkward little jumps to the sound of the tom-tom and his mother's voice" (155). While Perrin's narrative shows that Stephen has benefited from similar English customs which gave property and precedence to male heirs, he identifies Sunia's pleasure in bearing a male child as a peculiar characteristic of "Hindu womanhood" which gives "fresh impetus" to her "self-importance" (158). He also identifies Sunia as the source of further racial contamination for their son since she resists learning English, seems to possess "all the Oriental disregard for past or future," and exhibits ungovernable fits of rage that she fails to correct in their child as well as in herself (158).

Ironically, it is the return of the New Woman in this text that prompts Stephen to reevaluate his mixed marriage and life choices. Loo Larken, who has demonstrated her own downward class mobility by marrying a "railway man," though she says she still does "just what she fancies'" (169), violates Stephen's privacy by inviting him to discuss his feelings toward his wife. As he formulates his confession, Stephen feels that "suddenly all the satiety and weariness of the native woman that had been slowly deepening within him through all the arid months of the last two years confronted him as a harsh and complete reality, for which there would be no palliation, no possible relief. A repulsion that was almost physical pain assailed his heart and mind, his very veins. He felt he could not touch her, could not even listen to her; that if he went near her he should kill her" (175). When Stephen tells Loo that he has "grown to hate the sight" of his wife she responds, "But she is only a native. . . . You could get rid of her just when you wished if you gave her enough money. It is often done, though not so much in India as in Burmah" (180). Loo's knowledge about sexuality exposes the complicity that was frequently the price of the New Woman's relative freedom from Victorian gender roles.

In the end, Perrin saves Stephen the trouble of disposing of both his son and his Indian wife, and the authorial staging of these events shows the terrible self-righteousness, delusion, and hypocrisy that was reinforced when the New Imperialism joined with the "imperial feminism" of colonizing New Women like Loo Larken. Immediately after Stephen recognizes his murderous wishes toward Sunia, he learns that his son has drowned. Though he worries a little about how his wife, "with her elemental instincts and unschooled passions," will cope with their loss, his own "mind whispered that the child, for its own sake was better dead than living" (187). Shocked by her loss, Sunia returns to Hinduism and undertakes a pilgrimage to propitiate the goddess Kali (186). As a result, Sunia is conveniently absent when Stephen is urgently called home to England in order to arrange money matters related to his deceased uncle's estate, which he has suddenly inherited.

When his inheritance frees him from the need to return to his work in India, Stephen is tempted to take Loo Larken's advice, by remaining in England and simply abandoning Sunia. Unconstrained by any serious religious scruples, Stephen realizes that only his sense of "honour" prevents him from abandoning his wife, since the ceremony that united them was not registered and so is not legally binding. What Perrin does not acknowledge is that Stephen also realizes that Sunia does not have the economic means to contest his abandonment. When he tells his story to the English girl that he now wants to marry, she shows a proper female delicacy and class solidarity when she urges him to return to his Indian wife, repudiating the opportunistic ethics that Loo bluntly outlined, reminding him instead that "honour" and "sacrifice" are central to his identity as an upper-class Englishman (280).

The improbable conclusion of Perrin's novel shows the often unacknowledged importance of English class hierarchies in sustaining the colonial order in British India in the Edwardian era. Ultimately, Stephen returns to India to learn one final lesson: that maintaining class divisions is just as important as maintaining racial segregation. On his return to India, Stephen meets a old Indian man who remained loyal to the British during the Indian Uprising of 1857. Hearing his "simple history of love, faith, and heroism of the loyalty of a humble native servant" (301), Stephen recognizes that honor is central to the moral code that justifies British dominance in India. Once Dare has learned this lesson, Perrin rewards him when he discovers immediately afterward that his wife had drowned months before, when the canal works failed and the river Kali Nadi, the "waters of destruction," flooded the countryside. In devising this ending, Perrin invokes the mutiny, and the favorite colonial rape script associated with it, in order to whitewash her hero's sexual transgressions and return him to his proper place in the social order in England.

Imperial Feminism and Voices in the Night

Like Perrin's novel, Flora Annie Steel's *Voices in the Night* includes one easily recognizable New Woman in her plot, though her novel focuses on the other configuration of cross-racial romance that I have identified, since it describes the career of a pretty English girl, Genevievre Fuller, who falls in love and marries a Westernized Hindu, Chris Davenund. Steel's novel is designed to expose the "hideous" mistakes (73) made by this mixed-race couple and to illustrate the superior choices made by another New Woman, the chaste, and imperially minded Lesley Drummond, who, by the end of the novel, consents to marry Jack Raymond, an older colonizing man. In her strange and tangled narrative, Steel explores the "complex set of racial injunctions which operate in part through the taboo of miscegenation" (Butler, *Bodies*, 167) in British India. The resulting novel, so curiously devoid of passionate love, celebrates instead the erotic sacrifices that Steel regarded as a part of the white man's (and woman's) burden, epitomized by the rigid and seemingly sexless marriage of the lieutenant-governor of India and his wife, Lady Arbuthnot.

The importance of the theme of abjection, and its relation to female sexuality, are vividly displayed in this novel when Steel describes the futile efforts of a "sanitation" engineer, assigned to oversee the application of disinfectant to the streets around a "registered" brothel in Nushapore, the imaginary Indian city that provides the backdrop for this text. In the moral geography of this novel, the registered brothel marks the center of abjection, for here racial boundary crossings, illegitimate sexuality, and filth mingle together in a series of abject contaminations that cannot be washed away: "There was a strong smell of carbolic in Miss Leezie's house, for the bazaar on which it gave was being cleaned by half a dozen sweepers, a water-carrier, and the conservancy overseer in a uniform coat with brass badge; his part being to dole out the disinfectant and survey the proceedings from various doorsteps in advance of the slimy black sludge" (*Voices*, 147). Steel indicates that this ritual washing is far from routine; it is only performed on the day that an English official visits for an inspection. In defining this registered brothel as the epitome of abjection, a space filled with pollution, disease, and death, Steel reiterates many of the sordid details found in exposes like *The Queen's Daughters in India*.[13] But in imagining the private and public spaces beyond the compounds of Anglo-India in this novel, Steel defines "India" more generally as a world permeated by all kinds of abjection, as defined by body and food, by disease and death, and, perhaps most of all, by sexuality and reproduction.

In fact, Steel's novel offers two versions of the New Woman, one abjected and the other valorized. Genevievre Davenund embodies all the energies unleashed by the New Woman that Steel could assign to the zone of abjection. She presents Genevievre, nicknamed Viva, as a heartless English adventuress, a modern "vulgar girl of good taste" (72), who meets the high-caste Brahmin Chris Davenund at her mother's boardinghouse in London, a place frequented by "third-rate young men from the city, over whom she had wielded a cheap empire" (72). Finding Chris to be "better-looking and better-bred than any of her other admirers," Viva flirts with him.

Though Steel admits that Chris Davenund is "of better birth than the generality of those who brave the dangers of foreign travel" (87), he is represented, nonetheless, as lacking the moral judgment to assess Viva adequately, either before or after their marriage. As an outsider to British culture, he "could have no standard save that of books" (72). Sent to England to complete his education, Chris is disoriented, unable to recognize the signs of class in this foreign culture, so he misreads Viva's personal beauty as a sign of her virtue and integrity: "The superficial refinement of the girl, seen against the background of the only English life he knew, had made him think of the Lady in Comus" (72).

Though Chris and Viva avoid the moral complications suggested by Stephen Dare's marriage with Sunia because they elect a civil service at "the registrar" (74) in London rather than a public ceremony sanctified by the church, which would require Chris's conversion to Christianity, they face other obstacles as soon as they return to India. Expecting a social advance because of her marriage to a man whose father is an "unorthodox" Hindu "high up in Government service," Viva arrives in India only to discover that Davenund cannot find employment after his father's unexpected death, that "there was literally no place" (73) for him in Anglo-Indian society. Viva likewise finds herself associated with a Hindu mother-in-law who, after being widowed, has "reverted to the most bigoted austerity on her husband's death" (73).

In identifying the causes of the inevitable failure of Viva and Chris's marriage, Steel indicates her endorsement of Anglo-Indian values which conflate race with upper-class identity, moral probity, and sexual restraint. Chris is sufficiently Westernized to provide Viva with a home of her own, in a neighborhood miles away from his mother and family, and, as in Perrin's novel, domestic architecture becomes one measure of the degree of Westernization of the characters in this novel. Steel notes that in the racially mixed neighborhood of Shark's Lane, where Viva and Chris have lived for eighteen months when the novel begins, "a knowledgeable eye could infer the exact degree to which the social life within was at variance with the Western architecture in which it dwelt" (69). Unlike her Westernized Indian neighbors, Viva is apparently able to create an English-style home for her husband which displays the obligatory English signs of their rising class status: a piano, a dining room, and two bedrooms, one that is spartan and masculine, the other sweetly feminine. Steel describes Viva's bedroom in minute detail, noting the "roses on the walls, the hangings, the floor . . . roses even on the dressing table, trimmed like a rose itself" (220), but significantly it is not the marriage bed, but rather this staging ground of female vanity, that is the center of Viva's private life. In other words, Viva performs the English wife's proper role as consumer under the monopoly capitalism of the period, but in a marriage with the wrong type of man.

It is not domestic space, then, but rather Viva's unbridled sexuality, and Chris's failure to control it, that define this sexual union in Steel's view as racially and morally abject. Though Steel mutes any direct discussion of Viva's erotic interest or sexual relationship with her husband, she indicates signs of trouble in this marriage when Viva appears at breakfast, inappropriately dressed in a "pink negligée," wearing a "plentitude of powder" and smoking "a Turkish cigarette" (73). After Viva tells Chris, coolly, that she intends to claim "her full share of Western liberty" (72), she advises him to take a "second wife" (75) since, as a Hindu, he may marry or divorce in accord with Hindu law. Chris protests, expressing his love for Viva and his commitment to the highest Western ideals of romantic love and companionate marriage, values similar to those expressed by the Hindu heroes in Devi's *The Unfinished Song* and Tagore's *The Home and the World*. Viva asserts her racial authority when she argues that she is a "better judge of what an English lady can do" than is her Hindu husband (75) and later dismisses these romantic ideals bluntly, saying, "We girls have left it behind a bit in England, nowadays" (293).

Later, Viva publicly flouts the colonial mores which required Anglo-Indian wives to appear to live a life of scrupulous moral probity when she claims "her full share of Western liberty" (70) and publicly displays her sexual emancipation by flirting openly with other men, including the racially ambiguous and morally suspect Mr. Luncanaster, a man who is reputed to be an "awful sweep" (79), Anglo-Indian slang for a philanderer. This is just the first step on the slippery slope of Viva's moral decline. Because Chris lacks the proper "inherited" moral standards (79), he does not recognize that his wife has crossed into morally compromising territory. When Jack Raymond advises him to reassert his rights as a man and husband, Chris does not really understand because, as a Bengali intellectual, Steel imagines him as lacking the aggressive masculine instincts that Jack naturally exhibits.[14] In the end, Viva's frustrated materialistic ambitions and predatory sexuality are identified as irradicable marks of her class origins rather than her race, but it is her uninhibited sexuality that makes her, and New Women like her, into a source of embarrassment for Anglo-Indians like Steel who conflate race with upper-class identity in order to assert the colonizers' moral and intellectual superiority.

Steel displays what she regards as Chris's racial inferiority when she describes his nostalgic return to his home in the native quarters of the city, which expresses his unconscious reaction to the crisis in his marriage. Steel uses this journey to chart Chris's sequential surrender of Anglo-Indian standards by reference to three zones of abjection as defined by clothing and nakedness, pollution and bathing, and food and alms giving.[15] After Viva humiliates him in public by choosing to remain with Mr. Luncanaster at an important dance at the Residency, Chris wanders into the city and joins worshipers at the Siva Temple of Viseshwar. In order to enter the temple, Chris takes off his Western "garments of civilization" (195) and wraps himself in his wife's shawl to hide his nakedness. After a ritual bath, he allows the priest to apply his caste mark, which reignites his "pride of race" (117), but when he is recognized and denounced as a pollution-carrying outcast, he is driven from the temple. Reluctant to return to his home in Shark's Lane in daylight because of his state of near nakedness, Chris walks to the native quarters of the city, where he begs alms, transgressing another important Anglo-Indian boundary that marked the colonizers as the dispensers rather than the recipients of charity. Finally, Chris's sexual desire is awakened when he is offered food by a "slender slip of a girl about fourteen, with a long round throat poising the delicate oval of her face, and black lashes sweeping to meet the bar of her brows above her soft velvety eyes" (125). Realizing that he has inadvertently returned to his mother's house, Chris recognizes that this "extraordinarily beautiful" young woman is his cousin, Naraini.

The rest of the novel describes Chris Davenund's effort to reconcile his divided loyalties to British and Hindu cultures. While Chris feels tied to the former by his education, marriage, and work, he is drawn back to Hindu India by the gravitational force of his desire for Naraini, by his hope for reconciliation with his mother, and by the emotional appeal of Hinduism. Like *The Waters of Destruction* and many other Anglo-Indian novels of the period, the zones of abjection in Hindu society are ultimately defined by reference to the literal and metaphysical mother. By the end of the novel, Chris is faced with making a choice between "Right and Wrong, Higher and Lower, . . . old and new, Viva and Naraini" (377). Though he proves his commitment to protect the "Right," as the colonizers defined it, by heroically risking his life in order to frustrate an Indian nationalist plot to derail an English troop train, Chris subsequently gives Viva sufficient grounds for divorce when he "abandons" her, returns to his mother's home, and eventually reasserts his Hindu identity by marrying Naraini. Viva, likewise, returns to her proper place in the English class hierarchy, relieved that she has escaped from the "terrors" of Anglo-Indian life (402). Significantly, she bears no sign that she is carrying an unborn child who would remain a permanent reminder of her "mistaken marriage" to Davenund.

Because Steel, in contrast to Perrin, saw the New Woman as one expression of "inevitable" social change (3), she offers a second, imperially correct version of the New Woman in her heroine, Lesley Drummond. A young, unmarried woman, Lesley is characterized as a New Woman because she has the independent spirit, but not the unruly female sexuality, of Viva Davenund, and she has "led the life of a definitely independent woman in England for six years" (3) before traveling to India, without the protection of a father, brother, or uncle. Hired as a governess to look after Jerry Arbuthnot, the insufferable six-year-old son of the lieutenant-general and his wife, Lesley elects a strangely Victorian vocation. Handicapped by her occupation and by her obdurate racist disregard for Indians and Indian culture, she barely deigns to notice Indian men or women, let alone recognize their erotic appeal.

Though Lesley possesses the independence and pride of the New Woman, Steel denies her the self-conscious sexual agency that Viva constantly exhibits; Lesley, by contrast, is completely mystified by the meaning of her own sexuality. Displaying the "cool disdain, which is nowadays so often the prevailing expression of young womanhood for manhood" (1), Lesley does not recognize and act on her feelings for Jack Raymond, the "tall, spare" older man who, we learn, was once engaged to the aristocratic Lady Arbuthnot, until the novel is nearly complete. Strangely enough, it is Lady Arbuthnot who orchestrates a love triangle between herself, the obtuse Lesley, and her one-time lover, Jack Raymond. In fact, what draws Lesley into this triangle is her attraction not to Jack but rather to the beautiful Lady Arbuthnot, a name associated with the Anglo-Indian resistance to the social purity movement in the historical real of the 1890s (Levine, "Rereading," 588). While the triangulation of male homosocial desire is evident in the plots of so many Anglo-Indian novels, Steel's text hints at the sexual sources of Lesley's fascination, though class provides a convenient screen for why Lesley finds her employer so compelling. After prompting Jack to propose to Lesley, Lady Arbuthnot expediently steps aside.[16]

Steel's *Voices in the Night* also attempts to represent some of the ways that abjection functions in the world beyond the orbit of Anglo-Indian society. While she uses Chris Davenund to explore the zones of abjection in the public realm, when she moves him through India's streets, temples, and boardinghouses, Steel considers the zones of abjection in Indian family life in more detail through her melodramatic treatment of the private life of one of the old ruling families of the Muslim elite in Nushapore. In depicting this family, Steel unintentionally exposes some of the basic contradictions that arose in the 1890s, and later, when Anglo-Indians tried to adjust to new civic models that recognized women as "objects of desire" and, at the same time, as in need of "protection" (Hennessy and Mohan, 349). In describing the relationship between Jehan Aziz and his wife, Noormahal, Steel dramatizes why, in her view, some (elite) Muslim women seemed to require imperial protection because of the sexual degeneracy of aristocratic Muslim men.

Like Perrin, Steel uses the organization of domestic space in this Muslim family to illustrate the incompetence of the colonized; Aziz's wife and family live in an ancestral palace that has reverted to a "wilderness" (25) because he cannot afford to maintain it or to provide proper clothing, or even adequate food and medicine, for the members of his household. Abjection is located not only in the physical space of this household but also in the social arrangements that define the sexual dimensions of this marriage. As the narrator explains, the partners in this marriage "hate" each other and do not live together, though they remain legally and ritually connected because "in India the marriage tie is not a sentiment, it is a tangible right" (29). Jehan Aziz's wife, Noormahal, has many of the same physical qualities that Stephen Dare initially appreciated in his Indian wife (29), since she is "fair" and "still young, still comely" (29), but her husband prefers his "bachelor quarters" in old Delhi, where he enjoys the company of a professional courtesan, Dilaram. Nonetheless, Steel's narrator declares, "Noormahal felt none of the passionate repulsion which a Western woman would have felt" (30) when her husband fails to provide for her material needs and otherwise treats her with disrespect. The degeneracy of this family is symbolized, then, by the child who was "called into being" by these two "imperious, undisciplined natures" (32). Although Noormahal has given birth to a "pretty" but sickly son, his father's improvidence has reduced him to being the "heir to Nothingness" (29).

When plague strikes the population in the native quarters of this city, and the dead and the dying spread the zones of abjection from public to private space, Noormahal's little son is the first to die in this household, marking the extinction of his royal line in Nushapore. After another woman in the household dies of plague, Noormahal enters the zone of abjection herself when she helps bury the body.[17] Acting on new colonial mandates that defined Noormahal as in need of their protection, Jack Raymond and a male doctor break into her private quarters in order to offer medical help. Noormahal mistakenly thinks that these Englishmen have come to rape her, and kills herself by jumping into the household well to escape, becoming a casualty of these new colonial paradigms defining public and private life. Soon after, Jehan Aziz is killed in a freak accident, proving, as Steel's narrator proclaims, that "it is only the Spirit of Slaves that dies; the Spirit of Kings lives for ever" (418).

The only equivalent of the New Woman that Steel recognizes in either the Hindu or Muslim culture represented in this text is the sixteen-year-old Sobrai, one of the younger members of Noormahal's household. Sobrai, who is described as "a buxom creature, over-developed for her years, and overdressed in cheap finery of Manchester muslin at six pice a yard and German earrings at two annas a dozen" (21), has shrewdly assessed her unlikely marriage prospects in this degenerate family. After she finds four lost pearls, she decides to claim her sexual independence by leaving home and using them to raise the cash to pay the fees that will allow her to apprentice herself as a professional prostitute in a registered brothel that services British troops. Sobrai reasons, "If one had to amuse oneself, was it not better to do it openly in a recognized, almost respectable fashion, which was countenanced even by the Huzoors?" (36).

Steel's treatment of the licensed brothel in this text is deeply ambivalent, in part because she wants to retain the "model of masculinity" and heterosexuality that naturalizes male dominance, as her treatment of Jack Raymond, and the heroes in *On the Face of the Waters* and other novels, makes abundantly clear. These licensed brothels remain troublesome for Steel, and other Anglo-Indians who share her sympathies, then, because they expose the inconsistencies in colonial ideologies equating sexual and moral purity, since British soldiers made these establishments profitable.

By sexualizing Sobrai in ways that make her carry all the abjection that Steel associates with prostitution and other displays of illicit female sexuality, she disguises the threats to colonial culture posed by the registered brothel. Once Sobrai enters this house of prostitution, she finds a world even more regimented than her earlier life; here "all was rule and regulation. No freedom, no fun, no frivolity; in a way, no choice" (158). In one rare moment when she is left unsupervised, Sobrai reveals a "fierce faculty for obtaining personal gratification" that is, apparently, racially determined, when she is "seized" with a "dare-devil delight" and moves into the public space to display the exotic glamour that newly eroticizes her sexual and racial difference. Prompted to parade her talents before a crowd of rowdy English soldiers, Sobrai sings and then dances "not with the posturings and suggestions of the bazaar, but with the dignified gestures and scarcely perceptible swayings suited to her heavy robes, and to the words she sang" (162). By performing in this public space, rather than in the regimented world of the brothel, Sobrai inspires a riot, and in this way Steel avoids representing cross-racial sex between British soldiers and Indian prostitutes. The disorder Sobrai causes indicates, by synecdoche, that the entire Indian quarter of the city is both abject and female, as a body in need of purification. When the plague spreads disease and disorder throughout Nushapore, creating a revolutionary ferment as conflicts erupt between Muslims and Hindus over the need to dispose of the dead, the only solution, in Steel's view, is for colonial men to assert their natural, manly, imperial force.

Steel's novel ends in an orgy of improbability that is apparently intended to restore the political and moral order enforced by imperial hierarchies, but the symbols Steel invokes in her conclusion cannot bear the weight that she assigns to them. When a missing string of pearls is returned to Lady Arbuthnot and her young son recovers a politically sensitive letter containing governmental secrets, the integrity of colonial rule is restored. In the final pages of the novel, Lesley Drummond also agrees to marry Jack Raymond, ensuring that the colonial order will be reproduced (418). But by entering into this marriage, Lesley also enters a sexual zone that Steel worked throughout the novel to define as abject, characterizing it so broadly that it included all female bodies and all displays of female sexuality, abjecting, as a result, the reproductive capacities of colonizing men and women as well. Steel's novel shows, most of all, the dilemmas created at the turn of the century when Anglo-Indians like herself, and Lord Kitchener, defined sexual restraint as the most meaningful sign of the colonizers' right to rule. It also demonstrates how redefinitions of the sex and gender identities of British and Indian men between 1890 and 1910 disconnected the favorite rape script of the postmutiny period.

The Erotics of Difference in Life of My Heart

Life of My Heart (1905) illustrates, by contrast, that British feminism at the turn of the century could be used to authorize the liberation of female sexuality as well as its restriction. This cross-cultural romance is one of the most ideologically radical novels of this decade since it represents an Englishwoman who marries a working-class Muslim man, willingly sacrificing many of the privileges of race, class, and economic power that she otherwise would have enjoyed as a colonizing woman in India. Victoria Cross, the pseudonym of Vivian Cory, a long-time resident of British India, seems to have gleefully taken on the task of systematically breaking nearly every taboo that policed the color bar and prohibited cross-cultural and cross-class marriage in most Anglo-Indian romances. In detailing Frances's slow surrender to desire, Cross challenges every premise in the favorite rape script in the sexual imaginary of the postmutiny period and demonstrates, instead, that a superior "morality" does not necessarily make Englishwomen immune to the attractions of young colonized men.

Frances Wilson has many of the familiar attributes of the Anglo-Indian heroine since she is blond, blue-eyed, beautiful, well dressed, and rich, but she is also decidedly a New Woman. Having lost her mother when she was a child, Frances was privately educated; she has been instructed in Greek by an Oxford M.A., has read Indian history, and has learned "Hindustani and Persian with the ease of one already trained by a classical education" (17). Her excellent but "entirely theoretical" education has developed the "thinking power of the brain and the habit of deduction and inference, besides exciting and practising the imagination" (23). At twenty years of age, she is bored by the colonizing Englishmen she meets and is critical of the materialistic and seemingly passionless marriage arrangements of her class. Her father, General Wilson, is recently retired, and Cross defines him as one of the beneficiaries of the new monopolistic capitalism in this period since he supplements his military pension by drawing "some thousands in private income" that he obtained by speculating in railroad stocks (22). Frances has less need to marry than most conventional heroines in Anglo-Indian romances since she expects to inherit an independent income of four thousand pounds a year when she turns twenty-one (94).

Victoria Cross doubles the boundaries and amplifies the power of the taboos that Frances Wilson dares to break when she identifies Hamakhan, the handsome young Pathan who is the object of her heroine's attention, not only as a racial and cultural Other but also as a man who is widely separated from her heroine by his class and occupation.[18] Frances meets Hamakhan when he enters her home in order to renew the woven straw matting used on the floors. Frances is first attracted by the aesthetic qualities that colonial discourse previously denied to its racial others when she notices how the sunlight falls on Hamakhan's profile: "It was a proud, severe, and beautiful outline, of the noblest type, but one that from its very regularity would have had something of stony cruelty in it, save for the bloom, the soft, vivid bloom of youth upon it now" (11). Though she does not have a "sensual nature," having a mind "naturally cold and pure" (39), Frances nonetheless notes that Hamakhan's skin "looked soft as the softest velvet, and like velvet seemed to invite and seduce the touch" (11). Their transgressive relationship begins when Frances gives Hamakhan a large tip and allows him to see that she is attracted to him. Reading her gestures as a sexual invitation, Hamakhan immediately tries to kiss and embrace her.

Transforming a scene that could have been the prelude to a rape, Cross describes instead how Frances initially repulses Hamakhan but soon begins to imagine that "a tender love would grow up in her for him if once allowed to take root" (50). In a few short pages, Frances overcomes all the obstacles that are supposed to separate "pure" Englishwomen from Indian men. Cross explicitly challenges notions about the naturalness of "racial pride" when she describes how Frances looks at her handsome lover with "passion, delight, and—yes—pride. True, he was a chetai wallah, a man of the hills, a barbarian, poor, without an anna, except that gained by the toil of his coarsened palm; socially he would be looked upon with contempt everywhere; but, personally, what a glorious specimen of humanity" (58–59).

Like Stephen Dare, Frances exercises some of the powers that imperialism gave her when she takes advantage of her position as the memsahib in her father's house by hiring Hamakhan as a servant in order to enjoy a closer intimacy with him. Unlike Perrin, however, Cross reminds her readers that Englishmen often did this in earlier novels, and in earlier periods in Anglo-Indian life, when they were attracted to Indian women from a comparable class, noting, "These little things are so easy in the East" since "an ordinary individual there can gratify any little private penchant as easily as the Roman Augustus could buy a new slave" (73). But neither Frances nor Hamakhan is content with this arrangement for long. Frances discovers that proximity simply enflames her passion for Hamakhan, and she is tortured by her unfulfilled sexual desire.

What initially restrains Frances is not her pride of race but, the narrator contends, a "pride of womanhood" that makes her reluctant to surrender her virginity before marriage. Frances knows that "marriage with him would be impossible" since "the whole station, every single British soul in it" would oppose her desire to marry Hamakhan (65). Gradually, she accepts the fact that the "indulgence of her love for this Mohammedan, this native without the British pale, would mean secret, dishonourable flight, and it was this that revolted the proud, English trained-mind of the girl" (65). As she begins to consider living with Hamakhan without the benefit of marriage, Frances recognizes "the Great Border that divides the White from the Black," and sees herself as standing poised on the threshold that defines sexual abjection in Anglo-Indian society, "with her foot just hovering over it, with all smiling and safe around her, yet all dangerous, threatening, and uncertain before her" (77).

Cross inverts another potential rape scenario when she describes Frances in her bedroom, already undressed and lost in contemplation of the attractive image of her nearly naked body as she gazes in the mirror and longs for Hamakhan. When he suddenly enters her room, Frances welcomes rather than repulses him. When he then delivers his ultimatum, "If it is not marriage then it is farewell" (89), she agrees to elope with him.

By so outraging colonial taboos which assumed that colonial women's modesty and restraint were racially determined, Cross relocates the violence that prohibits miscegenation and shows explicitly how these taboos protected the gender identity and economic interests of colonizing men. While Perrin's and Steel's novels are organized around the splitting of the mother and the projection of these negative maternal traits onto the cultures of the colonized, Cross turns the readers' gaze back to the colonizing father. At a critical moment in their bedroom conversation, Frances's father bursts in on the couple, and, showing "the force of utter hatred and loathing" (90), he attacks Hamakhan and throws him down the staircase, returning him literally to his assigned place at the bottom of the colonial hierarchy. When her father invokes the typical imperial arguments about racial purity, asking his daughter, "Have you no pride of race, of blood? no self-respect?" (95), Frances coolly responds by noting that "there can be no immorality in mere colour" (95). Instead, she challenges the notion of British racial superiority itself by cataloguing the moral degeneracy of Anglo-Indian men, "I despise the men of my own race . . . a shooting, hunting, drinking, swearing set of unintellectual blockheads; stupid to talk to, hideous to look at, selfish and uninteresting to live with. I shall never marry one of these. Hamakhan is beautiful and clever; he can learn anything so quickly and easily. He suits me. I am exceptional in every way. Only an exceptional life would suit me" (95–96). This passionate declaration suggests one of the reasons why New Women in other novels, like Lesley Drummond or, as we shall see, Adela Quested in *A Passage to India*, are presented as obtuse, neurotic, and sexually conflicted modern women.

What makes this novel an important one in demonstrating the ideological work that rape was called upon to perform in the colonial imaginary is that Cross shows how "consent" remained a problem at the heart of colonial romances, even after the legal reforms of the 1880s. Frances is above the legal age of sexual consent, but she remains under her father's control until she inherits her fortune at the age of twenty-one. As a result, she must obtain his consent and cooperation in order to marry. Frances admits this when she tells her father, "If I tell you I want to marry this man, and ask you to give your consent and to help me for the one year which intervenes between now and my majority, what will you say?" (94). By articulating this request, Frances, and Cross, recognize how the laws of the 1880s shifted the focus of consent from young women to the men designated as their guardians, in India as well as in England. Likewise, she recognizes that Englishwomen's legal and economic status was further complicated by the marriage laws that remained in force in British India, since Frances would also lose many of her legal rights as an Englishwoman if she were to convert to Islam and marry according to Muslim law.

Because he sees this marriage as "monstrous, loathsome," and "immoral" (95), Frances's father refuses to help the couple, thinking he is acting to enforce Anglo-Indian taboos against miscegenation. He warns Frances that her lover will probably desert her in a few weeks since Oriental men are naturally "polygamous" (97). Frances counters, logically enough, by arguing that the economic arrangements of colonial society would militate against Hamakhan's desertion: "Why should he desert me? . . . A white wife, and when I can give him everything, everything in life? Of course I take my chance, but no more than in any other marriage. How many English marriages are happy? How many Englishmen keep other women besides their wives? How many divorces are there?" (97–98). Realizing that her father will not listen to this reasoned argument and that he is determined to "kill the man if he sees him again" (98), Frances pretends to submit to his judgment but leaves her home forever when she elopes with Hamakhan the next day.

In describing the progress of this romance, Cross not only flouts the repressive racial and sexual codes that provided the linchpin of imperial order in novels like Perrin's and Steel's, but she also breaks many of the most powerful taboos about the representation of the white female body and its desires, though her narrative also reveals the lingering traces of Byronic

Orientalism in her treatment of the lovers' sexual passion. Her debts to Byron are evident, for example, when Hamakhan lifts Frances onto his horse and they ride off together. Frances nearly swoons with desire as she holds on to his waist and notices that it is "a typical Eastern waist, full of vigour and strength, but slender and soft and with a yielding suppleness that renders an accidental touch even a danger and a temptation" (125). Likewise, Cross echoes Byron, and reveals the limits of her sympathy in imagining racial others, when she describes Hamakhan's "immoderate passion": "Most European women would have trembled before it, recognized something different here from the regulated, moderated, legalised desires of her own race; but Frances leaned to the untried, the strange, the terrible in everything, and she felt only wild exhilaration as they sped away over the plain, farther and farther away from home, protection, law, and her own race" (125). From this point on in the narrative, Frances masquerades in native clothing and adopts the veil. When she appears before Hamakhan for the first time in Eastern clothes, he predictably fetishizes Frances's white skin, which he regards as "the acme of beauty" (129).

In dramatizing her heroine's experiences in the rural working-class Muslim community of Brishamgur, where the couple seeks refuge, Cross breaks one literary taboo after another in challenging the boundaries that define abjection in Anglo-Indian culture, by reference to female sexuality and the female body. Though Cross omits the scene of sexual consummation, since it is apparently the erotic foreplay that matters most to her—and probably to her readers—she indicates the passion that the lovers share in many intimate scenes that center on their uncovered bodies. Moreover, Cross highlights the ways that maternity and abjection are defined differently in Hamakhan's culture when he asks Frances to display her barely pregnant body to his male friends. Though she is humiliated by this request, Frances reportedly loves Hamakhan "with a tenderness too deep to wish to disobey him or seem to make light of his wishes," so she stands unveiled in order that his friends may see the "swelling line that at present only gave to the slight perfect figure a shade more richness and maturity" (140).

In another episode, Cross violates one of the strongest taboos in Victorian and Anglo-Indian culture when Hamakhan, in a jealous rage, confronts Frances. When he threatens to "cut off" her breasts, she responds, tauntingly, with "Cut" (197), opening her robe to display "two slight girlish breasts, white as two snowy peaks capped with the rose of sunset, traversed faintly by small, clear blue veins. It was a sight to melt the verriest devil, and Hamakhan was not a devil, his faults were the faults of a fierce, wild race, and a certain inborn leaning towards cruelty" (198). Cross's narrator notes, however, that Frances's "British blood" (198) compels her to take this courageous and defiant stance, and contends that if Frances had "huddled terrified" or prayed for mercy, Hamakhan would have "slaughtered her relentlessly in his lust for inflicting pain" (198). Because she met him "fearlessly," he relented. While mutiny novels represent similarly desperate (though less explicit) gestures of racial pride as Englishwomen's last defense against rape and murder, Cross treats this defiance, instead, as proof of the authenticity and mutuality of the passion that these lovers share.

As a result of her boundary crossing, Frances enters a culture where the female body and maternity are celebrated rather than abjected. Frances observes that in this rural Muslim community "maternity is considered the crown of womanhood, far surpassing that of youth or beauty, and that with them a woman is proud and delighted to display it. Amongst the English, a woman regards the change in her figure with shame and hatred, and seeks at all costs to conceal it" (147). Cross, in fact, breaks another literary taboo that enforced the abjection associated with pregnancy and birth among the English colonizers when she dares to represent the heroine's tortured delivery of her first child and her decidedly unmaternal rejection of it when she discovers she has given birth to a girl. When Frances's labor begins, she longs for a "word of encouragement from sensible, motherly English lips" but knows that "none of these women would have touched her hand, now that she had passed beyond the barrier of her race" (204). Refusing to comply with the traditions that excluded colonized and colonizing men alike from the scene of birth, Hamakhan agrees to stay with Frances as she suffers through her labor in silence. Though this scene of childbirth seems designed to show that biological sex rather than race defines the most fundamental differences between these lovers, the narrator highlights Frances's elusive cultural superiority when Hamakhan watches her and wonders if "there is something more to be attained than the mere conquest of the flesh. What was this mysterious power that held those white, agonized, distorted lips together? that met and trampled upon nature and pain? In a woman it could not be soul; but this something, was it his?" (210).

Cross underlines the misogyny in both British and Muslim cultures when she notes that Frances and Hamakhan are both disappointed that she gives birth to "nothing but a daughter" (221), but at the same time she counters the gender conventions enforced by Orientalism by showing that Hamakhan's "tender domesticity" prompts him to try to reconcile his wife to their daughter. Later when she is pregnant with her second child, Frances asks Hamakhan whether he will take another wife if she fails again to deliver a son. Defying stereotypes, he responds, "Allah does not give everything to one man. I have enough; I am content" (309). Hearing these words, Frances feels she has gained insight into "the deepest, most sacred recesses" of Hamakhan's heart and exults in this evidence of the transforming power of their love: "Every word was contrary to his race instincts, his upbringing, his religion, his very nature; but each word came bright with truth from the furnace of white flame she had created in his being, in which were molten all his traditions, beliefs, ingrained desires, ambition, hopes, into passion for herself" (310–311).

In Cross's novel, such extravagant romantic love allows Frances and Hamakhan to transcend their racial and sexual differences, though her narrative hardly escapes Orientalism entirely. Challenging British and Anglo-Indian notions that her life with Hamakhan must be "degrading," (317), Frances observes instead her lover's devotion as he works "regularly, patiently, almost without food and drink through the long, hot day, returning to the one woman he loved and for whom he denied himself every pleasure, begging from no one, owing no man anything, innocent of causing suffering to man or beast; clean, honest, simple, bending his energies and his will to make another happy" (317–318). Their life together, Frances concludes, "came a good deal nearer the Christian ideal of existence" than did the "life of the average English subaltern, drinking, gambling, swearing, buried under debts, and . . . making love to his neighbour's wife" (318). Frances's meditation suggests why most Anglo-Indian romances novels typically end with the engagement or marriage ceremony of the couple rather than charting the heroine's life after marriage.

By describing the successive boundary crossings of her cross-cultural lovers, Cross suggests that it is the physical, social, and legal organization of colonial space that defeats these cross-cultural lovers, since Frances and Hamakhan spend the rest of the novel searching for the security of home. At the same time, Cross includes at least one episode that seems to reinstall the typical postmutiny script about interracial rape as the subtext of her love story when she describes how, during their stay in Brishamgur, several of Hamakhan's friends try to break into the house in order to rape Frances when he is working. Alone, with no servants to protect her, Frances recognizes, for the first time in her life, that she is vulnerable to sexual attack from Indian men and consents to live in seclusion, literally locked in each day by her lover, though she is nearly smothered by the heat and boredom of her isolation. Frances agrees to this seclusion because she realizes that if the intruders someday by "force or stratagem, or both, really gain possession of her," she would "have nothing but death to expect at Hamakhan's hands" since he would regard it as a sign of his as well as her "dishonour" (166). In other words, Cross seems, in the end, to reiterate colonial clichés about lawless Indian men, even though *Life of My Heart* resists many of these conventions.

Moreover, since Cross has characterized her lovers as "exceptional in every way," the other Indian men in this text suggest that violence rather than Hamakhan's tender love is the norm for colonized men. Two features of this episode, however, indicate how late-Victorian feminism disrupted this Orientalist myth. First, the village men regard themselves as Hamakhan's friends but refuse to acknowledge the sacredness of the bonds of love that should prompt them to regard Frances as a "sister" and extend to her the re-spect otherwise given to mothers in their community. Having already identi-fied Anglo-Indian men as similarly domineering, violent, and misogynistic, Cross designs a plot that shows how male gender identity overrides racial and cultural differences in British India at this time. Second, by describing Frances's fear that Hamakhan would reject and perhaps even kill her if she were gang raped, Cross identifies a concern that united colonizing and colo-nized women.

Having thus created a cross-cultural romance that dramatizes the ways that the biological and social expressions of sex and gender act to override racial and cultural differences, Cross is prompted, in the end, to reassert British "law" as the best means to protect both colonizing and colonized women from male aggression and violence. Driven out of Brishamgur by the sexual jeal-ousy of the men in his community, Hamakhan and Frances settle in a small, solitary house in Naimarabad, where Frances is able to sit in the open air, unobserved. Their idyll ends, however, when Frances is forced to recognize the limits of her romantic ethics of individualism when she abruptly discov-ers that Hamakhan's attitudes toward violence and death differ profoundly from her own. Responding to an urgent summons from a friend, Hamakhan leaves their home for several days and returns with a mysterious bag. When Frances awakens in the night to discover Hamakhan contemplating three bloody human heads that he has drawn out of the bag, she is horrified: "It seemed nothing could form an excuse, a justification, for those three livid, blood-stained faces beside them on the floor" (335). When Hamakhan re-marks that the men were Hindus, so "it is not at all unfitting for them to be murdered; rather, on the contrary, it was all to the glory of Allah" (336), Frances jumps to the conclusion that her lover has killed the men. She thus resumes the colonizer's role as moral instructor when she says, "It is horrible, abominable, and a religion that taught you all that is a religion to be ashamed of" (336). After Hamakhan tries to explain that he has not killed them but has pledged himself to carry them to the man who commissioned the murder, she invokes British law as the absolute standard of morality and conduct when she argues: "Hindoo or Mohommedan, it is a crime against the English law. Oh, why did you involve yourself in the wretched business when it was all nothing to you" (340).

Thus, in this odd turn from romance to a fantastic sort of allegory, Cross reasserts the hegemony of British standards of law and justice, by describing how Hamakhan's failure to recognize the reach of colonial law causes the tragic death of both lovers. Believing that Hamakhan "belonged now to her and himself no longer, but to the law" (352), Frances insists that she accompany him on his gruesome errand. Frances moves into the zone of abjection herself when, with startling self-involvement, she leaves their newborn daughter, apparently unattended, causing her certain death, in order to accompany Hamakhan. Cross does not justify Frances's abandonment; she simply notes that it is one of the moral dangers posed by the New Woman: "The maternal instincts had never been strong in her. Like the other simple natural elementary instincts, they seem to die off where there is excessive artificial mental cultivation" (345).

Several features of the final episode also characterize this text as more modern than the other Anglo-Indian romances and epics of the race that we have been considering.[19] When the police stop Hamakhan and Frances, with their incriminating bundle, they do not believe Hamakhan's explanation, and he refuses to implicate anyone who could corroborate his story. Reclaiming her racial privilege, Frances tells the police officer that she is English and swears, on her "honour," that Hamakhan is telling the truth, but she fails to convince the authorities. Seeing "that death was before them," Frances resolves to follow her lover "out of the warm, sunny house of life that she loved to the cold, black plain of Death, just as she had followed him from her father's house to the plains of the desert" (374).

By identifying death as the only solution that will allow both lovers to remain together permanently, Cross makes a classic return to tragedy, but her ending also shows how sensationalizing information technologies work in Anglo-Indian culture after 1900 to block the more universal appeal of this love tragedy and reinforce instead the gender ideologies that create two different versions of romance. Cross asserts the power of love when she notes that Hamakhan stabs himself in order to avoid arrest but overcomes his "instinct" to kill Frances so as to "seal her to him by her death" (380): "if his education and his life beside Frances had failed to extinguish his inborn lusts and instincts, it still had an influence, and left its trace upon his passion. She had been chaste, faithful, devoted to him, she had given up much, suffered much for him, and he would not deprive her of her life now to gratify himself" (379–380). Yet when Frances, like a twentieth-century Juliet, refuses the chance to live, and "obedient to the longing to gratify him to the last annihilating of her nature" (381), she demands that he kill her too, Cross shows how their *liebestod* is later misrepresented. Returning the readers' attention to Frances's body, and especially her breasts, Cross describes how her lover "raised his right arm, and with his last strength thrust the wet knife up to its hilt in the flesh between the breasts. Her wound stretched straight to the heart" (381). Ironically, when English officials gather beside Frances's body, they ask how this English girl could have cared "for such a brute" (382). Moreover, "sensational newspaper accounts" of this death further diminish its universal appeal by "sedulously" assuming that the dead girl "must be some very inferior person of the lower orders—a shop or dressmaker's assistant at most" (386). The women who gather beside the bodies, by contrast, "looked in silence at the dead body of the Pathan . . . and being women, did not wonder at all nor ask any question" (382). When her family learns of Frances's death, her father likewise declares that she got what she deserved, while her unhappily married sister wonders if "her sister's fate was worse than her own" (388). Though it is hardly a typical romance, Cross's *Life of My Heart* thus provides a dramatic illustration of how the sexualization of colonizing women could be used in conjunction with the new eroticization of colonized men to make the postmutiny rape script disappear.

The New Woman and The Unfinished Song

Swarnakumari Devi's *The Unfinished Song*, published originally in Bengali in 1898 and later translated into English by the author in 1913 (Tharu and Lalita, 237), treats a Hindu counterpart of the New Woman and represents the heroine's parallel awakening to romantic love. Like the Anglo-Indian cross-cultural romances discussed in this chapter, *The Unfinished Song* also imagines the possibilities of an interracial marriage between a nameless Englishwoman and an upper-class Hindu man, Romanath Roy. In contrast to these Anglo-Indian romances, Devi's novel begins after this cross-racial romance has failed and focuses, instead, on the young Hindu woman, Mrinaline, nicknamed Moni, who has the most to gain from the failure of this romance since the handsome Mr. Roy subsequently proposes marriage to her. Unlike

the colonizing women in all the Anglo-Indian novels I've read, Devi's heroine rejects the otherwise desirable Mr. Roy when she learns that he has abandoned his English fiancée.[20]

Like all the other heroines in this chapter, Moni is motherless, since
her mother died in her infancy, but unlike the English New Women, she has
a much more loving relationship with her father, noting that their mutual "devotion" is a compensation for the loss of her mother. Moni thus identifies
the unrecognized Oedipal grounds upon which abjection is erected in these
and so many other Anglo-Indian novels. Early in the novel, Devi identifies
two features that mark her heroine's status as a modern Indian woman, and
both invite comparison with the English New Women in the cross-racial romances we have already considered. Moni narrates her own story and explains that though she is a devoted Hindu, she is "still a spinster" at the age
of nineteen (12). Anticipating the readers' "still greater" surprise, she then
confesses that she "knew love before I entered wedlock" and that she "loved
a man without even expecting him to become my husband" (12). By these
comments, Moni indicates that her father is a social progressive who defied
the Hindu customs of arranged "child marriages," which would otherwise have
been contracted when Moni was a young girl. Her second comment indicates
that she has claimed her freedom to assess her partner's capacity for love and
his suitability for marriage herself, in defiance of Hindu customs prescrib-
ing nonconsensual marriage and female modesty, though it must be added,
for late twentieth-century readers, that the novel makes it clear that Moni has
not had any sexual relations with the man she loved. Moni's awakening to
mature, heterosexual love requires that she revise her view of "true love" as
requiring "self-abnegation" (16), a perspective that New Women like Loo
Larken and Viva Davenund could hardly have comprehended. By the end of
the novel, Moni tells the man she intends to marry that she now realizes "that
altercations and demands are also adjuncts of love, and in this way, love is
kept ever young" (218), indicating that Devi's heroine traverses a very different cultural and psychological landscape in order to arrive at this more
mature perspective on the emotional and moral basis for conjugal love.

The Unfinished Song also invites comparison with these cross-cultural
romances about English New Women because it is similarly concerned with
the arrangement of domestic space. Much of the novel takes place in the home
of Moni's Westernized sister and this domestic space resembles the domestic space described in countless Anglo-Indian romances. Moni's sister is married to a barrister who has been educated in England, and they have adopted
English customs of sociability. Like her sister, Moni does not observe purdah

and talks easily with her brother-in-law's unmarried male friends. In fact, like an English heroine, Moni meets Mr. Roy when he comes to their home to play tennis. Like Frances Wilson in *Life of My Heart*, Moni notices Mr. Roy's erotic appeal, observing that "he had finely cut aristocratic features, a well-shaped head with beautiful hair, and he wore a glossy jet black mustache" (35). It is not Roy's appearance, however, that is most seductive to Moni; it is the song he sings which holds her "spellbound," listening "like one in a trance" (37).

Like the imperially indoctrinated New Woman Lesley Drummond and, as we shall see, like Adela Quested as well, Moni is confused by her response when Mr. Roy asks her to marry him. Moni delays accepting his offer because something about the song he sings seems "unfinished," though she receives little support for her resistance either from her sister or from the culture at large. At the same time, Moni reminds the reader about the importance of marriage in the construction of Hindu women's gender identity when she says: "No Westerner can realise what a powerful influence matrimony has upon the life of a Hindu woman. Her husband is the representation of the Divine on earth to her, the object of her worship. There can be no mistake whoever he may be; he is the only one, and none other ever dare claim a thought in her mind" (43).

Moni later learns about Mr. Roy's past sexual history and, like the English New Women we have been considering, she judges his behavior by egalitarian moral standards. Because she "expected of man what man expects of woman" (65), she rejects Mr. Roy when she discovers that he is already engaged to an Englishwoman.[21] She maintains her view that Mr. Roy is "unworthy" (59) of her love because of her sense of moral outrage on behalf of an Englishwoman she has never met, even when her sister pressures her by telling her that she is being unreasonable. Mr. Roy also tries to overcome Moni's objections by trying to racialize the competition between these two women, arguing that his English lover was too assertive about her desires and "acted like one afflicted" if he did not visit her as often as she wished (71). Moni defends this unknown Englishwoman, saying to Roy, "What may have been a mere flirtation to you, was evidently to her the expression of deep-rooted feeling" (71). Thus, in refusing him, Moni acts on a sense of gender solidarity that Loo Larken and Lesley Drummond, like most New Women in colonial fiction, typically refuse. While Moni declares her faith in another kind of "manhood"(60), her more Westernized sister shows that she has accepted the colonizer's gender definitions and moral double standard in matters of sexuality. But she also articulates the racialized ethics of blame that

eventually undermined the favorite colonial rape script of an Indian man raping a "pure" Englishwoman in this period, when she tells Moni, "You know
that English girls are notorious for priding themselves on being able to cap-
tivate the affections of [Indian] men" (62).

In dramatizing Moni's struggle, however, Devi defines an alternate ideal
of mutually loving, companionate marriage that rejects, on one hand, an unqualified acceptance of the moral double standards imbedded in Western notions of romantic love and marriage and, on the other, the emerging Hindu
nationalist ideal of marriage in the 1880s which attempted to valorize the
"entire system of non-consensual, indissoluble, infant marriage" (Sarkar,
"Hindu," 226). Devi shows that Moni's sister and brother-in-law have completely internalized the colonizer's ideas of love, desire, and honor, carried
by the English language and literature they have studied and enforced by accepting Western notions of abjection. Moni, by contrast, wants to recover the
spiritual and ethical dimensions of love that British imperialism forced out
of romance.

Two resources support Moni in her resistance to the self-betraying marriage that Mr. Roy proposes. First, the English-speaking Moni must learn to
recognize "the dignity and beauty" of her "mother tongue" (90). What Moni
struggles with in her sister's house are the polite lies central to Anglo-Indian
gender arrangements, which required women to wink at any signs of their
men's lack of sexual fidelity and where "race" differences provided pat jus-
tifications for the betrayal, abandonment, and violence done to Indian women
and men. Moni is simply intolerant of this hypocrisy, and this causes a disease that her sister identifies as "hysteria."

Moni's other resource is her father's unqualified love and support, a
source of strength denied to all the English New Women discussed in this
chapter. Shortly after Moni returns to her father's house, she is able to hear
the rest of the "unfinished" song that allows her to find and marry Chotu,
the man she has loved since her childhood. In designing this ending, Devi
addresses two problems in contemporary Hindu marriage arrangements that,
according to Tanika Sarkar, remained unaddressed by the more orthodox and
patriarchal Hindu nationalist program in the 1880s and 1890s: the Hindu
woman's pain over the loss of her connections with her natal family and her
"longing for knowledge" ("Hindu," 231).

Throughout the novel, Moni's father supports her and endorses her reasons for refusing Roy's marriage offer. When she writes to her father, pro-
posing that she remain unmarried, saying, "I hear that in England many a
girl remains unmarried and spends her life in service to her country. Grant

me to do likewise, let me dedicate my life in service to the Motherland" (189–190), he asks, "Must you necessarily remain single in order to serve your country?" (190). His response identifies the polarized choices that colonizing women faced in nearly all Anglo-Indian romances of this period, choices which set independence and work against marriage and motherhood. By returning to her father's home, Moni heals the psychological scars created by the colonial "splitting" that Homi Bhabha has defined, and overcomes mistaken notions about love, filial duty, and self-sacrifice that were formed by the circumstances of her childhood. In consenting to marry Chotu, Moni establishes a marriage that will fulfill her needs for "liberty and self-reliance" (141). Moni's ultimate choice of a marriage partner thus demonstrates the promise of a new synthesis of cosmopolitan values that Anglo-Indian romances, including Forster's *Passage to India*, repeatedly rejected. Believing that an egalitarian marriage offers the soundest platform for Indian nationalism, Chotu declares his belief in a resolution that even the genial Forster ridicules when he says, "Honour to every lady. . . . Honour to every man, three cheers for India" (129).

Seeing beyond the colonizers' romances that imagine love in terms of conquest, Chotu promises Moni a marriage that includes all his devotion, offering, "my life, my soul, my being" (198). The marriage they celebrate is clearly informed by his deep appreciation for Moni's spirituality, ethics, and desires. As such, Moni's marriage illustrates what a few English New Women, like Mr. Roy's disappointed fiancée, were seeking in these cross-cultural marriages. Moni and Chotu's marriage is also one that escapes the erotic sacrifices, disciplined and enforced by British notions of sexual and racial purity and abjection, sacrifices that many Anglo-Indian writers, including Rudyard Kipling and Flora Annie Steel, thought were central to British imperial identity. Thus, Devi's *The Unfinished Song* discloses some of the rooms left empty in the house of fiction designed by British and Anglo-Indian writers who remained preoccupied with disguising the "utilitarian, materialist, and narrowly contractual" marriage arrangements of British colonizers (Sarkar, "Hindu," 226), and with justifying British attitudes toward the racial and sexual Others who shared the colonial contact zone of British India with them.

CHAPTER 7

Modernism, Irony, and the Erasure of Rape

RECONTEXTUALIZING *A PASSAGE TO INDIA*

Men are very slow in changing their philosophy about women. I
fancy their idea of the maternal relation is firmest fixed of all.
Sara Jeannette Duncan, "A Mother in India"[1]

*B*y the time that E. M. Forster's *Passage to India* was completed and published in 1924, Englishwomen's relation to the "historical real," and their participation in the "social contract" in Great Britain, had again been profoundly changed. In 1919, married and single middle-class women over thirty were given the right to vote, though five million younger and poorer single women could not vote until 1928 (Kent, 221). In the first decade following the Great War, some legal reforms were also directed toward improving British women's economic position. Some reforms were directed toward addressing the economic situation of unmarried women who had children. In 1918, the Bastardy Laws of 1872 were amended, doubling the amount men were to pay to support their illegitimate children. By 1923, the Matrimonial Causes Act legally removed the sexual double standard limiting the conditions for which women could file for divorce, and granting twice the amount previously paid for child support to women who won custody of their children (Kent, 221–222). Other obstacles blocking their access to jobs in the legal and other professions were eventually eliminated, for instance, with the passage of the Sex Disqualification Removal Act in 1928. These legal changes acknowledged many of the false premises of Victorian chivalry and gender arrangements and rectified some of the most obvious legal inequities in the social contract, especially in regard to women's sexual and reproductive capacities.

Significant changes were made, as well, in laws that more specifically regulated sexuality, inside as well as outside marriage. Rape laws, for instance, were altered in 1884, so wives could no longer be jailed for refusing conjugal rights to their husbands, and in 1891, husbands were forbidden to "forcibly imprison their wives in the matrimonial home to obtain their rights" (Pateman, 123). These legal changes concerning marriage, sexuality, and reproduction, however, did not adequately address deeper contradictions in the "sexual contract" that defined British women's relationship to men, the family, and the modern nation-state (6).

One sign of the continuing controversies about the modern woman's relation to the sexual contract that defined British social relations between 1890 and 1920 can be seen in the sudden appearance of a number of British novels that include representations of rape. Thomas Hardy's *Tess of the D'Urbervilles* (1891), for example, highlights the moral and ethical problems that cluster around coercion and sexual "consent" when a working-class single woman like Tess is raped by an upper-class man. A few years later, H. G. Wells, in *Ann Veronica* (1909), describes his heroine's escape from rape as part of her education as a modern woman. Wyndham Lewis, in *Tarr* (1918), coolly describes the brutal rape of his protagonist's lover, Bertha. All three of these novels suggest that more explicit treatments of rape emerged along with the liberalization of the sex and gender norms for the modern single woman in Great Britain in this period. Likewise, Hardy, in *Jude the Obscure* (1895), reconsiders the subject of marital rape in his representation of Sue Bridehead's harrowing relationship with Phillotson. John Galsworthy, in *The Man of Property* (1906), and Rebecca West, in *The Judge* (1922), among others, offer more complex perspectives on the psychological damage that wives suffer when they are raped by their husbands. In short, rape again became a politically and symbolically resonant theme in literature about contemporary domestic life in Great Britain in the two decades immediately before middle-class women were granted the vote in 1919, since it provided a means to explore persistent contradictions between the prevailing social and sexual contract and more modern views of law and justice, violence and sacrifice, love and sex.

At the same time, some of the changes in the sexual contract in force in Great Britain were countered by the growing acceptance, particularly among intellectuals and self-consciously experimental modernist writers, of Freudian theories concerning sex, desire, and violence, concepts which threatened to erase the reality of rape altogether. Freud had argued, since the 1890s, that "information received by our consciousness about our erotic life is especially liable to be incomplete, full of gaps or falsified" ("Psychogenesis,"18:167), but, by the 1920s, his theory about the inherent unreliability of any report about sexual experience had gained enough credibility that it began to be used inside as well as outside the courtroom to challenge the accuracy of women's testimony about rape.

Essays like Freud's "Totem and Taboo" (1912) provided further psychoanalytic justification for women's continued subordination to men, reframing many questions concerning women and rape, consent, marriage, and reproduction. Freud later famously summarized this essay, saying that "the work of civilization has become increasingly the business of men, it confronts them with ever more difficult tasks and compels them to carry out instinctual sublimations of which women are little capable," and concluded that women are more "hostile" to civilization than men ("Civilization," 21:103). In brief, "Totem and Taboo" reauthorized Victorian gender roles by creating a new fable about the origin of civilization. In this essay, Freud describes how the sons of the primal horde, galvanized by their "hatred of the father who stood so powerfully in the way of their sexual demands and their desire for power," acted together to kill the father. In order to maintain equality among them, the brothers replace "the law of the father" with a new "social contract" that provided impartial laws rather than force in order to regulate sexuality and other social relations.

Freud's myth about the origins of civilization in "Totem and Taboo" also reinscribes Orientalism because he assumes that the "women of the horde" had previously been "kept for the father's use alone," in a social arrangement resembling a harem. According to Carole Pateman, Freud's account of the origins of the social contract is inconsistent since it assumes rather than defends the initial premise that "that sexual relations are consensual and non-political" (105). It is also incomplete, in Pateman's view, because it excludes the father's prior crimes—the capture and rape of the mothers who gave birth to the sons of the primal horde—and it likewise does not acknowledge the overthrow of the "motherright," which had previously regulated and sanctified marriage.[2]

Although essays like "Totem and Taboo" were used to justify resistance to women's suffrage and other feminist reforms of the early twentieth century designed to alter the social contract, Freud's emerging theories on human sexuality provided powerful new arguments for the further liberalization of the sexual contract. According to Peter Gay, "On Narcissism" (1914) marked a "radical change" in psychoanalytic theory, as Freud began to reconsider his previous understanding of gender identity and sexual desire in light of changes in his ideas concerning "ego ideals," "perversion," and "sublimation." Once Freud recognized "that ego drives must be sexual in character" (341), he realized that "love for the self and love for others differ only in their object" (342).

The larger implications of this shift in Freud's thinking about sexual desire can be seen, for example, in two companion papers on homosexuality, translated into English in 1920 and 1923.[3] In the first of these essays, "The Psychogenesis of a Case of Homosexuality in a Woman," written in 1920, Freud speculates about the "origin" of lesbian desire. He describes his analysand as "a spirited girl," who, after "inspecting" the "genital organs" of "her slightly older brother," developed a "pronounced envy for the penis" (18:169). Freud then links "penis envy" with feminism when he notes that "she was in fact a feminist; she felt it to be unjust that girls should not enjoy the same freedom as boys and rebelled against the lot of woman in general" (18:169), and, after outlining her persistent attraction to an older woman, he identifies his analysand as a lesbian. Insisting that this beautiful girl showed no physical or mental traits that necessarily determined that her "object choice" would be another woman rather than a man, Freud concludes that the "mystery of homosexuality is therefore by no means so simple as it is commonly depicted in popular expositions" since "mental sexual character and object-choice do not necessarily coincide" (18:170).

In a roughly contemporaneous essay on male homosexuality, "Some Neurotic Mechanisms in Jealousy, Paranoia and Homosexuality," written in 1922 and translated into English the following year, Freud argues that typically "homosexual men have experienced a specially strong fixation on their mother" (18:171) and describes some of the psychological defenses generating what we might now call homophobia. He notes, for example, that "jealous and persecutory paranoiacs . . . project outwards onto others what they do not wish to recognize in themselves" (18:226). Freud concludes from these and other studies in this period that all humans are inherently bisexual, a premise that radically redefines homosexuality and its relation to abjection.[4] The new model of human sexuality that Freud developed in these essays separates homosexuality from the system of "morality" that had been used to condemn it, and helps to detach sexuality from inhibiting Victorian gender norms. These two essays on homosexuality provide a useful framework for understanding how Freud's new theories about sexuality acted to reveal the sexual content of the "homosocial" arrangements that appear in so many late nineteenth-century British and Anglo-Indian novels about colonial life. His analysis also shows why "sacrifice" remained a psychologically central, but ambivalent, concept in modern British and Anglo-Indian novels that focus on sex and gender relations in British India after World War I.

By the end of the Great War, British India had also witnessed irreversible political and social changes which altered the meaning and credibility of the favorite postmutiny rape script of a white woman threatened with rape by an Indian man. By 1919, this familiar rape script had grown so threadbare that the political work it once masked had become transparently obvious. For example, when Marcella Sherwood, an Englishwoman, was allegedly sexually assaulted during the social turmoil that followed the Amritsar Massacre, Sir Michael O'Dwyer ordered any Indian man passing through the street where the attack occurred to crawl. When Indian nationalists and others protested, O'Dwyer was eventually required to stand trial for his notorious "crawling" order and was found guilty of abusing his military command.[5] There were, of course, many other significant political and social changes that emerged after the war, but for the purposes of this study, this episode concerning Miss Sherwood demonstrates perhaps most clearly the profound reorientation in the political and symbolic order in British India in this period.

One of the features that makes *A Passage to India* unique among Anglo-Indian novels is that it incorporates some of these new "psychoanalytic" perspectives on truth and sexuality while, at the same time, relying upon the more conventional narrative techniques of the "ethnographic real."[6] After all, in a purely psychoanalytic novel, Adela's failure to comprehend the "real" India would not be significant, but in the novel that Forster published in 1924, Cyril Fielding and Mrs. Moore demonstrate that it is possible to transcend the cultural and personal barriers that prevent Adela from understanding India and Indians more fully.

Adela's enigmatic experience in the cave offers perhaps the most dramatic example of how these new psychoanalytic perspectives on the meaning of rape, sexuality, gender, and consent found expression in Forster's novel. In his early draft of *A Passage to India*, written in 1912, Forster described Adela's successful effort to avoid what was clearly a rape attempt by a stranger in the Marabar Caves:

> At first she thought that <she was being robbed,> he was <holding>\
> taking her hand\ as before/ to help her <out>, then she realised, and
> shrieked at the top of her voice. "Boum"<went> \shrieked [?]/ the
> echo. She struck out and he got hold of her other hand and forced
> her against the wall, he got both her hands in one of his, then felt at
> her <dress>\ breasts/. "Mrs. Moore," she yelled. "Ronny—don't let

him, save me." The strap of her Field Glasses, tugged suddenly, was drawn across her throat. She understood—it was to be passed once round her neck, <it was to> she was to be throttled as far as necessary and then . . . [Forster's suspension points] Silent, though the echo still raged up and down, she waited and when the breath was on her wrenched a hand free, got hold of the glasses and pushed them at \into/ her assailant's mouth. She could not push hard, but it was enough to <free her> hurt him. He let go, and then with both hands \on her weapon/ she smashed <him to pieces>\at him again/. She was strong and had horrible joy in revenge. "Not this time," she cried, and he answered—or <perhaps it was> the cave \did/.[7]

In the revised version of this episode that appears in the novel, Adela's experience in the caves is hollowed out, but it is not only rendered ambiguous and ironic, a gesture we might expect in a modernist text, it is redefined as unspeakable. In short, in *A Passage to India* rape is Orientalized and returned to the zone of abjection.

Ten years later, when asked what happened to Adela in the Marabar Caves, Forster, like Freud, insisted that the workings of female desire remained beyond words: "I tried to show that India is an unexplainable muddle by introducing an unexplained muddle—Miss Quested's experience in the cave. When asked what happened there, I don't know" (Forster, *Selected Letters*, 2:125–126). Yet, as I hope to show, because Forster's novel is not simply a high modernist text, because it attempts to combine the "psychoanalytic" with the "ethnographic real," it invites us to consider the significance of Forster's strategic silences about Adela's sexual desires. In other words, Forster's treatment of the two "uncolonized" women, Adela and Mrs. Moore, demonstrate some of the new conflicts posed by British women's redefined relationship to the social and sexual contract in the 1920s, conflicts that disappear when these women are only considered under the sign of British modernism.[8]

In staging the rape trial in *A Passage to India*, Forster uses Adela's testimony to dramatize the revolution that occurs when Freud's theory about the unreliability of reports about "erotic life" are applied in a colonial setting where the credibility of a white women's word had previously been regarded as sacrosanct. Forster's political intent in erasing the rape from *A Passage to India* is easy to recognize, especially when McBryde, the superintendent of police, blathers on about the Indian "psychology of crime" (187) or the "scientific" evidence proving that the "darker races are physically attracted by the fairer but not vice versa" (243). By dramatizing the psychological, social, and economic damage that Aziz experiences when he is falsely accused of rape, Forster exposes instead the destructive machinery of the sexual and racial regimes of Anglo-Indian life.

Forster's novel offers several other episodes, in addition to the trial itself, that help to display the ideological work once performed by this familiar rape script in the colonial imaginary. For example, when Fielding and Ronny Heaslop confront each other at the club after Adela's presumed sexual assault, Forster indicates that her personal testimony, rather than any personal trauma as a result of rape, is really what concerns the Anglo-Indians who rally around her. In the colonial imaginary, the real "martyr" is not Adela but Ronny Heaslop, the man who has promised to be her husband, the man whose honor is injured by this attack. Moreover, as rumors about this crime begin to circulate, suggesting the "unspeakable limit of cynicism untouched since 1857" (207), McBryde insists that "Mutiny records," rather than the "*Bhagavad Gita*," should be the Anglo-Indians' "Bible" in India (187). Though Forster underscores this theme when he again alludes to the Indian Uprising of 1857, by noting how the unfamiliar presence of children at the club evokes "the air of the Residency at Lucknow" (200), he shows that references to the historical archive cannot illuminate all the meanings assigned to this sliding signifier when he describes a "young mother—a brainless but most beautiful girl," who "sat on a low ottoman in the smoking room with her baby in her arms" (200). This woman steals the scene, taking over for the absent Adela: "This evening, with her abundant figure and masses of corn-gold hair, she symbolized all that is worth fighting and dying for; a more permanent symbol, perhaps, than poor Adela" (200). Part of my objective in writing this book has been to demonstrate why the woman who replaces Adela is not only "brainless and beautiful" but is also married and a mother. I would like to conclude this study by considering the echoing effects created when the colonial woman who was once imagined as a victim of rape becomes the "symbol" of "something else." My objective in this chapter is to explore what "else."

We can read Adela's mistaken claims about rape as an episode of colonial "ventriloquism," as Brenda Silver has brilliantly argued, but Forster admits that Adela has the power to awaken from her dream, whereas the Indian men in this text are compelled to live out the colonizers' worst nightmares. After Aziz is set free, Hamidullah asks Cyril Fielding ironically, "Is it a dream, and if so when did it start? And without doubt it is a dream that has not yet finished. . . . Of course some Indian is the culprit, we must never doubt that" (243). Charged with complicity in sustaining the divisive and contradictory myths that sustain the Raj, Cyril Fielding in this exchange is reduced to a guilty silence, as are many readers of this text.

I would like to move beyond critical standoffs about the ambivalent meanings of rape (or its absence) in this text by demonstrating how *A Passage to India* can be read as a hybrid novel, straddling the divide between the modernist and the modern, between psychological subjectivism and the "historical real," between narrative experimentalism and more conventional realist techniques. First, I would recall the phantom of Mrs. Moore, who is chanted back to life at the rape trial. Her presence reminds us that, by 1924, there were already several notorious Englishwomen in the realm of the "historical real" who had crossed over the racial boundaries that Adela and Cyril finally act to confirm. Because of her age, Mrs. Moore perhaps most obviously recalls the example of Annie Besant, who publicly and eloquently supported various Indian nationalist causes and was sentenced to house arrest because of it in 1917.[9] There is also Adela's strange claim that only Mrs. Moore "knows" about the events in the cave, recalling the esoteric knowledge articulated by other British women who crossed over: the Irish Theosophist Margaret Cousins; Vivekenanda's devotee, Margaret Noble; and Gandhi's companion, Mira Behn.

Likewise, though Adela only briefly fantasizes about a more intimate sexual relationship with Dr. Aziz, her reverie about cross-racial desire was enacted by other famous European women of her generation who dared to broach the racial, sexual, and political taboos of British India altogether by establishing marriages or more open sexual alliances with Indian men. Perhaps the most notorious examples were Nellie Sen Gupta, who worked as a trade union activist after her marriage in 1909; Agnes Smedley, an American socialist who established a sexual alliance with Virendranath Chattopadyaya in 1918; and Evelyn Trent, an American communist who married M. N. Roy, India's best known communist during this period, in 1917.[10]

The significance of Forster's choice to remove both Adela Quested and Mrs. Moore from the colonial scene in his novel can be better understood in relation to this modern historical/materialist context. Moreover when Forster characterizes Adela as both apolitical and implausibly obtuse about her own sexuality, he indicates how the New Woman, who was relatively successful in freeing herself from the constraints of Victorian sex and gender roles in the period between 1890 and 1914, was recaptured in the 1920s by Freudian psychology. As such, she, like Cyril Fielding, demonstrates what the ego must sacrifice in order to achieve heterosexual "maturity." In this way, Adela exposes the shifts in the meaning of sacred and profane love and, as a result, in the meaning of marriage, consent, maternity, and rape in the historical real of Great Britain and British India in the postwar decade.

Moreover, Mrs. Moore also becomes a more resonant figure when we see her in relation to the new ideologies defining Hindu nationalism in this decade. By the 1920s, as Tanika Sarkar has argued, Hindu nationalists shifted their attention from the Hindu wife to the mother, finding "a new centre of gravity" in the "loving relationship between the mother and the son" ("Hindu," 234). In most of *A Passage to India*, Forster ignores the impact of this "new and supreme deity within the Hindu pantheon—the Motherland, the reified woman" (Sarkar, "Hindu," 234–235), but his novel shows, nonetheless, how this ideological shift transformed the symbolic balance of imperial power since English and Indian mothers, both real and symbolic, exert a determining psychological force throughout this text. Although Cyril Fielding, like all the other Anglo-Indians in this novel, is insultingly dismissive about the Indian nationalists' project, he solves his quarrels with the mother finally and improbably by submitting to the conservative sex and gender regimes of the Raj.

Likewise, Forster's novel barely recognizes Indian women as political agents, representing them as timid, inarticulate beings or as voiceless shapes at the Bridge Party who stand with their "faces pressed into a bank of shrubs" (41). Yet there were, by the 1920s, a significant number of Indian women who had emerged from purdah and who took up positions as outspoken political activists. Their power to disrupt the colonial imaginary was enormous since they could no longer be portrayed as mute victims of Indian men. By voicing their own protests, this new generation of Indian women blocked a return to earlier colonial rape scripts in which "white men saved brown women from brown men." Indian nationalist women posed threats not only to the symbolic but also to the political order, as is evident in the case of the fervent nationalist Bhikaiji Cama (1861–1936), who served as a delegate to the International Socialist Congress in 1907. When British authorities failed to arrange her extradition while she worked in Paris to gather support for the Indian nationalists' cause, they illegally confiscated her property in India (Jayawardena, *Feminism*, 103–104).

In short, while subtle psychoanalytic readings of Forster's novel have revealed some of the dynamics of "colonial ventriloquism," they have not explained adequately why the beautiful Mrs. Blakeston is a "more enduring" symbol than Adela, why Forster silences Adela after the rape attempt, or why he overcompensates by removing both Adela and Mrs. Moore from the text. In the pages that follow, I will show how Forster's treatment of Adela Quested's nightmare in the cave—and Cyril Fielding's psychoanalytic reading of it—reveal the traces of Freud's new theories about sexuality, which transformed the entire sexual imaginary in British India after the Great War. When Adela leaves the Marabar Caves, she is presented as the victim of mystified sexual hysteria. When she leaves the courthouse, after her courageous refusal to mouth the lies required by the old colonial order, she realizes that she has come up against "something larger," though Forster prevents her from naming what this "something" is. This silence marks the closure that Forster would impose on her story and, as it turns out, on his narrative about the intimacy and love between Cyril Fielding and Dr. Aziz as well.

The function of the ethnographic real in *A Passage to India* becomes more visible when this novel is compared with two other hybrid novels from this period that treat gender, sexuality, and consent in British India: Sara Jeannette Duncan's *The Burnt Offering* (1909) and George Orwell's *Burmese Days* (1934). By observing how these three novels position themselves on the divide between the modern and the modernist, we can see why most Anglo-Indian writers avoided the techniques of high modernism in describing colonial life. All of these novels explore variations on Cyril Fielding's questions about the extent to which "kindness" can substitute for the "intoxication of the blood" in marriage and in social relations more generally. These questions apply in relation not only to the "queer nation" of India (*Passage*, 127) but to Great Britain as well. By comparing how each text responds to these questions about love, marriage, and reproduction, we can gain a more complete understanding of the challenges that representations of cross-racial desire posed to marriage, to the notions of sacred and profane love that were authorized by it, and to the racist gender arrangements that had previously ensured the reproduction of the colonial order.

Psychoanalyzing the New Woman

One of Forster's main concerns in *A Passage to India* is to consider the challenges posed by modern women in colonial society in British India. Though Forster previously expressed some sympathy for New Women with mildly socialist leanings, like Helen Schlegel in *Howard's End* (1910), *A Passage to India*, written during the most intense phase of the suffragette campaign, displays a reversal of this sympathy, indicating Forster's reservations about women's suffrage, feminism, and free love as it was practiced in the 1920s (Furbank, 180). When Adela joins Dr. Aziz in smoking a cigarette on the fateful day when he invites her to a picnic at the Marabar Caves, she makes one of several gestures that identify her as a New Woman.[11] It is the spectacle of "an English girl left smoking with two Indians" (83) that provokes Ronny Heaslop to such rudeness and prompts Aziz, in retaliation, to disclose the news that Adela intends to leave India soon, implying that she will not marry Heaslop. Ronny's difficulties interpreting Adela's desires and intentions in this scene, after she has been left alone with an Indian man, shows the uncertainty that the New Woman generated, especially after several famous women in the historical real had demonstrated their willingness to establish sexual alliances with Indian men.

In this and subsequent scenes, Ronny Heaslop recognizes that, because Adela is a New Woman, he cannot be certain that she will deny her sexual desire or submit to the chaste monogamy expected of colonial wives. Likewise, he cannot be sure that she will comply with colonial taboos against cross-racial unions, which otherwise enforced colonial marriage arrangements and restrained public expressions of alternatives to marriage as well as to heterosexuality. It is not only Adela's status as "new" to India, then, but also her potential sexual openness and unpredictability as an emancipated woman that make her experience in the Marabar Caves so open to question.

A second feature of Forster's representation of the modern woman in this text is his desacralized perspective on marriage, which marks one important departure from the formulas of earlier Anglo-Indian romances. Because the Christianity espoused by Ronny Heaslop and other Anglo-Indians is the "sterilized Public School brand" (257), marriage is reduced to a routine and spiritless civil rite. Moreover, Cyril Fielding, Adela Quested, and, ultimately, Mrs. Moore profess a dispassionate agnosticism which prompts them to regard marriage with even more skepticism. Fielding acknowledges a deep sadness when he first learns about Aziz's previous marriage and children. Anticipating his exclusion from the possibilities of heterosexual love and marriage, Fielding concludes: "He felt old. He wished that he too could be carried away on waves of emotion. . . . Kindness, kindness, and more kindness—yes that he might supply, but was that really all that the queer nation needed? Did it not also demand an occasional intoxication of the blood?" (127).

Later, Fielding confesses his profound reservations about marriage to Adela after she admits that she will not marry Ronny Heaslop. Irreverently, Fielding observes, "Marriage is too absurd in any case. It begins and continues for such very slight reasons. The social business props it up on one side, and the theological business on the other, but neither of them are marriage, are they?" (292). Fielding's admission that he is reluctant to shoulder the sacrifices of desire required for him to claim his place and power as patriarch under the Raj is compared with Adela's confession that her marriage to Ronny would legalize her own rape. Yet, later, when he discovers that he is unable to cross the race, class, and sexual boundaries that separate him from Dr. Aziz, Fielding sets in motion the chain of erotic sacrifices that prompts him eventually to marry Mrs. Moore's daughter, certainly one of the strangest unexplained mysteries of the novel.

Third, by shifting the grounds of rape and retribution from the streets and battlefields of the Indian Uprising of 1857 to the colonizers' courtroom, Forster acknowledges that India is becoming modern by, for example, representing the effects of the Liberal reforms in the judicial system in British India after the 1880s, when "sensitive" cases like Adela's provided tests of the reliability and loyalty of Indian judges.[12] Though Forster allows Adela to recover a more authentic voice during her electrifying testimony at Dr. Aziz's trial, the Indian judge, anxious to show his impartial efficiency, interrupts her before she can discover who did attack her. Like an analysand stunned by the recognition of the "gaps" in her recall of her sexual experiences, Adela is abruptly dismissed when the judge declares Aziz's innocence. I do not mean to suggest that the judge made a technical error. But by refusing to clarify what happened to her in the cave, Forster makes it impossible for readers to understand Adela's experience or assess the meaning of her refusal to continue to play the only acceptable part as a rape victim at Dr. Aziz's trial. Thus, Forster uses the insights of psychoanalytic thought to explode the standard colonial rape script by making Englishwomen's sexual experiences unspeakable. One of the effects of this choice is that he reassigns rape and its victims to the zone of abjection.

Moreover, by moving the scene of Adela's imaginary rape from the usual public or private spaces in British India, the streets or the home evoked by earlier colonial rape scripts, to the Marabar Caves, Forster reveals the void in the colonial imaginary that Indian nationalists made visible by their idealizing of native practices concerning marriage and motherhood. When Adela and Mrs. Moore enter the Marabar Caves, that site which encloses, if nothing else, the sacred ground of Mother India, they both experience a violation that prompts them to recognize the loss of their spiritual and moral power as Englishwomen and the thinness of their attachment to the modern secular state that British imperialism helped to support. At a time when Indian nationalists insisted on the sacred character of Indian domestic life and celebrated the beauty and power of Indian women's chastity, loyalty, and spirituality (Chatterjee, "Nationalist," 233–253), the more "modern" views of sex and gender adopted by the British paled by comparison.

Forster gestures to another force that created the "modern" English woman when he describes how, after her experience in the cave, Adela feels herself becoming a nameless body, suggesting how her new political rights were countered by the forces of postwar capitalism, both at home and abroad. In her hysteria, Adela feels that "everything now was transferred to the surface of her body, which began to avenge itself, and feed unhealthily" (214), and her function as a voiceless body is emphasized by Forster's decision to erase not only the rape attempt originally planned as part of her experiences in the cave but also her initial testimony about it. Though Adela apparently reports her charges against Dr. Aziz to the appropriate officials, Forster does not reproduce her words. This silence indicates Adela's choices: either she must describe her experience according to the rape script of colonialism's favorite melodrama or she must remain voiceless. Faced by this double bind, Adela assures herself of the reality of her experience by maintaining an echoing silence.

Finally, Forster recognizes the modernizing effects of Freudian psychology when he describes how Adela forgets, and then belatedly remembers, her "erotic" fantasies before she entered the cave. Forster thus shows his complicity with Freud's conservative gender models when she is only allowed to speak in order to retract her charges against Dr. Aziz. In other words, the "gaps" in Adela's story are used to show that the sexual repression of the modern woman discredits her autonomy and reliability as a political agent.

Some of the originality of *A Passage to India* can be seen in his strategic deployments of the ethnographic real, but other features of this text are brought to light when we consider Forster's use of more modernist techniques. Certainly, one interesting modernist feature of this text is Forster's use of colonial "splitting," when he divides the rape victim into two in order to deconstruct the standard colonial rape script of the young and beautiful Englishwoman raped by the Indian man. Thus, Adela, as the younger and presumably virginal woman, is assigned the symptoms of sexual hysteria while Mrs. Moore acts out the moral and existential crisis that has been part of rape narratives in the British tradition since, at least, Shakespeare's time. This procedure invites readers to consider the "sacrifices" of desire that previously made the rape script so compelling, but it also exposes new "erotic" sacrifices that Freud's theory about human sexuality brought into view.

Mrs. Moore is seldom recognized by Forster's critics as a victim of assault, sexual or otherwise, though Forster's text invites comparisons with Adela's "rape" when she feels throttled and suffocated after she enters into the cave and a "pad" settles on her mouth (Rajan, *Real*, 72). Like Adela's,

Mrs. Moore's first response, when she leaves the cave, is to look for "a villain" (163). Forster's irony keeps us from taking this attack very seriously since the "villain" proves to be an Indian baby, and the sinister pad is revealed by daylight to be the child's damp hand. It is perhaps Mrs. Moore's age that prevents most readers from assessing her panic and hysteria in terms of sexual trauma, though she exhibits symptoms that are typical of rape victims when she can no longer discriminate between a sacred union and the violence that is its opposite: she grumbles, "love in a church, love in cave, what is the least difference?" (224). While we might expect piety as the consequence of her disillusioned confrontation with the "undying worm itself" (231), Forster describes instead Mrs. Moore's movement into querulous agnosticism, paralysis, and retreat. When this side of her character is acknowledged at all, Mrs. Moore is viewed as a "withered priestess" (231) who, having been long ago initiated into the mysteries of sexuality and having already borne three children, can no longer be ravished by any but spiritual forces.[13]

Adela, by contrast, sees Mrs. Moore as offering her the only available cure for her "echo," casting her in the role of psychoanalyst. Indeed, Mrs. Moore identifies the talking cure as Adela's best chance for recovery when she insists that only by facing her own delusions about love and desire can Adela understand her experience and properly identify who—or what—assaulted her. Yet Mrs. Moore refuses to act on Victorian gender imperatives that demand that she provide this sympathy for Adela or to recognize the new psychoanalytic needs that modernism identified and Adela exhibits. Lost in a spiritual "muddledom," Mrs. Moore mourns instead the loss of her own authority as a mother, a loss intensified in the postwar sexual imaginary as it was reenvisioned by Freud. When Adela seeks her comfort and advice, saying, "You do nothing but good, you are so good" (228), Mrs. Moore says bluntly (and somewhat ungrammatically), "I am not good, no, bad" (228), and remains locked in self-pity: "Less attention should be paid to my future daughter-in-law and more to me, there is no sorrow like my sorrow" (231).

Mrs. Moore's reluctance to play the part of psychoanalyst for Adela coincides with her refusal to assume the new civic and ethical responsibilities assigned to Englishwomen after the vote was granted to them in 1919, as is evident in her unwillingness to testify at Dr. Aziz's trial. Moreover, her sudden flight from Anglo-India also exposes the force of powerful fears about the (homo)sexual possibilities that Freud's new theory of human bisexuality made available in the 1920s. Forster notes that Adela is "exceedingly fond" of Mrs. Moore (29) and shows throughout the text that her desire for intimacy with Mrs. Moore is more compelling than her desire for marriage with Ronny.

Moreover, Adela's intense relationship with Mrs. Moore echoes several of the details from Freud's 1920 essay about the origins of lesbian desire since he, too, charts "the transformation of feeling" that prompts his attractive young patient to "search for a substitute mother to whom she could become passionately attached" (18:158). It is from this case that Freud draws the revolutionary conclusion, "In all of us, throughout life, the libido normally oscillates between male and female objects" (18:158). In destroying the "deep and real" intimacy (219) that Adela hoped to establish between them, Mrs. Moore makes the lesbian potential in this relationship more visible by her unaccountable retreat. I do not mean to suggest that Adela and Mrs. Moore become lovers; I simply want to point out that after Freud articulated his new theory about the universality of bisexual desire, the gaps in Adela's and Mrs. Moore's stories, the obscurity of their motives, and their precipitous and mysterious banishment all create spaces that could be filled with other kinds of desire.

Forster's psychoanalytic modernism also finds expression in his characterization of Cyril Fielding and his relationship with Dr. Aziz. Cyril takes up the double roles that Mrs. Moore refuses, acting as Adela's psychoanalyst and as the "supervening light-giving consciousness" that defines the moral center of this text (Levenson, 21). Through Fielding's conversations with Adela, Forster identifies the only explanation offered by the text to elucidate her sudden, stunning repudiation of her claim that Dr. Aziz attempted to rape her. In their first conversation after the trial, Fielding offers to help Adela piece together the meaning of her experiences in the Marabar Caves when he argues that the most plausible explanation of her experience of near rape was that it was an "hallucination" (266). Adela obligingly (and perhaps ironically) fills in the Freudian assumptions about female sexual hysteria that prompt Fielding to make this guess: "You suggest that I had an hallucination there, the sort of thing—though in an awful form—that makes some women think they've had an offer of marriage when none was made" (266–267).[14] Later in this conversation, however, Adela shows that she has gone farther than Fielding in her commitment to "honesty" and her effort to understand the muddle created by her voicelessness. When she admits that she did not love Ronny, she also recognizes the possibility of marital rape in her anticipated marriage.

Moreover, Adela subsequently refutes Fielding's theory that she suffered from a sexual hallucination in the Marabar Caves. In other words, like the lesbian woman in Freud's 1920 essay, Adela refuses to participate in a continuing psychoanalytic dialogue or in the heterosexual compact it often normalized and enforced. Recognizing that any further effort to exact justice for the assault would simply reinforce the colonizer's paranoid nightmares, Adela identifies the guide as her probable attacker but says, indifferently, "It will never be known. It's as if I ran my finger along that polished wall in the dark, and cannot get further. I am up against something, and so are you. Mrs. Moore—she did know" (292).

Adela concludes this conversation by admitting that immediately before she entered the cave, she tried to convince herself that "tenderness," "respect," and "personal intercourse" could replace the "intoxications" of heterosexual romance (292). And when Fielding says, "I no longer want love" (292), she agrees. But seeing that no effort to explain the "truth" of her desires will transform the colonizing male's jealous paranoia about Indian men, Adela recognizes the larger psychological forces that she struggles against and declares her intention to retreat from India, to remain single, and "settle down to some career" at home (291). In thus aligning herself with Mrs. Moore and her unspeakable knowledge, Adela acknowledges the forces that Forster would banish from the novel when he sends Mrs. Moore to the bottom of the Indian Ocean and Adela herself back to a single (unrepresented) life in "feminist" England.

Unlike Adela, Fielding resists any invitation to apply psychoanalytic explanations to his own behavior, or to inquire into the nature of his sexual desires, even though his relationship with Dr. Aziz offers striking parallels with the reactions described in Freud's 1922 essay, "Some Neurotic Mechanisms in Jealousy, Paranoia and Homosexuality." In this essay, Freud identifies the unacknowledged erotic potential underlying the "homosocial contract" that structured so many nineteenth-century English and Anglo-Indian novels about India. Freud's essay thus illuminates the significance of Forster's choice of the two women who separate Fielding and Aziz, one living and one dead.

Fielding's chivalrous concern about Adela is often seen as the sole cause of the rupture that separates Fielding and Dr. Aziz after he is acquitted. In dramatizing the exchanges between Fielding and Aziz, as they lie on the roof of Mr. Zulfiquar's mansion, gaze "through mosquito nets at the stars" (278), call each other by their given names, and speak of justice and peace, Forster expresses a deep appreciation for Indian "civilization" and the homoerotic desires it aroused. Though he eloquently describes the promise of a consummation between these two deeply feeling and "civilized" men, as "the hand stretches out for ever, the lifted knee has the eternity though not the sadness of the grave" (280), Forster is less clear about the mechanism that evokes the colonial guilt that stops Fielding's homosexual desire in its tracks.

Freud's essay on male homosexuality offers a gloss, then, for the argument that Fielding picks with Aziz, suggesting as well how the colonial obsession with the rape of "white" women, when read in this context, reveals the paranoia and jealousy that guarded heterosexuality in British India. As such, the failure of this relationship exposes Fielding's surrender to the homosexual "paranoia" of the rest of Anglo-Indian culture. This exchange also shows new meanings in the language of "sacrifice" that became harder to ignore after Freud published his theory about the universality of bisexual desire. Fielding speaks about Adela's "sacrifice" when he urges Aziz to abandon his plans to charge her a large fee for legal damages, asking Aziz not to "treat her like a conquered enemy" (280). Reminding him of how brave Adela was in refusing to play the prescribed part in the rape script that would make her into a "national heroine," Fielding points out that Adela could have lied and claimed the adulation and limited power awarded to colonizing English women who, like Mrs. Hume, accepted such complicity and played the martyr's part.[15] With the "entire British Raj pushing her," Adela instead recanted her testimony and sent the whole "thing to smithereens" (281).

When Fielding's defense of Adela provokes Aziz to reveal his sexual jealousy, Fielding is unwilling to recognize or act on his friend's desires, thus setting the ultimate limit to their intimacy. Caught up in the drama of the colonizer's "old chivalry," Fielding is affronted when Aziz describes the version of interracial desire that most Anglo-Indian fiction worked relentlessly to deny. Facetiously, Aziz dictates the letter he would have Adela write: "Dear Dr. Aziz, I wish you had come into the cave; I am an awful old hag, and it is my last chance" (281). Offended by the vulgar expression of "this derived sensuality—the sort that classes a mistress among motor-cars if she is beautiful, and among eye-flies if she isn't," Fielding reasserts the racial "barrier" between himself and Aziz (268). Later, his political objections to "the old, old trouble that eats the heart out of every civilization: snobbery, the desire for possessions, creditable appendages" (241), become aesthetic ones. This turn away from politics to standards of "taste" makes Fielding into a more modernist hero, though it also reveals how his concern with aesthetics prevents him from achieving a more profound self-knowledge or the satisfaction of his deeper desires.

Dr. Aziz, on the other hand, embodies some of the configurations of desire that Freud made more visible when he liberated sexuality from Victorian morality and rigid gender norms. Aziz tries to make peace with Cyril by saying with "deep feeling" in his voice, "I will consult Mrs. Moore. . . Her opinion will solve everything. I trust her absolutely" (282). Aziz's acknowledgment of the power of maternal love only makes Fielding feel further alienated.

After Aziz corrects himself, saying, "I keep forgetting that she has left India. During the shouting of her name in court I fancied she was present. I had shut my eyes, I confused myself on purpose to deaden the pain" (282). Fielding reacts with guilty defensiveness. Having withheld the news that Mrs. Moore had, in fact, died shortly after leaving India, he protests: "You are so fantastic. . . . Miss Quested, you won't treat her generously; while over Mrs. Moore there is this elaborate chivalry. Miss Quested anyhow behaved decently this morning, whereas the old lady never did anything for you at all" (282). In this way, Forster identifies the rejection of the mother as the new touchstone of male heterosexual identity for Englishmen in the final years of the Raj.

Later in the text, Forster recognizes something murderous and psychoanalytically modern in Fielding's anger toward Mrs. Moore when he realizes that she has played an essential role in his separation from Aziz. Thinking back on his conversation with Aziz after the trial, Fielding admits that he had "tried to kill Mrs. Moore . . . on the roof of the Nawab Bahadur's house; but she still eluded him" (284). Though he clings to his good English common sense, reasoning that "facts are facts, and everyone would learn of Mrs. Moore's death in the morning," Fielding nonetheless acknowledges the psychological truth that "people are not really dead until they are felt to be dead. As long as there is some misunderstanding about them, they possess a sort of immortality" (283–284).

Fielding's resentment toward Mrs. Moore not only separates him from Aziz, but it also realigns him with Ronny Heaslop who, for his part, cannot forgive his mother for "mixing herself up with natives" (286). Ronny Heaslop is relieved, even glad, that his mother is dead. The source of his anger is clearly related to his power struggle with his mother, whom he sees as having undermined his authority in both the colonial hierarchy and the family. Like Orestes, Ronny is unrepentant after her death: "He had behaved badly to her, and he had either to repent (which involved a mental overturn), or to persist in unkindness towards her. He chose the latter course. How tiresome she had been with her patronage of Aziz! What a bad influence upon Adela!" (286).

Though Forster identifies the specific source of Heaslop's anger in this episode, he obscures the psychological origins of Fielding's similar guilt and its relation to his homosexual desires. The processes at work in both men can be illuminated by reference to Freud's "On Narcissism," which offers an analysis of the mother's role in structuring the sacrifices of desire that both heterosexuals and homosexuals must make. Judith Butler provides this provocative summary of Freud's argument: "A boy child begins to love through sacrificing some portion of his own narcissism, that the idealization of the mother is nothing other than that narcissism transferred outward, that the mother stands for that lost narcissism, promises the return of that narcissism, and never delivers on that promise. For as long as she remains the idealized object of love, she carries his narcissism, she is his displaced narcissism, and, in so far as she carries it, she is perceived to withhold it from him" (*Bodies*, 180). Compelled by this psychological and symbolic logic, Ronny, Cyril, and, indeed, all Englishmen who assume power in the final years of the Raj long to kill the mother.

Forster's veiled admission of the murderous anger toward the mother in *A Passage to India* suggests a new homosexual "origin" for the cultural paranoia and obsession that circulated rape stories, even as he enacts the "murder" of Mrs. Moore in order to return homosexuality to its previous zone of abjection in this text. When Mrs. Moore is chanted back to life by Aziz's sympathizers in the courtroom, she embodies the truth of Orestes' story and exposes imperialism's stake in repressing new sexual alternatives to it. As Forster's narrator explains, after Mrs. Moore's departure "a legend sprang up that an Englishman had killed his mother for trying to save an Indian's life—and there was just enough truth in this to cause annoyance to the authorities" (285). The conflict engendered by this fixation with the mother, and the jealousy and paranoia it produces in men like Ronny and Fielding, pervades all of Anglo-Indian culture. In this evocation of the lost mother, we can see that something fundamental has changed in the relationship between patriarchal and matriarchal power as it was conceptualized in the British empire after the death of Queen Victoria. It is no wonder that when Indian nationalists made Mother India the symbol of Indian unity, they provoked a crisis in the symbolic order of Anglo-Indian culture.

Forster is perhaps most radical in *A Passage to India* when he risks a frank description of Aziz's love for Cyril and for Mrs. Moore, and so offers a dimly glimpsed alternative to the Oedipal struggles with the mother that shape Fielding's desires. Aziz articulates the possibilities available in the East and newly liberated in the West when Freud detached sex from gender; when Aziz reminds Fielding, "We are not in the law courts. There are many ways of being a man" (300). Aziz's way is to allow love to bridge the racial divide separating him from both Fielding and Mrs. Moore. When Aziz acknowledges the sexual dimension of his love for Fielding, during their rooftop conversation, he shows his jealousy of Adela in precisely the terms Freud outlines in his 1922 essay on homosexuality. However, Aziz also shows that his deep affection for the motherly Mrs. Moore can coexist with his love for Fielding when, for example, he cries "like a child" after he hears of her death (290). In this way, Forster recognizes the "diverse cultural paths to male identity" available in Indian culture. Indian men, according to Stanley Kurtz, "display a different resolution altogether from that found in the Oedipus complex" (236), so that the son "gives up his immature genital attachment to the mother in return for the more sublime satisfaction of being immersed in a group of mothers" (142). This psychology, according to Kurtz, generates a greater tolerance toward male homosexuality in Indian culture.

Because Forster treats Fielding's and Aziz's intimacy and sexual jealousy with such subtlety, there is a strange and perhaps unintended irony in Fielding's abrupt and improbable late marriage to Mrs. Moore's daughter and in his last clumsy effort to establish a reconciliation with Aziz. Even Ralph Moore is more successful than Fielding in establishing a deeper connection with Aziz that allows the latter to feel his "great gratitude" for the "eternal goodness" of Mrs. Moore (350). Ralph's words, not Cyril's, allow Aziz to feel that he has broken free of the cycle of suffering that British imperialism creates in this text. For Fielding, however, there is no such resolution. Locked into hostility toward the mother, in denial about the grief over the sacrifices of desire required by life under the Raj, Fielding unaccountably marries Mrs. Moore's daughter.

One symptom of Fielding's "sacrifice" of desire can be found in his rigid refusal to recognize the appeal of Indian nationalism or the emotional power of the symbols of "Mother India" that so limits his sympathies for Aziz by the end of the novel. In their final conversations, Fielding declares his new allegiance to the Raj by belittling Aziz's nationalist hopes: "India a nation! What an apotheosis! Last commer to the drab nineteenth-century sisterhood! Waddling in at this hour of the world to take her seat" (361). By ending the novel with Fielding's cry, "Why can't we be friends now?"and the narrator's response, "No, not yet, no not there" (362), Forster marks the dead end of their relationship.

In other words, while Adela and Aziz illustrate the new sexual possibilities that were opened up by Freud's new theories about homosexuality, the conventional turn in Forster's plot returns them to the zone of abjection. Though Forster was understandably unwilling to reveal the male objects of his desire more frankly or to allow Fielding to step across the imaginary line that Anglo-Indian culture liked to pretend separated the races, he does show how central the Oedipal mother was in reorganizing the patterns of desire that modernism helped to circulate. By showing how "erotic life is liable to be . . . falsified," Forster demonstrates how rape can be made to disappear in

Anglo-Indian culture, but *A Passage to India* reveals his complicity, as well, in excluding alternatives to the heterosexual regimes of Anglo-India.

Looking beyond Rape

Sara Jeannette Duncan's novels, like Forster's, often featured active, recalcitrant New Women, but Joan Mills, the feminist socialist in *The Burnt Offering* (1909), presents the most radical combination of political allegiances that, according to Ann Ardis, placed the New Woman at the farthest remove from late Victorian gender norms and made her most disruptive to the status quo (Ardis, 14–15). Joan Mills differs from most New Women in Anglo-Indian novels because she exercises her political agency in order to win the vote for British women, she endorses the militant tactics of the suffragettes, and she assumes a more international perspective on workers' solidarity as articulated by socialists in the first decade of the twentieth century. In other words, Duncan's novel evokes the "ethnographic real" in describing Joan Mills as a modern, politically engaged woman who is unconstrained by conservative political and psychoanalytic revisions of her proper relation to the social contract.

Moreover, in bringing Joan Mills to British India in the decade before the Great War, and in narrating her cross-cultural romance with the Indian nationalist Bepin Behari Dey, Duncan creates a New Woman who multiplies the revolutionary challenges she poses to the gender, class, and race hierarchies of the Raj. Likewise, by including a second cross-cultural romance in this novel, between Rani Janaki Mukerjee and the Liberal home secretary, John Game, Duncan identifies Joan's counterpart by reference to the new Indian woman who began to emerge in the "historical real" in British India at this time.[16] In describing Janaki as a beautiful, articulate, cultured, Western-educated, self-assured, and politically engaged Hindu woman, Duncan creates a female character who embodies the political and social changes that are barely registered in most Anglo-Indian fiction, including Forster's brave novel. In the end, Duncan's plot takes a conservative turn that resembles Forster's and many other English modernist novels when she dramatizes how the personal sabotages the political in both these cross-cultural romances.

Joan Mills is a New Woman in every sense of the word. Unlike the heroine in Victoria Cross's *Love of My Heart*, she is a financially independent woman, with an income of £500 a year that she has inherited from her mother. Unlike any of the New Women in the romances I have described in previous chapters, Joan is a "great leader of the women's movement" in England and has been jailed twice in support of the suffragette cause (15–16). She is a political activist schooled by her father, Vulcan Mills, in socialist analysis of global economies, international politics, and class relations in England and in India. Finally, she is outspoken in criticizing the racism of her countrymen, and, unlike any of Forster's British characters, she is sympathetic to Indian nationalism and recognizes the potential for collaboration between British feminist socialists and politicized Bengali women, inside and outside purdah. Joan Mills thus helps us see what Adela Quested might have been.

Though I have found no written record of Forster's reading of Sara Jeannette Duncan's novels, Robin Lewis reports that Forster stayed with her in Simla during his tour of India in 1912–13 (28–29). In his journal Forster notes that he was impressed by Duncan's knowledge of local Indian culture and describes his impressions of a "modern wedding," between two Muslims who "sought to synthesize Western rationalism and traditional Muslim practices" (28–29), that she arranged for him to attend. Forster characterizes this ceremony, though, as "depressing, almost heart rending" and locates "the problem of India's future" in this failed effort to modernize one of India's fundamental rituals.[17] Marriage was no less problematic in postwar England or, indeed, in British India.

In *The Burnt Offering*, Duncan represents configurations of political and erotic desire that remain sadly out of reach for Fielding or for Adela,[18] though these possibilities were, perhaps, more hopefully envisioned in 1909, before women won the vote, before the Great War, and before Freud's revolution in his analysis of homosexuality. In her first appearance in the novel, Joan meets the man she is later to marry when she invites Bepin Behari Dey to enter their railway carriage after two English soldiers have violently ejected him from theirs. The first thing Joan does in Dey's presence is signal her identity as a New Woman by lighting a cigarette. Joan is traveling with her father, Vulcan Mills, a visiting Labour MP, whose politics, idealism, and passion for reform resemble those of Kier Hardie. Joan shares her father's socialist analysis and utopian zeal; she is "serious and modern, a combination with little vanity and no coquetry" (106) and is "obsessed by her father's mission and the political situation about her" (106).[19]

As an English visitor in Anglo-India, and an outsider by virtue of all of her allegiances, Joan, like Adela Quested, is appalled by the rigid race and class prejudices of the Anglo-Indian ruling elite, but, unlike Adela, she has a more comprehensive understanding of the dynamics of imperial power and openly criticizes the false premises of the Social Darwinist defenses of British racial superiority. Moreover, Joan shares with her father a quality that one of the Indian characters calls his "same-sightedness," and, like her father, Joan "will ask not what is your colour? what is your creed? but what are your morals and ideals'" (135). Duncan uses Joan to display the radical consequences of this "same-sightedness" when her heroine falls in love with an Indian man. Since she describes a heterosexual romance, Duncan is freer than Forster in her exploration of the new perspectives on sex and gender that are enacted in Joan's cross-cultural romance.

Joan's trenchant political critique of the racism of her contemporaries finds expression, for example, when she asks John Game whether many Englishmen fail the riding test that had been recently added to the civil service examination. When Game replies, "I should think not. Most Englishmen are naturally able to ride" (55), Joan replies ironically, "As all Englishmen are naturally able to govern" (55). Game defends himself, as Fielding does in *A Passage to India*, by saying, finally, "What about the opportunity of service? . . . I love my job. And . . . I shall defend it to the last" (88).

Likewise, when Joan happily admits the scandalous truth that white women are sometimes attracted to Indian men, her friend, Lucy, replies, "He is rather strikingly good-looking, isn't he—Mr. Dey? Those delicate, regular, aquiline features are quite the best Bengali type, I think" (120). Joan then calls attention to Lucy's unconscious racism when she counters, "Why place him as a type? I suppose if he is good-looking he is just good-looking as a human being, isn't he? One would think we were here to measure the skulls of these people" (120–121). Lucy's naive response, "Oh but we have. . . . It doesn't hurt them," provokes Joan's deadly ironic, "It only lacked that" (121). Unlike nearly all the characters in other Anglo-Indian novels, Joan recognizes how such scientific "knowledge" merely serves imperial purposes by keeping the castes, classes, and races apart.[20]

Most commentators on *The Burnt Offering* assess Joan's love for Dey as basically inauthentic, seeing it as an unnecessary "sacrifice" prompted by Joan's naive political idealism.[21] This interpretation, however, ignores the psychological role that Joan's father plays in this text and overlooks Duncan's subtle analysis of the ways that "consent" remains a central problem in the private and political worlds of British India. In describing the origins of Joan's desire for Bepin Behari Dey, Duncan subtly describes the interaction of the political and "psychological" registers of her desire. Early in the novel, Joan admits that she is a "little tired" of her participation in the socialist and feminist campaigns in England during the first decade of the century, acknowledging that these political causes did not fill the void created by her arid free-thinking agnosticism. Joan says: "Looking back, it is all tawdry and feverish, full of expediency and vulgarity. I love the larger peace and the deeper dream of India" (l24). Joan's recognition of the limits of liberal English feminism is intensified when she comes into contact with Indian women who are passionately committed to the cause of Indian nationalism. Even before she is engaged to Dey, Joan plans to stay in India to work with the women of the Roy family (and Duncan's choice of the name of the most famous Indian Communist at this time cannot be without its irony).[22] Joan pursues Dey frankly, then, not only because of his personal charm but also because he offers her new meaning in a modern world where love and marriage are otherwise stripped of their sacredness and "intoxication." Dey gives her the chance to be a part of something wider than the provincial world of Anglo-India and perhaps less self-interested than gambling in the colonial marriage market.

Duncan's narrator is ironic, and Joan is rueful, about the specious appeals of "Orientalism" that amplify her desire for Dey, and his for her, but as a modern feminist, she recognizes that she cannot pry apart her political and erotic desires. At the beginning of their relationship, Joan recognizes that Dey illustrates "what one had always understood of Orientals—they thought of women as inferior creatures. She would prove the contrary to Bepin. . . . And she found it very easy to do" (103). Duncan's narrator comments ironically on Joan's totalizing assumptions about Oriental men and on her feminist project to reform Dey by noting, "In a week he was saying to her with humble admiration, 'you have the intellect of a man,' upon which Joan proved that she had that of a woman so far as to be flattered" (103).

In describing the "esoteric jewel of an Oriental passion" (184) that develops between Joan and Dey, however, Duncan, in contrast to Forster, details Dey's motives and psychology in order to show the idealized role played by the wife and mother in Hindu nationalism in this period. When Dey protests against new colonial laws that prohibited Indians from possessing arms, for example, by telling Joan bitterly, "Your Government . . . will not let us be men" (192), Joan denounces these unjust laws, and Dey, calling her "Devi" (192) in response, recognizes her as a goddess. In detailing Dey's hope that he will succeed in "winning" Joan (192), Duncan notes that his "heart was full of certainty and gratitude and praise, and lyrical with love" (192–193), but she also reveals that he has been told "to use every effort to interest Miss Mills in the national movement" and "secure" her "for the Mother" before he thinks of himself. In carefully detailing the "sequence" of Dey's passion, Duncan indicates how the figure of Mother India acted to authorize his desire for Joan. While Duncan admits that Dey's "desire was ardent," she adds, "but it was not the flame that consumed him" (183). This remark does not necessarily identify Dey's love as inauthentic, though Duncan is unusual in recognizing how the feminine metaphors of love and power operated in the Indian nationalist ideology at the time (Sinha, *Colonial Masculinities*, 69–99).

Moreover, Duncan not only shows Dey's responsiveness to the metaphors of Indian nationalism, she also shows that Joan is susceptible to the appeal of being regarded as a "goddess," and in elaborating how Joan acts on her psychological as well as her political desires, she proves that Joan is her father's daughter. Vulcan Mills experiences a parallel "seduction" by unfamiliar Indian attitudes toward love, politics, leadership, and sacrifice (128). In exposing how the political and the psychological work together to shape Joan's, and her father's, desires, Duncan ironically identifies the particular seductions of intellectual men and women who are, like Joan and her father, "creatures of theory." Though Duncan indicates her appreciation for their "loyalty" to their beliefs in "same-sightedness," she also notes the quixotic excesses of their "obedience" to "any paper edict of the reason" (200). In other words, Duncan shows that Joan is seduced when Dey calls her a "goddess," because he feeds a hunger in Joan that has been created by the patriarchal organization of desire both under the Raj and in the modern capitalist state.

Like Forster, Duncan demonstrates that modern political subjects like Joan and her father cannot escape from the "sacrifices" of desire, either on the personal or the political level. Indeed, as Judith Butler argues, in the achievement of sexual maturity, erotic sacrifice cannot be avoided in any event; it can only be "repressed" (*Bodies*, 178). Unlike Forster, however, Duncan acknowledges the intercultural dynamic that at the turn of the century prompted the British to emphasize their sacrifices. This is particularly clear in an episode that explains the novel's title. When the Indian nationalist leader Thakore talks to her father about Dey's desire to marry Joan, he indicates the importance of sacrifice in Hindu culture when he urges: "Give her to India. . . . This is Kaliyuga. The gods ask sacrifice; and ours are not enough" (137). In his reply, Vulcan insists that only his daughter can give her consent to this marriage, saying that Joan "is my offering to your cause— and she is all I have. More than that. . . . I cannot say. . . . My daughter must choose her own husband" (137). Because she has accepted the political consequences of the civic model that her father describes here, which defines service and sacrifice as part of the modern citizen's moral obligation, Joan accepts Dey's proposal of marriage, though she realizes that this marriage will require much sacrifice: "If I—took this step—I should want to belong absolutely to the people—to live among them, wear their dress, adopt their habits, speak their language, think their thoughts" (196). For Duncan, this voluntary sacrifice is the price that women, and men, must pay for full participation in political and social life in British India or in England.

Like *A Passage to India*, *The Burnt Offering* stages a trial to define the central myth of colonial rule, but unlike Forster, Duncan moves from the register of the personal to the political, from the colonizers to the colonized, and from sex to gender, by focusing on the crime of sedition rather than on rape, though both crimes display the same fundamental conflicts that are reflected in Anglo-Indian notions of law, justice, freedom, and consent. This trial shows how imperial purposes override the liberties otherwise promised to the colonized and highlights the different punishments assigned to English and Indian defendants, since Vulcan Mills is deported, while an Indian nationalist is required to stand trial and is severely punished for the same crime. When Joan steps in to read her father's speech after his departure, Duncan also reveals how her gender short-circuits the political effect of her father's speech since the crowd of Bengali men that she addresses only see "the woman, the goddess, standing there for their sakes" and so cannot comprehend the "pungent" political message of the words she reads (259). Joan's speech in defiance of the laws of Anglo-India thus illustrates some of the power that seditious Englishwomen like Annie Besant later commanded. As such, Joan reveals the political as well as the psychological reasons why Forster removes Mrs. Moore from the scene of Dr. Aziz's trial.

Duncan compares Joan's romance with Dey with a second romance between Janaki Mukerjee and John Game in order to show that erotic sacrifices are similarly demanded of all participants in the racially segregated world of British India. Joan recognizes how and why the rhetoric of sacrifice works so well among the colonizers. For example, when John Game declares his love for her and reminds her of the heroic proportions of his sacrifice (229), she observes that he has confused dominance with love. Joan thus voices political objections that Adela can't put into words when she resists marriage with Ronny Heaslop: "You seem to think that by marrying me. . . . you would obtain some sort of influence over me, and even over my father—that you would be able to dictate our private beliefs and our public actions. This may be a natural official expectation, but. . . it is a very great mistake" (230). John Game later proves that Joan is correct in predicting that he wishes to "dictate" to her, when after she tells him that she plans to marry Dey, he responds by asking to speak to her father (231). Though Joan explains that she knows Dey is already married to a "child wife," and she understands the sacrifices she will face, Game tries to persuade her father to forbid the marriage by asking whether he realizes that "a Hindu husband could divorce her on the slightest pretext, but that she could never free herself from him? And that no British court could give her relief from these conditions?" (233). Oblivious to the double standards that still applied in English divorce cases until 1923, as well as to the political and erotic sacrifices required of colonial wives, Game cannot comprehend Joan's desire for Dey. He also cannot fathom her willingness to sacrifice herself to what she regards as the larger cause of India's national awakening, nor apparently can many of Duncan's critics.

The Burnt Offering differs most of all from *A Passage to India* because Duncan identifies an Indian counterpart for her politically engaged New Woman, when she describes Janaki, the elite Indian woman who has fallen in love with John Game, and characterizes her as ruled by intellectual and political as well as sexual passions. Widowed as a young woman before her marriage could be consummated, Janaki refused her progressive father's offer to arrange a second marriage, though she accepted his plan to send her to Oxford to study, and, as a result, she could "read an English newspaper and write a Persian poem" (37). Janaki's view of sex, gender, and love, however, has also been transformed by English notions about consent, as is clear when she tells her father, "I will marry, as the English do, according to my desire. I will seek my own husband as the English women do" (40).

In treating Janaki's erotic interest in John Game, Duncan illustrates the political as well as the personal consequences of her decision to "seek her own husband." Free to move between the worlds of the colonizer and the colonized, Janaki socializes with Englishmen and -women, and also enters the zenana, where she helps to create the revolutionary ferment that most British and Anglo-Indian novelists failed to recognize. Even though she has a Western education superior to that of most Anglo-Indian wives, Janaki is "patronized" by colonizing "ladies in high official position" (43), though they jealously watch "how the men would talk with her" and wonder whether some Englishman might like her well enough to wish to marry her (44). The Anglo-Indian men, blinded, like their wives, by their race and class prejudices and their unexamined assumptions about their own women's nonpolitical "nature," equate political passion with sexual permissiveness and see Janaki "as hot a little rebel as they make 'em" (204).

Ironically, though, it is not the political but the personal that causes Janaki to feel the heat of frustrated desire. Because John Game is a good liberal, he does not reject Janaki categorically because of her "race," as many other Anglo-Indian heroes do, but he fails, nonetheless, to recognize her as

an active free agent in love because of his dated understanding of Indian society. Game also fails to respond to Janaki's love because he is fixated on
the beautiful but superbly indifferent Joan Mills for the satisfaction of his
own long-delayed desires. Thus, Duncan, like Forster, confirms the barren-
ness of the essentially homosocial love affair with imperial power that limits
and deforms Anglo-Indian romances.

Though Duncan's novel ends with the failure of both cross-racial relationships, and with the dissolution of Joan's and Janaki's alliances with the
Hindu nationalists, the targets of her irony are harder to identify than Forster's
in *A Passage to India*. Duncan's plot acts to restore the balance of power under the Raj when death prevents the consummation of Joan's marriage. Dey
has been secretly involved in a terrorist plot to kill the viceroy, an act he hopes
will spark a revolution, a plan he keeps secret from Joan. Although the bomb
Dey throws misses the viceroy, he wounds a police officer and later shoots
himself while resisting arrest. Duncan's narrative seems, then, to confirm her
belief that political change in India should come gradually and peacefully,
as it did in her native Canada. Terrorism in India is pointless, as Janaki's guru
declares, since the colonizers, in due time, "will grant us our desire, the good
English, and leave to us our country" (164). However, as a result of Dey's
act of terrorism, John Game sustains slight "scratches" when he is thrown
out of the viceroy's carriage and dies shortly afterward from blood poisoning due to contact with the soil of India (314). Game's death thus ends Janaki's
romantic dreams.

Joan's subsequent discovery of the cause of Dey's death is also treated
with irony, when Duncan's narrator observes, "I do not know what revulsion
Joan Mills felt when the rite was revealed to which she had been so effective
a priestess; but it would be unwise, I think, to hope too much from it. It was
certainly not long before she had the tone of the philosopher for the loss of
both her lovers, though she placed them very differently in the category of
martyrdom. It would perhaps be accurate to say that for Bepin she had the
bow of acquiescence, for John the shrug" (316). Without the bonds of marriage to legitimize her participation in the Indian nationalist cause, Joan becomes politically irrelevant and is told by the ladies of the Roy household to
return to her father's home in England.

The final irony in *The Burnt Offering* is suggested by Janaki's response
to the news of John Game's death. Having lost the man she loved, Janaki joins
her father in renouncing the privileges granted to the fortunate few among
the colonized by their English colonizers. But unlike Moni in *The Unfinished
Song*, both father and daughter subsequently withdraw from political engage-

ment entirely, traveling instead, "from holy place to holy place," in order to gather "that wisdom of the heart which is the gift and the glory of the Mother whose children they are" (319). While Duncan and Forster thus expose the hypocrisies that find expression in colonial ideologies about the "white man's burden," Duncan insists that sacrifices are demanded from all modern citizens in the name of nationalism, from women as well as from men, and from the colonized as well as the colonizers.

When Duncan's realist novel is compared with Forster's more psychological and modernist text, the political limits of his use of the "ethnographic real" in *A Passage to India* become clearer. While Forster identifies Dr. Aziz as the real political "martyr" of his story, caught in a colonial imaginary obsessed with rapes that never occurred, he sacrifices both Mrs. Moore and Adela in working out the plot of the novel in order to obscure the homosexual alternatives to marriage and to discredit Indian nationalism itself. In the end, Forster, for all his objections to the empire, uses Fielding to trivialize Aziz's nationalist hopes and to censure his revolutionary dreams. After this display of loyalty, Fielding rejoins Anglo-Indian society and even hopes to reproduce. Duncan, by contrast, recognizes the power and legitimacy of Indian nationalism, though she also expresses her appreciation for moral and politically responsible liberal leaders like John Game who sacrifice themselves for the Raj. In the end, though, Duncan can find no new solution to these conflicts between *eros* and *polis*, and prevents all four of the characters in her cross-racial romance from marrying and reproducing.[23] With this unromantic ending, Duncan's avoids endorsing the racial hierarchies of the Raj that, for example, Alice Perrin celebrated so uncritically in *The Waters of Destruction*, but, at the same time, she suggests the delusions and inevitable defeat of her heroines' revolutionary hopes by underlining the ironies of Joan's and Janaki's return to their fathers' houses.

Domesticating Rape

While *A Passage to India* displays the psychological aspects of men's and women's sacrifices in colonial life and *The Burnt Offering* illustrates the political implications of these sacrifices, *Burmese Days* focuses entirely on men's sacrifices. This single focus gives the novel its peculiar flatness and, I would argue, the novel's hero his peculiar, self-destructive obtuseness. *Burmese Days* does recognize some of the contradictions about colonial race relations that Forster and Duncan screen out of their novels, contradictions that Frantz Fanon summarizes in his famous remark: "The originality of the colonial context is that the economic substructure is also a superstructure. . . . you are rich because you are white, you are white because you are rich" (*Wretched*, 40).

Like Duncan, Orwell also examines the rhetoric of sacrifice, but he shows that it is a cover for the political and economic exploitation of the colonial system where labor bears no correspondence to pay and where the colonizers' supposed sacrifices are simply a self-justifying "delusion" (60). Early in the novel, in a conversation with his Indian friend Dr. Veraswami, Flory insists that the Pax Britannica is based on "the lie that we're here to uplift our poor black brothers instead of to rob them" (33). But when the "fantastically loyal" Veraswami protests, Flory echoes Cyril Fielding when he lamely admits, "I'm here to make money, like everyone else. All I object to is the slimy white man's burden humbug. The Pukka Sahib pose" (33).

While Orwell's analysis of imperialism shows the traces of Freud's conservatizing model of the origins of the social contract in texts like "Totem and Taboo," where the sons band together to overthrow the father, his novel indicates why a new contract between colonizing and colonized men cannot be established. Flory, like most Anglo-Indians, is unwilling to renegotiate the sexual contract with colonizing or colonized women. Because the ideological contradictions in Orwell's text that result from this evasion are projected onto both colonizing and colonized women, they find dramatic expression in his starkly modern treatment of rape in this text.

Orwell presents a bitter indictment of the economic and political inequities in the relationships between colonizing and colonized men, but *Burmese Days* also shows a persistent blindness to the ways that the racial hierarchy in postwar British colonial life continued to enforce gender subordination, even after all Englishwomen were enfranchised in 1928. In imagining the Anglo-Indian society in Burma, which had been part of the Indian Empire for nearly forty years when the novel begins, Orwell describes a modern colonial world where sex and gender roles for men are no longer disciplined by Victorian morality, or even by the military code of honor that limits the recreational sex of British soldiers like those in Flora Annie Steel's *Voices in the Night*. Sex and gender roles for women, however, remain unrevised in this text. Though Orwell, like Forster, uses rape to illustrate the moral bankruptcy of Anglo-Indian life under the Raj, he makes colonizing women's fear of rape the butt of satire and ultimately consigns colonizing and colonized women alike to the zone of abjection. As a result, *Burmese Days* describes a modern colonial world devoid of honor, admiration, or love, a world in which rape is evacuated of its symbolic meanings.

John Flory, Orwell's ironic hero, embodies the dangers of a modern political subject who resists any introspection or psychological self-awareness. Because Flory sees no connections between his treatment of Burmese and English women, he repeatedly acts out his complicity in the racial, political, and sexual subordination of a colonial system he claims to abhor. Orwell's narrator apparently shares Flory's assumption that the sexual violations suffered by Burmese women have nothing to do with his critique of racism or his criticism of the social snobbery of colonizing women, and this omission, I would argue, is a common characteristic of British male modernist fiction in the period between World Wars I and II.

Orwell invites comparison with *A Passage to India* when John Flory, goaded by the ugly racism of the colonial bureaucrats at the Kyauktada Club, proposes that his Indian friend Dr. Veraswami be admitted to the all-white British club. Unlike Cyril Fielding, however, Flory does not even have the "small spark of courage" he needs to persist when others oppose Veraswami's membership, and he soon betrays his friend as well as his own principles. In an effort to explain this reversal, Orwell offers one of the only passages in the novel that provides a psychological perspective on Flory's inconsistent behavior. Flory has received a "third rate" imperial education similar to the one Kipling describes in *Stalky and Co*. As a result, he becomes a "good liar and a good footballer, the two things absolutely necessary for success in school" (56) and, in Orwell's jaundiced view, necessary for accommodation to life in one of the outposts of the British Empire. But Flory's education teaches him not only to lie to others but also to lie to himself. Flory's experiences in Burma thus produce a subject who is unwilling to "sacrifice" himself or his comforts in order to protect the British Empire. When the Great War begins, Flory refuses the call to military service because, as Orwell's narrator explains, "the East had already corrupted him" (59); "he did not want to exchange his whisky, his servants and his Burmese girls for the boredom of the parade ground and the strain of cruel marches" (59).

Orwell similarly alludes to the Indian Uprising of 1857 when he describes the careless violence of the colonizers that eventually provokes the Burmese to attack them after the Anglo-Indians take refuge in the British Club. Like Forster, Orwell mentions the famous defense of the Residency at Lucknow, though he deflates the heroic currency of these allusions even further by showing that the Burmese have little more than sticks and stones to use against the colonizers. Moreover, Orwell shows that the Anglo-Indians in this episode are blinded by a rage that is so excessive it renders them "half dazed." Ellis, for example, the Anglo-Indian who provokes this crisis by savagely beating a young nationalist, is portrayed as caught in the grip of hysterical rage, longing for "a real rebellion—martial law proclaimed and no quarter given!" so that "lovely sanguinary images moved through his mind. Shrieking mounds of natives, solders slaughtering them. Shoot them, ride them down, horses' hooves trample their guts out, whips cut their faces in slices" (221).

When the Resident's speech fails to dissipate the protesters, the Anglo-Indians assume a siege mentality, but "none of them thought to blame Ellis, the sole cause of their affair; their common peril seemed, indeed, to draw them closer together for a while" (227). When they realize that telegraph lines to the police headquarters have been cut, Flory recognizes the "seriousness of the situation" (229) and, feeling the pressure of Elizabeth's hand on his arm, he volunteers, like a hero in one of Henty's novels, to swim down the river and lead the colonial police in a counterattack. Although Flory succeeds in contacting the police, he proves himself to be more heroic than Henty's heroes, by Orwell's standards, for he disobeys his orders, and tells the police to shoot over the heads of the rioters rather than to shoot to kill (230). While Dr. Veraswami similarly proves his loyalty by joining the fray and fighting in defense of the Raj, Orwell designs a plot that prevents Flory and the doctor from receiving the usual rewards invariably distributed in Anglo-Indian mutiny novels.

At this point in the plot, Flory has come to see Elizabeth as a desirable wife, one who will reward him for his sacrifices, even though he once rejected such colonial rhetoric as "humbug." After his heroic adventures, Flory is too tongue-tied to express his desire to marry Elizabeth, partly because he recognizes the "devilish difficulty" of describing the "nature of the loneliness he wanted her to nullify" (162–163). He thus reveals the workings of a "colonial ventriloquism" of another sort since Flory mouths the colonial rhetoric of sacrifice in spite of himself. Unable to admit "the debaucheries, the lies, the pain of exile and solitude, the dealings with whores and moneylenders and pukka sahibs" (249), Flory launches into his proposal of marriage but is ironically cut short by an earthquake.

Orwell intervenes even more ironically in the plot when he introduces Flory's Burmese mistress, Ma Hla May, just at the moment when Elizabeth is ready to forgive Flory "everything" (237) after his successful efforts to alert the police "made him almost a hero in her eyes" (237). But Ma Hla May's perfectly timed exposure of Flory's sexual history destroys any chance that Elizabeth would accept him as a marriage partner. Caught in the meshes of the colonial imaginary, but no more so than Flory himself, Elizabeth is compelled by an "instinct" that was "deeper than reason or even self-interest" (225) and rejects Flory's marriage proposal. Her thinking echoes the rhetoric of many heroines in mutiny novels when they are threatened with rape: "Anything—spinsterhood, drudgery, anything—sooner than the alternative. Never, never would she yield to a man who had been so disgraced! Death sooner, far sooner" (225). Like Adela, Elizabeth is horrified by the prospect of marriage to a man she cannot respect, but Orwell's narrator belittles her concerns. In retrospect, Flory reevaluates the ethics of chivalry that prompted him so uncharacteristically to risk his life and succumbs to chagrin, killing himself in a messy suicide.

Burmese Days differs from both Forster's and Duncan's novels, then, because it reveals how the social contract is overwritten by the sexual contract for women in the modern postwar world. Because Flory consorts with Burmese concubines, who are categorically defined as his inferiors because of their race, gender, and class, he is able to avoid acknowledging the changes in the social contract that, in 1928, granted the vote to all British women and abolished the most powerful legal defenses of women's subordination to men. Unlike the self-sacrificing Dr. Aziz or the proudly solitary Fielding, or indeed unlike the Anglo-Indians in most of the novels I have surveyed in this book, Flory has lived openly with a number of Burmese women without the benefit of marriage. The most recent of his concubines, Ma Hla May, literalizes and embodies contradictions central to the persistent sexual contract defining colonial life. In economic terms, Ma Hla May is literally a slave since Flory "bought" her from her parents for three hundred rupees (46). Socially, she is treated like a prostitute, because Flory expects sex on demand and offers her, on occasion, a distanced, objectifying aesthetic appreciation, but even that is devoid of any expression of affection or respect. Though she is only one in a very long line of past mistresses, so long that Flory has lost count, Ma Hla May has persuaded "everyone, herself included, that she was Flory's legal wife" (46–47). In fact, according to Daphne Patai, Ma Hla May has legitimate reasons for her view: Burmese customary law, which was defined by Buddhist rather than Hindu or Muslim practices, would recognize her as Flory's wife since they had lived in open cohabitation for a sufficient period of time (39).

Because of the unacknowledged authority conveyed by his race and gender as well as his wealth and class, Flory retains the power to define the meaning and terms of his separation from Ma Hla May, but what facilitates the break is that she has not given birth to any children. Though he has paid, sheltered, and ostensibly "protected" Ma Hla May and has commanded her attention in return, Flory experiences no political or ethical conflict when he decides to dismiss her in order to appear as a respectable partner for Elizabeth Lackersteen. Reading their relationship entirely in economic terms, Flory throws Ma Hla May a few coins as severance pay and considers their relationship to be at a end.

Ma Hla May, by contrast, sees their separation in terms of divorce. Denied a proper settlement, and realizing she could not obtain justice in the courts of the colonizers, Ma Hla May seeks revenge by publicly exposing Flory for his sexual exploitation of her, significantly choosing a church as the site of this confrontation. Her tactic works only because the Englishmen in his community recognize the truth of her charges. Flory, and Orwell, show their resentment over the small power that Ma Hla May is able to claim in this episode by emphasizing her abjection. Ma Hla May identifies the real symbol of fear and loathing in this scene when she cries, "Look at me, you white men, and you women, too, look at me. . . . Look at this body that you have kissed a thousand times" (250).

As Ma Hla May's rhetoric indicates, it is not only colonized women who are assigned to the zone of abjection in the modern colonial world represented in *Burmese Days*; indeed, the zone of abjection in this text widens to include Mrs. Lackersteen, Elizabeth, and all the other memsahibs. A reference to rape allows Orwell to accomplish this rhetorical sleight of hand in the case of Mrs. Lackersteen. When she receives an anonymous letter that charges Dr. Veraswami with "inciting the natives to abduct and rape the European women," Orwell's narrator identifies the chain of association in the colonial imaginary that I have been tracing, but he identifies the fear of rape as the sick fantasy of stupid and neurotic memsahibs. The narrator comments that this letter had "touched Mrs. Lackersteen's weak spot. To her mind the words 'sedition,' 'nationalism,' 'rebellion,' 'Home Rule,' conveyed one thing and one only, and that was a picture of herself being raped by a procession of jet-black coolies with rolling white eyeballs" (124). Overinvolved in his hero's quarrels with the female authority, Orwell's narrator fails to see that Mrs. Lackersteen's response identifies a "weak spot" in the ideological and symbolic registers of twentieth-century British colonial culture.

Elizabeth Lackersteen's similarly appalling ignorance about sexuality and politics allows Flory initially to feel morally superior to her. When Elizabeth first meets Ma Hla May, for instance, she notes the sexual ambiguity that Freud identified and that Forster, Duncan, and a few other Anglo-Indians recognized in colonial life. The first time she sees Ma Hla May, she asks Flory, "Was that a man or a woman?" (78). When Flory lies, pretending Ma Hla

May is "one of the servants' wives," Elizabeth generalizes, "Oh. Is that what Burmese women are like?" (78). Ignoring the ways that the ethnographic appeal of Burmese culture solicits colonizing men and women differently, Flory tries to introduce Elizabeth to the "real" Burma, and is dismayed when she is appalled by the dancing, dirt, and especially by the overt sexuality that, according to the narrator, makes her feel a despised "kinship" with Burmese women, a kinship not of her making (107). But when Elizabeth begins to recognize the discrepancies in the colonial categories of "black" and "white," asking him, for example, if Eurasians are "degenerate," a premise Social Darwinism legitimized, Flory fails to correct her because he does not want to explain how he knows so much about Eurasian and Burmese women.

While *Burmese Days* otherwise insists on the difference that race makes in this colonial culture, Elizabeth Lackersteen is eventually characterized in the same terms and reveals the same contradictions in the sexual contract that Ma Hla May more obviously embodies. Early in the novel, Elizabeth is presented, and indeed like many New Women, she regards herself, as engaged in polite prostitution. Orphaned and without resources, Elizabeth is sent out to join the family of her father's brother and his wife, like many of the young Englishwomen in fiction of the period who cheerfully travel to India in the "fishing fleet" to find an appropriate, upwardly mobile British husband. Shamed by having to work to support herself while in Paris, Elizabeth sees marriage unsentimentally, as a better business arrangement. Urged by her aunt to "marry anybody, literally anybody," and threatened with the object lesson about a girl who "failed to get married" while in India and returned to England to work "as a kind of lady help, practically a servant" (88), Elizabeth is eager to oblige.

Unwilling to recognize the psychological forces that identify Flory's obsessive display of male hypersexuality as the modern replacement for the homosociality that organized nineteenth-century Anglo-Indian society, Orwell shifts rape from the public to the private sphere in order to assign Elizabeth to the zone of abjection. Elizabeth is desperate to marry because her uncle, the man whom colonial culture assigned to be her protector, tries several times to rape her. Unlike Forster, however, Orwell treats Elizabeth's sexual harassment by her uncle as an ironic but mundane fact of colonial life. This is what makes Elizabeth a modern woman when she, like one of Freud's patients, is "horrified" to discover that "some men are capable of making love to their nieces" after her uncle pinches her leg "in a way that simply could not be misunderstood" (159). Later, Mr. Lackersteen makes a second "spirited attempt to rape her" (209) and continues to "pester her unceasingly. . . . Almost

under the eyes of the servants . . . pinching and fondling her in the most re-
volting way" (242). Caught in a double bind because she is afraid to tell her
aunt about her husband's outrageous behavior, Elizabeth silently resists the
sexual exploitation that Freud himself repressed in his later work, and looks
for a respectable excuse to leave her uncle's household.

What defines Orwell's treatment of rape as psychoanalytically modernist, and what makes these rape attempts possible, is not a lasciviousness projected onto the native man but what these images covered up in the colonial
imaginary: the failure of mother-right in this colonial world. Elizabeth, like
Adela Quested and Joan Mills, comes to India as a motherless child, but
Orwell gives her none of the legacies that Joan or even Adela enjoys. Elizabeth is the daughter of a New Woman rather than a New Woman herself, and
the descriptions of Elizabeth and her suffragette mother indicate one way that
Orwell apparently defended his leftist politics from the challenges of the generation of feminists who succeeded Joan Mills. Orwell describes Elizabeth's
mother as "an incapable, half-baked, vapouring, self-pitying woman who has
shirked all the normal duties of life on the strength of sensibilities which she
did not possess. After messing about for years with such things as women's
Suffrage and Higher Thought, and making many abortive attempts at literature, she had finally taken up painting" (80). When Elizabeth's alcoholic father dies, leaving her mother with an income of £150 a year, her mother fails,
not surprisingly, to "live on three pounds a week in England," and takes Elizabeth with her to try to live more cheaply in Paris, hardly a reprehensible course
of action. Yet Orwell ridicules this mother's efforts to support herself and her
child and adds further irony by describing how she dies of self-generated pto-
maine poisoning (84). In Orwell's novel, then, the murderousness toward the
mother that Ronny Heaslop expresses in *A Passage to India* when he lets down
his guard spreads to include Burmese and British women alike.

Although she is the daughter of a feminist suffragette, Elizabeth has
apparently been well trained by reading Anglo-Indian romances and soon falls
under the spell of an empty and illusory romance with the polo-playing newcomer, Verrall. While he amuses himself by flirting with Elizabeth, Verrall
proves himself to be immune to any compelling heterosexual desire and shows
repeatedly that he "abhors" women (185–186). After his flirtation with Elizabeth runs its course, he decamps, and soon after, Flory commits suicide, humiliated by Ma Hla May. Elizabeth then accepts a marriage proposal from
Mr. Macgregor, the highest official in this little colonial world, but Orwell's
narrator invites his readers to despise her choice, noting ironically how "she

fills with complete success the position for which Nature had designed her from the first, that of a burra memsahib" (263).

As Orwell's novel makes clear, in the postwar symbolic order, rape appears as an unremarkable and pervasive correlative of modern sexual relations and more aggressive models of male heterosexual identity. Like many other British writers in the modern period, Orwell assigns rape to the private domain of the family, out of the reach of political or ethical censure, where it has remained until very recently. As long as he harasses one of his own kin, a young woman in his own household, Mr. Lackersteen, like Flory, remains confident that he will be protected by a social contract that defined any illicit aspect of sexual life as "private."

Orwell recognizes one of the consequences of the gradual liberalization of laws defining colonial relations, as well as sex and marriage, in the twentieth century, when he shows how British notions of privacy could be used to shelter colonized and colonizing men alike from charges of rape. While the villain of this colonial drama, U Po Kyin, was known to have committed "many and many a rape" (124), he remains as immune from prosecution as is Mr. Lackersteen, as long as he confines his attempts to women of his own race. Given this modern reconfiguration of sexuality and violence under the Raj, rape becomes a fact of life that could unite colonizing and colonized women. This is why, perhaps, Orwell prevents Elizabeth from acting more positively on the "kinship" she feels with colonized women in this text, and why modern patriarchal colonial cultures would assign all rape victims to the zone of abjection.

In conclusion, the failure of the cross-racial romances in both *A Passage to India* and *The Burnt Offering* show why the deep divisions between *eros* and *polis* in Anglo-Indian society could no longer be maintained by a reiteration of older nationalist allegories about the rape of white women by Indian men. At the same time, both these novels envision modern marriage as a self-willed sacrifice and recognize the new multiple possibilities of desire that are projected onto eroticized racial Others, whose appeal is amplified by an "ethnographic real" that commodifies and circulates it (Apter, 300).

When *A Passage to India* is read in relation to *Burmese Days*, on the other hand, we can see how the "grain of resentment in all chivalry" (237) that Forster identifies in Anglo-Indian society is magnified and becomes a cover for the blinding resentment directed against women of all races and classes in Orwell's novel. Orwell's ostensible target is the hypocrisy of Anglo-Indian life, but he is unapologetic about the catalogue of the colonizing men's illicit and exploitative boundary crossings: Flory with his hundred unremembered prostitutes as well as the mistress who proves to be his nemesis, Lackersteen with his obsessive desire to rape the attractive young niece he is duty bound to protect, and Verrall with his unscrupulous indifference to any responsibilities except those owed to his horses and the advancement of his career. Orwell imagines no solutions and offers no way out of this bleak and loveless colonial world.

Read in this context, *A Passage to India* shows, finally, its humanism as well as its modernism. While it re-Orientalizes rape in ways that normalize the existing sexual contract in British India, it does not take the misogynist turn so apparent in Orwell's novel, despite all the resistance to the heterosexual and cross-racial plots that it displays. At the same time, Forster's novel shows the legacy of his psychoanalytic modernism when it assigns the mother to a new place in the restructuring of sexual desire under British modernism, even as it refuses to represent other alternatives to marriage as a means to symbolize the reconciliation between colonizer and colonized. After more than fifty years of Anglo-Indian romances, it is hardly surprising that a brilliant, original, and courageous author like Forster did not present interracial marriage as a solution to colonial conflicts in his novel nor envision life beyond the Oedipal battles for and with the mother that defined the male colonizer's relation to the Raj in the modern period. It is sad, however, that Forster's reticence prevented him from sharing the solutions that he discovered in coming to India, even though he did not write about them.[24]

Conclusion

A Glance at Rape in Postcolonial Fiction

᠅᠅᠅᠅᠅

*I*n this book, I have charted the rise and fall of the most familiar rape script in the colonial imaginary of Anglo-Indian fiction, a plot which features pure Englishwomen threatened with rape by Indian men. My objective has been to expose the primary scripts about sexuality, violence, and power that made this particular rape narrative meaningful to British and Anglo-Indian readers. In many ways, it is the postcolonial literature about India, and the criticism about it, that, in duplicating and elaborating this particular rape script, has created the illusion that rape stories were everywhere in nineteenth-century colonial texts; they were not. So it is here that I would locate our own postcolonial version of the ghost of Miss Wheeler. The graphic and brutal representation of the rapes of colonial women in John Masters's *Nightrunners of Bengal*, for example, tell us more about the rape scripts at work in our own time, as does the more sensitive treatment of Daphne Manners's rape by Indian hoodlums in *The Jewel in the Crown*.[1]

Postcolonial Indian writers have another story to tell, as I would like to demonstrate with a brief summary of Manohar Malgonkar's disturbing *The Devil's Wind: Nana Saheb's Story*. As Malgonkar's subtitle indicates, this novel asserts Nana Saheb's innocence in the most famous rape story of the Indian Uprising of 1857, the massacre of Englishwomen and children at the Bibighar in Cawnpore (Kanpur). The burden of Nana Saheb's rebuttal clearly expresses the ways that British colonial histories of the Indian Mutiny of 1857 continue to be revised to support the ideological demands of contemporary Indian nationalism. Malgonkar's narrative shows how and why postcolonial intellectuals need to "write back," revising in this case the rape scripts concerning power and violence that helped to hold the Raj in place. As Nana

Saheb observes, "Our revolt had thrown up a surfeit of British heroes but no villains to balance them against, and they needed villainy of the requisite magnitude to serve as a backdrop for heroism. How hollow would Havelock's victories have seemed if I, Nana Saheb, had not been their principal objective!" (253).

In cataloguing the violence suffered by the colonized during the British retaliatory campaign after the massacre at Kanpur in 1857, Malgonkar's novel details the "orgy of killing, rape, and vandalism" perpetrated by Colonel James Neill and his soldiers, events that are censored in nearly all British mutiny novels and, in fact, in many British nineteenth-century imperial histories as well. Thus, Malgonkar reveals why "romances" and "boys' adventures" about the mutiny were the preferred form, since in these genres the moral uprightness of the heroes is an uncontested given, which means, as the narrator in G. A. Henty's *Times of Peril* insists, that British soldiers simply do not rape. Malgonkar counters such claims with numerous graphic representations of the rapes of Indian women by Englishmen that challenge colonial myths about the purity and righteousness of the British acts of "revenge." Malgonkar's novel thus invokes imperial history to correct it, by maintaining that British soldiers did, indeed, rape as well as pillage and burn as they swept through the countryside: "Women were dragged out screaming and pounced upon in bazaars, so that the word 'rape' itself acquired a plurality, a collective connotation, and people spoke of villages and townships raped, not of single women" (245).

By bringing Nana Saheb back to the well at Kanpur, Malgonkar also displays the epistemological power of the colonizer, evident in all these novels and histories. He describes Kanpur as a razed city and details the monuments erected to consecrate the most cherished myths of the Raj. Nana Saheb stops at the shrine at the Bibighar and reads the inscription:

SACRED TO THE PERPETUAL MEMORY OF A GREAT COMPANY OF CHRISTIAN PEOPLE CHIEFLY WOMEN AND CHILDREN WHO, NEAR THIS SPOT WERE CRUELLY MURDERED BY THE FOLLOWERS OF THE REBEL DHONDU PANT OF BITHOOR AND CAST, THE DYING WITH THE DEAD INTO THE WELL BELOW ON THE 15TH DAY OF JULY 1857.

Forbidden, like all other Indians, to enter the enclosure around the memorial and fired by slow anger over the colonizers' lies, Nana Saheb exonerates himself, "Despite the most exhaustive inquiries, no one has been able to establish that I was anywhere near the Bibighar or even that anyone had seen me in Kanpur when the slaughter occurred, as hundreds had seen Hodson shooting the heirs of the Mogul emperor or as thousands had witnessed the public hangings of the remaining princes by Metcalfe and Boyd" (299). He then wonders where the memorials are to the Indian women and other innocent people who also died when British forces struck back in 1857.

The broadside that Nana Saheb is given a few minutes later likewise displays some of the forces that caused the subaltern's subordination under the Raj; the original document, he is told, was written in Urdu and inscribed in blood by Zaffar Ali. It describes how Ali was flogged by Neill's soldiers and "made to lick the blood on the floor of the Bibighar"; it pledges his son to "avenge this desecration on the General's descendants" (303–304). This message was copied and circulated secretly, like the chapatis, throughout the countryside.

Yet, though Malgonkar exonerates Nana Saheb as well as the Rani of Jhansi, Tantya Topi, and other Indian leaders of the Uprising of 1857, he assigns blame for the massacre at Bibighar to an Indian woman, Hussainy Begam. Nana Saheb declares that neither he nor the sepoys had anything to do with the murder of the English survivors at the Bibighar, "if only out of religious scruples, no Indian soldier would bring himself to murder captive women and children, no matter who ordered him to do so" (218). But this declaration seems to reproduce the same absolute polarities of romance that are evident in many British and Anglo-Indian Mutiny novels.

Likewise, Malgonkar's description of the woman he identifies as responsible for organizing the massacre shows similar marks of abjection linked to her gender; Nana Saheb recalls, "The name conjures a witchlike creature, withered and permanently bent under a dripping dungbasket, her hair standing like wire. She was shrieking wildly and beating her breast when I last saw her. She had just been told that her daughter had been burned alive in the burning of Daryagani" (218). Though British accounts of the mutiny often claimed that she was his mistress, Nana Saheb, like Dr. Aziz in *A Passage to India*, is offended to be associated with such a hideous woman.

The Devil's Wind also describes the afterlife of Eliza Wheeler. Malgonkar's handling of her story, like his identification of Hussainy Begam as the madwoman responsible for the massacre at Kanpur, shows that while he is able to address the parts of this rape script that concern colonial violence and power by a fairly simple process of inversion, the themes concerning sexuality and power are not so simply handled. In Malgonkar's version, Nana Saheb is deeply in love with Eliza Wheeler; he finds her to be that "certain kind of woman who, the very first time you see her, bruises your heart in some way. You are held captive not so much by her physical charms as by some magnetic attraction which has no meaning for anyone else" (92). As this passage shows, the eroticization of violence compounds the eroticization of racial difference in our times.

In the opening pages of this love story, Malgonkar simply reverses the values associated with "whiteness" in British mutiny novels. Eliza is the second daughter of Major General Hugh Wheeler and his young and pretty Indian wife; early in the novel Eliza declares that, unlike her mother, she will not marry a "white man" (102). But when the rebellion begins in Kanpur, Malgonkar resorts to postcolonial "splitting" in order to separate Nana Saheb from the man who rapes Eliza Wheeler. In his version, Eliza is abducted by soldiers of the Muslim leader, Nizam Ali. This part of the story begins to sound much more like the colonizers' favorite rape script since it too circles around reproduction. Kept in captivity, Eliza is forcibly converted to Islam, married to Nizam Ali, and then repeatedly raped because he has no sons and wants a legitimate heir. As in many of the colonizers' novels, Nizam Ali's first wife is a co-conspirator in the subsequent rapes. Later Eliza explains that her torture went on for days, with "the two women swearing obscenely and admonishing me to be complaisant, and then holding me down and cleaning me up, preparing me for the man to come tearing into me like a crazed bull" (235). In this version, religion substitutes for race as the sign of abjection.

In Malgonkar's story, the raped woman is allowed to kill her rapist, to survive, and later to describe her ordeal to Nana Saheb. This part of the story is meant to point in a hopeful direction, but unfortunately it strains credulity most. Like a typical mutiny hero, Nana Saheb rescues Eliza Wheeler, though he must kill Nizam Ali's wife in order to release her, indicating the diminished power of the ethics of chivalry in our time. When Eliza begins her terrible story, Nana Saheb gently tells her, "You don't have to tell me," and she responds, "Who am I to tell, then, how I became pregnant? There is no one left. I'll go mad if I don't tell someone" (233). Eliza insists that she cannot return home since she will be "jeered at because I am going to be a mother, carrying a child implanted by numerous acts of rape, knowing that I couldn't even say for certain who the father was" (234). Eliza's comment identifies women as the definers and enforcers of the racial and sexual codes that rape victims violate when they become pregnant. Women are not, however, the framers of the *zina* laws in force today in Pakistan, nor do women act alone to enforce the laws or the shame and ostracism that often add to the rape victim's sufferings.[2]

Improbably, then, Nana Saheb offers Eliza Wheeler shelter, arranges for the adoption of the child she is forced to bear, and later marries her, fathering a daughter and living contentedly with her. In the end, *The Devil's Wind*, like a good ghost story, identifies the source of the illusions that haunt so many British and Anglo-Indian versions of this rape story about the Indian Uprising of 1857. Eliza Wheeler does not die after she kills her attacker; she is allowed to play the part of Nana Saheb's faithful wife, accompanying him in his exile first in Nepal and later in Turkey, bringing Nana's story to a close that resembles the conclusion of Robert Armitage Sterndale's *The Afghan Knife*. Indian women who have been raped more recently, during, for example, the communal violence in Surat in 1992 or in Bombay in 1993, do not tell stories that end so happily. Many Hindu women who were raped and engraved with the name "Pakistan Zindabad" were not welcomed back into their families after their savage violations, nor were many Muslim women who were raped and marked with the sign of "om" on their foreheads.[3]

Studies like this one will not prevent rape. As I write this conclusion, I am confronted with painful evidence that rape, and the fear of it, continue to haunt the lives of most modern women in India, in Pakistan, in Great Britain, and, perhaps most of all, in the United States. I realize that a study like this cannot hope to alter the powerful forces that have multiplied the number of rapes, both reported and unreported, in the postmodern, postcolonial world that we now inhabit. I hope, however, that this analysis will raise awareness about the ways that literature has lent, and continues to lend, itself to the circulation of the most pernicious "scripts" that conflate power, sex, and reproduction and so make rape seem to be an excusable crime in times of peace as well as in war.

NOTES

Introduction

1. For Burke's comments, see *Parliamentary Papers* (1771–1774): 17:671. For analysis, see Kramnick (136). See also Marshall (*Impeachment*) and (*British*); Musselwhite; and Suleri. Percival Spear identifies Warren Hastings as the "real founder of the British domination in India" (2:92).
2. Burke, "Speech in Opening the Imperial Impeachment, 19 February 1788," in *Works* (10:83–89). See also Kramnick (137).
3. Suleri discusses the effects of this rhetoric on Burke's audiences (59–63).
4. See Ali; and Kabbani. Karkar and Ross offer a particularly interesting discussion of these tales of seduction (esp. 41).
5. Suleri (59–63). Rosane Rocher's effort to "disaggregate" Edward Said's Orientalism has been especially helpful. Teltscher (*India Inscribed*); Majeed; and Stokes offer excellent summaries of colonial policy in this period. For more general studies analyzing Said's *Orientalism*, see Ahmad (*In Theory*) and ("Between"); Breckenridge and Van der Veer; Mackenzie (*Orientalism*) and ("Edward Said"); Lowe; Dennis Porter; Robbins; and Turner. While British colonialism certainly reveals the European colonizer's imposing power and desire for political, economic, cultural, religious, and linguistic domination, I agree with Rocher's argument that recent scholars have overlooked the differences between the specific colonial policies of the group of colonial administrators originally called Orientalists, including Warren Hastings and Sir William Jones, and the positions of the group called Anglicanists, including, most notoriously, Thomas Macaulay. Said's appropriation of the term "Orientalists" has created considerable confusion, especially among literary critics.
6. See Said's *Orientalism* and his more recent *Culture and Imperialism*; Mannoni; Fanon; Donaldson; Sharpe (*Allegories*); and Alloula. I have named these particular critics because their work has been especially influential. Others, of course, could be mentioned, particularly among more psychoanalytically inclined scholars. Literary critics, like Eric Meyer, who find the master text of Orientalist discourse in Byron's poetry, repeat Said's Orientalist bias in privileging Islamic over Hindu culture, since, in all but a few vapid lyrics like "Stanzas to a Hindoo Air," Byron avoids representing Hindu culture.

7. On Fanon, see Gates.
8. I have derived these statistics from Gupta's bibliography of novels about India. See also Brantlinger (esp. 199); and the less reliable survey of novels on the Indian Mutiny by Shailendra Dhari Singh. I use "Anglo-Indian" in its nineteenth-century usage throughout to refer to British residents in British colonies in India or to British-Indian political relations. "Eurasian" was the term most commonly used in the nineteenth century to denote mixed-race peoples.
9. For details, see Spear; Stokes (*Peasant*); Metcalf (*Aftermath*); and Malleson, among many other sources. I discuss histories and fiction about the Uprising of 1857 in more detail in chapters 3, 4, and 5.
10. On the impact of Victorian formulations of chivalry, see Paxton ("Mobilizing").
11. See Metcalf (*Aftermath*, 290–291).
12. In the more than fifty novels of the period that I read, I found no explicit representations of rape except in James Grant's *First Love and Last Love*. On Paul Scott's fiction, see Rubin's interesting study.
13. Responding to the work of Michel Foucault, Teresa de Lauretis develops this term to refer to all the forces that install sex and gender differences (1–30).
14. Roy Porter makes a generally persuasive argument in urging caution in projecting contemporary ideas about rape into the historical past ("Rape," 216–236). This project has been made possible by several fine recent studies of rape, including: Higgins and Silver; Clark (*Women's Silence*); Edwards (*Female Sexuality*) and (*Policing*). The classic study is, of course, Brownmiller, but see also feminist studies by Estrich; Plaza; MacKinnon ("Feminism") and (*Feminism Unmodified*); and Bell; to name only a few important works.
15. For analysis of interracial rape, see Scully; Smith; Hall ("Mind") and (*Revolt*); and Angela Davis. I discuss Scully's findings in more detail in chapter 5.
16. These examples are cited in the 1933 edition of the *Oxford English Dictionary*. The first edition of the *Oxford English Dictionary* (1898) lists no entry for "rape," meaning sexual assault, one of many signs of how profoundly rape was censored in the Victorian period.
17. While McClintock is describing British imperialism in Africa in a slightly later period, her description nonetheless captures the unevenness in the kinds of power and the skill in commanding it that, in my view, also typifies colonial relations in British India, especially before 1857 (McClintock, 15).
18. See Trevelyan (305). To my knowledge, he was the first historian to investigate this claim systematically.
19. See Sinha (*Colonial Masculinities*) and ("Chattams," 98–116); Tanika Sarkar ("Bankimchandra") and ("Hindu Wife"); and Carroll. See also Hirschmann and Lewis for earlier work on this topic.
20. I refer, of course, to Gayatri Chakravorty Spivak's famous essay, "Can the Subaltern Speak," as well as the important work of Ranajit Guha and the Subaltern Studies Group.
21. Special thanks to Sanjay Joshi for help with this example from Urdu and to Jim Wilce for his help with the Bengali term.
22. Philippa Levine brought this example to my attention. For details, see Ballhatchet (10, 82–83, 140–142).

23. I borrow this term from Gatens (135). There has been considerable debate among feminists as well as other social theorists, especially those influenced by the work of Michel Foucault, about whether rape can be best defined in terms of "violence" or "sex." Like Vikki Bell, I see rape as incompletely assessed by either of these rubrics since it is also fundamentally about power, and how and when people assert it. Shani D'Cruze's analysis of "rape scripts" provides one way to include these issues of power and deliberate choice. While my project, like Gatens's study, accepts some of Foucault's insights about how discourse structures sexuality, as is evident, for instance, in our common use of "genealogy," I agree with her in insisting that the material and ethical dimensions that shape power, violence, and sexuality must also be included in a full analysis of rape.

24. For details on these legal controversies, see especially Philippa Levine (*Victorian Feminism*); and Kent. On the formation of "feminist imperialism," see Burton (127–205).

25. When the Contagious Diseases Acts, which authorized the arrest and forcible examination of women suspected of carrying venereal disease, were applied in India, they gave colonial officers another arena to act on Social Darwinist theories about gender, sex, and race. See Hutchins; Metcalf (*Aftermath*); Greenberger; Parry (*Delusions*); Memmi; and Nandy (*Intimate*), who argue that Social Darwinism was one of the most powerful discourses in legitimizing British imperialism in India. The stability of notions of "race" has recently been called into question by a number of critics. See, for example, Gilman; Thomas; and Young. Far less attention has been paid to the role of feminist discourse in both promoting and resisting the establishment of the Raj, but see Burton; Chaudhuri and Strobel; Melman; Strobel; Mills; Ware; Moira Ferguson; and Paxton ("Disembodied Subjects"). For studies that emphasize the interaction between British and Indian notions of gender, see Alexander and Mohanty; Sinha (*Colonial Masculinities*); Stoler ("Making"); Nair ("Question"); and Jayawardena (*White Woman's*) and her earlier (*Feminism*).

26. Spivak recommends a more fully "worlded" analysis of imperialism and its relation to nineteenth-century feminism in a famous essay ("Three").

27. On the fears about "black" on "white" rape in the United States, see Angela Davis's classic analysis. See also Ware (176–224); and Hall (*Revolt*) and ("Mind"). On rape and racial scares elsewhere, see Inglis; and Stoler ("Carnal Knowledge") and ("Sexual Affronts"). Global perspectives on economic systems may also help provide some explanation for parallels between the retaliatory violence and racial antagonism after the Mutiny in India and the brutal epidemic of lynching directed at black men in the 1870s and 1880s in the United States, for which rape narratives in both cases served as a provocation and cover.

28. On representations of India in earlier periods of British literature, see Laura Brown; Jyotsna Singh; and Drew. See also more general recent surveys by Cronin; Crane; Inden; and Halbfass.

29. No discussion of the formations of Indian nationalism would be complete without acknowledgment of the work of Partha Chatterjee (*Nation*), (*Nationalist Thought*), and ("Nationalist"); Gyan Prakash (*After Colonialism*) and (*Bonded*

Histories); and the brilliant feminist revisionary critiques of Tanika Sarkar ("Hindu Wife") and Mrinalini Sinha (*Colonial Masculinities*). Hubel (*Whose India*) presents a particularly astute analysis of many of the techniques used by Anglo-Indian novelists and British historians to avoid recognizing Indian Nationalism as a powerful force in this period.

30. For interesting discussions of the role of rape in eighteenth-century English novels, see Eagleton; Frances Ferguson; and Jacobus ("In Parenthesis").

31. John Drew catalogues representations of Indian women in Romantic poetry. See also Marilyn Butler's persuasive analysis of the displacements accomplished by Romantic poetry (*Romantics*). On the epic form and imperial ideologies, see Quint.

32. On Hardy's treatment of rape, see Rooney. Certainly one of the most important analyses of rape in Forster's *Passage to India* is Brenda Silver's brilliant essay in the same collection.

33. Munich ("What," 154). See Lloyd Davis's introduction and other essays in his collection (*Virginal Sexuality*) on important changes in the representation of women's sexuality in the Victorian period.

34. I borrow this term from Mary Louise Pratt's very useful and provocative analysis of travel writing about the Americas (1–11). Anthony D. King, in his neglected *Colonial Urban Development*, makes a strong and materially grounded argument for the "hybrid" nature of British colonial culture in India. See also more recent work by Young; and Thomas.

35. Several excellent recent studies analyze literature about colonial life written by British authors with no direct experience of it. See, for example, Bongie; Bivona; Susan Meyer; and Perena.

36. Bakhtin, *The Dialogic Imagination* (11–12). For other details, see Paxton ("Mobilizing Chivalry").

37. Many literary and colonial discourse critics who begin with the assumption that colonial subjects are always already inscribed by the polarities of colonial discourse don't often recognize the destabilizing, if not positively liberating, effects of literary language in contrast to the more utilitarian languages of missionaries, statesmen, scientists, or physicians.

38. The classic source on Oriental language training for British men is Cohn ("Command").

39. See especially Green (*Dreams*) and (*Seven*); and Sandison. Green's assessment is accepted somewhat uncritically by Bristow. Surprisingly, Jameson (*Political Unconscious*) simply reproduces rather than interrogates the categorical imperative that prompted Henty, Stevenson, and Kipling to rename their novels "romances." On the long-standing conventions that were overridden by this semantic switch, see Langbauer; and McKeon.

40. I have borrowed the term "ethnographic real" from Emily Apter's fine essay ("Ethnographic," 299–343), though she uses this term in a somewhat different context.

41. Wurgaft discusses Rudyard Kipling's cultural location with comprehensive finesse (101–152, esp. 104).

42. There are a number of studies that support McClintock's description of the

double binds faced by colonizing women: see esp. Hennessy and Mohan; Stoler ("Carnal Knowledge," 51–52); Strobel; Ardener and Callan; and Callaway. On the specific conditions of Anglo-Indian women writers in the 1880s and 1890s, see Sainsbury; Parry's important study (*Delusions*); and my essay ("Disembodied Subjects").

43. On changes in the publishing industry that made this strategy effective, see Tuchman. Moore-Gilbert (*Kipling*) offers some useful background on the publishing options available in British India.

44. I am especially indebted to the work of Tanika Sarkar, Mrinalini Sinha, Kumari Jayawardena, and Joanna Liddle and Rama Joshi in developing this regrettably brief summary. In a study of this length, I could not include Indian novels that were more widely representative of all the ideological and literary possibilities in circulation in the first three decades of the twentieth century. Others will, I hope, continue the pioneering work of critics like Gayatri Spivak, Meenakshi Mukerjee, Susie Tharu and K. Lalita, Rajeswari Rajan, and many others whose scholarship has helped to make my study possible.

45. My analysis of sati draws on important work by Nandy ("Sati"); Mani; Spivak ("Can the Subaltern Speak?"); Yang; and Gilmartin.

46. On the activities of Victorian feminists and their relation to the "social purity" movement in India, see Philippa Levine ("Rereading") and ("Venereal"); Ballhatchet; and Burton.

47. Homi K. Bhabha develops this useful concept (*Location*, 132). I am deeply indebted to this book and to Bhabha's earlier essays, especially ("Signs"), ("Other Question"), ("Representation"), and (*Nation*).

48. See the important new scholarship on colonial cultures and homosexuality, homoeroticism, and gender identity in Boone ("Vacation Cruises"); Christopher Lane (*Ruling Passion*); and Behdad (*Belated Travelers*) and ("Eroticized Orient"). Much has been written about the ways that Forster's sexuality finds, or doesn't find, expression in *A Passage to India*; see, for example, Dellamora (*Apocalyptic Overtures*) and (*Masculine Desire*).

CHAPTER 1   *Rape, the Body, and the Sacrifices of Desire*

1. See Alloula (*Colonial*, 3).

2. In focusing on Burke's writing rather than the much more diffuse impact of the new translations by Sir William Jones, Charles Wilkins, and other Orientalist scholars that he consulted, Sara Suleri reproduces Said's conflation of the narrowest and the most expansive definitions of Orientalism (24–48). While historians and critics of an earlier generation understood the Orientalist school to refer specifically to British colonial administrators who, like Jones and Hastings, favored policies whereby Indian subjects would be governed according to indigenous laws and practices of Hinduism or Islam, postmodern critics typically follow Said's lead in finding evidence of a larger Orientalism evident in the traces of solipsism and ethnocentricity in nearly all Western texts about the Orient, from Aeschylus' *Persians* and Euripides' *Bacchae* to the texts of present-day scholars writing about the Middle East.

3. My analysis of the impact of the translations of Sanskrit texts on British Romantic poetry has been made possible by several excellent studies that followed the pioneering work of Raymond Schwab and Edward Said. See especially Rocher; Teltscher (*India Inscribed*); Majeed; and Leask. On the "Indian sublime," see Suleri (24–48).

4. See also Watkins. Trivedi reassesses Byron's treatment of Muslim culture but omits any discussion of rape (82–104).

5. Lisa Lowe offers an intelligent critique of such undiscriminating assessments of Orientalism (see esp. 8).

6. See Lynn Hunt's interesting analysis of similar patterns in popular French fiction written during the French Revolution. See also Gatens (54).

7. Inderpal Grewal identifies the Indian zenana as the nearest equivalent of the harem but uses these terms interchangeably (5). I follow her example.

8. *Byron's Letters* (8:147–148). Further evidence of Byron's antifeminism can be seen in one letter, for example, where Byron complained, "Two faults are unpardonable in a woman,—she can read and write" (2:132). For more on Shelley's view of romantic love, see Nathaniel Brown; and Mellor.

9. See Ali for a comprehensive discussion of Scheherazade's role in *The Arabian Nights*.

10. Lovell (*Conversations*, 73).

11. Curran (*Shelley's Annus*) explores the impact of Shelley's reading of the *Vend Avesta*, but he does not comment on Shelley's reading of the translations of Sir William Jones or Charles Wilkins. Likewise, John Drew is very cautious in the conclusions he draws about Shelley's exposure to this scholarship. Neither considers how the notes to Southey's "The Curse of Kehama" may have introduced Shelley to Jones's works. Evidence of Shelley's continued interest in India can be found, for instance, in a letter he wrote in 1822 to Thomas Love Peacock, inquiring about the possibility of going to India as a secretary in the court of some maharajah; he received a discouraging reply and did not live long enough to pursue this desire (Drew, 235).

12. I adopt the more modern spelling of Sakuntala and Dusyanta throughout, though I retain Jones's spelling when I refer to his translation by name or to details particular to it.

13. There has been some critical debate about the form of "The Curse of Kehama" and "Laon and Cythna." Wilkie argues that Southey's poem is a "romance" (*Romantic Poets*, 36). Curran argues that Shelley's goals are "more to be associated with epic than romance" (*Poetic Form*, 147). Byron's violation of the usual codes defining the hero's sexuality and gender relation have made "Sardanapalus" unmentionable or uncategorizable. For a more general discussion of epic and empire, see Quint.

14. I cite all passages from the 1810 edition of "The Curse of Kehama," published by Longman, Hurst, Rees, Orme, and Brown, readily available on microfilm. Since this edition does not provide line numbers, I cite canto and page number rather than line number in parentheses throughout. See Marilyn Butler ("Revising") for changes in Southey's reputation.

15. See Inderpal Grewal's interesting discussion of women and freedom of movement (159–229).
16. In chapter 42 of *Tess of the D'Urbervilles*, Tess cuts off her eyebrows and folds a cloth around her face to prevent unwanted male attention.
17. Southey was well aware of the significance of sati at the time. Carnall reports that he read the Baptist Missionary Society's *Annual Review* for 1802, which included several reports of sati (*Robert Southey and His Age*, 207–208). As Miller notes, the temple of Jaganath in Puri was also one of the first temples to incorporate *devadasi*s who performed the *Gita Govinda* as part of regular temple rituals (*Dark Lord*, 6).
18. Lata Mani has argued that these episodes of "human sacrifice" also raise questions about how English concerns about sati between 1790 and 1830 served "to protect the entire community from its own violence" by contemplating those who could be imagined as "victims outside itself" (20). On sati, see also Yang; and Spivak ("Can"). I follow these authors in adopting a modern spelling for sati.
19. Clark (*Men's Violence*, 47, 60) documents the changes in rape laws in this period.
20. This logic also exposes some of the assumptions that define rape victims who are not beautiful or pure as beneath notice.
21. All parenthetical citations refer to the second edition of Burke's essay, *A Philosophical Enquiry into the Origin of Our Ideas of the Sublime and Beautiful*, available in facsimile.
22. Southey also evokes Burke's theory of the sublime to align Kailyal with the forces of good. When Kailyal petitions the god Indra to stop Kehama's "irresistible career," and learns that he cannot stop the Almighty Rajah, she asks to return to earth, saying, "The Gods / Are feeble here; but there are higher Powers / Who will not turn their eyes from wrongs like ours" (72). Southey's cheerful confirmation of his heroine's moral superiority, evidenced by her "purity" and "faith," echoing the gender ideals embedded in Burke's theory of the sublime, are reproduced endlessly in Anglo-Indian novels.
23. I cite from Neville Rogers's edition of "Laon and Cyntha" throughout.
24. Compare Cythna's reaction to her child with that of the slave mother in Elizabeth Barrett Browning's "Pilgrim at Tinker Creek," who is driven to kill her child because it constantly reminds her of the man who raped her.
25. Wolfson ("Problem") discusses Byron's "gender bending" in insightful ways. Sardanapalus's contemptuous brother-in-law regards him as an effeminate coward who has dallied in the harem and turned his back on his manly duties as emperor. These complaints about the sexual obsessions of Oriental leaders are repeated endlessly in nineteenth-century British and Anglo-Indian fiction about India. For a discussion of the effect of Napoleon's career on British Romantic poets, see Marilyn Butler (*Romantics*).
26. I cite from Frederick Page's edition of "Sardanapalus," which provides act, scene, and line references.
27. For another view, see Kensall (315–332).

28. Intent on protecting Sardanapalus's role as tragic victim and valorizing Byron's homoeroticism, Christensen argues rather fantastically that "'Sardanapalus' is *The Wealth of Nations* in drag" (289). See Garber; McClintock; and Boone ("Vacation Cruises") for excellent discussions of cross-dressing and colonial culture.

29. With the dissolution of the College of Fort William in 1831, the work of the Asiatic Society took other directions. For details, see Knopf (*British Orientalism*).

30. I have derived these statistics from Gupta's bibliography.

31. In addition to Alloula's brilliant analysis of how postcards represent the harem, many other studies have analyzed how travel literature, memoirs, advertising, and film have contributed to the formation of common patterns in colonial discourse about the harem. I have especially benefited from the studies by Melman; Apter; Lowe; Shohat; Grewal; and Behdad ("Eroticized Orient"). Croutier surveys paintings of harem life by British and French painters, and beautifully reproduces numerous examples.

32. Janaki Nair has argued that Englishwomen who wrote accounts of life in the Indian zenana avoided recognizing their own subordination by "making 'visible'" colonized women's subordination ("Zenana," 25). I contend that Anglo-Indian women were not universally "thwarted" in recognizing their own subordination in Paxton ("Disembodied Subjects").

33. For an analysis of American captivity tales from the same period, see Namias.

34. See Shohat (72) for more discussion of these "sites of contradiction," though she draws most of her examples from films and mentions only a few novels.

35. These terms are from Zonana (592–617). Melman has shown that when Victorian women travelers entered the closed female world of the harem, they wrote accounts that not only countered erotic male fantasies about harem life but often turned these observations back on Western men by noting, for example, that Muslim women enjoyed some legal rights denied to European women in marriage, divorce, and inheritance (108). They also noted differences in the way that Oriental women and men treated the female slaves they owned (109). The fascination with the Englishwoman imprisoned in the "harem" of an Indian man persisted long past 1833, when the Emancipation Act officially outlawed African slavery in British territories. Vron Ware offers an explanation by noting that British feminists, particularly in Quaker and Baptist groups, remained actively involved through at least the 1860s in international efforts to outlaw slavery in the United States and elsewhere. See also Moira Ferguson. Of course, "bond slavery" persisted and remained an open challenge to imperial defenses of empire, as Gyan Prakash (*Bonded Histories*, 1–2) has powerfully argued. Studies by Inderpal Grewal; and Partha Chatterjee (*Nationalist Thought*) have been especially helpful in developing my arguments in chapters 1–2.

36. I agree with Hennessy and Mohan that the passage of the Married Women's Property Act in 1882 marked a fundamental change in the "sexual imaginary" of late nineteenth-century England, a theme I explore in subsequent chapters.

37. In developing this summary of late eighteenth-century and early nineteenth-century colonial history, I have found particularly helpful the scholarship that

explores the boundaries between literature and history by Rocher; Majeed; Leask; MacKenzie (*Orientalism*); Teltscher (*India Inscribed*); Dennis Porter; Williams and Chrisman; Moore-Gilbert (*Kipling*) and (*Writing*); Sinha (*Colonial Masculinities*); Tanika Sarkar ("Hindu Wife") and ("Bankimchandra"); Carroll; and Metcalf (*Ideologies*).

38. See especially Hunt for a demonstration of how the French Revolution changed the representation of paternity and inheritance in French novels during this period. Nancy Armstrong offers an influential analysis of how British fiction consolidated new middle-class notions of chastity in the eighteenth and nineteenth centuries

39. For an interesting discussion of *Vathek*, see Kabbani (31–32).

40. Behdad discusses the role of the black eunuch in eighteenth-century French harem tales, in his fine essay ("Eroticized Orient," 119–122).

41. See Mellor (*Romanticism*, 32–33).

42. On the impact of missionary accounts, see especially Mani.

43. For biographical details, see Taylor (*Story*); Misra's analysis of Taylor's novels (*Raj*, 65–112); and Lyall. I was unable to obtain a first edition Taylor's *Ralph Darnell* (1865), so all citations refer to the compact, single-volume reprint.

44. For a well-informed discussion of the importance of this episode in British histories of the Raj, see Teltscher ("Fearful Name," 30–64).

45. I have adopted Taylor's idiosyncratic spelling for Suraj-ud-Daula throughout.

46. The force of Orientalist conventions apparently blinds B. J. Moore-Gilbert in his incorrect summary of Sozun's role in Darnell's life (*Kipling*, 52).

47. See Ian Duncan's wonderful analysis of Scott's fiction (esp. 131).

48. Celik and Mitchell present fascinating analyses of how world exhibits influenced the ways of seeing the Orient. Grewal (133–178) discusses the shaping force of Romantic notions of travel, though I see Byron's role as more central to the creation of new colonial "subjectivities" and equations of travel with certain kinds of "freedom."

49. For a detailed discussion of Kate's relation with the women of the zenana in Kipling's *Naulahka*, see Paxton ("Secrets," 139–162). Though Anna Leonowens's *Romance of the Harem* (1873) treats "harem" life in Siam, it also focuses on divorce. See also Laura E. Donaldson's analysis of Leonowens' romance (32–51); and Morgan's discussion (221–265). For a discussion of feminism and imperialism in the late nineteenth century, see Burton's excellent study.

50. See Isabel Armstrong (172–187).

Chapter 2   *The Temple Dancer*

1. Margolin (12).

2. I refer to the work of Gyan Prakash (*Bonded Histories*). My analysis of the larger context of Indian nationalism draws on the work of Partha Chatterjee in (*Nation*), (*Nationalist Thought*), and ("Nationalist"); as well as Tanika Sarkar ("Hindu Wife") and ("Bankimchandra"); and Mrinalini Sinha (*Colonial Masculinities*). For another perspective on Indian nationalism, see Hubel (147–178). Grosz points out that rape as a social event can be read either from the inside

or the outside (from the point view of the victim or of the rapist): thus its representation can provide a means to explore the "interface" between "privatized experience and signifying culture" (*Volatile Bodies*, 10).

3. For important studies on the *devadasi*, see Srinivasan; Margolin; Singha and Massey; Oldenberg; and Ramesh and Philomela. See also Buonaventura.

4. I cite from Avriel Goldberger's translation of *Corinne* (92).

5. In distinguishing the position of the "Orientalist" from that of the "missionary," I am indebted to Rocher; and Cohn ("Notes"). Thanks to Lata Mani for bringing the latter text to my attention. On the legacies of Wilberforce and the Clapham sect, see Majeed; Teltscher (*India Inscribed*); and Hutchins. Gayatri Spivak's famous formulation about how Englishmen save "brown women from brown men," in my opinion, projects imperial attitudes onto earlier nineteenth-century texts, where religion rather than "race" is the primary categorical term.

6. See Stocking; and Arnold (*Colonizing*) and (*Imperial Medicine*). On the role of sexuality, see Philippa Levine ("Venereal") and ("Rereading"); and Ballhatchet.

7. I rely on the definition of "abjection" offered by Julia Kristeva in *Powers of Horror* (9–10) and as developed by Judith Butler (*Bodies*, esp. 180). For further explanation, see my discussion of this term in chapter 6.

8. I cite from the more readily available *Luxima* (1859) throughout. In plot and characterization, this version differs little from the rare earlier version, *The Missionary* (1811). For biographical details on Owenson, see Campbell.

9. I draw here on Javed Majeed's analysis of erotic love in Jones's translations and original poetry (87–121). Jones's translation of the *Gita Govinda* also illustrated to English readers how the spiritual could be combined with the erotic in a text central to the Bhakti tradition of Hindu philosophy and devotional practice.

10. Drew discusses this landscape in some detail (240–242). He notes that Shelley ordered Jones's complete works in December 1812, shortly before he began work on "Alastor," but there are no published letters proving that Shelley actually read Jones's translation of *Sacontala*, so Drew cautiously focuses instead on the influence that Owenson's novel exerted on Shelley's "Alastor." For an analysis of the appeal of *Sacontala* and the *Bhagavadgita* for deists like Shelley, see Rocher (esp. 227–228).

11. For details, see Taylor's autobiography.

12. My reading of sati here draws upon the scholarship of Mani and Carroll.

13. Further evidence of Penny's debts to evangelical literature can be found in her direct allusion to Southey's "Curse of Kehama," when one of the minor characters, Miss Frost, is startled by a Hindu priest and thinks of "bygone ages" when there was no paternal "Government to put a value of human life." Miss Frost then envisions the "world famed Juggernaut car" and the fanatical devotees who prostrate themselves before it or throw their children underneath the wheels of this "cruel car" (*Romance* 170).

14. James Blythe Patton's *Bijli* (1898) and I.A.R. Wylie's *Daughter of Brahma* (1912) indicate the survival of Shelley's and Taylor's more liberal views of the *devadasi*. Patton shows an informed appreciation for the traditions of *tuwa'if* dancing, locates his nautch girl in an all-Indian context, and eliminates any contact with

Englishmen. Likewise, by presenting her as a Muslim rather than a Hindu, Patton excludes the spiritual dimensions that makes the temple dancer a more disruptive figure in Victorian colonial discourse about India. Bijli is thus free to act out the unrecognized tensions that underlie Penny's *Romance of the Nautch Girl* by describing the dancing girl as torn by her desire to pursue a career as a devoted artist, on one hand, and her longing for all the fulfillments of married love, on the other. Wylie, in *The Daughter of Brahma*, allows the interracial marriage of a second-generation English colonist with a beautiful *devadasi*, but, in the end, the dancer dies so that the hero may live a more conventional life married to the Englishwoman he has grown to love.

Chapter 3 *Mobilizing Chivalry*

1. Spear, *History of India* (2:141).
2. Bhabha (*Location*) provides an interesting overview of the causes of the uprising of 1857 and the role of rumor. Influential Indian histories include Chandra (esp. 94–97); and Guha. See Stokes (*Peasant*, 1–15) for an excellent recent, and succinct, historiographical survey.
3. For other discussions of the reports of rapes and reprisals, see Metcalf (*Aftermath*); and Brantlinger (199–224). Broehl argues that news of the massacre at Cawnpore "inflamed" British ferocity and retribution as no other event in the Mutiny; he reports that many officers, including John Nicholson, "firmly believed" that Englishwomen had been raped and "dishonored" in this war (141). For a comprehensive list of Mutiny novels, see Gupta; and the less reliable survey by Shailendra Dhari Singh. Earlier drafts of this chapter were presented at the Nationalisms and Sexualities Conference, Harvard University, June 17, 1989, and at the Bunting Institute, Radcliffe College, Oct. 31, 1990. See also Paxton ("Mobilizing Chivalry").
4. I was unable to obtain a first edition of James Grant's *First Love and Last Love*, so I cite from the edition included in *The Complete Works of James Grant* (vol. 16).
5. I cite from the first edition of G. A. Henty, *Rujub, the Juggler*.
6. Taylor typically signed his writing with the name Meadows Taylor, though librarians sometimes categorize him under his full name of Philip Meadows Taylor.
7. For a fuller discussion of how these novels employ the structures of chivalric romances, see Paxton ("Mobilizing Chivalry"). The starting point for my analysis of the "epic" features of these novels is Bakhtin's magisterial study, *The Dialogic Imagination*.
8. I am indebted to Joplin's "The Voice of the Shuttle Is Ours," which first appeared in the *Stanford Literature Review* 1, no. 1 (Spring 1984): 25–53. For the reader's convenience, I cite from the revised version of this essay included in Higgins and Silver (35–64).
9. For a convenient summary, see Sinha (*Colonial Masculinities*, 160–162). On James Mill's influence on Thomas Babington Macaulay, see Majeed (esp. 123–194).

10. *Parliamentary Papers*, 1837–1838 (52).

11. To my knowledge, Trevelyan was the first to make this claim. Sharpe says that official inquiries could produce no evidence of "systematic rape and torture at Cawnpore or any place else," but she provides no documentation to substantiate these claims ("Unspeakable," 32). Trevelyan summarizes the depositions of sixty-three witnesses, official reports by civil officers of the districts, and two published narratives (xi–xii).

12. For useful studies on the rape of Lucrece, see Ian Donaldson and Bryson. Richard Jenkins argues that classical texts, including Livy's version of the rape of Lucrece, were moved to the center of the British curriculum in the second half of the nineteenth century. Hulme documents how other Latin texts, like Virgil's treatment of Aeneas's idyll with Dido, reshaped colonial discourse about the Americas.

13. Stoler ("Making," 641). On the Ilbert Bill, see Sinha ("Chathams," 98–116) and (*Colonial Masculinities*). See also Hirschmann. For other views of the role of Indian women in the ideology of Indian nationalism in this period, see Sangari and Vaid.

14. Michie argues that women's bodies could not be described in Victorian novels. I contend that this generalization does not apply to the bodies of nonwhite women. Rape, of course, remained a common theme in popular Victorian melodramas.

15. Bakhtin argues that this delay is characteristic of "romances" (151).

16. As cited by Ian Donaldson (29).

17. See Taylor (*Story*, 445). See also Mansukhani (1–12). As an "uncovenanted" officer, Taylor received his commission in India, was entitled to less pay, and was excluded from the most prestigious posts in the colonial administration, like Indians who also served in this capacity.

18. For details about George Chesney's *The Dilemma*, see Paxton ("Mobilizing Chivalry," 5–30); and Brantlinger (211–212).

19. Compare Taylor's descriptions of Seeta with his portrait of Mary Palmer, painted a few years after their marriage in 1831, and reproduced in Taylor (*Letters*).

20. For another reading of Seeta's interracial marriage, see Jyotsna Singh (79–89).

21. Perhaps this failure of imagination can be explained personally since Taylor's wife died in 1844. Some critics have claimed that Taylor later established a permanent alliance with one or more Indian women, but he never remarried; see Amur.

22. Sinha provides a good summary of the emphasis on masculinity and its relation to colonial ideologies in this period (*Colonial Masculinities*, 1–68). Bongie and Christopher Lane (*Ruling Passion*) offer important and path-breaking analyses of the New Imperialism.

23. Cited by Sinha (*Colonial Masculinities*, 39–40). Several other scholars, including Bongie and Wurgaft, also cite this letter.

24. See Hennessy and Mohan's interesting discussion of the impact of these laws on colonial fiction and Sainsbury (esp. 167).

25. See Gregg's review, "The Indian Mutiny in Fiction" (218–231).

26. Brantlinger sees the acid defense as "nonsense" and diagnoses Bathurst's prob-

lem, somewhat dismissively, by saying that he is "gun shy" (217). Both these implausibilities display, it seems to me, the increasing pressure on the conservative and patriarchal definitions of female honor that Henty wanted to valorize. See also Nadis.

27. In *On the Face of the Waters*, Steel notes that Englishwomen at home were more threatened by rape and by efforts to police it than were Indian women; her heroine is "comforted" when she veils herself and remembers: "It was not England where a lonely woman might be challenged all the more for her loneliness. In this heathen land, that down-dropped veil hedged even a poor grass-cutter's wife about with respect" (68). For details on Steel's ambivalent feminism, see Paxton ("Disembodied Subjects," 387–409).

28. Holton (22). For an interesting discussion of Alice Gissing as a "New Woman," see Saunders (303–324).

29. For an informative discussion of the role played by Nicholson and Lawrence in the conservative defense of empire, see Wurgaft.

30. Terrible parallels can be found between the untold stories of rape during the mutiny of 1857 and recent wars in Bosnia and in India. On the latter, see Purshottam Agarwal (29–57).

CHAPTER 4   *Hostage to History*

1. Bhabha (*Location*, 132).

2. Jameson simply accepts and reproduces this appropriation of "romance" rather than interrogates it (*Political Unconscious*, 206–280). Martin Green (*Dreams*) and (*Seven*) takes another tack in cataloguing the features of this genre, though he does not address the significance of earlier uses of romance. Stieg (2–15), uses the term "romance" in ways that reproduce the derision that male authors often heaped upon it in the 1890s and later. For an interesting discussion of the links Jameson finds between "romance" and "allegory," see Jameson ("Third World").

3. For interesting histories of the Rani of Jhansi, see Fraser (272–96); and Lebra-Chapman. See also Spivak ("Rani").

4. Langbauer offers a useful discussion of Victorian "romances" (12–61). For a more general reconsideration of the role of "romance" in the development of the British novel tradition, see McKeon.

5. I am indebted to Koestenbaum's excellent discussion of "romance" (esp. 152–153).

6. See Weeks for details on the social and political effects of this act. Dellamora (*Masculine Desire*) provides a fascinating overview of the consequences of these changes in British literature of this period.

7. With more than eighty boys books to his credit, G. A. Henty was, of course, one of the recognized masters of this form of romance. His boy's book about the Mutiny, *In Times of Peril* (1881), in contrast to *Rujub, the Juggler* (1893), which was supposedly written for a mature audience, provides a formula that is repeated by many imitators. For other analyses of this genre of boys' adventure, see Jeffrey Richards (12–33, 72–106); Katz (30–57); Dunae (105–21). For

more general discussions, see Brantlinger; John Mackenzie (*Propaganda*); and McClintock.

8. Shailendra Dhari Singh (78) identifies this passage as central to many of the novels written in the later years of the century. Bongie includes an insightful discussion of the "New Imperialism" (33–49).

9. James Fitzjames Stephen has been long identified as an important spokesman for the New Imperialism. See Metcalf (*Aftermath*, 318); and Sinha (*Colonial Masculinities*, 39–40), for two important examples.

10. Hume Nisbet's status as an "Anglo-Indian" writer is questionable, but I am following B. J. Moore-Gilbert's lead in considering *The Queen's Desire* (1893) in this context (*Kipling*, 103). Nisbet's preface reminds us that opportunities for cheaper world travel and an increasingly more cosmopolitan culture in the 1890s allowed freer circulation of ideas about India and began to erase some of the differences that distinguished metropolitan from Anglo-Indian Orientalism. His critique of his upper-class English officers may also express Nisbet's Scottish perspective.

11. All citations refer to the three-volume edition of *The Star of Fortune*. Hilda Gregg, in her review of mutiny novels published in *Blackwood's Magazine* in 1897, casts doubt on the accuracy of Muddock's memories by noting that he apparently has forgotten much of his Indian experience since in his novel *The Great White Hand* he improbably describes the Hindu Nana Sahib as swearing "by the Prophet" (Gregg, 224–225).

12. Katz offers an interesting discussion of comparable underground retreats (34).

13. Several other male romances of this period describe male heroes confined by Indian women. When Frank Malcolm, the hero in Louis Tracy's *The Red Year* (1908), is befriended by the Princess of Delhi, who intervenes many times to save him from death, the hero manfully resists all her advances, erotic and otherwise. Likewise, in Charles Pearce's *Red Revenge* (1901), when Hooseinee Khanum, a dancing girl at the court of Nana Sahib, lures the hero, Dick Heron, to her quarters and locks him in, she displays the "ungovernable" passion that is one of the qualities most persistently attributed to the Oriental woman in all these texts. As soon as Hooseinee kisses him, Dick knows that she is "an enemy" (36) and manfully resists all her efforts to rape him.

14. I have borrowed Trin T. Minh-ha's more general discussion of the unmet desires that are created by histories that are rigorously based on "facts" (119–120).

15. These two poems, and many others, are published in full in P. C. Joshi's collection.

16. Cited by Lebra-Chapman (133–134).

CHAPTER 5   *Lost Children*

1. Bell (378).

2. My comparison of *Kim* and *Gora* is informed by Spivak ("Burden," 275–299). For useful background in defining the political positions of Tagore's characters in *Gora*, see Knopf's classic study (*British Orientalism*); Borthwick; and Hubel.

On Tagore's fiction, see also Naravane; and Edward Thompson (*Rabindranath Tagore*).

3. For details, see Scully (343).

4. I am most persuaded by Wurgaft (esp. 103). Kipling's attitudes toward the British Empire have been widely debated; for major positions, see especially Parry ("Contents," 49–63); Said (*Culture*, 132–162); McClure; S. P. Mohanty (21–40); David ("Children," 124–142); and Behdad (*Belated Travelers*, 73–91).

5. Viswanathan presents one of the most comprehensive surveys of these educational practices in India.

6. Nupur Chaudhuri (517–536) summarizes the social conditions and practices defining motherhood for colonizing women in British India in this period.

7. The racial heritage of Kim, as the child of an Irish recruit, was also ambiguous, since the racial status of the Irish was open to question at this time (as it was throughout the nineteenth century), as McClintock shows (52–53). The significance of Kim's class has been given much less attention, but its importance is dramatically revealed when Kim's life is compared with that of Indian orphan otherwise very much like him in Mulk Raj Anand's *Coolie* (1936).

8. See Stoler ("Carnal Knowledge," 78–80) on orphanages in British India.

9. See Low's interesting discussion (esp. p. 97). McClintock makes a similar point but does not discuss Kim's avoidance of cross-gender passing (69–71). See also Plotz.

10. Kipling further disguised these questions about Kim's sexuality by revising his age downward by ten months in later editions of this novel. In Said's edition of *Kim*, the age at which Kim leaves St. Xavier's is set at "fourteen years and ten months" (212), but in earlier editions, including Morton N. Cohen's edition for Bantam, Kipling identifies him as "fifteen years and eight months old" when he leaves school.

11. Kim's career offers interesting parallels with the Eurasian character, Dick Smith, in Flora Annie Steel's *Miss Stuart's Legacy*.

12. Although Hubel does not discuss *The Story of Sonny Sahib*, she discusses several of Duncan's other novels and provides useful background on Duncan's complex ironies concerning colonial life.

13. See "Meditations for a Savage Child," in Adrienne Rich, *The Fact of a Doorframe: Poems Selected and New, 1950–1984* (New York: Norton, 1986), 179–183.

14. For details on the relation between colonial mothers and children, see Paxton ("Disembodied Subjects").

15. Perhaps this is a sign of Oliphant's greater license as a male author describing the education prescribed for colonizing women. Sara Jeannette Duncan is more ironic, and distanced, in describing Helen Peachy's "education," in her *Simple Adventures of a Memsahib*.

16. The Age of Consent Bill was passed in England in 1885, but the age of consent debate in India continued throughout this period. See Sinha (*Colonial Masculinities*, 138–180).

CHAPTER 6   *Mixed Couples*

1. Penny (*Question*, 178).
2. On nationalism and "romance," see Ross; Sommer (*Foundational*); and Ahmad ("Jameson's"). I am indebted to Butler (*Bodies*) in my analysis of the new processes that "eroticized" racial difference in this period. See also Butler (*Gender Trouble*); Paxton ("Secrets," 139–187).
3. The most important study of these romances remains Parry (*Delusions*, esp. 70–130). See also Stieg; and Sainsbury. On Diver's series, see Parry (*Delusions*, 79–83); and David (*Rule*, 162–169) for other readings.
4. In addition to Maud Diver's Sinclair series, see also her *Candles in the Wind* (1909); Alice Perrin's *The Charm* (1910); Victoria Cross's *Self and Other* (1911); I.A.R. Wylie's *Daughter of Brahma* (1912). For Englishwomen who marry or seriously consider marrying Indian men, see Fanny Farr Penny, *A Mixed Marriage* (1903), and *A Question of Colour* (1926); Alice Perrin, *The Stronger Claim* (1903), and *The Anglo-Indians* (1913); and Ethel Savi, *Mock Majesty* (1923), to name only a few.
5. Borthwick provides this dating for the novel. In her otherwise useful analysis, Hubel overlooks the significance of this date and considers the novel in the context of the late 1890s. In the 1880s, as Sinha (*Colonial Masculinities*) and Tanika Sarkar ("Hindu") and ("Bakimchandra") have both shown, Hindu nationalists were centered on Hindu marriage practices rather than on the less divisive theme of Mother India that emerged later. For relevant background, see also Knopf ("Rammohun Roy," 21–45).
6. For a useful analysis of the cultural context and the importance of romantic love in this novel, see Borthwick (esp. 132).
7. Sainsbury (163–87) offers an intelligent critique of some of Hennessy and Mohan's claims about the interaction and effects of these two acts. On the impact of the consent debates, see Sinha (*Colonial Masculinities*, 138–180).
8. Stieg ("Indian Romances") offers perhaps the best example, though many of the scholars working on male adventure stories express this assumption as well.
9. Although Butler's primary example is an American novel from a somewhat later period that represents cross-racial marriage, Nella Larsen's *Passing* (1929), her analysis raises provocative questions about similar themes in Anglo-Indian fiction.
10. King (*Colonial*) documents how Indian cities were dramatically redesigned during the late nineteenth and early twentieth centuries in an effort to separate the "native" quarters of the city from the governmental, residential, and military zones of the colonizers. Homes constructed by English colonials in late nineteenth- and early twentieth-century British India display the distinctive colonial requirements for the visual organization of indoor and outdoor space to keep natives and servants at the prescribed proper distance. See also Metcalf (*Imperial Vision*); and Grewal (esp. 166–178). Callaway (*Gender*) discusses colonial domestic space in British Africa at the same time. Mitchell offers a brilliant analysis of changes in public and private space in Egypt.
11. For Butler's discussion of abjection, see (*Bodies*, 8).

12. See Grosz (*Sexual Subversions*, 78) on abjection as the "struggle against the mother" in Kristeva's theory.

13. For details, see Burton (157–66); and Philippa Levine ("Venereal Disease," 579–602); for the political consequences of the timing and publication of Andrew and Bushnell's research, see Levine ("Rereading," 585–612).

14. I draw, of course, on Sinha's discussion of the formation of the "effeminate" Bengali (*Colonial Masculinities*, esp. 1–32).

15. Tarlo (esp. 33–37) surveys English perceptions of Indian clothing and "nakedness."

16. Lesley's fascination with Lady Arbuthnot's physical beauty can be compared with Irene Renfield's similar obsession with Clare Kendry's beauty, which opens up the possibility of a more fulfilling lesbian relationship between these women, a relation Irene rejects in the end.

17. Julia Kristeva reminds us in *Powers of Horror* that "the utmost of abjection . . . is death infecting life" (3–4).

18. Stoler ("Carnal Knowledge," 76–88) argues persuasively that class was often a major concern in the assessment of interracial marriages and the children produced by them in India and other colonial cultures.

19. Thompson (*Night*) describes another kind of passionate closeness in the heroine's attachment to the "jungle" and to her father. This novel includes a near rape when the Eurasian, Victor Stone, pursues the heroine, though she literally sets a snare for him, injuring him and his horse and allowing her to escape.

20. Devi's novel is less concerned with tracing the zones of abjection than are comparable Anglo-Indian romances, but the English translation is prefaced by a biographical sketch of Devi, by E. M. Lang, that more than compensates. Lang refers to the same zones of abjection charted in these novels and reveals intimate details that would be unthinkable in a sketch about an English author, detailing Devi's status as a widow, her diet, her bathing habits, and her dedication to maintaining her chastity by refusing to remarry. Hubel (137) identifies E. M. Lang as a "friend" of Devi; his preface nonetheless demonstrates the arrogance so often licensed by British imperialism. Ignoring a long tradition of Indian women's literary accomplishments, Lang identifies Devi as the first Indian woman to publish a novel (4), and condescendingly estimates its literary value by applying, as his only standard, the author's knowledge of English culture.

21. Hubel discusses Moni's efforts to apply the same moral standards to her future husband as she would expect of herself, but she overstates Moni's and her father's "traditionalism," as if there were only two positions on these issues rather than a wide range of positions in the 1880s. Not recognizing the significance of the decision by Moni's father not to seek a partner for Moni when she was very young, Hubel underestimates his progressiveness. I see his intervention in "arranging" Moni's marriage at the end of the novel as a more benevolent and playfully ironic gesture since he has been close enough to his daughter throughout her life to have seen her attraction to Chotu.

CHAPTER 7   *Modernism, Irony, and the Erasure of Rape*

1. Sara Jeannette Duncan, "A Mother in India" (*Pool*, 14).
2. Moira Gatens presents an interesting counterargument (76–91).
3. All passages from the "The Psychogenesis of a Case of Homosexuality in a Woman" are from Freud (18:145–172). My reading of the significance of these changes has been shaped by Judith Butler (*Bodies*, 57–91, 167–185); and Grosz (*Volatile Bodies*, 52–61). See also Gay (339–342).
4. All passages from "Some Neurotic Mechanisms in Jealousy, Paranoia, and Homosexuality" are from Freud (18:223–232). On "abjection," see Judith Butler (*Bodies*, esp. 2–3, 167–185). For a more specific historical perspective on the construction of British women's sexuality in this period, see Shelia Jeffreys. For a more general discussion of women writers, World War I, and modernism, see Gilbert and Gubar.
5. For details, see G. K. Das (esp. 7); Parry ("Politics," 27–43). Several Indian critics have argued persuasively that Forster's *Passage to India* represents Anglo-Indian society before 1914; that is, before the crisis created by World War I and by the Amritsar Massacre in 1919. Robin Lewis also cites K. Natwar-Singh's statements about the dated perspective evident in *Passage* (108–09). Other evidence of social and political change are beyond the limits of this study, but see Frances B. Singh (265–78).
6. I am indebted to Apter (299–325) for this evocative term, though she applies it in a somewhat different context.
7. Forster (*Manuscripts*, 242–243). Silver provides further details on this aspect of the publication history of *A Passage to India*. On the uses of rape in other colonial contexts, see Stoler ("Making," 634–660).
8. Sharpe argues that critics have gone as far as they can perhaps go in considering Adela's experience in the cave in relation to Forster's understanding of Eastern metaphysics or Freudian psychology; Sharpe recalls the history of the mutiny instead (*Allegories*, 113–135). In an earlier essay, Sharpe traces the path which leads from the haunted work to that which haunts it "in the Mutiny accounts" ("Unspeakable," 41). Silver, by contrast, reads Adela's retraction and refusal to identify the man who attacked her as a sign of solidarity with the colonized (130). On the critical silence about homosexuality, see Lisa Lowe (102–135); and Suleri (132–148). For other important readings of Forster's novel, see Gillian Beer; John Beer; Christopher Lane ("Volatile Desire," 188–212); Paul Armstrong; Mason; Sahni; and Showalter.
9. For details on Besant, see Paxton ("Complicity," 158–176).
10. For details about these women, see Jayawardena (*White*, 154, 233, 231).
11. In the 1890s English social conservatives like Elizabeth Lynn Linton trivialized the New Woman's political potential and reacted, instead, to her gestures of class insubordination. She especially singles out the New Woman's indiscreet cigarette smoking with men (Ardis, 25).
12. Forster's focus on the consequences of the liberal reforms of the 1880s rather than on the more recent Morley-Minto reforms in 1906 or the Montague-Chelmsford report in 1919 is perhaps what creates the dated feeling of this novel.

13. See essays by Hughes (129–136); and Phillips (121–140).

14. Susan Edwards discusses the emergence of this type of "hallucination" and its relation to rape charges (*Female Sexuality*, 96–99). See also Stimpson's interesting analysis of the relationship between space and desire in women's, and especially in lesbian, writing.

15. I refer to the case of Mrs. A. O. Hume and Greedhare Mehtar, discussed in Sinha (*Colonial Masculinities*, 53).

16. Compare Spear (181–194) with Partha Chatterjee (*Nationalist Thought*, 85–130). Hubel also offers a revisionist survey and critique (13–44). On the interaction between Hindu Nationalists and Indian feminists, see Sarkar ("Hindu Wife," 213–235); Sinha (*Colonial Masculinities*, esp. 151–180); and Grewal (179–232); for details about English feminists, see Jayawardena (*Feminism*, 73–108).

17. See also Forster (*Selected Letters*, 1:159–160).

18. For details on Duncan's life in India, see Fowler. Perhaps Duncan's experience as a Canadian woman and successful author before she married Everard Cotes gave her a greater sense of detachment in assessing Anglo-Indian life. Cotes directed the Indian News Agency for several years during their marriage, which helps account, I think, for Duncan's trenchant and specific political commentary. Duncan's outsider position writes itself into her novels, especially in her skepticism about the stability of the category of race in organizing the hierarchies of Anglo-Indian life. Duncan's first Anglo-Indian heroine, Helen Peachey Browne, from *The Simple Adventures of a Memsahib* (1893), is athletic, vigorous, and vaguely emancipated but steers clear of temptations to insubordination, sexual and otherwise. Duncan presents interesting versions of the New Woman in the actress Hilda Howe, in *Hilda: A Story of Calcutta* (also called *The Path of a Star*) (1899), and the doctor Ruth Pearce, in *Set in Authority* (1906). See also Hubel (45–70).

19. Dean identifies Duncan's political position as a "Pink Tory" (14–18) and argues that she is particularly astute in showing the fissures in Orientalist discourse (138–139).

20. Dean argues that Joan is deceived because of her "desire to sacrifice herself for Indian culture" (149).

21. Sommer (*Foundational Fictions*, 40–44). In a related essay, Sommer argues that "allegory is a type of double vision akin to irony, meaning that on one level it narrates and on another level it throws doubt on the validity of its narration" ("Allegories," 67).

22. Much has been written about the construction and uses of colonial knowledge. See, for example, Thomas Richards; Spivak ("Neocolonialism" 220–51); and Veena Das (58–79).

23. I borrow these terms from Sommer ("Allegories," 60–82).

24. In drawing these comparisons, I do not intend to castigate Forster for not writing the novel that a feminist postcolonial critic might desire. Moffat argues eloquently that *A Passage to India* reflects his appreciation for and practice of "the art of leaving out what [one does] not want to say" (33). I heartily agree with her argument.

Conclusion

1. Rubin explores the afterlife of the theme of rape in postcolonial literature about India.
2. The effects of the introduction of *zina* laws in Pakistan are summarized by Mehdi.
3. For details, see Purshottam Agarwal (29–30); and Abdulali (196–206).

BIBLIOGRAPHY

Works Cited

Abdulali, Sohaila. "Rape in India: An Empirical Picture," in Rehana Ghandailly, ed. *Women in Indian Society: A Reader*. New Delhi: Sage, 1988.

Agarwal, Bina, ed. *The Structures of Patriarchy: State, Community, and Household in Modernising Asia*. New Delhi: Kali, 1988.

Agarwal, Purshottam. "Sarvarkar, Surat, and Draupadi: Legitimizing Rape as a Political Weapon," in Tanika Sarkar and Urvashi Butalia, eds. *Women and Right-Wing Movements: Indian Experiences*. London: Zed Books, 1995, 29–57.

Ahmad, Aijaz. "Between Orientalism and Historicism: Anthropological Knowledge of India," *Studies in History* n.s. 7, 1 (1991): 133–63.

———. "Jameson's Rhetoric of Otherness and the 'National Allegory,'" *Social Text*, no. 17 (Fall 1987): 3–25.

———. *In Theory: Classes, Nations, Literatures*. London: Verso, 1992.

Alexander, M. Jacqui, and Chandra Talpade Mohanty, eds. *Feminist Genealogies, Colonial Legacies, Democratic Futures*. London: Routledge, 1996.

Ali, Muhsin Jassim. *Scheherazade in England: A Study of Nineteenth-Century English Criticism of the "Arabian Nights."* Washington, D.C.: Three Continents Press, 1981.

Alloula, Malek. *The Colonial Harem*. Minneapolis: U of Minnesota P, 1986.

Amur, G.S. "Meadows Taylor and the Three Cultures," in M. K. Naik, S. K. Desai, and S. T. Kallapur, eds. *The Image of India in Western Creative Writing*. Madras: Macmillan, 1971, 1–12.

Anand, Mulk Raj. *Coolie*. Delhi: Hind Pocket Books, 1972. First ed. 1936.

Apter, Emily. "Ethnographic Travesties: Colonial Realism, French Feminism, and the Case of Elissa Rhäis," in Gyan Prakash, ed. *After Colonialism: Imperial Histories and Postcolonial Displacements*. Princeton: Princeton UP, 1995, 299–343.

Arberry, A. J. , trans. *The Koran Interpreted*. 2 vols. London: George Allen and Unwin, 1955.

Ardener, Shirley, and Hillary Callan. *The Incorporated Wife*. London: Croom Helm, 1984.

Ardis, Ann. *New Women, New Novels: Feminism and Early Modernism*. New Brunswick: Rutgers UP, 1991.

Armstrong, Isabel. "So What's All This about the Mother's Body? The Aesthetic, Gender, and the *Polis*." *Women: A Cultural Review* 4, 2 (1993): 172–187.

Armstrong, Nancy. *Desire and Domestic Fiction: A Political History of the Novel.* New York: Oxford UP, 1987.

Armstrong, Paul B. "Reading India: E. M. Forster and the Politics of Interpretation." *Twentieth-Century Literature* 38, 4 (Winter 1992): 365–385.

Arnold, David. *Colonizing the Body: State Medicine and Epidemic Disease.* New York: Oxford UP, 1987.

———. *Imperial Medicine and Indigenous Societies.* Manchester: Manchester UP, 1988.

Ashcroft, Bill, Gareth Griffiths, and Helen Tiffin, eds. *The Empire Writes Back: Theory and Practice in Post-Colonial Literatures.* New York: Routledge, 1989.

Bakhtin, Mikhail. *The Dialogic Imagination: Four Essays.* Trans. Caryl Emerson and Michael Holquist. Austin: U Texas P, 1981.

Balibar, Etienne, and Immanuel Wallerstein. *Race, Nation, Class: Ambiguous Identities.* London: Verso, 1992.

Ballhatchet, Kenneth. *Race, Sex, and Class under the Raj.* London: Weidenfeld and Nicholson, 1980.

Beer, Gillian. "Negation in *A Passage to India*," in John Beer, ed. *"Passage to India": Essays in Interpretation.* London: Macmillan, 1985, 44–58.

Beer, John. ed. *"Passage to India": Essays in Interpretation.* London: Macmillan, 1985.

Behdad, Ali. *"Belated Travelers": Orientalism in the Age of Colonial Dissolution.* Durham: Duke UP, 1994.

———. "The Eroticized Orient: Images of the Harem in Montesquieu and his Precursors," *Stanford French Review* 13, 2–3 (1989): 109–126.

Bell, Vikki. "Beyond the 'Thorny Question': Feminism, Foucault, and the Desexualization of Rape," *International Journal of the Sociology of Law* 19 (1991): 83–100.

Bhabha, Homi K. *The Location of Culture.* London: Routledge, 1995.

———. *Nation and Narration.* London: Routledge, 1990.

———. "The Other Question: Difference, Discrimination, and the Discourse of Colonialism," in Francis Barker et al., eds. *Literature, Politics and Theory.* London: Methuen, 1986, 148–172.

———. "Representation and the Colonial Text: A Critical Exploration of Some Forms of Mimeticism," in Frank Gloversmith, ed. *The Theory of Reading.* Sussex: Harvester, 1984, 93–122.

———. "Signs Taken for Wonders: Questions of Ambivalence and Authority under a Tree outside Delhi, May 1817," *Critical Inquiry* 12, 1 (1985): 144–165.

Bivona, D. *Desire and Contradiction: Imperial Visions and Domestic Debates in Victorian Literature.* Manchester: Manchester UP, 1990.

Blain, Virginia, Patricia Clements, and Isobel Grundy, eds. *The Feminist Companion to Literature in English: Women Writers from the Middle Ages to the Present.* London: Batsford, 1990.

Bongie, Chris. *Exotic Memories: Literature, Colonialism, and the Fin de Siècle.* Ithaca: Cornell UP, 1991.

Boone, Joseph A. "Vacation Cruises; or, The Homoerotics of Orientalism," *PMLA* 110, 1 (Jan. 1995): 89–107.

Borthwick, Meredith. *The Changing Role of Women in Bengal, 1849–1905*. Princeton: Princeton UP, 1984.

Brantlinger, Patrick. *Rule of Darkness: British Literature and Imperialism, 1830–1914*. Ithaca: Cornell UP, 1988.

Breckenridge, Carol, and Peter Van der Veer, eds. *Orientalism and the Post Colonial Predicament: Perspectives on South Asia*. Philadelphia: U of Pennsylvania P, 1993.

Bristow, Joseph. *Empire Boys: Adventures in a Man's World*. London: Harper Collins Academic, 1991.

Broehl, Wayne G. *Crisis of the Raj: The Revolt of 1857, through British Lieutenants' Eyes*. Hanover: U of New England P, 1986.

Brown, Laura. *The Ends of Empire: Women and Ideology in Early 18th Century English Literature*. Ithaca: Cornell UP, 1993.

Brown, Nathaniel. *Sexuality and Feminism in Shelley*. Cambridge: Harvard UP, 1979.

Brownmiller, Susan. *Against Our Will: Men, Women, and Rape*. New York: Simon and Schuster, 1975.

Bryson, Norman. "Two Narratives of Rape in the Visual Arts: Lucretia and the Sabine Women," in Sylvia Tomaselli and Roy Porter, eds. *Rape: An Historical and Social Enquiry*. London: Blackwell, 1987, 152–173.

Buonaventura, Wendy. *Serpent of the Nile: Women and Dance in the Arab World*. London: Saqi, 1989.

Burke, Edmund. *A Philosophical Enquiry into the Origins of Our Ideas of the Sublime and Beautiful*. Ed. James T. Boulton. London: Blackwell, 1987. First ed. 1757.

―――. *The Complete Works of the Right Honourable Edmund Burke*. 10 vols. Boston: Little, Brown, 1866–1869.

Burton, Antoinette. *Burdens of History: British Feminists, Indian Women, and Imperial Culture, 1865–1915*. Chapel Hill: U of North Carolina P, 1994.

Butler, Judith. *Bodies That Matter: On the Discursive Limits of Sex*. London: Routledge, 1993.

―――. *Gender Trouble: Feminism and the Subversion of Identity*. London: Routledge, 1990.

Butler, Marilyn. "Revising the Canon," [London] *Times Literary Supplement*, Dec. 4–10, 1987, 1349, 1359–1360.

―――. *Romantics, Rebels, and Reactionaries: English Literature and Its Background, 1760–1830*. Oxford: Oxford UP, 1981.

Byron, George Gordon, *Lord Byron's Letters and Journals*. Ed. Leslie Marchand. 12 vols. Cambridge: Belknap Press of Harvard UP, 1973–1982.

―――. *Byron's Poetical Works*. 3 vols. Ed. Frederick Page. Oxford: Oxford UP, 1970.

Callaway, Helen. *Gender, Culture, and Empire: European Women in Colonial Nigeria*. Urbana: U of Illinois P, 1988.

Campbell, Mary. *Lady Morgan: The Life and Times of Sydney Owenson*. London: Pandora, 1988.

Carnall, Geoffrey. *Robert Southey*. London: Longmans, 1964.

Carnall, Geoffrey. *Robert Southey and His Age: The Development of a Conservative Mind*. London: Oxford UP, 1960.

Carroll, Lucy. "Law, Custom, and Statutory Social Reform: The Hindu Widows' Re-marriage Act of 1856," *Indian Economic and Social History Review* 20, 4 (1983): 363–388.

Celik, Zeynep. *Displaying the Orient: The Architecture of Islam at Nineteenth-Century World's Fairs*. Berkeley: U of California P, 1992.

Chandra, Bipan. *Modern India*. New Delhi: National Council of Educational Training and Research, 1976.

Chatterjee, Partha, "The Nationalist Resolution of the Women's Question," in Kumkum Sangari and Sudesh Vaid, eds. *Recasting Women: Essays in Indian Colonial History*. New Brunswick: Rutgers UP, 1990, 233–253.

———. *Nationalist Thought and the Colonial World: A Derivative Discourse*. London: Zed Books, 1986.

———. *The Nation and Its Fragments: Colonial and Postcolonial Histories*. Princeton: Princeton UP, 1993.

Chaudhuri, Nupur. "Memsahibs and Motherhood in Nineteenth-Century Colonial India," *Victorian Studies* 31, 4 (Summer 1988): 517–536.

Chaudhuri, Nupur, and Margaret Strobel, eds. *Complicity and Resistance: Western Women and Imperialism*. Bloomington: Indiana UP, 1992.

Chesney, George. *The Dilemma*. New York: Abbott, 1908. First ed. 1876.

Christenson, Jerome. *Lord Byron's Strength: Romantic Writing and Commercial Society*. Baltimore: Johns Hopkins UP, 1993.

Clark, Anna. "Rape or Seduction? A Controversy over Sexual Violence in the Nineteenth Century," in London Feminist History Group. *The Sexual Dynamics of History: Men's Power, Women's Resistance*. London: Pluto Press, 1983, 13–27.

———. *Women's Silence, Men's Violence: Sexual Assault in England, 1770–1845*. London: Pandora, 1987.

Cohn, Bernard S. "The Command of Language and the Language of Command," in Ranjit Guha, ed. *Subaltern Studies IV: Writings on South Asian History and Society*. Delhi: Oxford UP, 1988, 276–329.

———. "Notes on the History of the Study of Indian Society and Culture," in Cohn. *An Anthropologist among the Historians and Other Essays*. Delhi: Oxford UP, 1987, 136–171.

Crane, Ralph. *Inventing India: A History of India in English-Language Fiction*. Basingstoke: Macmillan, 1992.

Croker, Bithia Mary. *Mr. Jervis*. Philadelphia: Lippincott, 1895. First ed. 1894.

Cronin, Richard. *Imagining India*. Basingstoke: Macmillan, 1989.

Cross, Victoria [Vivian Cory]. *Life of My Heart*. London: Scott, 1905.

———. *Self and the Other*. London: T. Werner Laurie, 1911.

Croutier, Alev Lytle. *Harem: The World behind the Veil*. New York: Abbeville Press, 1989.

Curran, Stuart. *Shelley's Annus Mirabilis: The Maturing of an Epic Vision*. San Marino, Calif.: Huntington Library, 1975.

———. *Poetic Form and British Romanticism*. New York: Oxford UP, 1986.

Das, G. K. "*A Passage to India*: A Socio-Historical Study," in John Beer, ed. *'Passage to India': Essays in Interpretation*. London: Macmillan, 1985, 1–15.

Das, Veena. "Gender Studies, Cross-Cultural Comparison, and the Colonial Organization of Knowledge," *Berkshire Review* 2 (1986): 58–79.

David, Deirdre. "Children of Empire: Victorian Imperialism and Sexual Politics in Dickens and Kipling," in Anthony H. Harrison and Beverly Taylor, eds. *Gender and Discourse in Victorian Literature and Art.* DeKalb: Northern Illinois UP, 1992, 124–142.

———. *Rule Britannia: Women, Empire, and Victorian Writing.* Ithaca: Cornell UP, 1995.

Davin, Anna. "Imperialism and Motherhood," *History Workshop Journal* 5 (1978): 9–65.

Davis, Angela Y. "Rape, Racism, and the Myth of the Black Rapist," in *Women, Race and Class.* New York: Random House, 1983, 172–201.

Davis, Lloyd. *Virginal Sexuality and Textuality in Victorian Literature.* Binghamton: SUNY P, 1993, 143–157.

D'Cruze, Shani. "Approaching the History of Rape and Sexual Violence: Notes toward Research," *Women's History Review* 1, 3 (1993): 377–396.

Dean, Misao. *A Different Point of View: Sara Jeannette Duncan.* Montreal: McGill Queen's UP, 1991.

De Lauretis, Teresa. *Technologies of Gender: Essays on Theory, Film, and Fiction.* Bloomington: Indiana UP, 1987.

Dellamora, Richard. *Apocalyptic Overtures: Sexual Politics and the Sense of an Ending.* New Brunswick: Rutgers UP, 1994.

———. *Masculine Desire: The Sexual Politics of Victorian Aestheticism.* Chapel Hill: U of North Carolina P, 1990.

De Staël, Germaine. *Corinne; or, Italy.* Trans. Avriel H. Goldberger. New Brunswick: Rutgers UP, 1987.

Devi, Swarnakumari. *The Unfinished Song.* London: T. W. Laurie, 1913.

Diver, Maud. *The Dream Prevails.* London: John Murray, 1936.

———. *The Englishwoman in India.* London: Blackwood, 1903.

———. *Far to Seek.* London: John Murray, 1938. First ed. 1921.

———. *Lilamani: A Study of Possibilities.* London: Hutchinson, 1919. First ed. 1910.

———. *The Singer Passes.* London: Blackwood, 1931.

Donaldson, Ian. *The Rape of Lucrece: A Myth and Its Transformation.* Oxford: Clarendon Press, 1982.

Donaldson, Laura E. *Decolonizing Feminisms: Race, Gender, and Empire Building.* Chapel Hill: U of North Carolina P, 1992.

Doniger, Wendy, and Brian K. Smith, trans. *The Laws of Manu.* London: Penguin, 1991.

Drew, John. *India and the Romantic Imagination.* Delhi: Oxford UP, 1987.

Dunae, Patrick A. "Boy's Literature and the Idea of Empire, 1870–1914," *Victorian Studies* 24 (1980): 105–121.

Duncan, Ian. *Modern Romance and Transformations of the Novel: The Gothic, Scott, Dickens.* Cambridge: Cambridge UP, 1992.

Duncan, Sara Jeannette. *The Burnt Offering.* New York: Lane, 1910. First ed. 1909.

———. *Hilda, A Story of Calcutta.* New York: Fredrick Stokes, 1898.

———. *The Pool in the Desert.* New York: Penguin, 1984. First ed. 1903.

Duncan, Sara Jeannette. *Set in Authority*. London: Constable, 1906.

―――. *The Simple Adventures of a Memsahib*. New York: Appleton, 1893.

Eagleton, Terry. *The Rape of Clarissa: Writing, Sexuality, and Class Struggle in Samuel Richardson*. Oxford: Blackwell, 1982.

Edwards, Susan. *Female Sexuality and the Law: A Study of Constructs of Female Sexuality as They Inform Statute and Legal Procedure*. Oxford: Robertson, 1981.

―――. *Policing "Domestic" Violence: Women, The Law, and the State*. London: Sage, 1989.

Ellis, Kate Ferguson. *The Contested Castle: Gothic Novels and the Subversion of Domestic Economy*. Urbana: U of Illinois P, 1989.

Emeneau, Murray, and T. Burrow, eds. *A Dravidian Etymological Dictionary*. Oxford: Clarendon, 1984.

Estrich, Susan. *Real Rape*. Cambridge: Harvard UP, 1987.

Fanon, Frantz. *Black Skin, White Masks*. Trans. Charles Lam Markmann. New York: Grove Press, 1967.

―――. *The Wretched of the Earth*. Trans. Constance Farrington. New York: Grove Press, 1963.

Ferguson, Frances. "Rape and the Rise of the Novel," *Representations* 20 (Fall 1987): 88–112.

Ferguson, Moira. *Subject to Others: British Women Writers and Colonial Slavery, 1670–1834*. New York: Routledge, 1992.

Figueria, Dorothy Matilda. *Translating the Orient: The Reception of "Sakuntala" in Nineteenth-Century Europe*. Albany: SUNY P, 1991.

Forster, E. M. *The Hill of Devi: Being Letters from Dewas State Senior*. London: Arnold, 1953.

―――. *The Manuscripts of "A Passage to India."* Ed. Oliver Stallybrass. London: Edward Arnold, 1972.

―――. *A Passage to India*. San Diego: Harcourt, Brace, and World, 1984.

―――. *Selected Letters of E. M. Forster*. Eds. Mary Lago and P. N. Furbank. 2 vols. Cambridge: Cambridge UP, 1985.

Foucault, Michel. *Discipline and Punish: The Birth of the Prison*. Trans. Alan Sheridan. New York: Random House, 1979.

―――. *The History of Sexuality*. Vol. 1: *An Introduction*. Trans. Robert Hurley. New York: Vantage, 1980.

Fowler, Marian. *Redney: A Life of Sara Jeannette Duncan*. Toronto: Anasai, 1983.

Fraser, Antonia. *The Warrior Queens*. New York: Knopf, 1989.

Freud, Sigmund. "Civilization and Its Discontents," in *The Standard Edition of the Complete Works of Sigmund Freud*, vol. 21. Ed. James Strachey. London: Hogarth Press, 1961, 59–145.

―――. "The Psychogenesis of a Case of Homosexuality in a Woman," in *The Standard Edition of the Complete Works of Sigmund Freud*, vol. 18. Ed. James Strachey. London: Hogarth Press, 1920–1922, 147–172.

―――. "Some Neurotic Mechanisms in Jealousy, Paranoia, and Homosexuality," in *The Standard Edition of the Complete Works of Sigmund Freud*, vol. 18. Ed. James Strachey. London: Hogarth Press, 1920–1922, 223–232.

―――. "Totem and Taboo," in *The Standard Edition of the Complete Works of*

Sigmund Freud, vol. 13. Ed. James Strachey. London: Hogarth Press, 1913–1914, 1–161.

Furbank, P. N. *E. M. Forster: A Life.* New York: Harcourt, Brace, Jovanovich, 1978.

Garber, Marjorie. *Vested Interests: Cross Dressing and Cultural Anxiety.* New York: Harper Perennial, 1992.

Gates, Henry Louis. "Critical 'Fanonism,'" *Critical Inquiry* 17 (1991): 457–470.

Gatens, Moira. *Imagining Bodies: Ethics, Power and Corporeality.* London: Routledge, 1996.

Gay, Peter. *Freud: A Life for Our Times.* New York: Norton, 1988.

Gilbert, Sandra M., and Susan Gubar. "Soldier's Heart: Literary Men, Literary Women and the Great War," in *No Man's Land: The Place of the Woman Writer in the Twentieth Century.* Vol 2: *Sex Changes.* New Haven: Yale UP, 1989, 258–323.

Gilman, Sander L. "Black Bodies, White Bodies: Toward an Iconography of Female Sexuality in Late Nineteenth-Century Art, Medicine, and Literature," *Critical Inquiry* 12, 1 (1985): 204–242.

Gilmartin, Sophie. "The Sati, the Bride, and the Widow: Sacrificial Women in the Nineteenth-Century," *Victorian Literature and Culture* 25, 1 (1997): 141–158.

Girard, René. *Violence and the Sacred.* Trans. Patrick Gregory. Baltimore: Johns Hopkins UP, 1972.

Grant, James. *First Love and Last Love: A Tale of the Indian Mutiny,* in *The Complete Works of James Grant,* vol. 16. London: Routledge, n.d. First ed. 1868.

Green, Martin. *Dreams of Adventure, Deeds of Empire.* New York: Basic Books, 1970.

———. *Seven Types of Adventure Tales: An Etiology of a Major Genre.* University Park: Pennsylvania State UP, 1991.

Greenberger, Allen. *The British Image of India: A Study in the Literature of Imperialism, 1880–1960.* New York: Oxford UP, 1969.

Gregg, Hilda. "The Indian Mutiny in Fiction," *Blackwood's Magazine* 161 (Feb. 1897): 218–231.

Grewal, Inderpal. *Home and Harem: Nation, Gender, Empire, and the Cultures of Travel.* Durham: Duke UP, 1996.

Grosz, Elizabeth A. *Sexual Subversions: Three French Feminists.* Sydney: Allen and Unwin, 1989.

———. *Volatile Bodies: Toward a Corporeal Feminism.* Bloomington: Indiana UP, 1994.

Guha, Ranajit. *Elementary Aspects of Peasant Insurgency in Colonial India.* Delhi: Oxford UP, 1983.

Gupta, Brijen Kishore. *India in English Fiction, 1800–1970.* Metuchen: Scarecrow, 1973.

Halbfass, Wilhelm. *India and Europe: An Essay in Understanding.* Albany: SUNY P, 1988.

Hall, Jacquelyn Dowd. "The Mind That Burns in Each Body: Women, Rape and Racial Violence," in Ann Snitow, Christine Stansell and Sharon Thompson, eds. *Powers of Desire: The Politics of Sexuality.* New York: Monthly Review Press, 1983, 329–349.

———. *The Revolt against Chivalry: Jesse Daniel Ames and the Women's Campaign against Lynching.* New York: Columbia UP, 1983.

Hennessy, Rosemary, and Rajeswari Mohan. "The Construction of Women in Three

Popular Texts of Empire: Towards a Critique of Materialist Feminism," *Textual Practice* 3, 3 (1989): 323–359.

Henty, G. A. *In the Days of the Mutiny.* New York: Griffin and Farran, 1893.

———. *In Times of Peril.* New York: Burt, 1888. First ed. 1881.

———. *Rujub, the Juggler.* 3 vols. London: Chatto and Windus, 1893.

Higgins, Lynn A., and Brenda R. Silver, eds. *Rape and Representation.* New York: Columbia UP, 1991.

Hirschmann, Edwin. *White Mutiny: The Ilbert Bill Crisis in India and the Genesis of the Indian National Congress.* Delhi: Heritage, 1980.

Holton, Sandra Stanley. *Feminism and Democracy: Women's Suffrage and Reform Politics in Britain, 1900–1918.* Cambridge: Cambridge UP, 1986.

Hubel, Teresa. *Whose India? The Independence Struggle in British and Indian Fiction.* Durham: Duke UP, 1996.

Hughes, Peter. "Mothers and Mystics: An Aspect of *Howard's End* and *A Passage to India*," in Richard J. Watts and Urs Weidmann, eds. *Modes of Interpretation: Essays Presented to Ernst Leisi.* Tübingen: Gunter Narr, 1984, 129–136.

Hulme, Peter. *Colonial Encounters: Europe and the Native Caribbean, 1492–1797.* London: Methuen, 1986.

Hunt, Lynn Avery. *The Family Romance of the French Revolution.* Berkeley: U of California P, 1992.

Hutchins, Francis G. *The Illusion of Permanence: British Imperialism in India.* Princeton: Princeton UP, 1967.

Inden, Ronald. "Orientalist Constructions of India," *Modern Asian Studies* 20, 3 (1986): 401–446.

Inglis, Amirah. *The White Women's Protection Ordinance: Sexual Anxiety and Politics in Papua.* New York: St. Martin's Press, 1975.

Jacobus, Mary. *First Things: The Maternal Imaginary in Literature, Art and Psychoanalysis.* London: Routledge, 1995.

———. "In Parenthesis: Immaculate Conceptions and Feminine Desire," in Mary Jacobus, Evelyn Fox Keller, and Sally Shuttleworth, eds. *Body/Politics: Women and the Discourses of Science.* New York: Routledge, 1989, 11–28.

Jacobus, Mary, Evelyn Fox Keller, and Sally Shuttleworth. *Body/Politics: Woman and the Discourses of Science.* New York: Routledge, 1989.

Jameson, Fredric. *The Political Unconscious: Narrative as a Socially Symbolic Act.* Ithaca: Cornell UP, 1981.

———. "Third-World Literature in the Era of Multinational Capital," *Social Text*, no. 15 (Fall 1986): 65–88.

Jayawardena, Kumari. *Feminism and Nationalism in the Third World.* London: Zed Books, 1986.

———. *The White Woman's Other Burden: Western Women and South Asia during British Colonial Rule.* New York: Routledge, 1995.

Jeffreys, Sheila. *The Spinster and Her Enemies: Feminism and Sexuality, 1880–1930.* London: Pandora, 1985.

Jenkins. Richard. *The Victorians and Ancient Greece.* Cambridge: Harvard UP, 1980.

Jones, Sir William. "On the Mystical Poetry of the Persians and Hindus," *Asiatick Researches* 3 (1792): 165–183.

————, trans. *Sacontala; or, The Fatal Ring: An Indian Drama, by Calidas* [Khalidasa]. London: Edwards, 1792.

Joplin, Patricia Klindienst. "The Voice of the Shuttle Is Ours," in Lynn A. Higgins and Brenda Silver, eds. *Rape and Representation*. New York: Columbia UP, 1991, 35–64.

Joshi, P. C., ed. *Rebellion, 1857: A Symposium*. Calcutta: K. P. Bagchi, 1986.

Kabbani, Rana. *Europe's Myths of Orient*. Bloomington: Indiana UP, 1986.

Karkar, Sudhir. *Intimate Relations: Exploring Indian Sexuality*. Chicago: U of Chicago P, 1987.

Karkar, Sudhir, and John Munder Ross, *Tales of Love, Sex, and Danger*. New York: Unwin, 1986.

Katz, Wendy R. *Rider Haggard and the Fiction of Empire: A Critical Study of British Imperial Fiction*. Cambridge: Cambridge UP, 1987.

Kensall, Malcolm. "The Slave Woman in the Harem," *Studies in Romanticism* 31, 3 (Fall 1992): 315–332.

Kent, Susan Kingsley. *Sex and Suffrage in Britain, 1860–1914*. Princeton: Princeton UP, 1987.

King, Anthony D. *Colonial Urban Development: Culture, Social Power, and Environment*. London: Routledge and Paul, 1976.

Kipling, Rudyard. *The Jungle Books*. Ed. Daniel Karlin. London: Penguin, 1992. First ed. 1897.

————. *Kim*. Ed. Edward Said. London: Penguin, 1989. First ed. 1902.

————. *The Naulahka: A Story of West and East*. London: Heinemann, 1892.

————. *Something of Myself: For My Friends, Known and Unknown*. Garden City: Doubleday, 1937.

Knopf, David. *British Orientalism and the Bengal Renaissance*. Berkeley: U of California P, 1969.

————. "Rammohun Roy and the Bengal Renaissance: An Historiographical Essay," in V. C. Joshi, ed. *Rammohun Roy and the Process of Modernization in India*. New Delhi: Vikas, 1975, 21–45.

Koestenbaum, Wayne. *Double Talk: The Erotics of Male Literary Collaboration*. New York: Routledge, 1989.

Kramnick, Isaac. *The Rage of Edmund Burke: Portrait of an Ambivalent Conservative*. New York: Basic Books, 1977.

Kristeva, Julia. *Powers of Horror: An Essay on Abjection*. Trans. Leon S. Roudiez. New York: Columbia UP, 1982.

Kurtz, Stanley N. *All the Mothers Are One: Hindu India and the Cultural Reshaping of Psychoanalysis*. New York: Columbia UP, 1993.

Lacquer, Thomas. *Making Sex: Body and Gender from the Greeks to Freud*. Cambridge: Harvard UP, 1990.

Lane, Christopher. *The Ruling Passion: British Colonial Allegory and the Paradox of Homosexual Desire*. Durham: Duke UP, 1995.

————. "Volatile Desire: Ambivalence and Distress in Forster's Colonial Narratives," in Bart Moore-Gilbert, ed. *Writing India, 1757–1980*. Manchester: Manchester UP, 1996, 188–212.

Lane, Edward William, trans. *The Thousand and One Nights; or, The Arabian Nights Entertainment.* 3 vols. London: John Murray, 1847. First ed. 1838.

Langbauer, Laurie. *Women and Romance: The Consolations of Gender in the English Novel.* Ithaca: Cornell UP, 1990.

Lawrence, James H. *The Empire of the Nairs.* Delmar, N.Y.: Scholars' Facsimiles, 1976. First ed. 1811.

Leask, Nigel. *British Romantic Writers and the East: Anxieties of Empire.* Cambridge: Cambridge UP, 1992.

Lebra-Chapman, Joyce. *The Rani of Jhansi: A Study in Female Heroism in India.* Honolulu: U of Hawaii P, 1986.

Leonowens, Anna. *The Romance of the Harem.* Richmond: U of Virginia P, 1991.

Levenson, Michael H. *Genealogy of Modernism: A Study of English Doctrine, 1908– 1922.* Cambridge: Cambridge UP, 1984.

Levine, June Perry. *Creation and Criticism: A Passage to India.* Lincoln: U of Nebraska P, 1971.

Levine, Philippa. "Rereading the 1890s: Venereal Disease as Constitutional Crisis in Britain and British India," *Journal of Asian Studies* 55, 3 (Aug. 1996): 585– 612.

———. "Venereal Disease, Prostitution, and the Politics of Empire: The Case of British India," *Journal of the History of Sexuality* 4, 4 (1994): 579–602.

———. *Victorian Feminism, 1850–1900.* Tallahassee: Florida State UP, 1987.

Lewis, Robin Jared. *E. M. Forster's Passages to India.* New York: Columbia UP, 1979.

Liddle, Joanna, and Rama Joshi. *Daughters of Independence: Gender, Caste and Class in India.* London: Zed, 1986.

Lovell, Ernest J. Jr., ed. *Conversations with Lord Byron.* Princeton: Princeton UP, 1966.

Low, D. A. *Lion Rampant: Essays in the Study of British Imperialism.* London: Frank Cass, 1973.

Low, Gail Ching-Liang. "White Skins, Black Masks: The Pleasures and Politics of Imperialism," *New Formations* 9 (1989): 83–103.

Lowe, Lisa. *Critical Terrains: French and British Orientalisms.* Ithaca: Cornell UP, 1991.

Lyall, Alfred C. *Studies in Literature and History.* Freeport: Books for Libraries, 1968.

McClintock, Anne. *Imperial Leather: Race, Gender and Sexuality.* London: Routledge, 1995.

McClure, John A. *Kipling and Conrad: The Colonial Experiences.* Cambridge: Harvard UP, 1981.

Mackenzie, John M. "Edward Said and the Historians," *Nineteenth-Century Contexts* 18, 1 (1994): 9–25.

———. *Orientalism: History, Theory, and the Arts.* Manchester: Manchester UP, 1995.

———. *Propaganda and Empire: The Manipulation of British Public Opinion, 1880– 1960.* Manchester: Manchester UP, 1984.

———, ed. *Imperialism and Popular Culture.* Manchester: Manchester UP, 1986.

McKeon, Michael. *The Origins of the English Novel, 1600–1740.* Baltimore: Johns Hopkins UP, 1987.

MacKinnon, Catherine A. "Feminism, Marxism, Method, and the State: Toward a Feminist Jurisprudence." *Signs: Journal of Women in Culture and Society* 8 (1983): 635–658.

————. *Feminism Unmodified: Discourses on Life and Law*. Cambridge: Harvard UP, 1987.

Mainwaring, M. (Mrs.). *The Suttee; or, The Hindu Converts*. London: A. K. Newman, 1830.

Majeed, Javed. *Ungoverned Imaginings: James Mill's History of British India and Orientalism*. Oxford: Clarendon Press, 1992.

Malgonkar, Manohar. *The Devil's Wind: Nana Saheb's Story*. New Delhi: Penguin, 1988.

Malleson, G. B. *History of the Indian Mutiny of 1857–58*. 3 vols. London: n.p., 1896.

Mani, Lata. "Contentious Traditions: The Debate on Sati in Colonial India," in Kumkum Sangari and Sudesh Vaid, eds. *Recasting Women: Essays in Colonial History*. New Brunswick: Rutgers UP, 1990, 88–126.

Mannoni, Octave. *Prospero and Caliban: The Psychology of Colonization*. Trans. Pamela Powesland. New York: Praeger, 1956.

Mansukhani, G. S. *Philip Meadows Taylor: A Critical Study*. Bombay: New Book, 1951.

Margolin, Frederique Affel. *Wives of the God-King: The Rituals of the Devadasi of Puri*. Delhi: Oxford UP, 1985.

Marshall, J. P. *The British Discovery of Hinduism in the Eighteenth Century*. Cambridge: Cambridge UP, 1970.

————. *The Impeachment of Warren Hastings*. London: Oxford UP, 1965.

Mason, Philip. *The Glass, the Shadow and the Fire*. New York: Harper and Row, 1975.

Masters, John. *Nightrunners of Bengal*. London: Joseph, 1951.

Mehdi, Rubya. "The Offence of Rape in the Islamic Law of Pakistan," in Jennifer Tempkin, ed. *Rape and the Legal Process*. London: Sweet and Maxwell, 1987, 185–195.

Mellor, Anne K. *Romanticism and Gender*. New York: Routledge, 1993.

Melman, Billie. *Women's Orients: English Women and the Middle East, 1718–1918: Sexuality, Religion and Work*. Ann Arbor: U of Michigan P, 1992.

Memmi, Albert. *The Colonizer and the Colonized*. Boston: Beacon Press, 1967.

Metcalf, Thomas R. *The Aftermath of the Revolt in India, 1857–1870*. Princeton: Princeton UP, 1964.

————. *An Imperial Vision: Indian Architecture and Britain's Raj*. Berkeley: U of California P, 1988.

————. *New Cambridge History of India*. Vol. 3, Pt. 4: *Ideologies of the Raj*. Cambridge: Cambridge UP, 1994.

Meyer, Eric. "'I Know Thee Not, I Loathe Thy Race': Romantic Orientalism in the Eye of the Other," *ELH* 58 (1991): 657–699.

Meyer, Susan. *Imperialism at Home: Race and Victorian Women's Fiction*. Ithaca: Cornell UP, 1996.

Michie, Helena. *The Flesh Made Word: Female Figures and Women's Bodies*. New York: Oxford UP, 1987.

Miller, Barbara Stoler, trans. *Love Song of Our Dark Lord* [*Gita Govinda*]. New York: Columbia UP, 1977.

————. *Theater of Memory: The Plays of Kalidasa*. New York: Columbia UP, 1984.

Mills, Sara. *Discourses of Difference: An Analysis of Women's Travel Writing and Colonialism.* New York: Routledge, 1991.

Misra, Udayon. *The Raj in Fiction: A Study of Nineteenth-Century British Attitudes toward India.* Delhi: B. R. Publishing, 1987.

Mitchell, Timothy. *Colonizing Egypt.* Cambridge: Cambridge UP, 1988.

Mitter, Partha. *Much Maligned Monsters: The History of European Reactions to Indian Art.* Oxford: Clarendon Press, 1977.

Moffat, Wendy. "*A Passage to India* and the Limits of Certainty," *Journal of Narrative Technique* 20, 3 (Fall 1990): 331–341.

Mohanty, S. P. "Kipling's Children and the Colour Line," *Race and Class* 31 (1989): 21–40.

Money, Edward. *The Wife and the Ward; or, A Life's Error.* London: Routledge, 1859.

Moore-Gilbert, Bart. *Kipling and "Orientalism."* New York, St. Martin's, 1986.

————, ed. *Writing India, 1757–1900: The Literature of British India.* Manchester: Manchester UP, 1996.

Morgan, Susan. *Place Matters: Gendered Geography in Victorian Women's Travel Books about Southeast Asia.* New Brunswick: Rutgers UP, 1996.

Muddock, J. E. *The Great White Hand; or, The Tiger of Cawnpore.* London: Hutchinson, 1896.

————. *The Star of Fortune, A Story of the Indian Mutiny.* London: Chapman Hall, 1895.

Mukerjee, Meenakshi. *Realism and Reality: The Novel and Society in India.* Delhi: Oxford UP, 1985.

Munich, Adrienne Auslander. "What Lily Knew: Virginity in the 1890's," in Lloyd Davis, ed. *Virginal Sexuality and Textuality in Victorian Literature.* Binghamton: SUNY P, 1993, 143–157.

Musselwhite, David. "The Trial of Warren Hastings," in Francis Barker et al., eds. *Literature, Politics and Theory.* London: Methuen, 1986, 77–103.

Nadis, Mark. "G. A. Henty's Idea of India," *Victorian Studies* 8 (1964): 49–58.

Naik, M. K., S. K. Desai, and S. T. Kallapur, eds. *The Image of India in Western Creative Writing.* Madras: Macmillan, 1971.

Nair, Janaki. "Uncovering the Zenana: Visions of Indian Womanhood in English-women's Writing, 1813–1940." *Journal of Women's History* 2, 1 (1990): 8–33.

————. "On the Question of Agency in Indian Feminist Historiography," *Gender and History* 6 (April 1994): 82–100.

Namias, June. *White Captives: Gender and Ethnicity on the American Frontier.* Chapel Hill: U of North Carolina P, 1993.

Nandy, Ashis. *The Intimate Enemy: Loss and Recovery of Self under Colonialism.* Delhi: Oxford UP, 1983.

————. "Sati: A Nineteenth-Century Tale of Women, Violence, and Protest," in Nandy. *At the Edge of Psychology: Essays in Politics and Culture.* New Delhi: Oxford UP, 1980, 1–13.

Naravane, Vishwanathan S. *An Introduction to Rabindranath Tagore.* Columbia: South Asia Books, 1978.

Nisbet, Hume. *The Queen's Desire: A Romance of the Indian Mutiny.* London: F. V. White, 1893.

Oldenberg, Veena Talwar. "Lifestyle as Resistance: The Case of the Courtesans of Lucknow, India," *Feminist Studies* 16, 2 (Summer 1990): 259–287.

Oliphant, Philip Lawrence. *Maya: Tale of East and West*. London: Constable, 1908.

Orwell, George. *Burmese Days*. New York: Time, Inc., 1950. First ed. 1934.

Owenson, Sydney [Lady Morgan]. *Luxima, The Prophetess: A Tale of India*. London: Charles Westerton, 1859.

———. *The Missionary*. London: Stockdale, 1811.

Parliamentary Papers 17 (1771–1774).

Parry, Benita. "The Contents and Discontents of Kipling's Imperialism," *New Formations* 6 (1988): 49–63.

———. *Delusions and Discoveries: Studies in the British Imagination, 1880–1930*. Berkeley: U of California P, 1972.

———. "The Politics of Representation in *A Passage to India*," in John Beer, ed. *"A Passage to India": Essays in Interpretation*. London: Macmillan, 1985, 27–43.

Patai, Daphne. *The Orwell Mystique: A Study in Male Ideology*. Amherst: U of Massachusetts P, 1984.

Pateman, Carole. *The Sexual Contract*. Stanford: Stanford UP, 1988.

Patton, James Blythe. *Bijili, the Dancer*. Boston: Page, 1898.

Paxton, Nancy L. "Disembodied Subjects: English Women's Autobiographies under the Raj," in Sidonie Smith and Julia Watson, eds. *De/Colonizing the Subject: Gender and the Politics of Women's Autobiography*. Minneapolis: U of Minnesota P, 1992, 387–409.

———. *George Eliot and Herbert Spencer: Feminism, Evolutionism, and the Reconstruction of Gender*. Princeton: Princeton UP, 1991.

———. "Mobilizing Chivalry: Novels about the Indian Uprising of 1857," *Victorian Studies* 36, 1 (Fall 1992): 5–30.

———. "Resistance and Complicity in the Writings of Annie Besant and Flora Annie Steel," in Nupur Chaudhuri and Margaret Strobel, eds. *Western Women and Imperialism: Complicity and Resistance*. Bloomington: Indiana UP, 1992, 158–176.

———. "Secrets of the Colonial Harem: Gender, Sexuality, and the Law in Kipling's Indian Fiction," in Bart Moore-Gilbert, ed. *Writing India: Literature about British India, 1757–1990*. Manchester: Manchester UP, 1996, 139–187.

Pearce, Charles E. *Red Revenge: A Romance of Cawnpore*. London: Stanley Paul, 1909.

Penny, Fanny Emily Farr. *A Mixed Marriage*. London: Methuen, 1903.

———. *The Romance of a Nautch Girl*. London: Sonnenschein, 1898.

Perera, Suvendrini. *Reaches of Empire: The English Novel from Edgeworth to Dickens*. New York: Columbia UP, 1991.

Perrin, Alice. *The Anglo-Indians*. London: Methuen, 1914. First ed. 1912.

———. *The Charm*. London: Methuen, 1910.

———. *Waters of Destruction*. London: Chatto and Windus, 1905.

Philips, K. J. "Hindu Avatars, Moslem Martyrs, and Primitive Dying Gods in E. M. Forster's *A Passage to India*," *Journal of Modern Literature* 15, 1 (Summer, 1988): 121–140.

Platt, John T. *The Dictionary of Urdu, Classical Hindi, and English*. New Delhi: Munshriram Manaharlal, 1988.

Plaza, Monique. "Our Damages and Their Compensation," *Feminist Issues* 1, 3 (1981): 23–35.

Plotz, Judith. "The Empire of Youth: Crossing and Double-Crossing Cultural Barriers in Kipling's *Kim*," in Francina Butler, Barbara Rosen, and Judith A. Plotz, eds. *Children's Literature*, vol. 20. New Haven: Yale UP, 1993, 111–131.

Porter, Dennis. "Orientalism and Its Problems," in Patrick Williams and Laura Chrisman, eds. *Colonial Discourse and Postcolonial Theory: A Reader*. New York: Columbia UP, 1993, 150–161.

Porter, Roy. "Rape—Does It Have a Historical Meaning?" in Sylvia Tomaselli and Roy Porter, eds. *Rape: An Historical and Social Enquiry*. Oxford: Blackwell, 1986, 216–236.

Prakash, Gyan, ed. *After Colonialism: Imperial Histories and Postcolonial Displacements*. Princeton: Princeton UP, 1994.

———. *Bonded Histories: Genealogies of Labour—Servitude in Colonial India*. Cambridge: Cambridge UP, 1990.

Pratt, Mary Louise. *Imperial Eyes: Studies in Travel Writing and "Transculturation."* New York: Routledge, 1992.

Quint, David. *Epic and Empire: Politics and Generic Form from Virgil to Milton*. Princeton: Princeton UP, 1993.

Rajan, Rajeswari Sunder. *Real and Imagined Women: Gender, Culture and Postcolonialism*. London: Routledge, 1993.

———, ed. *The Lie of the Land: English Literary Studies in India*. Delhi: Oxford UP, 1992.

Ramesh, Asha, and H. P. Philomena. "The Devadasi Problem," in Kathleen Barry, ed. *International Feminism: Networking Against Female Sexual Slavery*. New York: Feminist Press, 82–88.

Richards, Jeffrey, ed. *Imperialism and Juvenile Literature*. Manchester: Manchester UP, 1989.

Richards, Thomas. *The Imperial Archive: Knowledge and the Fantasy of Empire*. London: Verso, 1993.

Robbins, Bruce. "Colonial Discourse: A Paradigm and Its Discontents," *Victorian Studies* 35, 2 (Winter 1992): 209–214.

Rocher, Rosane. "British Orientalism in the Eighteenth Century: The Dialectics of Knowledge and Government," in Carol A. Breckenridge and Peter Van der Veer, eds. *Orientalism and the Post Colonial Predicament: Perspectives on South Asia*. Philadelphia: U of Pennsylvania P, 1993, 215–249.

Rooney, Ellen. "'A Little More Than Persuading': *Tess* and the Subject of Sexual Violence," in Lynn A. Higgins and Brenda R. Silver, eds. *Rape and Representation*. New York: Columbia UP, 1991, 87–114.

Ross, Marlon B. "Romancing the Nation-State: The Poetics of Romantic Nationalism," in Jonathan Arac and Harriet Ritvo, eds. *The Macropolitics of Nineteenth-Century Literature: Nationalism, Exoticism, and Imperialism*. Philadelphia: U of Pennsylvania P, 1991.

Rubin, David. *After the Raj: British Novels of India since 1947*. Hanover, N.H.: UP of New England, 1986.

Sahni, Chaman L. *Forster's "A Passage to India": The Religious Dimension*. Atlantic Highlands: Humanities Press, 1981.

Said, Edward W. *Culture and Imperialism*. New York: Knopf, 1993.

———. *Orientalism*. New York: Random House, 1978.

Sainsbury, Alison. "Married to the Empire: The Anglo-Indian Domestic Novel," in Bart Moore-Gilbert, ed. *Writing India, 1757–1990: The Literature of British India*. Manchester: Manchester UP, 1996, 163–187.

Sanday, Peggy Reeves. *Women, Power, and Male Dominance: On the Origins of Sexual Inequality*. New York: Cambridge UP, 1982.

Sandison, Alan. *The Wheel of Empire: A Study of the Imperial Idea in Some Late Nineteenth- and Early Twentieth-Century Fiction*. New York: St. Martin's Press, 1967.

Sangari, Kumkum, and Sudesh Vaid, eds. *Recasting Women: Essays in Colonial History*. New Brunswick: Rutgers UP, 1990.

Sarkar, Tanika. "Bakimchandra and the Impossibility of a Political Agenda," *Oxford Literary Review* 16, 1–2 (1994): 177–204.

———. "The Hindu Wife and the Hindu Nation: Domesticity and Nationalism in Nineteenth-Century Bengal," *Studies in History* 8, 2 (1992), 213–235.

Saunders, Rebecca. "Gender, Colonialism, and Exile: Flora Annie Steel and Sara Jeannette Duncan in India," in Mary Lynn Broe and Angela Ingram, eds. *Women's Writing in Exile*. Chapel Hill: U of North Carolina P, 1989.

Savi, Ethel Winifred. *Mock Majesty*. London: Putnam's, 1923.

Schwab, Raymond. *The Oriental Renaissance: Europe's Rediscovery of India and the East, 1680–1880*. New York: Columbia UP, 1984.

Scott, Sir Walter. *The Surgeon's Daughter and Castle Dangerous*. New York: Harper and Brothers, 1829. First ed. 1827.

Scully, Pamela. "Rape, Race, and Colonial Culture: The Sexual Politics of Identity in the Nineteenth-century Cape Colony, South Africa," *American Historical Review* 100, 2 (April 1995): 335–359.

Sedgewick, Eve Kosofsky. *Between Men: English Literature and Male Homosocial Desire*. New York: Columbia UP, 1985.

Sharpe, Jenny. *Allegories of Empire: The Figure of Woman in the Colonial Text*. Minneapolis: U of Minnesota P, 1993.

———. "The Unspeakable Limits of Rape: Colonial Violence and Counter-Insurgency," *Genders* 10 (Spring 1991): 25–46.

Shelley, Percy Bysshe. "Laon and Cyntha; or, The Revolution of the Golden City, a Vision of the Nineteenth Century," in *The Complete Poetical Works of Percy Bysshe Shelley*. 4 vols. Ed. Neville Rodgers. Oxford: Clarendon Press, 1975.

———. *Letters*. 2 vols. Ed. Fredrick L. Jones. Oxford: Clarendon Press, 1964.

Shohat, Ella. "Gender and Culture of Empire: Toward a Feminist Ethnography of the Cinema," *Quarterly Review of Film and Video* 15, 1–3 (May 1991): 45–84.

Shortt, John. "The Bayadère; or, Dancing Girls of Southern India," *Transactions of the Anthropological Society of London* 3 (1867–1869): 182–194.

Showalter, Elaine. "*A Passage to India* as 'Marriage Fiction': Forster's Sexual Politics," *Women and Literature* 5, 2 (1977): 3–16.

Silver, Brenda, "Periphrasis, Power, and Rape in *A Passage to India*," in Lynn A.

Higgins and Brenda R. Silver, eds. *Rape and Representation*. New York: Columbia UP, 1991, 115–137.

Singh, Frances B. "*A Passage to India*, the National Movement, and Independence," *Twentieth Century Literature: A Scholarly and Critical Journal* 35, 2–3 (Summer/Fall 1985): 265–278.

Singh, Jyotsna. *Colonial Narratives, Cultural Dialogues: "Discoveries" of India in the Language of Colonialism*. London: Routledge, 1996

Singh, Shailendra Dhari. *Novels on the Indian Mutiny*. New Delhi: Arnold-Heinemann, 1973.

Singha, Rina, and Reginald Massey. *Indian Dances: Their History and Growth*. London: Faber and Faber, 1967.

Sinha, Mrinalini. "Chathams, Pitts, and Gladstones in Petticoats: The Politics of Gender and Race in the Ilbert Bill Controversy, 1883–84," in Nupur Chaudhuri and Margaret Strobel, eds. *Western Women and Imperialism: Complicity and Resistance*. Bloomington: Indiana UP, 1991, 98–116.

———. *Colonial Masculinities: The 'Manly Englishman' and the 'Effeminate Bengali' in the Late Nineteenth Century*. Manchester: Manchester UP, 1995.

Smith, Valerie. "Split Affinities: The Case of Interracial Rape," in Marianne Hirsch and Evelyn Fox Keller, eds. *Conflicts in Feminism*. London: Routledge, 1990, 271–287.

Sommer, Doris. "Allegories and Dialectics: A Match Made in Romance," *Boundary* ser. 2, 18, 1 (1991): 60–82.

———. *Foundational Fictions: The National Romances of Latin America*. Berkeley: U of California P, 1991.

Southey, Robert. *The Curse of Kehama*. London: Longman, Hurst, Rees, Orme, and Brown, 1810.

Spear, Percival. *A History of India*, vol. 2. Harmondsworth: Penguin, 1973.

Spivak, Gayatri Chakravorty. "The Burden of English," in Rajeswari Sunder Rajan, ed. *The Lie of the Land: English Literary Studies in India*. Delhi: Oxford UP, 1992, 275–299.

———. "Can the Subaltern Speak?" in Cary Nelson and Lawrence Grossberg, eds. *Marxism and the Interpretation of Culture*. Urbana: U of Illinois P, 1988, 271–313.

———. "Neocolonialism and the Secret Agent of Knowledge," *Oxford Literary Review* 13, 1–2 (1991): 220–251.

———. "The Rani of Sirmur," in Francis Barker, Peter Hulme, Margaret Ivesen, and Deane Lexley, eds. *Europe and Its Others*, vol. 2. Colchester: U of Essex, 1985, 128–151.

———. "Three Women's Texts and a Critique of Imperialism," in Robyn R. Warhol and Diane Price Herndl, eds. *Feminisms: An Anthology of Literary Theory and Criticism*. New Brunswick: Rutgers UP, 1993, 798–814.

Srinivasan, Amrit. "Reform or Conformity? Temple 'Prostitution' and the Community in the Madras Presidency," in Bina Agarwal, ed. *The Structures of Patriarchy: State, Community, and Household in Modernising Asia*. New Delhi: Kali, 1988, 175–198.

Stavrianos, L. S. *Global Drift: The Third World Comes of Age*. New York: William Morrow, 1981.

Steel, Flora Annie. *The Complete Indian Housekeeper and Cook*. London: Heinemann, 1889.

———. *The Garden of Fidelity: The Autobiography of Flora Annie Steel, 1847–1929*. London: Macmillan, 1930.

———. *On the Face of the Waters*. London: Heinemann, 1896.

———. *A Tale of Indian Heroes, Being the Stories of the Mahabarata and the Ramayana*. New York: F. A. Stokes, 1923.

———. *Voices in the Night*. London: Heinemann, 1900.

Sterndale, Robert Armitage. *The Afghan Knife*. New York: Brentano's, 1899. First ed. 1879.

Stieg, Margaret F. "Indian Romances: Tracts for the Times," *Journal of Popular Culture* 18, 4 (Spring 1985): 2–15.

Stimpson, Catharine R. *Where the Meanings Are: Feminism and Cultural Space*. New York: Routledge, 1989.

Stocking, George W. *Victorian Anthropology*. New York: Free Press, 1987.

Stokes, Eric. *The English Utilitarians and India*. Oxford: Clarendon Press, 1959.

———. *The Peasant Armed: The Indian Revolt of 1857*. Oxford: Clarendon Press, 1986.

Stoler, Ann L. "Carnal Knowledge and Imperial Power: Gender, Race, and Morality in Colonial Asia," in Micaela di Leonardo, ed. *Gender at the Crossroads of Knowledge: Feminist Anthropology in the Postmodern Era*. Berkeley: U of California P, 1991, 51–101.

———. "Making Empire Respectable: The Politics of Race and Sexual Morality in 20th century Colonial Cultures," *American Ethnologist* 16, 4 (1989): 634–660.

———. "Sexual Affronts and Racial Frontiers: European Identities and the Cultural Politics of Exclusion in Colonial Southeast Asia," *Comparative Studies in Society and History* 34, 3 (July 1992): 514–551.

Strobel, Margaret. *European Women and the Second British Empire*. Bloomington: Indiana UP, 1991.

Suleri, Sara. *The Rhetoric of English India*. Chicago: U of Chicago P, 1992.

Tagore, Rabindranath. *Gora*. [English trans.] London: Macmillan, 1925.

———. *Home and the World*. Trans. Surendranath Tagore. London: Macmillan, 1919. First Indian ed. 1916.

Tarlo, Emma. *Clothing Matters: Dress and Identity in India*. Chicago: U of Chicago P, 1996.

Taylor, John Edward, ed. *Letters from Meadows Taylor Written during the Indian Rebellion*. London: n.p., 1857.

Taylor, Meadows. *Confessions of a Thug*. London: Bentley, 1839.

———. *The Letters of Philip Meadows Taylor to Henry Reeve*. Ed. Patrick Caddell. London: Oxford UP, 1947.

———. *Ralph Darnell*. 1 vol. London: Tench and Tübner, 1897. First ed. 1865.

———. *Seeta*. London: Kegan Paul, Tench, and Tübner, 1872.

———. *The Story of My Life*. London: Blackwood, 1878.

Taylor, Meadows. *Tara: A Mahratta Tale*. London: Kegan Paul, Tench, and Tübner, 1874.

———. *Tippoo Sultaun: A Tale of the Mysore War*. London: Paul, 1880. First ed. 1840.

Teltscher, Kate. *India Inscribed: European and British Writing on India, 1600–1800*. Delhi: Oxford UP, 1995.

———. "The Fearful Name of the Black Hole: Refashioning an Imperial Myth," in Bart Moore-Gilbert, ed. *Writing India, 1757–1990: The Literature of British India*. Manchester: Manchester UP, 1996, 30–51.

Tharu, Susie, and K. Lalita, eds. *Women Writing in India: 600 B.C. to the Present*. 2 vols. New York: Feminist Press, 1991.

Thomas, Nicholas. *Colonialism's Culture: Anthropology, Travel and Government*. Princeton: Princeton UP, 1994.

Thompson, Edward John. *Night Falls on Siva's Hill*. London: Heinemann, 1929.

———. *The Other Side of the Medal*. Ed. Mulk Raj Anand. New Delhi: Sterling Publishers, 1989. First ed. 1925.

———. *Rabindranath Tagore: Poet and Dramatist*. Delhi: Oxford UP, 1991.

Tidrick, Kathryn T. *Empire and the English Character*. London: Tauris, 1990.

Tomaselli, Sylvia, and Roy Porter, eds. *Rape: An Historical and Social Enquiry*. London: Blackwell, 1987.

Tracy, Louis. *The Red Year: A Story of the Indian Mutiny*. London: White and Co., 1908.

Trevelyan, G. O. *Cawnpore*. London: Macmillan, 1865.

Trinh, T. Minh-ha. *Woman, Native, Other: Writing Postcoloniality and Feminism*. Bloomington: Indiana UP, 1989.

Trivedi, Harish. *Colonial Transactions: English Literature and India*. Manchester: Manchester UP, 1994.

Tuchman, Gail. *Edging Women Out: Victorian Novelists, Publishers and Social Change*. New Haven: Yale UP, 1989.

Turner, Bryan S. *Orientalism, Post-Modernism, and Globalism*. London: Routledge, 1994.

Varma, Devendra P. *The Gothic Flame*. New York: Russell and Russell, 1957.

Vishwanathan, Gauri. *Masks of Conquest: Literary Study and British Rule in India*. New York: Columbia UP, 1989.

Ware, Vron. *Beyond the Pale: White Women, Racism, and History*. London: Verso, 1992.

Watkins, Daniel P. *Social Relations in Byron's Eastern Tales*. Rutherford, N.J.: Farleigh Dickinson UP, 1987.

Weeks, Jeffrey. *Sex, Politics, and Society: The Regulation of Sexuality since 1800*. London: Longmans, 1989.

Wilkie, Brian. *Romantic Poets and Epic Traditions*. Madison: U of Wisconsin P, 1965.

Williams, Patrick, and Laura Chrisman, eds. *Colonial Discourse and Post-Colonial Theory: A Reader*. New York: Columbia UP, 1993.

Wolfson, Susan J. "'A Problem Few Dare Imitate': Sardanapalus and 'Effeminate Character,'" *ELH* 58 (1991): 867–902.

Wollstonecraft, Mary. *A Vindication of the Rights of Woman: The Norton Critical Edition*. Ed. Carol H. Poston. New York: Norton, 1988.

Wurgaft, Lewis. *The Imperial Imagination: Magic and Myth in Kipling's India.* Middletown, Ct.: Wesleyan UP, 1983.

Wylie, Ida Alexa Ross. *The Daughter of Brahma.* London: Mills and Boon, 1912.

Yang, Anand. "Whose Sati? Widow Burning in Early Nineteenth-Century India," *Journal of Women's History* 1 (1989): 8–33.

Young, Robert. *Colonial Desire: Hybridity in Theory, Culture and Race.* London: Routledge, 1994.

Zonana, Joyce. "The Sultan and the Slave: Feminist Orientalism and the Structure of *Jane Eyre*," *Signs* 18:3 (Spring 1993): 592–617.

Works Consulted

Annan, Noel. "Kipling's Place in the History of Ideas," in Andrew Rutherford, ed. *Kipling's Mind and Art: Selected Critical Essays.* Stanford: Stanford UP, 1964, 97–125.

Apter, Emily. "Female Trouble in the Colonial Harem," *Differences: A Journal of Feminist Cultural Studies* 4:1 (1992): 205–224.

Arnold, William Delafield. *Oakfield; or, Fellowship in the East.* London: n.p., 1973. First ed. 1854.

Bardhan, Kalpana. "Being a Woman in South Asia," *Journal of Women's History* 2 (Spring 1990): 200–219.

Boone, Joseph A. *Tradition, Counter Tradition: Love and the Form of Fiction.* Chicago: U of Chicago P, 1987.

Boulger, Demetrius C. *Lord William Bentinck.* Oxford: Clarendon Press, 1892.

Bourdieu, Pierre. *Language and Symbolic Power.* Ed. John B. Thompson. Trans. Gino Raymond and Matthew Adamson. Cambridge: Harvard UP, 1991.

Carroll, Margaret D. "The Erotics of Absolutism: Rubens and Mystification of Sexual Violence," *Representations* 25, 3 (Winter 1989): 3–30.

Chakravorty, Uma. "The World of the Bhakti in South Indian Traditions—the Body and Beyond," *Manushi* 50–52 (1989): 18–28.

Cobham, Alfred. *Edmund Burke and the Revolt against the Eighteenth Century: A Study of the Political and Social Thinking of Burke, Wordsworth, Coleridge, and Southey.* London: Allen and Unwin, 1960.

Crook, Nora. *Kipling's Myths of Love and Death.* New York: St. Martin's Press, 1989.

Eastman, David. "Robert Southey and the Intellectual Origins of Romantic Conservatism," *English Historical Review* 104 (April 1989): 308–331.

Edwardes, Allen. *The Rape of India: A Biography of Robert Clive and a Sexual History of Hindustan.* New York: Jullian Press, 1960.

Forrest, R. E. *Eight Days.* London: Smith, Elder, 1891.

Gallop, Jane. *Thinking through the Body.* New York: Columbia UP, 1988.

Geertz, Clifford. *Works and Lives: The Anthropologist as Author.* Stanford: Stanford UP, 1988.

Goonatilake, Susantha. *Crippled Minds: An Exploration Into Colonial Culture.* New Delhi: Vikas, 1982.

Goonetilleke, D.C.R.A. *Images of the Raj: South Asia in the Literature of Empire.* New York: St. Martin's Press, 1987.

Graham, Kenneth. "Beckford's Adaption of the Oriental Tale in *Vathek*," *Enlightenment Essays* 5 (Spring 1974): 24–33.

Gray, Maxwell [Mary Gleed Tuttiett]. *In the Heart of the Storm*. New York: Appleton, 1891.

Habermas, Jürgen. *The Theory of Communicative Action*. Trans. Thomas McCarthy. Boston: Beacon, 1984.

Haggis, Jane. "Gendering Colonialism or Colonizing Gender? Recent Women's Studies Approaches to White Women and the History of British Colonialism," *Women's Studies International Forum* 13, 1–2 (1990): 105–115.

Hammami, Reza, and Martina Rieker. "Feminist Orientalism and Orientalist Marxism," *New Left Review* 170 (1988): 93–106.

Hardy, Kay, ed. *"The 1001 Nights": Critical Essays and Annotated Bibliography*. Cambridge: Dar Mahjar, 1985.

Hooks, Bell. *Yearning: Race, Gender, and Cultural Politics*. Boston: South End Press, 1990.

Hunter, W. W. *The Old Missionary*. New York: Anson Randolph, 1895.

Hyam, Ronald. *Britain's Imperial Century, 1815–1914: A Study of Empire and Expansion*. London: Batsford, 1976.

———. *Empire and Sexuality: The British Experience*. Manchester: Manchester UP, 1990.

Islam, S. *Kipling's 'Law': A Study of His Philosophy of Life*. London: Macmillan, 1975.

Jain, M. P. *Outline of Indian Legal History*. Bombay: N. M. Tripathi, 1966.

Jeffreys, Shelia, ed. *The Sexuality Debates*. New York: Routledge, 1987.

Kemp, Sandra. *Kipling's Hidden Narratives*. London: Blackwell, 1988.

Kingsley, Henry. *Stretton*. 3 vols. London: Tinsley, 1869.

Kingston, W.H.G. *The Young Rajah*. London: Thomas Nelson, 1909. First ed. 1876.

Kipling, Rudyard. *The Light that Failed*. Ed. J. M. Lyon. London: Penguin, 1988. First ed. 1897.

———. *Letters of Marque*. New York: Collier, 1891.

Krishnaswamy, Santha. *The Woman in Indian Fiction in English*. Atlantic Highlands: Humanities Press, 1984.

Kumar, Radha. *The History of Doing: An Illustrated Account of Movements for Women's Rights and Feminism in India, 1800–1990*. London: Verso, 1993.

Lawrence, G. A. *Maurice Derring; or, the Quadrilateral*. London: Tinsley, 1864.

McBratney, John. "Imperial Subjects, Imperial Space in Kipling's *Jungle Book*," *Victorian Studies* 35:3 (1992): 277–293.

Mackenzie, John M. *The Empire of Nature: Hunting, Conservation, and British Imperialism*. New York: St. Martin's, 1988.

Mayo, Katherine. *Mother India*. New York: Harcourt, 1927.

———. *Slaves of the Gods*. London: Cape, 1929.

Mohanty, Chandra Talpade. "Under Western Eyes: Feminist Scholarship and Colonial Discourses," *Boundary* ser. 2, 12, 3/4 (Spring/ Fall 1984): 333–358.

Mohanty, Chandra Talpade, Ann Russo, and Lourdes Torres, eds. *Third World Women and the Politics of Feminism*. Bloomington: Indiana UP, 1991.

Pafford, Mark. *Kipling's Indian Fiction*. New York: St. Martin's Press, 1989.

Pal, Pratapaditya, and Vidya Dekejia. *From Merchants to Emperors, British Artists and India, 1757–1930*. Ithaca: Cornell UP, 1986.

Patwardhan, Daya. *A Star of India: Flora Annie Steel, Her Works and Her Times*. Poona: Griha Prakashan, 1963.

Pearce, Charles E. *The Star of the East: A Romance of Delhi*. London, 1912.

Penny, Fanny Emily Farr. *Caste and Creed*. London: White, 1890.

———. *A Question of Colour*. London: Hadder and Stoughton, 1926.

Perrin, Alice. *East of Suez*. London: Chatto and Windus, 1909. First ed. 1901.

———. *A Free Solitude*. London: Chatto and Windus, 1907.

———. *Idolatry*. Leipzig: Tauchniz, 1909. First ed. 1907.

———. *Into Temptation*. London: F. V. White, 1894.

———. *The Stronger Claim*. London: Harrap, 1925.

———. *The Woman of the Bazaar*. London: Cassell, 1926. First ed. 1914.

Rao, K. Bhaskara. *Rudyard Kipling's India*. Norman: U of Oklahoma P, 1967.

Rubin, Gayle. "The Traffic in Women: Notes on the 'Political Economy' of Sex," in Rayna Reiter, ed. *Toward an Anthropology of Women*. New York: Monthly Review Press, 1975, 157–210.

Ruswa, Mirza Hadi. *Umrao Jan Ada*. Trans. Kushwant Singh. Calcutta: Orient Longman, 1961.

Silverman, Kaja. "White Skin, Brown Masks: The Double Mimesis; or, With Lawrence in Arabia." *Difference* 1, 3 (1989): 3–54.

Sleeman, Sir W. H. *Rambles and Recollections of an Indian Official*. Rev. and annotated by Vincent A. Smith. Karachi: Oxford UP, 1973. First ed. 1844.

Steel, Flora Annie. *The Hosts of the Lord*. London: Heinemann, 1900.

———. *Indian Scene: Collected Short Stories of Flora Annie Steel*. London: Arnold, 1933.

———. *The Law of the Threshold*. New York: Macmillan, 1924.

———. *Mistress of Men, a Novel*. New York: Frederick Stokes, 1917.

Stepan, Nancy. *The Idea of Race in Science: Great Britain, 1800–1960*. New York: Archon Books, 1982.

Tanner, Laura E. *Intimate Violence: Reading Rape and Torture in Twentieth-Century Fiction*. Bloomington: Indiana UP, 1994.

Taylor, Meadows. *The Noble Queen*. London: Paul, 1986. First ed. 1886.

Thurston, E. *Castes and Tribes of Southern India*. Madras: n.p., 1900.

Trevelyan, G. O. *Competitionwallah*. London: Macmillan, 1864.

Wentworth, Patricia. *The Devil's Wind*. London: Andrew Melrose, 1912.

Wilson, Angus. *The Strange Ride of Rudyard Kipling*. New York: Viking, 1978.

Woolf, Leonard. *Growing: An Autobiography of the Years 1904–1911*. New York: Harcourt Brace, 1961.

Wylie, Ida Alexa Ross. *My Life with George: An Unconventional Autobiography*. New York: Random House, 1940.

INDEX

ABOUT THE AUTHOR

Nancy Paxton is an associate professor in the Department of English at Northern Arizona University. She is the author of *George Eliot and Herbert Spencer: Feminism, Evolutionism, and the Reconstruction of Gender.*